The Timeline Book of Science

Forthcoming books in the same series:

The Timeline Book of the Arts
The Timeline Book of Great Ideas
The Timeline Book of History

The Timeline Book of Science

George Ochoa and Melinda Corey

A Stonesong Press Book

Ballantine Books • New York

Copyright © 1995 by The Stonesong Press, Inc.

All rights reserved under International and Pan-American Copyright Conventions. Published in the United States by Ballantine Books, a division of Random House, Inc., New York, and simultaneously in Canada by Random House of Canada Limited, Toronto.

Library of Congress Cataloging-in-Publication Data

Ochoa, George.
    The timeline book of science / George Ochoa and Melinda Corey.
        p.   cm.
    "A Stonesong Press book."
    Includes bibliographical references and index.
    ISBN 0-345-38265-X
    1. Science—History—Chronology.   I. Corey, Melinda.   II. Title.
Q125.024   1995
509—dc20   94-11865
                                                            CIP

Cover design by Richard Hasselberger

Typography by Noble Desktop Publishers

A Stonesong Press Book

Manufactured in the United States of America

First Edition: March 1995

10 9 8 7 6 5 4 3 2 1

Photo research by Photosearch, Inc., New York City

In memory of
José Verdi Cevallos, physician and poet,
and
Harriet Griggs Guild, physician and pathfinder

TABLE OF CONTENTS

ACKNOWLEDGMENTS

We are indebted to Kerry Benson and Risa Schneider, diligent researchers and contributors. We also thank Tom Brown for keyboarding much of the manuscript and Mudit Tyagi for his editorial assistance. Finally, we thank Paul Fargis and Sheree Bykofsky of The Stonesong Press and Ginny Faber, our editor at Ballantine.

INTRODUCTION

A timeline is a record of change; *The Timeline Book of Science* is a record of stunning change. In no field of human endeavor have things been altered more quickly, dramatically, and irreversibly than in our knowledge of the physical universe and our ability to manipulate it. The most rapid and visible changes have taken place in just the last two centuries, originating mostly in Europe and America, but many of the deepest changes took place much earlier in distant places. It is obvious that microwave ovens, television, computers, the theory of relativity, and the model of the atom are products of scientific knowledge; it may be less obvious that so are bread, the dog, the pipeline, the concept of angles, and the year.

The Timeline Book of Science charts chronologically, from prehistory to the present, how we came to know what we know about nature and have what we made. It is a story with many twists and turns, frequent shifts of locale, and a decidedly uneven pace. For millions of years the tale hardly moves at all; after the development of agriculture it moves gradually but slowly; then in the last few hundred years it moves at a blinding pace. A physician from ancient Rome would have had much in common, technologically, with a physician in seventeenth-century Italy, but both would have great difficulty figuring out what to do with a CAT scanner in a late-twentieth-century hospital, much less how to drive home on the expressway after work.

It is no accident, then, that most of this book deals with the few hundred years since the sixteenth and seventeenth centuries, when people like Copernicus, Galileo, and Francis Bacon brought about a fundamental shift in humanity's approach to studying nature, a change known as the scientific revolution. Yet *The Timeline Book of Science* also outlines other important stories of scientific progress: how early humans spread out of Africa across the world and invented such technologies as fish hooks, sewing needles, and the use of fire; how farmers and herders domesticated wild plants and animals; how Chinese experimenters invented silk, paper, and gunpowder while Chinese astronomers first recorded what became known as Halley's Comet; how the Hindus developed a system of numerals that was passed to the Arabs and from them to Europeans; and how Mayans in Central America independently developed their own system of numerals.

INTRODUCTION

The Timeline Book of Science ranges over as many different topics as it does periods and locales. It charts the growth of the disciplines usually taught in school—biology, chemistry, physics, and the earth sciences. But it also maps the rise of technology, engineering, archaeology, paleontology, mathematics, medicine, psychology, computer science, and the exploration of earth and space. It concentrates on the physical sciences but nevertheless includes entries on linguistics and the social sciences—anthropology, sociology, economics, political science.

Throughout, the timeline reports action. It tells what was discovered, invented, suggested, argued, and disproved—by whom, when, where, and why. It notes wrong steps as well as right ones, established ideas as well as controversial ones. There are exploded theories such as the four humors and phlogiston (material supposedly lost in combustion); outmoded procedures such as medical bleeding; and obsolete inventions, such as the Stanley Steamer. There are the sometimes meandering, sometimes steady processes by which modern theories were developed (chemical bonding, molecular genetics) and modern technologies created (electronics, satellites). There are controversies mostly restricted to earlier times—the scientific debate over Darwin's theory of evolution—and the controversies of the present day—who first settled the Americas; where is the mass that astronomers call "missing"?

Lest the accumulation of events become overwhelming, *The Timeline Book of Science* includes sidebars that spotlight moments in the story. Some of these are serious (how the bubonic plague was blamed on European Jews), others humorous (how an English town incorporated a dinosaur into its coat of arms). Some offer more detail on how a discovery was made and why it was significant, while others bring out the human side of scientists and inventors (such as Charles Goodyear, who never made a penny from his invention of vulcanized rubber). Other sidebars quote the reflections, observations, and quips of scientists and eyewitnesses from Aristotle on nature to Einstein on the atomic bomb.

In the Stanley Kubrick film *2001: A Space Odyssey* (1968) there is a sequence in which a hairy ancestor of humans, having learned how to use a bone as a weapon, hurls it into the air; the next thing we know, a human-made spacecraft is orbiting the earth. If the devil is in the details, then this account of our development, however evocative, leaves much to be explained. How do we know what we know about the universe and ourselves? What are we still trying to discover? How did we come to own the technologies we possess; why is it they sometimes seem to own us? With the year 2001 now much closer than it was, *The Timeline Book of Science* is written to help answer these questions.

A NOTE TO THE READER

The Timeline Book of Science is arranged by year and within a year by category. The categories are as follows:

ARCH	Archaeology
ASTRO	Astronomy, space science, space exploration
BIO	Biology, biochemistry, agriculture, ecology
CHEM	Chemistry
EARTH	Earth sciences (geology, oceanography, meteorology), earth exploration
MATH	Mathematics
MED	Medicine
MISC	Miscellaneous
PALEO	Paleontology
PHYS	Physics
PSYCH	Psychology, neuroscience, artificial intelligence
SOC	Social sciences (anthropology, sociology, economics, political science), linguistics
TECH	Technology, engineering

In the timeline, B.C. dates are indicated by negative numbers, A.D. dates by positive numbers.

Throughout prehistory, antiquity, and the early Middle Ages, it is often difficult to place exact dates. Therefore, most of the dates in this book up to the year A.D. 1000 should be considered approximate (with certain exceptions, such as May 28, 585 B.C., the precise date of a solar eclipse predicted by the Greek philosopher Thales). After A.D. 1000, dates can generally be considered exact unless marked with a *c.* for *circa*.

This timeline is primarily a record of action—experiments, achievements, discoveries, assertions. To avoid clutter, birth and death dates of those performing the actions have mostly been left out. However, the birth and death dates of many of the scientists and inventors named in the timeline are included in the Appendix.

B.C.

−2,500,000　In East Africa the hominid (humanlike) species *Homo habilis* makes the first stone tools. **TECH**

−1,800,000　*Homo erectus* evolves. This hominid species will eventually be the first to leave Africa and learn the use of fire. **PALEO**

−1,000,000　*Homo erectus* populations begin to move out of Africa into Asia and from there ultimately to Europe. **EARTH**

−500,000　*Homo erectus* discovers the use of fire. The earliest firm evidence is found at Zhoukoudian, near Beijing, China. *See also* 13,000 B.C. **TECH**

−400,000　*Homo erectus* invents the spear. **TECH**

−100,000　The earliest anatomically modern *Homo sapiens* populations evolve in Africa. There is still debate about whether *Homo sapiens* moved out of Africa to spread across Asia and Europe, or simply evolved independently in different regions from local *Homo erectus* populations. **PALEO**

−48,000　*Homo sapiens* reaches the continent of Australia from southeast Asia. **EARTH**

−38,000　The Cro-Magnon people *Homo sapiens sapiens* appear in Europe, the Middle East, and North Africa. These anatomically modern humans will replace the existing Neanderthal populations. Along with other modern human populations in places as far apart as Australia and southern Africa they will invent art, develop specialized tools, and exhibit cultural differences over place and time. **TECH**

−33,000　Early Europeans make body ornamentation such as beads and pendants, the first known form of art. **TECH**

−28,000　Europeans mark notches on bones and stones to tally numbers. **MATH**

−28,000　Flutes, the earliest musical instruments, appear in Europe. **TECH**

−28,000　Europeans make the first known sculptures from stone, bone, antler, and horn. Some are of animals, some of exaggerated female shapes called Venuses. **TECH**

−24,000　Europeans invent sewing needles made of bone. **TECH**

–24,000	The fish hook and fishing line are in use in Europe.	**TECH**
–20,000	The bow and arrow have been invented and are in use in Spain and North Africa.	**TECH**
–20,000	Primitive oil lamps are invented. They are probably fueled by animal fat in hollowed-out stones, with wicks of plant fiber.	**TECH**
–20,000	Humans in Europe make paintings on cave walls.	**TECH**

ENVIRONMENTAL DISASTER

*P*remodern peoples are commonly viewed as having lived in harmony with nature, while modern civilization is seen as degrading the environment and exterminating species. This idealized view masks a darker fact: whether their economy is hunter-gatherer or industrial-capitalist, humans have a long history of taking what they can until the supply runs out. A case in point is that of the first known people in the Americas— the ancestors of today's Native Americans, the Clovis culture.

The Clovis culture is named for stone tools first discovered in 1952 at a site near Clovis, New Mexico, that dates from about 9500 B.C. Similar tools dating from about the same time have since been found across North America. The Clovis people are widely believed to have been the original discoverers of America, although some archaeologists place the date for the earliest human migration into the Americas as early as 35,000 years ago. The Clovis people migrated from Siberia into Alaska across the land bridge that then existed across the Bering Strait. By about 10,500 years ago their descendants reached the southern tip of South America.

The arrival of the Clovis people coincides with a remarkable wave of species extinctions. Just before the Clovis people arrived, the American wilderness was abundant with big mammals: mammoths, mastodons, giant ground sloths, giant beavers, saber-toothed cats, camels, horses. By about 9000 B.C., shortly after the Clovis people's arrival, all these species became extinct. Within the span of a few centuries, North America lost 73 percent of its genera of large mammals, South America about 80 percent.

What happened to all these animals? Beginning with the works of American geoscientist Paul Martin in 1973, many scientists have argued that the Clovis people hunted these species to extinction. Never having seen humans, the animals would not have feared them, and the humans would have had no reason to hold back. The arrival of the first Americans may well have been marked by an environmental disaster as great as any other in human history.

-13,000	The spear thrower and harpoon are invented.	**TECH**
-13,000	Huts built from mammoth bones and maps drawn on bone appear in Mezhirich in eastern Europe.	**TECH**
-13,000	Humans begin making their own fires. Previously they had relied on "found" fires, which they carefully carried and maintained. *See also* 500,000 B.C.	**TECH**
-12,000	Dogs, descendants of the Asian wolf, are domesticated in Iraq.	**BIO**
-10,000	Herding begins with the domestication of goats in Iran.	**BIO**
-10,000	By this time the ancestors of Native Americans have crossed the land bridge from Siberia to Alaska, entering the Western Hemisphere, though some archaeologists place the first crossing as early as 33,000 B.C.	**EARTH**
-9000	Mass extinctions of large animals in North and South America may be caused by the intrusion of human hunters, the ancestors of Native Americans.	**BIO**
-8000	Agriculture is invented in northern Iraq with the farming of wheat and barley.	**BIO**
-8000	Potatoes and beans are cultivated in Peru, rice in Indochina.	**BIO**
-8000	Polynesians in the East Indies and Australia begin to spread out over the islands of the South Pacific.	**EARTH**
-8000	The first cities appear in Iraq and other sites in the Near East, including Jericho in Palestine.	**TECH**
-8000	In Mesopotamia (modern Iraq), clay tokens are used to tally shipments of grain and animals. This system will be the basis for the first system of numeration and writing. *See* 3500 B.C.	**TECH**
-7700	Sheep are domesticated in Iran.	**BIO**
-7000	From 7000 to 6000 B.C. the pig and the water buffalo are domesticated in China and East Asia, the chicken in South Asia.	**BIO**
-7000	New forms of wheat are cultivated in Syria and Turkey. Sugarcane is cultivated in New Guinea. Flax is grown in Southwest Asia. In Mexico, maize, squash, peppers, and beans are grown.	**BIO**
-7000	Mortar is used with sun-dried brick in Jericho.	**TECH**
-7000	Clay pottery is made in Turkey and the Near East. *See also* 6000 B.C.	**TECH**
-7000	Woven cloth is invented in Anatolia, now Turkey.	**TECH**
-6500	Trepanning, the drilling of a hole in the skull as a treatment for head injuries, is practiced in Europe and Asia. In some regions it will continue through the Middle Ages and even into the beginning of the twentieth century.	**PSYCH**

A BORING PROCEDURE

L ong before modern brain surgery there was trepanation, the removal of bone by boring a small hole in the human skull. In Russia, Europe, and the Near East, trepanation was practiced as long ago as the Neolithic period, or New Stone Age (9000–6000 B.C.). In some places it was common as recently as the Middle Ages. Trepanned skulls have even been found associated with the Inca civilization (thirteenth to sixteenth centuries A.D.) of Peru.

Trepanation may have been done sometimes as a religious ritual, but in many cases it appears to have been a medical treatment for a blow to the cranium and the resulting hematoma, or swelling filled with blood. Cranial drilling was intended to cure head injuries by allowing evil spirits to escape from the heads of the possessed. As late as the nineteenth century, trepanning was used to treat migraine headaches and epilepsy.

The procedure varied by place and time, with more than a dozen possible methods of scraping and grooving the skull to remove bone without damaging the underlying dura, a fibrous membrane that protects the brain. The Incas were trained to anaesthetize the patient with herbs and nerve pressure, and there is evidence that some cultures successfully used primitive antibiotics to stave off infection.

−6400	Cattle are domesticated in Turkey, probably from the long-horned wild ox called the auroch, or uru. Aurochs will become extinct in 1627. **BIO**
−6000	Modern-style wheat for bread is grown in Southwest Asia. Citrus fruit is domesticated in Indochina. **BIO**
−6000	The first pottery is used for food preparation and consumption. *See also* 7000 B.C. **TECH**
−5000	The llama and alpaca are domesticated in Peru. **BIO**
−5000	Irrigation is invented in Iraq. **TECH**
−5000	Nuggets of metal, including gold, silver, and copper, are used as ornaments and for trade. **TECH**
−4200	Egyptians invent the first known calendar with a 365-day year broken into twelve thirty-day months plus five days of festivals. It will be the basis for the Roman and modern Gregorian calendars. The date of invention is uncertain and may be as late as 2700 B.C. **ASTRO**
−4000	The horse is domesticated in Ukraine. The first known horse riders are the Ukrainian Sredny Stog culture. **BIO**
−4000	The first sail-propelled boats appear. **TECH**

–4000	The Egyptians mine and smelt copper ores.	**TECH**
–4000	Bricks are fired in kilns in Iraq.	**TECH**
–3600	Bronze, an alloy of 90 percent copper and 10 percent tin, is invented in the Middle East. Harder and more versatile than copper, this new metal ushers in the Bronze Age, the age of the Trojan War, Gilgamesh, and the Exodus. *See also* 1400 B.C., Iron Age.	**TECH**
–3500	Wine and beer are developed by Sumerians in western Iran.	**TECH**
–3500	The Egyptians use papyrus boats to travel on the Nile.	**TECH**
–3500	The plow is introduced in Sumeria.	**TECH**
–3500	The Sumerians develop cuneiform, the earliest known form of writing. This system, based on pictograms wedged into clay tablets, grows out of the earlier use of clay tokens. *See also* 8000 B.C.	**TECH**
–3300	Between now and 2500 B.C., speakers of proto-Indo-European begin to spread across a vast region from western Europe to central Asia. The homeland of this nomadic horse culture may have been the steppes of Ukraine and Russia. Their language will give rise to the Indo-European languages, including the branches called Germanic (English, German), Italic (Latin, French), Slavic (Russian), Indo-Iranian (Sanskrit), Baltic (Lithuanian), Celtic (Gaelic), and Greek, Albanian, Armenian, and Anatolian (Hittite).	**SOC**

THE LAST OF THE WINE

*T*he earliest inventions—fire, bows and arrows, wheeled carts—are the most difficult to place in time. New excavations and methods of analysis can overthrow the hoariest of received opinions on who invented what when. A case in point is the first manufacture of wine.

For a long time, the earliest evidence of wine manufacture came from Egypt from about 3000 B.C. Then, in 1991, Canadian graduate student Virginia Badler made a new claim about a dirty fragment of pottery from a Sumerian site in western Iran dating from about 3500 B.C. The interior of the pottery, housed at the Royal Ontario Museum, was stained red. Some archaeologists thought it was paint; Badler thought it was wine.

Chemists at the University of Pennsylvania put the issue to the test by analyzing the reddish residue with infrared spectroscopy, a method that distinguishes chemicals by the wavelengths of light they absorb. They found that the residue was rich in tannic acid, an organic substance found almost without exception in grapes. Badler was proven right and the date for the invention of wine was pushed back five hundred years.

METHUSELAH'S BIRTHDAY

*I*n North America, about 2700 B.C., a bristlecone pine began growing in the White Mountains of what is now California. That tree, now known as Methuselah, is still alive, making it the oldest-known living tree, at about 4,700 years of age. Bristlecone pines are believed to have a potential lifespan of 5,500 years and are rivaled in longevity only by the giant sequoias, which may live to 6,000. If no one cuts it down, Methuselah may still be alive in the twenty-eighth century A.D.

–3300	The wheel is invented in Sumeria (southern Iraq). It is put to use in hauling carts and making pottery.	**TECH**
–3100	The Egyptians invent an early form of hieroglyphics.	**TECH**
–3000	Hieroglyphic numerals are used in Egypt.	**MATH**
–3000	The candle is introduced in Egypt and Crete.	**TECH**
–3000	Cotton fabric is woven in India.	**TECH**
–3000	Dyes for cloth are in use in China and Egypt.	**TECH**
–2980	Imhotep, an Egyptian physician, architect, and counselor to King Zoser, flourishes between now and 2950 B.C. Often called the world's first scientist, he writes the first known medical manuscript and designs the step pyramid, or Pyramid of Zoser, the world's first large stone structure.	**MISC**
–2900	The Sumerians develop symbols for syllables, a key step in the evolution of writing.	**TECH**
–2900	Egyptian pharaoh Cheops or Khufu supervises the building of the Great Pyramid of Giza.	**TECH**
–2850	Egyptian pharaoh Chefren or Khafra orders the building of the Great Sphinx at Giza.	**TECH**
–2700	According to legend, Chinese emperor Shen Nung investigates and experiments with herbs and acupuncture. The *Pen Tsao* (*The Herbal*) is later attributed to him; he will be considered the founder of Chinese medicine.	**MED**
–2600	In the first recorded seagoing voyage, Egyptians searching for cedarwood sail to Byblos in Phoenicia.	**EARTH**
–2600	According to legend, silk manufacture begins in China.	**TECH**

–2595   Legendary Chinese emperor Huang-ti lives. The medical text *Nei Ching*, later attributed to him, claims there are four steps to developing a medical diagnosis: observation, auscultation (listening to sounds that arise within organs), interrogation, and palpation (touching)—i.e., look, listen, ask, and feel.   **MED**

–2500   The construction of Stonehenge begins in southwestern England, near Salisbury, and is completed about 1700 B.C. The monument, with its concentric circles of stones, ditches, and holes, serves both religious and astronomical purposes. Some stones are aligned with the rising and setting of the sun and moon at the summer and winter solstices.   **ASTRO**

–2500   Glass ornaments appear in Egypt.   **TECH**

–2500   During the next few centuries the Sumerians develop a system of standard weights and measures, including such units as the shekel, the mina, the log, the homer, the cubit, and the foot.   **TECH**

–2500   The oldest written story, the Sumerian *Epic of Gilgamesh*, may have first appeared in written form around this time.   **TECH**

–2400   Divination, the interpretation of omens perceived in natural phenomena, is used for medical purposes in Mesopotamia. The body organs of sacrificed animals are thought to reveal a patient's fate.   **MED**

–2300   Maps of lands and cities appear in Mesopotamia.   **TECH**

–2296   The Chinese record the first known sighting of a comet.   **ASTRO**

Stonehenge, England. (*Great Britain Ministry of Works*)

–2000	The Park of Intelligence is founded as China's first zoo. **BIO**
–2000	The Babylonians develop positional notation based on the number 60. **MATH**
–2000	Horsedrawn battle chariots and metal riding bits are invented in the Near East. **TECH**
–2000	The palace of Minos in Crete has light and air shafts and interior bathrooms with their own water supply. **TECH**
–2000	Using wooden ships, the Minoans of Crete become the world's first sea power. **TECH**
–1900	The Babylonians discover the Pythagorean theorem more than one thousand years before Pythagoras (c. 530 B.C.). **MATH**
–1800	Babylonian astronomers begin to compile records of celestial observations, including star catalogs. **ASTRO**
–1800	The Babylonians develop multiplication tables. **MATH**
–1800	Leavened bread is invented in Egypt. **TECH**
–1775	Mesopotamian physicians are ruled by the Code of Hammurabi, which includes the earliest known system of medical ethics. **MED**
–1700	Rye is cultivated by eastern Europeans, whose growing season is not long enough to generate wheat. **BIO**
–1700	The Sumerians develop squares and square roots, cubes and cube roots, and quadratic equations. They also calculate an approximate value for pi. **MATH**
–1700	Egyptian mathematicians develop a system of geometry, a ciphered numeral system, and tables of values for fractions. **MATH**
–1700	The Babylonians use windmills for irrigation. **TECH**
–1600	Egyptians use castor oil as a laxative. **MED**
–1600	Egyptian medical remedies and procedures are documented in papyrus manuscripts, especially those discovered in modern times by Edwin Smith and George Ebers (*see* 1872). Topics include arthritis, hookworm infection, and surgery for head injuries. **MED**
–1600	The Phoenicians, or Canaanites, invent the world's first purely phonetic alphabet, based on symbols for sounds, not things or syllables. This alphabet is the ancestor of all modern Western alphabets. **TECH**
–1500–1000 B.C.	The ancient Hindus derive reserpine, the first modern sedative-antihypertensive, from the root of the *Rauwolfia serpentina* plant. Hindus also become the first to perform successful skin grafting and plastic surgery of the nose. **MED**
–1500	The Egyptians use the shadow cast by a gnomon, a vertical stick, to tell time. **TECH**

–1500	The Chinese under the Shang dynasty (c. 1523–c. 1027 B.C.) develop a system of writing. **TECH**
–1470	The Aegean volcanic island of Thera (Santorini) explodes. The ashes and tidal wave bring an end to the powerful Minoan civilization of Crete, permitting the rise of the Mycenaean Greeks and the Phoenicians. **EARTH**
–1400s	The shadow of the Needle of Cleopatra in Heliopolis, Egypt, is used to estimate the solstices, seasons, and time of day. **ASTRO**
–1400	Using oared ships and guided by the stars, the Phoenicians learn to navigate in the open sea. **TECH**
–1400	The Hittites of Asia Minor (now Turkey) develop a practical method for smelting iron, ushering in the Iron Age. Bronze (*see* 3600 B.C.) is gradually replaced as the dominant metal. The revolution reaches Europe by 1000 B.C. **TECH**
–1350	The Chinese develop decimal numerals. **MATH**
–1300	The Chinese devise a working calendar by this time, if not earlier. **ASTRO**
–1200	The dye known as Tyrian purple is invented by the Phoenicians. Obtained from a Mediterranean snail, it will be a favorite of the rich and powerful throughout antiquity. **TECH**
–1200	The Egyptians dig the first of several canals from the Nile River to the Red Sea. **TECH**
–1200	Linen is woven from flax stalks in Egypt. **TECH**
–1200	The Olmec civilization of Mesoamerica (Mexico and Central America) raises pyramids and massive stone monuments. **TECH**
–1000	The Chinese develop the counting board, the forerunner of the abacus. **MATH**
–1000	Between now and c. 900 B.C., Aesculapius, the Greek (later Roman) god of medicine, becomes known as a deity. Aesculapian cults build temples where the sick congregate to be healed. **MED**
–1000	The Chinese burn coal for fuel. **TECH**
–1000	The Chinese store ice to use for refrigeration. **TECH**
–800	Egyptian physicians give drugs, along with magic spells, to heal the sick. The association between cause and effect is noticed, the basis of empirical medicine. **MED**
–800	By now, Egyptians are using sundials with six time divisions to tell time. The sundial is introduced in Greece by the sixth century B.C. **TECH**
–763	The Babylonians are the first to record a solar eclipse. **ASTRO**
–750	The arch is in use among the Etruscans in Italy. **TECH**

–700   The Chinese begin keeping records of comets, meteors, and meteorites.   **ASTRO**

–700   During the Chou dynasty (c. 1027 B.C.–256 B.C.), two doctrines evolve to form the basis of Chinese medicine. One is the doctrine of yin and yang, the two principles of masculinity, light, and heaven (yang) and femininity, darkness, and earth (yin). The other is that of the five elements or phases: metal, wood, water, fire, and earth. It is believed that humans require equilibrium among the two principles and five elements to remain in good health.   **MED**

–700   The Assyrians introduce the aqueduct.   **TECH**

–668   The reign of Ashurbanipal, king of Assyria, begins (ends 627 B.C.). He establishes a library in his capital at Nineveh, which is destroyed c. 612 B.C.   **MISC**

–650   The Lydians of Asia Minor introduce the first standard coinage.   **TECH**

–625   Thales of Miletus, a Greek philosopher, astronomer, and mathematician, is born in present-day Turkey (d. 547 B.C.). Among other things, he will theorize correctly that solar eclipses are the result of the moon's passing in front of the sun. See also May 28, 585 B.C.   **MISC**

–600   The Japanese practice massage and acupuncture, adopted from the Chinese as healing therapies.   **MED**

–600   The Zapotecs of Mesoamerica invent a system of hieroglyphics, the earliest known writing in the Americas.   **TECH**

May 28, 585 B.C.   A solar eclipse, predicted by Greek mathematician Thales of Miletus, occurs during a battle between the Lydians and Medes. The warring parties take it as an omen and make peace.   **ASTRO**

–585   Thales develops deductive geometry. The Theorem of Thales, that an angle inscribed in a semicircle is a right angle, is attributed to him, though he may have learned it from the Babylonians.   **MATH**

–585   Thales studies magnetism.   **PHYS**

–580   Thales theorizes that water is the fundamental element of which all other substances are made.   **CHEM**

–570   The diluvial doctrine, a theory proposing that the earth's surface was transformed by great floods, begins to develop and spread. The concept can be traced to the early Greek thinkers Xenophanes and Anaximander. Diluvialism will flourish in the seventeenth and eighteenth centuries A.D.   **EARTH**

–547   Greek philosopher and astronomer Anaximander dies. During his career, he introduced the idea of evolution, claiming that life begins in marshy slime conditions and slowly evolves onto drier areas.   **BIO**

–547	Greek philosopher and astronomer Anaximander dies. During his career, he introduced the idea of evolution, claiming that life begins in marshy slime conditions and slowly evolves onto drier areas. **BIO**
–530	Greek philosopher and mathematician Pythagoras argues that the earth is a sphere and that the sun, moon, stars, and five visible planets (Mercury, Venus, Mars, Jupiter, Saturn) revolve around the earth in eight concentric spheres, rotating independently. The friction between the spheres generates harmonious, virtually inaudible sounds called the music of the spheres. **ASTRO**
–530	Pythagoras is the first Greek to learn that the morning star and evening star are the same object. He names this planet Aphrodite, after the goddess of love known by the Romans as Venus, hence the planet's modern name. **ASTRO**
–530	Pythagoras proves the so-called Pythagorean Theorem, that the square of the hypotenuse of a right triangle is equal to the sum of the squares of the other two sides. *See* 1900 B.C., the Babylonians. **MATH**
–530	The idea that the brain is the center of higher activity will be credited to Pythagoras. **MED**
–510	Greek traveler Hecataeus draws the first recognizable map of the Mediterranean world. **EARTH**
–500	Hanno of Carthage navigates down the west African coast and describes, among other things, the gorilla. **BIO**
–500	Phoenician navigators are believed to have reached the Atlantic Ocean, sailing as far as Cornwall, England, to the north, where they established tin mines, and circumnavigating Africa to the south. **EARTH**
–500	By now the abacus, the first significant calculating device, is known in Egypt. **MATH**
–500	The work known as the *Sulvasutras* ("Rules of the Cord") summarizes Indian geometry. **MATH**
–500	Chinese philosopher Confucius is one of the first to discuss human nature and how it can be modified. **PSYCH**
–500s	The sundial is in use in Greece. *See* 800 B.C., Egypt. **TECH**
–470	The Greek Alcmaeon becomes the first known physician to dissect human bodies. Because of objections to human dissection, anatomy studies will decline until the works of Mondino De'Luzzi in 1316. **MED**

Hippocrates. (*National Library of Medicine*)

—460   Greek physician Hippocrates is born on Cos (an island off Turkey, known later as Kos). He will set medicine free of the shackles of philosophy and religion by being the first to record case histories, practice bedside observations, and provide physicians with moral inspiration and ethical standards. The Hippocratic oath, administered to new physicians, will become the best known of the Hippocratic writings, but its original authorship will remain uncertain.   **MED**

—450   The Greek philosopher Leucippus epitomizes the study of rationalism by stating that every event has a natural cause, ruling out supernatural intervention as an explanation.   **MISC**

—440   Greek philosopher Democritus theorizes that the Milky Way is made up of many stars, that matter is composed of invisible particles called atoms, and that the moon is similar to the earth.   **MISC**

—430   Greek philosopher Empedocles of Acragas (Agrigentum) speculates that the world is made up of four elements: earth, air, water, and fire. *See also* 350 B.C., Aristotle.   **CHEM**

—428   Greek natural philosopher and mathematician Anaxagoras dies. The author of *On Nature*, he is imprisoned for suggesting that the sun is a big, hot stone rather than a deity and that the moon is an inhabited body that borrows light from the sun.   **ASTRO**

-420   Greek mathematician Hippias introduces the first curve beyond the circle and the straight line, the trisectrix or quadratrix. **MATH**

-420   Greek mathematicians discover incommensurable line segments. **MATH**

-420   Greek physician Hippocrates believes, incorrectly, that only women suffer hysteria, claiming it is caused by a "wandering uterus." He does present accurate descriptions of mania, phobias, paranoia, and melancholia. **PSYCH**

-414   Greek mathematician Theaetetus is born (*d.* 369 B.C.). He will study the five regular solids and develop the theorem that there are five—and only five—regular polyhedra. **MATH**

-408   Greek philosopher Eudoxus of Cnidus is born (*d.* 355 B.C.). He will develop a model of celestial motion involving a complex combination of rotating spheres. He will also establish the geometric theory of irrational numbers. **MATH**

....

"To do nothing is sometimes a good remedy."—Hippocrates, Greek physician; c. 400 B.C.

....

-400   By now the Babylonians have established the zodiac circle, the band in the sky that includes the apparent paths of the sun, moon, and planets. Horoscopes become available describing the presumed influence of the sun, moon, and planets given their position in the zodiac at the time of one's birth. **ASTRO**

-400   Philolaus, a member of the Pythagorean school, argues that the earth, sun, moon, planets, and stars are all in motion around a "central fire." This is the earliest known theory of a moving earth. **ASTRO**

-400   In Chaldea, horoscopes become available based on the planets' positions in the constellations of the zodiac at the time of one's birth. **ASTRO**

-400   By now the Greeks have formulated three famous problems that will puzzle mathematicians for centuries: squaring the circle, duplicating the cube (*see* 360 B.C., Menaechmus) and trisecting the angle. By the nineteenth century it will be shown that the three problems are unsolvable using the straightedge and compass alone. **MATH**

-400   Greek philosopher Democritus argues that objects in the external world radiate beams that induce perceptions in the human mind. **PHYS**

-400   Greeks working for Dionysius of Syracuse, Sicily, invent the catapult, the first artillery weapon. **TECH**

-390   Greek astronomer Heracleides is born in Pontus, now part of Turkey (*d.* c. 320 B.C.). He will be the first to argue that Venus and Mercury orbit the sun. **ASTRO**

−387   Plato founds the Academy in Athens, often considered the world's first university.   **MISC**

....

"To be acceptable as scientific knowledge a truth must be a deduction from other truths."—Aristotle, Greek philosopher; fourth century B.C.

....

−384   Greek philosopher Aristotle is born (*d*. 322 B.C.). After studying under Plato, he will write on logic, ethics, poetics, rhetoric, metaphysics, politics, and nature. His teachings on biology, medicine, and the physical world will be transmitted to Europe, mainly through Arab scholars, during the Middle Ages. These views will be considered authoritative until the scientific revolution (c. 1550 to 1700) calls them into question.   **MISC**

HOW DO YOU KNOW THE EARTH IS ROUND?

*M*ost people today accept that the earth is round, but many would be hard put to defend this claim. After all, as seen from a casual stroll or even from an airplane, the earth looks flat. Without resorting to pictures from space (which a conspiracy theorist might reject as fake), how can you prove that the earth is round?

This question was answered more than two thousand years ago by the Greek philosopher Aristotle (384–322 B.C.), who argued that one can see the earth's shape clearly during a lunar eclipse. As the moon passes under the earth's shadow, the shape of the shadow is always round. This effect might sometimes be produced by a flat disk, but not always. For example, the sun would sometimes strike the disk edge on, producing a shadow in the shape of a straight line. Only a sphere will always produce a round shadow.

For the unconvinced, Aristotle pointed out that travelers going north or south saw new stars appear over the horizon ahead, while stars that had been visible disappeared under the horizon in the rear. Ships going out to sea disappeared hull first, whichever direction they took. These effects could be explained only by a round earth.

As it turns out, the earth is not a perfect sphere but an oblate spheroid, a sphere slightly flattened at its poles and slightly bulging at the equator. English physicist Isaac Newton (1642-1727) showed that this effect would result from the earth's rotation. However, Aristotle's conclusion, still roughly correct, has been held by educated people ever since.

-372   Greek botanist Theophrastus is born (*d.* c. 287 B.C.). He studies un-
        der Plato and Aristotle, carrying on the tradition of biology and con-
        centrating on the plant world. He will be considered the founder of
        botany.   **BIO**

-370   Between now and 350 B.C., Diocles of Carystos writes the first
        Greek herbal.   **MED**

-360   Greek mathematician Eudoxus of Cnidus introduces a new theory
        of proportion: a definition of equal ratios that deals with the prob-
        lem of comparing ratios of incommensurable magnitudes. He also
        develops the axiom of continuity that serves as the basis for the
        method of exhaustion.   **MATH**

-360   Greek mathematician Menaechmus discovers conic sections, the
        curves later known as the ellipse, parabola, and hyperbola. He uses
        conics to provide a solution to the problem of duplicating the cube.
        See c. 400 B.C.   **MATH**

....

*"For ourselves, we may take as a basic assumption, clear
from a survey of particular cases, that natural things are
some or all of them subject to change."—Aristotle,
Greek philosopher; fourth century B.C.*

....

-360   Greek mathematician Dinostratus uses the trisectrix or quadratrix
        of Hippias (*see* c. 420 B.C., Hippias) to provide a solution to the
        problem of squaring the circle (*see* c. 400 B.C.).   **MATH**

-352   The Chinese report the first recorded supernova.   **ASTRO**

-350   Chinese astronomer Shin Shen prepares a star catalog with about
        eight hundred entries.   **ASTRO**

-350   Aristotle classifies animals. He will be considered the founder of
        classical biology and zoology.   **BIO**

-350   In *De caelo* (*On the Heavens*), Aristotle defines chemical elements
        as constituents of bodies that cannot be broken down into other
        parts.   **CHEM**

-350   Aristotle theorizes that the universe is arranged in concentric shells
        with the earth dominating at the center, then water, air, and fire. A
        fifth shell, the site of the heavenly bodies, is unchanging and incor-
        ruptible, composed of a fifth element, ether.   **EARTH**

-350   Aristotle writes on disease, comparative anatomy, embryology, and
        psychology. His approach to disease is grounded in the theory of
        four humors (blood, phlegm, yellow bile, and black bile), four quali-
        ties (hot, dry, moist, and wet), and four elements (earth, fire, air,
        and water). Despite evidence to the contrary, Aristotle's ideas will
        dominate medicine for centuries.   **MED**

THE APPIAN WAY

*T*he world's first all-weather road system was built to facilitate modern warfare. Following their defeat in the Samnite Wars, particularly their humiliation at the Battle of the Caudine Forks along the rocky Apennines in 321 B.C., the Roman military began to develop more effective attack formations and better transportation routes through uneven terrain. The formation, the legion, allowed troops to scatter when facing troublesome roads, then reunite easily when conditions improved. The improved transportation route was the Via Appia, or Appian Way.

The Roman censor Appius Claudius Caecus ordered construction of the Appian Way, a paved road uniting Rome and Capua, to be usable by troops in all weather. Begun in 312 B.C., the road was built of multiple layers of durable materials, the top layer composed of a mixture of concrete, rubble, and stones set in mortar. The road was instrumental in facilitating Roman victory in future wars with the Samnites.

Equally important was the Appian Way's various political uses. It was crucial to building commercial interests and sustaining cultural links with and political control over the provinces. Over time, several roads were built to link Rome with other cities and colonies, including the Via Flaminia (Flaminian Way), which headed north to link Italy with the Latin colony of Ariminum. In all, the Roman road system covered more than fifty thousand miles and crossed through thirty countries. Only remnants of the roads still exist.

−350	In his *Organon* Aristotle systematically outlines the rules of logic. **MISC**
−350	Aristotle claims that memory is based on three principles of association: similarity, contrast, and contiguity. He argues that arousing violent emotions through drama has a cathartic effect on human audiences, allowing viewers to purge themselves of aggressive impulses. **PSYCH**
−340	Greek physicist Strato is born (*d.* 270 B.C.). Like Aristotle, he will detect the acceleration of falling bodies but state incorrectly that heavier bodies fall faster than lighter ones. **PHYS**
−335	Aristotle founds the university called the Lyceum in Athens. His lectures there will be collected into about 150 volumes, fifty of which will survive to modern times. **MISC**
−330	Athenian female physician Agnodike challenges a law prohibiting women from practicing medicine on other women. As a result of her successful efforts at assisting women in childbirth, the law is changed and Athenian women are allowed to practice medicine. **MED**

–320	The Greek philosopher Theophrastus writes the first systematic book on botany, describing over five hundred plant species. **BIO**
–320	Mathematicians Aristaeus and Euclid write on conics, the curves formed by a plane intersecting a cone. **MATH**
–314	Theophrastus of Eresus writes *Peri Lithon* (*On Stone*), which catalogs the mineral substances then found in Athenian trade. This short treatise is the first known geology text. **EARTH**
–312	The Roman consul Appius Claudius begins building the Appian Way, which will stretch 132 miles from Rome to Capua and later be extended to Brundisium (Brindisi). Initially covered by gravel and later by stone, it will be the best road yet built. **TECH**
–300s	By now the Babylonians have developed a symbol for zero. **MATH**
–300	Greek adventurer Pytheas sails into the Atlantic, voyaging as far as Scandinavia and the Baltic Sea. En route he observes and describes tides, a phenomenon little known in the Mediterranean. **EARTH**
–300	Euclid, a Greek in Alexandria, Egypt, writes his *Elements*, a textbook summarizing and systematizing Greek mathematics, including plane and solid geometry and the theory of numbers. It will be accepted in the West as a basic reference until the modern age. **MATH**
–300	A classic work of Chinese mathematics, the *Chou pei suan ching*, is written. **MATH**
–300	Chinese mathematicians use a system of "rod" symbols for numerals (sometimes written, sometimes represented by physical rods) to carry out calculations of large numbers. **MATH**
–300	The third century B.C. is a golden age of Greek mathematics, due largely to the work of Euclid, Apollonius of Perga, and Archimedes at Alexandria, Egypt. **MATH**
–300	Indian mathematicians develop the Brahmi numerals, a decimal system of numeration without a place-value notation. **MATH**
–300	Alexandria's Greek school of medicine is founded. **MED**
–300	Ptolemy I, ruler of Egypt, founds the university in Alexandria called the Museum. Its library will be the largest yet known. **MISC**
–295	Greek physician Praxagoras distinguishes between veins and arteries. The name *arteries* is derived from this physician's mistaken belief that arteries carry air. **MED**
–287	Greek scientist, mathematician, and inventor Archimedes is born (*d.* 212 B.C.). He will discover the law of specific gravity and study the mathematics of the lever. Among his inventions will be the Archimedean screw, a device to lift water and loose materials such as sand. **MISC**

-280   Greek anatomist Herophilus divides nerves into sensory and motor, names the first section of the small bowel the duodenum, and names the prostate gland. After studying the function of the arteries and veins, Herophilus advocates bloodletting, which will be used as a therapeutic for more than two thousand years.   **MED**

-280   The Colossus of Rhodes, a 105-foot-high statue of the sun god, is completed.   **TECH**

-280   Sostratus of Cnidus builds a 300-foot lighthouse on Pharos near Alexandria, Egypt. Projecting light from a series of concave mirrors, it will become one of the seven wonders of the ancient world.   **TECH**

....

"Give me a firm spot on which to stand, and I will move the earth."—Greek mathematician and inventor Archimedes on the lever, one of his principal areas of research; third century B.C.

....

-270   Greek scientist Ctesibius invents a popular new version of the ancient water clock, a device that tells time according to the steady accumulation of water in a chamber.   **TECH**

-260   Greek mathematician and scientist Archimedes calculates the value of pi.   **MATH**

-260   The Roman numeral system is at an advanced stage. It will survive in Europe until the Middle Ages, when it will be gradually replaced by Arabic numerals. *See* 1202, Fibonacci.   **MATH**

-260   While sitting in a public bath Archimedes discovers the law of specific gravity now known as Archimedes' principle: a body dropped into a fluid displaces a volume of fluid equal to its own volume.   **PHYS**

-260   Greek scientist Archimedes works out the mathematics of the lever.   **TECH**

-250   The *Chui-chang suan-shu* (*Nine Chapters on the Mathematical Art*) is among the most influential Chinese books of mathematics. It contains more than two hundred problems on engineering, surveying, calculation, agriculture, and right triangles as well as solutions to problems in simultaneous linear equations using positive and negative numbers.   **MATH**

-250   From now until 48 B.C., the Alexandrian medical school enjoys its greatest prominence. It is the only center in the ancient world where human dissection is regularly practiced for scientific reasons.   **MED**

–250   The Chinese book *Mo Ching*, written by followers of the philosopher Mo-tzu, contains a statement of the first law of motion that will be stated in 1687 by Isaac Newton in his *Principia*: a body continues in a state of rest or in uniform motion unless acted upon by outside forces.   **PHYS**

–240   Chinese astronomers make the first known observation of Halley's Comet. *See* 1705, Halley.   **ASTRO**

–240   Eratosthenes of Cyrene, librarian at Alexandria, Egypt, correctly calculates the diameter of the earth as about 8,000 miles and the circumference as about 25,000 miles. *See also* 1684, Picard.   **EARTH**

–225   Greek mathematician Apollonius of Perga, known in antiquity as the Great Geometer, publishes his *Conics*, which makes several important advances in the study of these curves.   **MATH**

–214   The Great Wall of China is begun by Emperor Shih Huang Ti, founder of the Ch'in dynasty. It will eventually extend 1,500 miles from the Pacific Ocean to central Asia.   **TECH**

–200s   Greek astronomer Aristarchus of Samos is the first person known to argue that the earth revolves around the sun. He also proposes that day and night are caused by the earth's rotation and makes estimates of the sun's distance and size that are several orders of magnitude too small. *See also* 1650, Wendelin.   **ASTRO**

–200   The Greeks invent the astrolabe, a device for measuring the positions of heavenly bodies.   **ASTRO**

–170   Scholars working for Eumenes II of Pergamum, in Asia Minor, invent parchment, a writing material made from hides. It will compete effectively with the more ancient writing vehicle, papyrus.   **TECH**

–165   The Chinese make the first recorded observations of sunspots.   **ASTRO**

–150   Greek astronomer Hipparchus of Nicaea correctly calculates the distance of the moon from the earth as about 240,000 miles.   **ASTRO**

–140   Chinese philosopher Han Ying makes the first known reference to the hexagonal structure of snowflakes.   **CHEM**

–140   Hipparchus compiles the first trigonometric table. His table of chords helps to introduce the systematic use of the 360° circle.   **MATH**

–101   The Romans become the first to employ water power to mill flour.   **TECH**

–100s   Hipparchus compiles a star catalog and discovers changes in the equinoxes caused by the wobbling of the earth as it rotates. He argues that the earth is motionless at the center of the universe, a view that will dominate European thinking until the time of Copernicus. *See* 1543, Copernicus. *See also* 140, Ptolemy.   **ASTRO**

–100s   Hipparchus invents a system of magnitude for measuring the brightness of stars, the basis for the modern system. *See also* 1856, Pogson.   **ASTRO**

–100   Greek astronomer Posidonius of Apamea erroneously calculates that the earth's circumference is 18,000 miles. This value will be accepted as true through the Middle Ages, while the correct value (deduced by Eratosthenes in 240 B.C.) will be forgotten.   **EARTH**

–100   Chinese mathematicians use negative numbers.   **MATH**

–100   In Syria the process of glassblowing is invented.   **TECH**

–99   The Roman physician Asclepiades opposes the theory of humors put forth by Hippocrates. Asclepiades teaches that the body is composed of disconnected atoms, separated by pores, and orderly motion of the atoms must be maintained. He attempts to cure disease through exercise, bathing, and varying the diet. This theory is revived in different forms far into the eighteenth century.   **MED**

–63   A primitive system of shorthand is developed by former slave Marcus Tullius Tiro.   **TECH**

–60   In the poem *On the Nature of Things*, the Roman philosopher Lucretius speculates, as had Democritus (*see* 440 B.C.), that matter is made of atoms.   **PHYS**

–52   Chinese astronomer Ken Shou-ch'ang builds a stellar observation device called an armillary ring, which consists of a metal circle representing the equator.   **ASTRO**

–50   Mayan written records begin in Mesoamerica. Though writing in the New World did not begin with the Maya (*see* 600 B.C., the Zapotecs), they were to give it its greatest refinement, using a mix of ideographic and phonetic elements. The Maya classic period will last from A.D. 250 to 900.   **TECH**

–46   Following the advice of Greek astronomer Sosigenes, Julius Caesar institutes the Julian calendar, a reform of the Roman calendar based on estimates that the year is 365¼ days rather than 365 days. This calendar alternates three regular years of 365 days with one leap year of 366 days. With the reforms proclaimed by Pope Gregory XIII in 1582, this calendar will become the basis for the one now in use throughout most of the world. *See* October 15, 1582.   **ASTRO**

–44   In May and June, Roman and Chinese observers report a red comet visible in daylight. Many Romans believe it to be the departed spirit of Julius Caesar, exalted to divine status after his assassination on March 15. The red color is probably due to dust in the air from recent eruptions of Mount Etna in Sicily.   **ASTRO**

−44   From March to May, Mount Etna in Sicily undergoes a series of eruptions. Volcanic dust darkens the skies. Three years of crop failures are reported by the Chinese.   **EARTH**

−40s   The Tower of Winds in Athens is built by Andronikos of Kyrrhestes. Its timekeeping device combines a water clock and eight solar clocks.   **TECH**

−28   From now until 1638, Chinese astronomers keep continuous records of sunspot activity.   **ASTRO**

−27   The Roman Pantheon, an early domed building, is begun this year.   **TECH**

A.D.

20   Greek historian and philosopher Strabo summarizes the geographical knowledge of his day in *Geographia*.   **EARTH**

43   In *De situ orbis* ("A Description of the World"), Roman geographer Pomponius Mela divides the earth into the climatic zones: North Frigid, North Temperate, Torrid (equatorial), South Temperate, and South Frigid.   **EARTH**

50   Roman philosopher Seneca speculates that there is change and imperfection beyond the moon, contrary to prevailing belief in the unchanging heavens.   **ASTRO**

50   Roman poet Lucius Junius Moderatus Columella suggests that grain and legume crops be rotated and fields be "dunged" to preserve the earth's fertility. Previously Romans have used a mixture of blood and bone as fertilizer.   **BIO**

50   Roman encyclopedist Aulus Cornelius Celsus writes the first organized medical history, which describes the four cardinal symptoms of inflammation: redness, swelling, heat, and pain.   **MED**

50   Greek engineer Hero, or Heron, of Alexandria invents a primitive steam engine, but it is never put to productive use.   **TECH**

60   Greek physician Pedanius Dioscorides compiles the first systematic pharmacopeia. This famous herbal, *De materia medica*, describes more than five hundred plants and thirty-five animal products. Ninety of the plants he mentions will still be in use in the twentieth century. *See also* 1544.   **MED**

70   Roman natural philosopher Pliny the Elder publishes *Natural History*, a thirty-seven-volume work on zoology, botany, astronomy, and geography. It will become as famous for its errors as for the facts it propagates throughout the Middle Ages.   **BIO**

70   In China the religion of Buddhism (imported from India, where it was founded in the sixth century B.C.), introduces faith healing, hypnotism, autosuggestion, and meditation arts as components of medical practice.   **MED**

75   Greek mathematician Hero, or Heron, of Alexandria publishes the *Metrica*, in which he demonstrates Heron's formula for the area of a triangle.   **MATH**

79   Mount Vesuvius erupts near Naples, burying the towns of Pompeii and Herculaneum. The buried towns, rediscovered fifteen centuries later, in 1592, will serve as a spur to early archaeologists. *See also* 1592.   **ARCH**

90   In Rome, multiple aqueducts provide 250 gallons of water per day to the citizenry.   **TECH**

100s   The Chinese note that a magnetic sliver, allowed to turn freely, always points north–south. *See also* 1180, Neckam.   **PHYS**

THE ERUPTION OF MOUNT VESUVIUS
August 24, 79

*M*eanwhile on Mount Vesuvius broad sheets of fire and leaping flames blazed at several points, their bright glare emphasized by the darkness of night....

They [his uncle's household] debated whether to stay indoors or take their chance in the open, for the buildings were now shaking with violent shocks, and seemed to be swaying to and fro as if they were torn from their foundations. Outside, on the other hand, there was the danger of falling pumice stones, even though these were light and porous....

We also saw the sea sucked away and apparently forced back by the earthquake; at any rate it receded from the shore so that quantities of sea creatures were left stranded on dry sand....

At last the darkness thinned and dispersed like smoke or cloud; then there was genuine daylight, and the sun actually shone out, but yellowish as it is during an eclipse. We were terrified to see everything changed, buried deep in ashes like snowdrifts.

> —Eyewitness impressions of the disaster that destroyed the towns of Pompeii and Herculaneum, from Pliny the Younger, in *Letters (translated by Betty Radice, 1969)*

100   In China it is discovered that dried chrysanthemum flowers can kill insects. The Chinese proceed to develop a powder from these flowers and invent the first insecticide.   **BIO**

100   A female alchemist known as Mary the Jewess, living in the first or second century, invents or at least elaborates such types of chemical apparatus as a three-armed still, a hot-ash bath, the water bath later named the *bain-marie* in her honor, and the dung bed. Her writings combine practical techniques, mystical imagery, and theoretical ideas.   **CHEM**

100   Alexandrian mathematician Menelaus writes on spherical geometry in his *Spherics*.   **MATH**

100   Mathematician Nicomachus of Gerasa, near Jerusalem, writes the *Introductio arithmeticae*, which uses mathematics in the service of neoplatonic philosophy.   **MATH**

100   Indian physician Charaka presents ethical standards to be required of those caring for the sick, including purity, cleverness, kindness, good behavior, and competence in cooking.   **MED**

105   Chinese inventor Tsai Lun devises paper, a writing surface that can be produced cheaply from wood, rags, or other substances containing cellulose (as opposed to papyrus, made from an Egyptian reed, or parchment, made from hides). It will not reach Europe until 1320.   **TECH**

106   In central Asia, traders from China meet to barter Chinese silk and spices with Roman traders of gems, precious metals, glassware, pottery, and wine.   **MISC**

117   Between now and 138, Greek physician Soranus of Ephesus serves as a respected authority on gynecology, obstetrics, and infant diseases. His treatise on pediatrics contains the earliest description of rickets.   **MED**

122   Hadrian's Wall is built in Britain to defend against northern tribesmen, including the Picts. The wall, built mainly of stone, runs seventy-two miles, from the Tyne to the Solway.   **TECH**

125   Zhang Heng of China refines the armillary ring, first introduced in 52 B.C. and used for observing the stars.   **ASTRO**

126   Between now and 145, during the Shun Ti reign, the Taoist religious leader Chang Tao-ling composes a guide to charms and incantations for curing disease.   **MED**

128   Imported wheat from Egypt and North Africa lowers grain prices and decreases the number of Roman farmers, who cannot compete with foreign prices.   **BIO**

140   In the *Megalé syntaxis tēs astronomias*, later known as *The Almagest*, the Alexandrian astronomer, geographer, and mathematician Claudius Ptolemaeus (Ptolemy) synthesizes the geocentric Ptolemaic system that will dominate Western cosmology until the Copernican revolution of 1543. In Ptolemy's system all the heavenly bodies revolve around a fixed earth. It will come to western Europe by way of Arabic translation in 827.   **ASTRO**

140   Ptolemy introduces the concept of epicycles, hypothetical small circles on which each planet moves. Epicycles were used to account for apparent anomalies in planetary motion that were not correctly explained until Kepler's works in 1609.   **ASTRO**

140   Ptolemy's *Almagest* includes a table of chords and writings on trigonometry.   **MATH**

....

"Every animal is sad after coitus except the human female and the rooster."—Claudius Galen, Greek physician and scholar; second century A.D.

....

160   Greek physician and anatomist Claudius Galen dissects animals, applying the results (sometimes mistakenly) to humans. He shows the importance of the spinal cord, uses the pulse as a diagnostic tool, and describes the flow of urine to the bladder. He also describes respiration and proves that the arteries carry blood, but he incorrectly explains the passage of blood through the heart. Right and wrong, his pronouncements will carry medical authority for the next seventeen centuries.   **MED**

160   Galen establishes the doctrine of vitalism, which claims that a force that is neither chemical nor mechanical is responsible for the processes of life. He specifically identifies animal spirits in the brain, vital spirits in the heart, and natural spirits in the liver.   **MED**

180   The first known alchemy manuscripts appear in Egypt.   **CHEM**

185   The Chinese observe a supernova in the constellation Centaurus that remains visible for twenty months.   **ASTRO**

190   The Chinese calculate pi to five decimal places: 3.14159.   **MATH**

250   Greek mathematician Diophantus devises solutions to problems that represent the beginnings of algebra. His problems include ones that must be solved with whole numbers, known as Diophantine equations.   **MATH**

250   The Mayan classic period begins in Mesoamerica (Mexico and Central America). Lasting until 900, the classic Maya civilization will make great advances in agriculture, astronomy, mathematics, writing, and architecture.   **MISC**

∙∙

"Scourges, pestilence, famine, earthquakes, and wars are to be regarded as blessings, since they serve to prune away the luxuriant growth of the human race."—Quintus Septimius Florens Tertullianus (Tertullian), Carthaginian churchman; A.D. 195

∙∙∙∙∙∙∙∙∙∙∙∙∙∙∙∙∙∙∙∙∙∙∙∙∙∙∙∙,∙∙∙∙∙∙∙∙∙∙∙∙∙∙∙∙∙∙∙∙∙∙

270	In China, Wu dynasty alchemists manufacture gunpowder by combining sulfur and saltpeter.	TECH
Aug. 29, 284	The Coptic calendar is introduced in Egypt and Ethiopia.	TECH
300	Zosimos of Panopolis, Egypt, writes a summary of alchemy.	CHEM
300	During their classic period, the Mayans use sweat baths for medicinal purposes.	MED
304	Integrated pest management begins in China when Hsi Han records how to use specific types of ants to control other insect pests attacking mandarin oranges.	BIO
350	The Chinese invent an early form of printing using blocks of raised, reversed symbols smeared with ink.	TECH
390	Roman matron St. Fabiola is influential in the founding of the first general public hospital in western Europe.	MED
400	Alexandrian philosophers coin the term *chemistry* to denote the process of change in material substances.	CHEM
400	Indian texts called the *Siddhantas* contain the first trigonometric use of half-chords, the predecessor of the modern sine function.	MATH
400	Indian physician Susruta describes plastic surgery operations for earlobe deformity, skin grafting, and rhinoplasty (nasal reconstruction).	MED
400	The Chinese invent the wheelbarrow.	TECH
406	Rye, oats, and spelt (wheat for animal feed) are brought to Europe by such invaders as the Alans, Sciri, and Vandals.	BIO
410	Alexandrian mathematician Proclus is born (*d.* 485). He will preserve information on Greek mathematics before Euclid, particularly in his summary of the lost work of Eudemus, *History of Geometry* (c. 335 B.C.).	MATH
433	St. Patrick spreads Christianity throughout Ireland. By 795 Irish monks, following the path of the navigator St. Brendan, are believed to have reached Iceland.	EARTH

Sept. 4, 476   The last Roman emperor, Romulus Augustulus, is deposed by the Goths under Odoacer. This date traditionally marks the end of the western Roman empire and of classical antiquity, with its heritage of art and learning. The Middle Ages that follow in Europe are considered to last roughly until the mid-fifteenth century, when the Renaissance (fifteenth through seventeenth centuries) will revive and extend classical art, scholarship, and science. *See* May 30, 1453, Constantinople.   **MISC**

499   Indian mathematician Aryabhata writes the *Aryabhatiya*, a summary of astronomical and mathematical knowledge. Among other things, he recalculates the Ptolemaic measurements of celestial motion and suggests that the earth rotates.   **ASTRO**

500   Polynesians begin settling the islands of Hawaii.   **EARTH**

529   St. Benedict founds the monastic order of Benedictines, under whom care of the sick becomes a part of monastery life. The era is marked by the belief that saints and miracles can heal the sick and dying.   **MED**

529   Byzantine emperor Justinian closes the Academy and the Lyceum, two universities in Athens, founded respectively by Plato in 387 B.C. and Aristotle in 335 B.C. The closing is motivated by the Christian church's distrust of pagan learning.   **MISC**

537   The church of Hagia Sophia in Constantinople takes full advantage of the art of dome design, with a large dome placed on a square support and pierced with many windows.   **TECH**

552   Silkworms are smuggled from the Far East at the order of Byzantine emperor Justinian, thus introducing silk production to Constantinople.   **BIO**

560   Eutocius's commentaries on Archimedes and Apollonius preserve many of their mathematical ideas.   **MATH**

595   Hindu numerals make their first appearance on a plate where the date 346 is written in decimal-place value notation. At this time the Hindu system includes only nine numerals—the tenth, the zero, will not appear until later (*see* 876). Hindu numerals will be adopted by the Arabs and later by the West. *See* 820, Muhammad ibn al-Khwārizmī.   **MATH**

600   Chinese mathematicians Zu Chong-zhi and his son Zu Geng-shi calculate pi to seven decimal places.   **MATH**

600   Eastern and northern European agricultural production improves with the refinement by the Slavs of the coulter (a blade that cuts vertically into the ground in advance of the plowshare) and moldboard plow.   **TECH**

NUMERAL ENVY

*I*n 529 the Byzantine emperor Justinian closed the philosophical schools of Athens, including the Academy, founded by Plato some nine centuries earlier, in 387 B.C. Now regarded as an archetypal victory of ignorance over knowledge, this move was made to defend the state religion, Christianity, from what was then perceived as pagan influences.

Some of the Academy's scholars moved to Syria, where they founded centers of Greek learning. However, they regarded their new home as an academic backwater and expressed disdain for the level of knowledge of non-Greeks. On hearing of this, Syrian bishop Severus Sebokht was moved, writing in 662, to let the Greeks know that "there are also others who know something." Noting that the Hindus in particular had made great advances in astronomy and mathematics, Sebokht praised their "valuable methods of calculation, and their computing that surpasses description. I wish only to say that this computation is done by means of nine signs." This is now considered the first explicit mention anywhere of the Hindu numeral system; based on ten but at the time still lacking the zero. This system would later (c. 820) be adopted by the Arabs and still later by the entire Western world.

Thus, the first mention of Hindu numerals was an indirect result of Justinian's distaste for Greek learning and the Greeks' distaste for everyone else's.

---

602 | Priests from Korea introduce the Chinese calendar and astronomy to Japan. **ASTRO**

620 | Indian mathematician Brahmagupta uses negative numbers. His *Brahma-sphuta-siddhānta* treats trigonometry, algebra, and mensuration. **MATH**

Sept. 20, 622 | The Arab prophet Muhammad (c. 570–632), founder of the religion of Islam, flees from his native city of Mecca to Medina. Muslims will date their calendars from this event, called the Hegira, or flight. After his death, Muhammad's followers will establish an Arab empire stretching from Spain, North Africa, and the Middle East to central Asia. In the following centuries the Arabs will sponsor a revival of science and learning that will greatly influence European civilization. **MISC**

628 | Sugar is introduced to Constantinople by soldiers returning through India from fighting in Persia (Iran). **TECH**

635   The Chinese observe that a comet's tail always points away from the sun. *See also* 1540, Peter Apian.   **ASTRO**

642   The Arabs conquer Alexandria, Egypt, the ancient site of Hellenistic learning. Although they destroy its museum and library, the Arabs will preserve, translate, and extend the scientific and mathematical knowledge of the Greeks.   **MISC**

662   Syrian bishop Severus Sebokht makes the earliest specific reference to Hindu numerals. *See* 595 for their earliest occurrence.   **MATH**

673   Callinicus, an alchemist in Constantinople, invents Greek fire, a chemical mixture (perhaps naphtha, potassium nitrate, and calcium oxide) that burns on water and is useful in naval battles.   **TECH**

675   The first sundial in England is erected in Newcastle.   **ASTRO**

700s   Independently from the Hindus, the Maya of Mesoamerica (Mexico and Central America) have developed a system of positional notation based on twenty and using zero as a place holder. With this system they are able to calculate enormous numbers.   **MATH**

700   The Chinese invent porcelain, a form of pottery that eventually reaches Europe under the popular name *china*.   **TECH**

700   Windmills are invented in Persia (Iran). The Crusaders will bring the idea to Europe in the twelfth century.   **TECH**

701   By now the Arabs have introduced spices from Indonesia to the Mediterranean world. This commercially successful innovation will one day provide an incentive to European explorers seeking easy access to the East.   **MISC**

708   Safer than local water and said by some to have medicinal powers, tea becomes a commercially popular drink in China, though it has been known there since prehistoric times. It will come to Europe in the seventeenth century.   **TECH**

721   Arab alchemist Jabir ibn Hayyan, or Geber, is born (*d.* c. 815). He will draw on ancient Greek alchemy to try to turn base metals into gold and discover the elixir of life or a panacea, a substance that can cure any disease. In the course of these fruitless efforts he will make important discoveries in chemistry, including aluminum chloride, acetic acid, nitric acid, and white lead.   **CHEM**

750   Geber distills acetic acid from vinegar to create the first pure acid known.   **CHEM**

751   After learning papermaking techniques from Chinese prisoners, Muslim engineers construct the first paper mill in Muslim territory. A Chinese-influenced paper mill will open in Baghdad, Iraq, in 793.   **TECH**

765   Three-field crop rotation, which allows land to be productive for two out of three years, is first mentioned in European texts. It will later be popularized by Carolingian king Charlemagne.   **BIO**

770   Hindu works on mathematics are translated into Arabic as the Arabs begin to synthesize, then extend the discoveries of Greek and Indian mathematicians.   **MATH**

770   Iron horseshoes come into widespread use in Europe.   **TECH**

780   Arab mathematician Muhammad ibn al-Khwārizmī is born in Khwarizm, now Uzbekistan (*d.* 850). His translated works will introduce Hindu-Arabic notation to Europe. His name, al-Khwārizmī, is the source of the modern word *algorithm*.   **MATH**

800   Chinese mathematicians solve equations with the method of finite differences.   **MATH**

800   French ecclesiastic St. Bernard forbids Cistercian monks from studying medical books, declaring that prayer is the only remedy allowed to treat the sick.   **MED**

800   Persians elevate the professional standards of their physicians by requiring examinations before licensing.   **MED**

808   Islamic translator Hunayn ibn Ishaq is born (*d.* 873). He will translate many volumes of Greek natural science, including works by Plato, Aristotle, Hippocrates, and Galen.   **MISC**

820   Having borrowed Hindu numerals (now known as Arabic numerals) from India, Muhammad ibn al-Khwārizmī outlines rules for computing with these numerals. In *Al-jabr wa'l muqabalah*, known as *Algebra* in Europe, he features these numerals and the system of positional notation, in which the symbol for zero serves as a place marker. This work also shows how to solve all equations of the first and second degree with positive roots. *See also* 1202, Fibonacci.   **MATH**

827   Ptolemy's synthesis of Greek astronomy, *Megalé syntaxis tēs astronomias* (c. 140), is translated into Arabic as *Al magiste*, or *The Greatest*. It becomes known to history as *The Almagest*.   **ASTRO**

836   Arab mathematician Thabit ibn Qurra is born in Haran, now Turkey (*d.* 901). He will translate Greek works into Arabic and work on solving the problem of Euclid's fifth postulate.   **MATH**

850   The astrolabe, used for astronomical observations, is refined by Arab scientists.   **ASTRO**

850   The Arabs begin drinking coffee, a beverage that will not spread to Europe until hundreds of years later.   **MISC**

BEFORE GUTENBERG

*I*n 1454, German printer Johannes Gutenberg founded the modern publishing industry when he set the Latin Bible in lead-alloy movable type
and printed it on a wood printing press. But Gutenberg was not the first
to invent printing or movable type. The first experimenters with the printing
process were the Sumerians, who cut into cylindrical stones symbols representing a signature, and pressed the image into clay that was then baked. The
technique of reversed characters being inked onto paper was first developed
by the Chinese, who engraved images onto wood blocks as early as the eighth
century; the first such book, The Diamond Sutra, was printed in 868. By the
eleventh century, both Chinese and Korean printers were using clay, wood,
bronze, and iron to develop movable type. The Chinese printer Pi Sheng was a
leader in the field of setting individual ideograms in clay type.

858   Arabian astronomer Abū-'Abd Allāh Muhammad ibn Jābir ibn Sinān
al Battāni (Albatemius) is born in Haran, Turkey (d. 929). He will refine Ptolemy's system, introduce trigonometry as an astronomical
tool, recalculate the length of the year, and improve measurements
of the precession of the equinoxes.   **ASTRO**

863   The Cyrillic alphabet is developed by Macedonian missionary Cyril
and his brother Methodius. Eventually it is used by Russian and various other peoples.   **TECH**

868   The first printed book, *The Diamond Sutra*, is manufactured in
China.   **TECH**

870   A Viking named Ottar sails more than one hundred miles north of
the Arctic Circle to become the first human known to cross the
Arctic Circle by sea.   **EARTH**

874   A Viking named Ingolfur Arnarson lands in Iceland, leading to the
first permanent settlement there.   **EARTH**

876   The symbol for zero appears in India.   **MATH**

880   Arab alchemists and physicians distill wine to produce alcohol. **CHEM**

880   Persian physician and alchemist Ar-Razī, or Rhazes, uses what will
be called plaster of Paris to form cast material for holding broken
bones in place. Later he will be the first to give authentic descriptions of smallpox and measles. He will also divide all substances
into animal, vegetable, or mineral. His Greco-Arabic medical encyclopedia, *Continens*, translated into Latin in 1279, will be a major
source of therapeutic knowledge for three centuries.   **MED**

900   The horse collar is in use in Europe. This innovation completes the transformation of the horse into a powerful farm animal, allowing for still greater food production in northern Europe. *See also* the 600 invention of the moldboard plow.   **TECH**

900   The classic Mayan civilization (begun c. 250) collapses.   **MISC**

940   With the Dunhuang star map Chinese astronomers invent a map-projection technique of the kind later called the Mercator projection. *See* 1568.   **ASTRO**

980   Persian physician Avicenna is born (*d.* 1037). His medical writings will be considered some of the most important textbooks in medical education from the twelfth to the seventeenth centuries.   **MED**

982   Icelander Erik Thorvaldson, or Erik the Red, discovers Greenland. A Viking colony is begun there in 986. *See also* 1576.   **EARTH**

1000   The Maoris, a Polynesian people, colonize New Zealand. Within a few hundred years they will exterminate most of the island's unique animal species, including the large flightless birds called moas.   **EARTH**

1000   By now the Malagasy people, originally from Indonesia, have colonized the island of Madagascar off eastern Africa. They exterminate much of that island's unique fauna, including gorilla-sized lemurs and flightless elephant birds.   **EARTH**

1000   A Viking named Bjarne Herjulfson becomes the first European to see the Americas when he sails west past Greenland to Newfoundland, Canada. Two years later, Leif Eriksson will travel there to found the short-lived colony of Vinland.   **EARTH**

1000   Eskimos arrive at Greenland, and competition begins to develop between their group and the Vikings. In 1415 the Viking colony will end and Greenland will be left to the Eskimos.   **EARTH**

1000   By this time Polynesians have traversed 14 million square kilometers (5.6 million square miles) of ocean and occupy a triangle from New Zealand north to Hawaii and east to Easter Island.   **EARTH**

1000   In China the pivoting needle on a magnetic compass is discovered and becomes an important aid to navigators. By 1100 this knowledge is picked up by Arab traders through contacts with the Indonesian islands.   **EARTH**

1000   Persian or other Asian travelers introduce the concept of the seven-day week to the Chinese. Before this, ten-day weeks were common in China.   **TECH**

1000   The Bridge of the Ten Thousand Acres in Foochow, China, is constructed.   **TECH**

1006	A bright "guest star" or supernova, visible for a number of years, is observed in China, Japan, various Islamic lands, and Europe. **ASTRO**
c. 1010	Arab astronomer ibn Yunus compiles two centuries of observations in *The Large Astronomical Tables of al-Hakim*, used by future Arab astronomers. **ASTRO**
c. 1025	Arab physicist Abū 'Ali al-Hasan ibn al-Haytham (Alhayen) is one of the first scientists to study optics. He analyzes lenses, develops parabolic mirrors, and theorizes that vision is the result of light falling on the eye, not light emanating from the eye, as had been previously thought. **PHYS**
1027	As acupuncture becomes more systematic, China's reigning emperor requests that copper models of the human body be made to illustrate the principles of this form of medical therapy. **MED**
1041	Movable type of Chinese ideograms, fashioned from clay blocks, is used in China by printer Pi Sheng. **TECH**
c. 1050	Arab poet, scientist, and mathematician Omar Khayyám is born (*d.* 1123). His *Algebra* will go beyond al-Khwārizmī's (*see* 820) to include equations of the third degree. **MATH**
c. 1050	The crossbow, the first mechanized hand weapon, is introduced into France. It uses a device such as a two-handed crank to increase the tension of the bow and therefore the force of the bolt or arrow. **TECH**
c. 1050	More efficient iron plows are used in northern Europe instead of wooden plows. **TECH**
July 4, 1054	Chinese, Japanese, and Arab astronomers report a supernova that remains visible for twenty-two months. Its residue now forms the Crab Nebula. **ASTRO**
c. 1065	Jewish rabbi, physician, and philosopher Moses Maimonides becomes known for his medical teachings. In the twentieth century the invocation known as the Prayer of Maimonides will be used at some medical school graduation ceremonies. **MED**
1066	During William the Conqueror's invasion of England, the bright phenomenon now called Halley's Comet is sighted. **ASTRO**
1067	To prohibit international development of its invention of gunpowder, China outlaws the exportation of sulfur and saltpeter. **TECH**
1071	Forks as eating utensils are introduced to Venice and western Europe from the Byzantine Empire, but they are slow to gain general acceptance. **TECH**
c. 1075	The Arab astronomer Arzachel theorizes correctly that the orbits of planets are elliptical, not circular. **ASTRO**

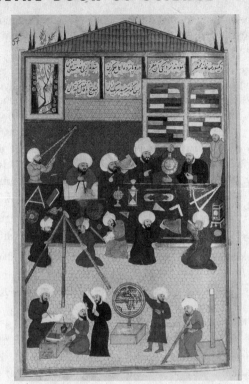

Persian miniature of an Arab scientist using early navigational instruments. (*Topkapi Museum, Istanbul*)

1086	The magnetized compass is popularized by Shen Cha, an official working with the Chinese water systems. **TECH**
c. 1100s	Latin translators such as Adelard of Bath, Michael Scot, and Gerard of Cremona introduce Arabic works on astronomy and mathematics to medieval Europe. These works, based ultimately on ancient Greek learning, eventually become the foundation of European science. **MISC**
c. 1100	The Chinese demonstrate the cause of solar and lunar eclipses. **ASTRO**
1100	Arab physician Ibn Zuhr (Avenzoar) is the first to describe the parasite, an itch mite, causing the highly contagious skin disease scabies. **MED**
c. 1100	A history of science by Arab writer Abu'l Fath al-Chuzini includes tables of specific densities and observations on gravity. **PHYS**

1120　　The use of latitude and longitude measurements, in degrees, minutes, and seconds, is introduced by an Anglo-Saxon scientist known as Welcher of Malvern.　　**TECH**

1137　　The Abbey of St. Denis near Paris, designed by Abbé Suger, becomes the first major building to make use of flying buttresses, a system of architectural support that permits the building of gigantic cathedrals. The new architecture is known as Gothic.　　**TECH**

....

"The dull mind rises to truth through that which is material."—Abbé Suger, architect and builder of the Abbey of St. Denis, the first important example of Gothic architecture; opened in 1137

....

1142　　Adelard of Bath translates Euclid's *Elements* into Latin.　　**MATH**

1148　　Soldiers returning from the Crusades in the Middle East introduce sugar to Europe.　　**TECH**

c. 1159　　Between now and 1173, Benjamin of Tudela travels east through Islamic lands, keeping a written account of his journey. Though he is the first western European to do so, his status as a Jew prevents his account from being influential in the Christian world.　　**EARTH**

1175　　Gerard of Cremona, Italy, translates Ptolemy's astronomical compendium *The Almagest* into Latin, along with other Greek and Arab works.　　**ASTRO**

1176　　In England, rabbits are introduced as local livestock.　　**BIO**

1180　　English scholar Alexander Neckam is the first European to note that a magnetic needle always points north–south (*see also* China, 100s). Three centuries later, this discovery contributes to the navigation feats of the age of exploration.　　**PHYS**

1180　　In England, glass windows are used in houses.　　**TECH**

1184　　The cathedral at Sens, France, becomes one of the earliest examples of Gothic architecture and technology. It is designed by architect William of Sens. *See also* 1137, St. Denis.　　**TECH**

1189　　In France, the first paper mill in Christian Europe is opened. *See also* 1276 and 1494.　　**TECH**

1193　　Indigo is imported from India for use in dyeing fabrics.　　**TECH**

c. 1194　　Viking explorers reach Spitzberg, 450 kilometers north of the Arctic Circle. This is the farthest north the Vikings go.　　**EARTH**

1200s　　Coal, known as a fuel in China since 1000 B.C., is mined in England by early in this century. *See* 1233, Newcastle.　　**TECH**

c. 1200   Medical instruction becomes more theoretical and scholarly, spreading to medical schools at Montpellier, Paris, Oxford, and Bologna.   **MED**

1202   Italian mathematician Leonardo Fibonacci publishes his *Book of the Abacus*, which introduces Arabic numerals and positional notation to Europe, though these are not fully adopted for three hundred years. *See* 820, al-Khwārizmī.   **MATH**

c. 1220   Scottish naturalist Michael Scot translates Aristotle's classifications of animals into Latin.   **BIO**

c. 1220   Jordanus Nemorarius publishes *Mechanica*, describing a law of the lever and the law of the composition of movements.   **PHYS**

1225   Cotton is first manufactured in Spain.   **TECH**

1233   Coal is first mined in Newcastle, England. The mine is so successful that it generates the phrase "carrying coals to Newcastle," connoting an unnecessary activity.   **TECH**

1237   Chinese physician Chen Tzu-ning publishes his *Fu Jen Liang Fang*, the first Asian monograph on the diseases of women.   **MED**

1240   European shipbuilders construct vessels with rudders, an innovation borrowed from the Arabs.   **TECH**

c. 1245–1247   Franciscan friar Giovanni da Pian del Carpini leads a conversion mission into Mongol lands. His account of these travels, *Liber tartarorum*, becomes the first opportunity for Westerners to read an accurate description of central Asia.   **EARTH**

1249   English scholar Roger Bacon notes that lenses can be used for improving eyesight. Eyeglasses appear in China and Europe at about the same time; it is not clear where they were invented first.   **TECH**

1249   Gunpowder, developed in China, is mentioned for the first time in European writings by scientist Roger Bacon.   **TECH**

c. 1250   German scientist Albertus Magnus introduces Aristotle's ideas on botany and biology to Europe. His *De vegetabilibus* classifies plants and vegetables and describes the function and structure of various plant parts.   **BIO**

c. 1250   Albertus Magnus discovers the element arsenic.   **CHEM**

1250   Crusaders returning to Europe from Arab lands help spread acceptance of Arabic numbering and decimal systems.   **MATH**

1259   Construction begins on an observatory at Maragha, Iran.   **ASTRO**

c. 1260   An observatory is built at Beijing, China.   **ASTRO**

1264   Bakers' marks, the forerunner to trademarks, are used for the first time in England. Through them bakers identify their wares with individualized icons slashed into the bread.   **TECH**

c. 1265   During the Kamakura period (1185–1333), Japanese swordsmiths reach their technical apex. Their *tachi* (slashing swords) are sharp enough to behead an enemy with one stroke.   **TECH**

....

"It seems wonderful to everyone that sometimes stones are found that have figures of animals inside and outside.... Avicenna says that the cause of this is that animals, just as they are, are sometimes changed into stones."
—Albertus Magnus, German theologian and scholar, on fossils; thirteenth century

....

1267   The Council of Venice forbids Jews to practice medicine among Christians.   **MED**

1269   William of Moerbeke translates the major scientific and mathematical treatises of Archimedes into Latin.   **MATH**

1269   French scholar Pèlerin de Maricourt (Petrus Peregrinus) performs early experiments with magnets, describing magnetic poles and refining the use of a magnet as a compass.   **TECH**

1269   Tolls are charged on some roads in England.   **MISC**

c. 1270   The Polish scientist known as Witelo writes a book on optics called *Perspectiva*, which became part of a work that was the most influential treatise on optics until the seventeenth century.   **PHYS**

1270   British physician and chemist Roger Bacon researches optics and refraction, the bending of a light ray as it passes from one medium into another. *See* 1249, eyeglasses.   **PHYS**

1272   The Alphonsine tables, planetary charts whose compilation was ordered in 1250 by Alphonso X of Castile, are completed. They will remain in use until the 1500s.   **ASTRO**

c. 1276   Italian scientist Giles of Rome writes a treatise, *De formatione corporis humani in utero*, on the development of the human fetus. It includes a discussion of the timing of the soul's entry into the fetus and the biological importance of each of the two parents.   **BIO**

1276   Papermaking begins in Italy, in the city of Montefano.   **TECH**

c. 1280   Arab physician Alquarashi is the first to identify the pulmonary transit of blood, from the right to the left ventricle via the lungs.   **MED**

1288   The first known gun, a small cannon, is made in China.   **TECH**

1289   Block printing is used for the first time in Europe.   **TECH**

c. 1290   French surgeon Henri de Mondeville advises doctors to cleanse wounds and let them dry without salves or wine-soaked dressings. He also recommends applying pressure to stop bleeding and advocates the use of sutures.   **MED**

1291   In Venice, glassmakers learn to produce clear glass (only colored glass has been available since glass ornaments first appeared in Egypt about 2500 B.C.). The colorless glass will make modern mirrors and windowpanes possible.   **TECH**

c. 1292   A new type of vessel, the great galley, is developed in Venice. These long, shallow boats are driven by multiple rows of oarsmen and can carry a great deal of cargo.   **TECH**

1295   French physician Lanfranchi becomes the first to describe a brain concussion and the symptoms of a skull fracture.   **MED**

1298   Venetian merchant Marco Polo publishes *Divisament dou monde*, describing his travels (1275–1295) in China. The book will inspire future explorers.   **EARTH**

1300s   Mechanical clocks, driven by the force of gravity on weights, are invented in Europe.   **TECH**

1300   The False Geber, an anonymous alchemist writing under the name Geber, discovers sulfuric acid, the most powerful acid yet known.   **CHEM**

WHEN GLASS LOST ITS COLOR

For thousands of years after sand was fired into glass objects in the Near East around 2500 B.C., this now commonly clear material was usually produced only in color. Impurities lent color to glass, and a workable decolorization process had yet to be invented.

By the end of the thirteenth century, the technique of adding clarifying substances to make glass clear was perfected in Venice, which had become, and to this day remains, a world center for exquisite glass production. One way Venetian glass manufacturers retained their monopoly on certain glassmaking processes was to move in 1291 to an isolated island where materials were hoarded, techniques kept secret, and penalties assessed on trespassers and talkative employees.

To infuse glass with color, impurities can still be useful. Here are some common compounds added to glass to produce popular colors:

Blue	Cobalt and copper
Bottle Green	Oxidized iron
Brown	Iron and sulfur
Purple	Chromates
Red	Copper or selenium
Ruby	Gold

1300   Spanish alchemist Arnau de Villanova distills alcohol for the first time, producing brandy from wine.   **TECH**

1303   Chinese mathematician Chu-Shi-kié (Chu Shih-chieh) writes the *Precious Mirror of the Four Elements*, which marks the apex of Chinese algebra. It contains simultaneous equations, equations of degrees up to fourteen, the Horner transformation method, and the arithmetic triangle later called the Pascal triangle.   **MATH**

1304   Theodoric of Freibourg, Germany, accurately explains several aspects of the formation of rainbows.   **PHYS**

1312   Europeans reach the Canary Islands off Morocco for the first time.   **EARTH**

1316   Italian anatomist Mondino De'Luzzi writes the first book in history devoted entirely to anatomy.   **MED**

1320   Paper, a Chinese invention (*see* 105), reaches Europe, largely replacing vellum, a parchment made from the skins of animals such as the calf or lamb.   **TECH**

1328   English philosopher and mathematician Thomas Bradwardine publishes his *Tractatus de proportionibus*, in which he broadens the theory of proportions and proposes an alternative to Aristotle's (incorrect) law of motion.   **MATH**

1333   In Venice the first botanical garden since antiquity is established.   **BIO**

Aug. 26, 1346   English king Edward III uses longbows and cannons loaded with gunpowder at the battle of Crécy, France. The longbows are more important to Edward's victory, but gunpowder is the weapon of the future.   **TECH**

c. 1348   Bubonic plague, called the black death, begins to sweep Europe after devastating Asia and North Africa. A large part of the Old World's population will die from the plague.   **MED**

c. 1350   French philosopher Jean Buridan proposes the concept of impetus, which is similar to the later concept of inertia as articulated in Newton's first law of motion (*see* September 1687, Newton).   **PHYS**

c. 1360   French mathematician Nicole d'Oresme generalizes Thomas Bradwardine's theory of proportions (*see* 1328), suggests notations for fractional powers, argues that irrational powers are possible, and develops the graphic representation of functions known as the latitude of forms.   **MATH**

1370   John of Arderne, the earliest known English surgeon, writes extensively on modern surgery, the use of irrigation (cleansing by flushing with water), and the repair of anal fistulas.   **MED**

1391   English writer Geoffrey Chaucer's *Treatise on the Astrolabe* explains how to construct and use this instrument for measuring the position of stars.   **ASTRO**

1400s   Coffee, which originated in Ethiopia, begins to gain popularity as a beverage in Arab countries. It will reach most of Europe by the midseventeenth century.   **TECH**

Protective clothing used by doctors and others who visited plague houses (1720 engraving). (*Germanisches National Museum, Nuremburg*)

BLAMING THE JEWS

*B*ubonic plague, known in medieval times as the black death, is known today to be caused by the bacterium Yersinia pestis, a microbe transmitted to humans by the bite of fleas from infected hosts, especially rats. However, in the mid-fourteenth century, when the black death moved like a wave across Central Asia, the Middle East, North Africa, and Europe, its cause was a mystery. Its sufferers experienced chills, high fever, vomiting, diarrhea, and the formation of buboes, or painful inflammations of lymph nodes, most commonly in the groin. Black hemorrhages might form and the disease turn into pneumonic plague, in which the patient's lungs became infected, leading swiftly to death. The pneumonic form was particularly contagious, transmitted from one person to another by water droplets in the air.

Unchecked by medical knowledge, this lethal epidemic decimated the population. Sufferers grappled for a way to explain its destruction. Many Christians, considering it divine punishment for moral wrongdoing, turned to prayer and acts of penance. Others took a course as virulent as the disease itself: blaming the Jews.

In communities throughout Provence, Catalonia, Aragon, Switzerland, southern Germany, and the Rhineland, Jews were accused of poisoning Christian water sources. Violence erupted against Jews. In some areas, governments resisted the clamor for retribution, but others abetted the Christian protests. Hundreds of Jewish communities were destroyed. Jews in western Europe were burned, tortured, imprisoned, and exiled in numbers large enough to shift the center of European Jewry permanently eastward.

c. 1400   Italian architect Filippo Brunelleschi begins the first archaeological digs in Rome.   **ARCH**

1400   English monks Johann Sprenger and Heinrich Kraemer publish *The Witches' Hammer*, claiming in it that witches are devil possessed and should be killed. Although this book has a long, influential history in Europe, by the twentieth century researchers will theorize that most "possessed" people in the 1400s were in fact mentally ill.   **PSYCH**

c. 1402   Emperor Yung-lo of China encourages overseas conquest. Admiral Cheng-ho's fleet sails as far west as the Red Sea, visiting Mecca and Egypt as well as Indonesia, Malaya, and Sri Lanka.   **EARTH**

1418   Prince Henry the Navigator of Portugal opens an observatory and school for navigation at Sagres on Cape St. Vincent, Portugal. His goal is to find a way around Africa to reach the trade riches of China.   **EARTH**

1418	Portuguese navigators discover and claim Madeira. **EARTH**
1427	The Portuguese navigator Diogo de Sevilha discovers the Azores, an island chain more than seven hundred miles west of Portugal. **EARTH**
1428	Mongol astronomer Ulūgh Beg builds an observatory at Samarkand featuring a quadrant, a device to measure stellar positions, that is 180 feet high. **ASTRO**
1430s	Ulūgh Beg publishes a new star map and tables of star positions, improving on Ptolemy's work. **ASTRO**
1436	Italian artist Leon Battista Alberti writes on using mathematical principles to achieve perspective in art. **TECH**
1439	The military forces of French king Charles VII become the first to make systematic use of gunpowder artillery. **TECH**
1440	German scholar Nicholas of Cusa argues that space is infinite and that the stars are suns, each with its own inhabited planets. **ASTRO**
c. 1450	It is discovered that transporting soil up from the valleys in the Andes mountains makes the higher regions arable. **BIO**
c. 1450	The idea of bodily humors remains central to European medicine as the Middle Ages draw to a close. Purging, cupping, bloodletting, and leeching are all in ordinary use to control the body's balance of blood, phlegm, yellow bile, and black bile. **MED**
1450	The Dutch harquebus becomes the first firearm small enough to be carried and fired by a single person. **TECH**
1450	The Chinese are printing pages using movable wooden type, an innovation that will soon (*see* 1454) spread to Europe. **TECH**
1451	Nicholas of Cusa, a German scholar, introduces the idea of using concave lenses to amend nearsightedness. Previously, only convex lenses for farsightedness were used. **TECH**
c. 1452	Between now and 1519, Leonardo da Vinci makes notes proposing the marine origin of fossils. Knowing it would be thought heretical, da Vinci does not publicly reveal this observation. **EARTH**
May 30, 1453	Constantinople falls to the Ottoman Turks, marking the end of the Byzantine, or Eastern Roman, Empire and the traditional end of the Middle Ages. The city will become known as Istanbul. Christian scholars fleeing the Muslims help bring the knowledge of classical learning to western Europe, contributing to the flourishing of arts, letters, and sciences in the Renaissance (fifteenth to seventeenth centuries). **MISC**
1454	With a printing press of his own invention, using movable metal type, Johannes Gutenberg of Mainz, Germany, prints three hundred copies of the Bible in Latin. This first printed book is now called the Gutenberg Bible. **TECH**

1456	Sugar is made more widely available in England. **TECH**
1457	The first medical publication printed, a calendar, advises physicians as to when purging should be most therapeutic. **MED**
c. 1460	Prince Henry the Navigator dies (*b.* 1394). By this time Portuguese explorers have sailed down the west coast of Africa as far as present-day Gambia. **EARTH**
1470	The mainspring, a spiral string whose gradual unwinding powers a clock, is invented. **TECH**
1472	German mathematician and astronomer Regiomontanus (Johann Müller) makes the first scientific study of the comet that will later become known as Halley's Comet (*see* December 25, 1758). **ASTRO**
Feb. 19, 1473	Astronomer Nicolaus Copernicus is born in Torun, Poland (*d.* 1543). His *De revolutionibus orbium coelestium* (1543), proposing that the earth and planets revolve around the sun, will revolutionize the field of astronomy. **ASTRO**
1473	The first medical dictionary is printed. **MED**
1473	The atomic theory of Democritus becomes known to Western scholars with the translation into Latin of Lucretius's *On the Nature of Things* (60 B.C.). **PHYS**
1474	Regiomontanus publishes his *Ephemerides astronomicae*, a compendium of celestial coordinates that will prove useful to navigators. *See* February 29, 1504, Columbus. **ASTRO**
1474	After 425 years under construction, Winchester Cathedral in England is completed. **TECH**
c. 1475	Aristotle's *Meteorologia* and Ptolemy's *Geographia* are translated into Latin. **EARTH**
1476	In Venice, Aristotle's fourth-century B.C. work on animal structure, function, reproduction, physiology, and development is published under the title *De animalibus*. It is the first zoological compilation. **BIO**
1479	The first book set from metal type in England is printed by William Caxton: *The Game and Playe of Chesse*, a Latin work translated into French. **TECH**
1481	German cleric Konrad von Megenberg's *Buch der Natur*, the first printed book to contain animal figures, is published. **BIO**
1483	Greek botanist and philosopher Theophrastus (372–287 B.C.) is posthumously honored when his treatise on botany *De historia et causis plantarum* is published in Treviso. This work is considered the earliest on scientific botany. **BIO**
1487	Portuguese navigator Bartholomeu Dias discovers the southernmost tip of Africa, the Cape of Good Hope. **EARTH**

1487   John II of Portugal, Prince Henry the Navigator's grand-nephew, organizes an expedition through the Mediterranean and the Red Sea under the leadership of Pero de Covilhão.   **EARTH**

1490   The *Tabulae directionum* of German mathematician and astronomer Regiomontanus is published posthumously. In this work and *De triangulus*, not published until 1533, Regiomontanus first organizes trigonometry as a discipline, making numerous advances in the field. He also applies algebraic methods to geometric problems. **MATH**

1490   Italian scientist and artist Leonardo da Vinci describes capillary action, the rise of fluids in a small-diameter (capillary) tube.   **PHYS**

Oct. 12,   Italian mariner Christopher Columbus (1451–1506), leading a fleet
1492   of three ships from Spain, becomes the first European since the Vikings (*see* 1000) to reach the Americas. Unlike the Vikings, Columbus will open the Western Hemisphere to wholesale colonization by Europe.   **EARTH**

1492   Italian mathematician Francesco Pellos introduces the decimal point.   **MATH**

1492   Through the voyages of Christopher Columbus several foods, including allspice, peppers, plantain, and pineapples, are made known to Europe.   **TECH**

Sept. 25,   Columbus's second voyage sets sail from Cadiz, Spain. This 17-ship ex-
1493   pedition will explore Dominica, Puerto Rico, Cuba, and Jamaica.   **EARTH**

1493   A town crier is directed by Paris officials to order all those who have the "greater pox" (syphilis) to leave the city—or be thrown into the Seine. By 1496 syphilis will be epidemic in Europe.   **MED**

1494   Italian mathematician Luca Pacioli publishes his *Summa de arithmetica, geometria, proportioni et proportionalita*. This highly influential work includes not only the first printed material on algebra but also useful information on double-entry bookkeeping.   **MATH**

1494   The first English paper mill opens.   **TECH**

c. 1497   Italian navigator Amerigo Vespucci explores the coast of the continental area south of the islands discovered by Columbus. Vespucci maintains that this land is not Asia but a "new world."   **EARTH**

1497   Italian mariner Giovanni Caboto (John Cabot), sailing for the English, reaches Newfoundland and Nova Scotia. He becomes the first European since the Vikings (*see* 1000) to reach the mainland of North America.   **EARTH**

Nov. 22,   Portuguese navigator Vasco da Gama becomes the first European to
1497   round the southernmost part of Africa, the Cape of Good Hope, and reach Asia, arriving in India in 1498.   **EARTH**

May 1498   Columbus departs from Spain on his third voyage, commanding a fleet of six ships. After stopping at Trinidad, the fleet reaches the Paria Peninsula on the coast of Venezuela on August 5, marking Columbus's first visit to the mainland of the Americas.   **EARTH**

1500   German engineer Ulrich Rulein von Kalbe writes *Bergbuchlein*, the first known mining manual.   **EARTH**

c. 1500   Italian painter and scientist Leonardo da Vinci dissects human bodies and records his anatomical findings in accurate, detailed drawings.   **MED**

1501   German botanist Leonhard Fuchs is born in Wemding, Bavaria (*d.* 1566). *Fuchsia*, a genus of tropical shrubs and trees, will be named for him, as will the color fuchsia after the purplish-red of the shrub's flowers.   **BIO**

1501   From now to 1587, a pandemic outbreak spreads through Europe of a disease characterized by fever, headache, sweating, and a black tongue. It is initially called Mobus Hungaricus (the Hungarian disease) but later will be regarded as an outbreak of typhus.   **MED**

May 9, 1502 Columbus departs from Cadiz, Spain, on his fourth and final voyage to the Americas. On this voyage, Columbus visits Santo Domingo, the Cayman Islands, Jamaica, Cuba, and Honduras. He then sails south along the coasts of Nicaragua and Costa Rica looking for a sea passage to India but never finds one. After being marooned in Jamaica for a year, he arrives back in Spain on November 7, 1504, and dies two years later, on May 20, 1506.   **EARTH**

1503   The properties of rubber are noted for the first time by Europeans during Columbus's fourth voyage. This substance, made of latex from the plant *Hevea brasiliensis* or *Parthenium argentatus*, first came to the explorers' attention in the form of a ball used in various games by the native Americans. *See* 1615, rubber.   **TECH**

Feb. 29,   Using German mathematician and astronomer Regiomontanus's
1504   *Ephemerides astronomicae* (1474), Columbus correctly predicts a total lunar eclipse, casting awe into the local Native Americans.   **ASTRO**

1504   German inventor Peter Henlein devises the first watch, a clock small enough to fit in a pocket.   **TECH**

1506   The Laocöon sculpture (first century B.C.) is discovered near Santa Maria Maggiore, Italy. It will influence Renaissance sculptors such as Michelangelo.   **ARCH**

1507   The name *America* appears on a map for the first time. German cartographer Martin Waldseemüller names the newly discovered lands for Amerigo Vespucci, an Italian explorer reputed to have been the first to recognize that these areas were not part of Asia. *See* c. 1497.   **EARTH**

1510   French barber and surgeon Ambroise Paré (*d.* 1590) is born near
              Laval, Mayenne. He will be considered the father of modern surgery
              for his common-sense treatments of injury and disease. At a time
              when other surgeons are treating gunshot wounds with boiling oil,
              Paré treats them with salves and cleanliness. And when colleagues
              are cauterizing bleeding arteries—without anaesthesia—Paré learns
              to tie off arteries to stop blood loss.   **MED**

1510   Scientist and artist Leonardo da Vinci designs a horizontal water
              wheel, a forerunner of the water turbine.   **TECH**

LEONARDO'S SCIENCE

*I*talian Renaissance artist Leonardo da Vinci is well known. Leonardo
the scientific investigator has been less well appreciated. Yet his note-
books, particularly the two previously unknown ones found in Madrid
in 1965, reveal the Italian artist and thinker as a man who merged the
worlds of science and art to better understand the mechanics of life now
and the possibilities of technology.

A brief sampling of Leonardo's scientific achievements shows not only
his ability to intertwine the disciplines of the arts and sciences but to balance theoretical pursuits and the activity of practical tasks:

- *In 1494, while serving as artist and scientist to the court of Lodovico
  Sforza in Milan (one year before completing the painting* The Last
  Supper), *he devised plans to harness the waters of the Arno River.*
- *As military engineer for Cesare Borgia in 1502–1503, Leonardo ex-
  plored problems of swamp reclamation.*
- *While examining mathematical theory in Florence, he studied anatomy
  at the city's hospital of Santa Maria Nuova.*
- *During a time of great artistic achievement (his* Mona Lisa *was created
  in 1503), he furthered his study of anatomy by analyzing the movements
  of birds in flight and carrying out a variety of cadaver dissections that
  culminated in a book of life drawings,* Anatomy *(1508, unpublished).*
- *While architect and engineer to French king Louis XII from 1506 to
  1513, Leonardo also undertook scientific studies of botany, geology,
  and hydraulic power.*

*His other areas of exploration included rock stratification, the making of
eyeglass lenses, and inquiries into flying machines. Whether theoretical,
artistic, or practical, Leonardo's explorations were experiments in vision.
He believed that the key to understanding the world was* saper vedere, *"to
know how to see."*

| 1512 | Hieronymus Brunschwygk publishes his *Big Book* (an expansion of his *Little Book* of 1500), on chemical apparatus and techniques such as stills, furnaces, and distillation. **CHEM** |

| 1513 | Exploring Florida, Ponce de León of Spain is the first European to reach the portion of North America that is now the United States. **EARTH** |

| Sept. 25, 1513 | Traveling through Panama, Spanish explorer Vasco Nuñez de Balboa becomes the first European to see the Pacific Ocean from the Americas. **EARTH** |

| 1513 | Orange and lemon trees are introduced to Florida by Spanish explorer Ponce de León. **TECH** |

| 1514 | Copernicus writes his first account of his heliocentric theory, that the earth and the planets move around the sun. His writings circulate quietly for years, but he does not publish a complete account until 1543. **ASTRO** |

| 1514 | Plus (+) and minus (–) signs are first used in equations for addition and subtraction. **MATH** |

| 1514 | French physician Pierre Brissot opposes the current method of bloodletting, in which physicians drain blood from the veins farthest from the pathogenic lesion. Brissot claims that blood withdrawal from a surgically opened vein should be near the lesion to be effective. For this heresy he is banished by the French Parliament. **MED** |

| Dec. 31, 1514 | In Brussels, Flemish anatomist Andreas Vesalius (d. 1564) is born. He will create the first accurate illustrated book on the structure of the human body, marking the beginnings of the modern study of anatomy. He will oppose Galen's theories on anatomy, proving them incorrect. Vesalius will also oppose Aristotle's view that the heart is the seat of life, claiming that role instead for the brain and nervous system. **MED** |

| 1517 | Spanish explorer Francisco Fernández de Córdoba becomes the first European to discover the Yucatán Peninsula and find the remains of Mayan civilization. **EARTH** |

| 1517 | Henry VIII's physician, Thomas Linacre, writes a new Latin translation of Galen's medical treatises. Physicians all over Europe now realize they had been placing their full confidence in distorted, secondhand versions of the famous physician's work. **MED** |

| Sept. 23, 1518 | England's Royal College of Physicians is founded. **MED** |

| 1519 | Chocolate, peanuts, sweet potatoes, and vanilla, among other foods, are found in use in Mayan communities. **BIO** |

The Great Temple at Tenochtitlán, reconstructed by Ignacio Marquina. (*American Museum of Natural History*)

1519	Hernando Cortés sails from Cuba to Mexico, where he encounters Aztec civilization, with its capital at Tenochtitlán, the present-day site of Mexico City. In time the Spanish destroy the Aztec civilization. **EARTH**
Sept. 20, 1519	Ferdinand Magellan, a Portuguese navigator wounded while fighting for his country against Morocco but denied a pension, offers his services instead to Spain. Charles V decides to sponsor Magellan on a westward voyage to circumnavigate the globe. Magellan departs today with five ships. **EARTH**
1520	The rifle is developed by German gunmaker August Kotter. **TECH**
Apr. 27, 1521	Fighting with natives in an area that will come to be known as the Philippines, Magellan dies. **EARTH**
Sept. 1522	A ship from Ferdinand Magellan's fleet returns to Spain, the first to circumnavigate the globe. Magellan himself and four of his five ships failed to complete the trip. The lone surviving ship is led by Juan Sebastián de Elcano. **EARTH**
1524	Commissioned by France to search for a northwest passage, Italian navigator Giovanni da Verrazano becomes the first European to enter New York harbor. **EARTH**
1524	The Hospital of the Immaculate Conception in Mexico City is built by Hernando Cortés. It is the first hospital on the American continent. **MED**

1525   Christoff Rudolf introduces the square root symbol (√⁻) and makes use of decimal fractions in *Die Cass*.   **MATH**

1525   In Rome the first Latin transcription of the works of Hippocrates (*see* 460 B.C.) is published.   **MED**

1527   Swiss-born chemist and physician Philippus Aureolus Theophrastus Bombast von Hohenheím (Paracelsus) publicly burns Galen's and Avicenna's works, whose theories of humors he rejects, claiming that the purpose of alchemy is to make medicines that will cure and treat disease. Although he is ridiculed for his belief in astrology and an elixir of life, Paracelsus stresses the importance of minerals, especially zinc, in treating disease.   **MED**

1529   Sweet rather than bitter oranges are introduced from Asia to Europe by the Portuguese. Bitter oranges had been available for centuries.   **BIO**

1530   Italian physician and poet Girolamo Fracastoro writes *Syphilis sive morbus Gallicus*, giving this sexually transmitted disease its modern name and recognizing its venereal cause.   **MED**

1530   Spanish explorer Gonzalo Jiménez de Quesada becomes the first European to learn about the potato, from Native Americans in Colombia. It will become a staple of Old World as well as New World cooking.   **TECH**

1530   Dutch mathematician Gemma Frisius suggests that the local time of a prime meridian should be the standard time in determining longitude.   **TECH**

1531   Tobacco is commercially grown in the Spanish West Indian colonies.   **BIO**

1532   Bills of mortality, showing that the population can be estimated from birth and death rates, are introduced in England. They are the first attempt at vital statistics.   **MED**

1535   Italian mathematician Niccolò Tartaglia works out a method for solving cubic equations. The solution is later published by mathematician Geronimo Cardano. *See* 1545, Cardano.   **MATH**

c. 1536   Sarsaparilla is promoted as an antisyphilitic drug.   **MED**

1540   In *Astronomicum caesareum*, German astronomer Petrus Apianus (Peter Bennewitz) observes that the tails of comets always point away from the sun, as the Chinese had previously discovered. *See* 635.   **ASTRO**

1540   In his *Narratio prima de libris revolutionum*, German mathematician Georg Joachim Iserin von Lauchen (Rhäticus or Rheticus) offers a summary of the heliocentric system developed but not yet published by Copernicus.   **ASTRO**

1540   *On Pyrotechnics*, by Italian mine supervisor Vannoccio Biringuccio, discusses ore processing, smelting, distillation, and other such topics. This posthumous opus is considered the first important work on metallurgy.   **CHEM**

1540   Francisco Pizarro reaches Peru and, within two years, destroys a second New World civilization, that of the Incas of Peru. *See* 1519, Cortés.   **EARTH**

1540   German instrument maker Georg Hartman discovers magnetic inclination or dip and is believed to be the first to measure magnetic declination on land.   **EARTH**

1540   During an expedition in 1540–1542, Fernando Vásquez de Coronado becomes the first European to see the Grand Canyon.   **EARTH**

1540   Swiss-born chemist and physician Paracelsus is the first to use tincture of opium, which he calls laudanum for medical purposes.   **MED**

1540   Prussian physician Valerius Cordus (1515–1544) discovers sulfuric ether, though it does not become widely used as an anesthetic until the nineteenth century.   **MED**

1540   Italian physician Pietro Andrea Mattioli uses mercury to treat syphilis, but this popular cure is painful and often kills the patient. Mattioli also advocates oil of scorpions to treat the plague.   **MED**

1541   During an expedition in 1539–1542 led by Spanish explorer Hernando de Soto, the first Europeans see the Mississippi River, in what is now the United States.   **EARTH**

1541   During an expedition in 1541–1542, Spanish explorer Francisco de Orellana becomes the first European to see the Amazon River and cross South America from ocean to ocean.   **EARTH**

1542   In Leipzig, Germany, a botanical garden is established.   **BIO**

1542   German botanist Leonhard Fuchs (*see also* 1501) describes peppers, pumpkins, and corn (maize) from the New World in his botanical masterpiece *De historia stirpium*. His work makes no attempt to classify plants, instead emphasizing firsthand observation of plant habits, locales, and characteristics.   **BIO**

1543   Shortly before the death this year of Polish astronomer Nicolaus Copernicus (*b.* 1473), his *De revolutionibus orbium coelestium* (*On the Revolutions of Celestial Bodies*) is published. This work argues that the earth and the planets travel around the sun, in contradiction to the prevailing geocentric world view codified by Ptolemy (c. 140) and accepted ever since. Like Ptolemy, though, Copernicus argues that planetary motion is basically circular, with epicycles to account for observed anomalies. The publication of this work marks the beginning of what is now known as the Copernican revolution in astronomy.   **ASTRO**

June 1, 1543　Flemish anatomist Andreas Vesalius publishes *De corporis humani fabrica* (*On the Structure of the Human Body*), the first accurate human anatomy text.　　**MED**

....

"Since nothing stands in the way of the movability of the earth, I believe we must now investigate whether it also has several motions, so that it can be considered one of the planets."
—Nicolaus Copernicus, Polish astronomer, on his theory that the earth is one of several planets moving around the sun; in De revolutionibus orbium coelestium, 1543

....

1544　Italian physician and botanist Pietro Andrea Mattioli publishes an Italian version of the classic botany text *De materia medica* by Dioscorides, a Greek physician and herbalist. *See* 60.　　**BIO**

1545　Italian mathematician Geronimo Cardano publishes his *Ars magna*, a landmark book on algebra often considered to mark the beginning of modern mathematics. It includes Tartaglia's method for solving cubic equations (*see* 1535) and Ludovico Ferrari's method for solving quartic equations. It also includes methods for working with negative numbers.　　**MATH**

c. 1545　French surgeon Ambroise Paré devises artificial limbs for war-injured soldiers. These "hands" include individually moving fingers and a holder for a quill pen.　　**MED**

1546　Astronomer Tycho Brahe (*d.* 1601) is born at Skøane, Denmark, now part of Sweden. Tycho will set a new standard for precision in astronomical measurements. He will also make important observations of the supernova of 1572 and the comet of 1577.　　**ASTRO**

1546　Italian physician Girolamo Fracastoro formulates the first theory suggesting that the tiny, autonomous living entities called bacteria are what cause disease.　　**MED**

1546　In *De natura fossilium*, German metallurgist Georgius Agricola (Georg Bauer) coins the word *fossil* for anything dug from the earth, including rocks in the shape of bones and shells.　　**PALEO**

1547　In London the St. Mary's of Bethlehem Hospital establishes a separate asylum for the insane. It will become known as Bedlam, a term that will become synonymous with a place or state of uproar and confusion.　　**MED**

1550　Italian scientist Geronimo Cardano publishes a book on natural history that implies a belief in evolutionary change.　　**BIO**

c. 1550　In Yucatán, Mexico, during the postclassic period, Mayan Indians roast green corn, then leave it to produce mold, which is used to treat wounds, cuts, ulcers, and intestinal infections.　　**MED**

c. 1550–
1700

This period in Europe will become known as the scientific revolution. During this time scientists such as Copernicus, Galileo, Harvey,
Pascal, and Newton and philosophers such as Francis Bacon transform the modern world's approach to understanding nature.
Traditional deference to classical authorities on nature, such as
Aristotle, is replaced by reliance on the empirical methods of science.   **MISC**

1551

German astronomer Erasmus Reinhold publishes *Tabulae
prutenicae*, astronomical tables based on Copernicus's heliocentric
theory that improve on the thirteenth-century Alphonsine tables.
See 1272.   **ASTRO**

1551

German-Swiss physician and naturalist Konrad von Gesner begins
publication of what will be considered the most authoritative zoological study since Aristotle, his *Historiae animalium* (1551–1558,
1587). It includes lists and descriptions of each known animal
species and their physical appearance, emotions, habits, locale, diseases, and uses for mankind.   **BIO**

1551

German mathematician Georg Joachim Iserin von Lauchen
(Rhäticus or Rheticus) produces detailed trigonometric tables.   **MATH**

1551

Italian physician Bartolommeo Maggi proves that gunshot wounds
are not poisonous.   **MED**

1551

Italian anatomist Gabriel Fallopius describes the tubes that carry the
human ovum from the ovary to the uterus. These passages, which
will become known as the Fallopian tubes, are where fertilization
takes place.   **MED**

1552

The convex lens is developed by Italian physicist Giambattista della Porta and used to refine the camera obscura, an artist's tool for
tracing that had been invented by Roger Bacon three centuries
earlier.   **TECH**

1553

English mariner Richard Chancellor opens a northeastern sea route
to Russia, encouraging trade between the two countries.   **EARTH**

1554

Italian naturalist Ulisse Aldrovandi publishes his systematic study of
plant classification, *Herbarium*.   **BIO**

1554

French physician Jean-François Fernel publishes his work called
Medicina, the first modern medical textbook.   **MED**

1555

French naturalist Pierre Belon describes the homologies (basic simi-
larities) in the body plans of vertebrates.   **BIO**

1556

Tobacco is introduced to continental Europe by Franciscan monk
André Thevet, who brings seeds of the plant to Spain from a trip to
Rio de Janeiro.   **BIO**

51

| 1556 | *De re metallica* (*Concerning Metallic Things*), by German physician Georgius Agricola (Georg Bauer), now published posthumously, is the first important work on mineralogy.   **EARTH** |

1556

| Jan. 24, 1556 | The deadliest earthquake in recorded history devastates Shansi, China, with a death toll in the hundreds of thousands.   **EARTH** |

| 1556 | French surgeon Pierre Franco is the first to perform a suprapubic lithotomy, or incision into the bladder to remove stones.   **MED** |

| 1557 | English mathematician Robert Recorde makes the first known use of the modern equals (=) sign.   **MATH** |

| 1559 | Ice cream is developed in Italy, by a freezing process using ice and salt.   **TECH** |

| 1560 | Italian physicist Giambattista della Porta founds the first scientific association designed for the exchange of information, the Academia Secretorum Naturae, or Academy of the Mysteries of Nature.   **MISC** |

| Feb. 15, 1564 | Galileo Galilei is born in Pisa, Italy (*d.* 1642). Often considered the founder of the experimental method, he will become known for his achievements in astronomy, physics, and mathematics as well as a clash with the Roman Catholic church over his support for the heliocentric theory (that the earth and planets revolve around the sun).   **MISC** |

| 1565 | Swiss scientist Konrad von Gesner's *De rerum fossilium* (*On Things Disinterred from the Earth*) contains the first illustrations of fossils.   **BIO** |

| 1565 | Tobacco is introduced from Florida to England by explorer John Hawkins. *See also* 1556.   **BIO** |

| 1565 | Muskets are in use in Europe.   **TECH** |

| 1565 | The lead pencil (or lead) is seen for the first time in a woodcut from a book about fossils by Swiss-German naturalist Conrad von Gesner.   **TECH** |

| 1567 | Bologna's botanical garden is founded.   **BIO** |

| 1568 | The first map to use the Mercator projection appears. Designed by Flemish cartographer Gerardus Mercator (Gerhard Kremer), this map employs a cylindrical projection that distorts the sizes of areas in order to preserve their shapes.   **EARTH** |

| 1568 | Ambroise Paré recognizes the difference between syphilis (called the greater pox) and smallpox (the lesser pox).   **MED** |

| 1570 | Geographer Abraham Ortelius of Antwerp publishes his *Theatrum orbis terrarum*, which contains seventy maps and is the first comprehensive atlas of the world.   **EARTH** |

1572   A supernova as bright as Venus is observed in the constellation Cassiopeia by Chinese astronomers and Danish astronomer Tycho Brahe. This stellar explosion remains visible to the naked eye for sixteen months. Tycho calls it a *nova* in his *De nova stella* (*On the New Star*) the following year. His hypothesis that this supernova is farther away than the moon contradicts traditional belief by indicating that change can happen in the celestial sphere.   **ASTRO**

....

"Science without conscience is the death of the soul."
—François Rabelais, French scholar, satirist,
and monk; sixteenth century

....

1572   Pigeons are used to transport messages in Haarlem, the Netherlands.   **BIO**

1572   In Rafael Bombelli's *Algebra*, complex numbers are applied to solve equations for the first time. Bombelli also uses continued fractions to approximate roots.   **MATH**

c. 1574   Italian philosopher Giordano Bruno is accused of heresy and forced to leave the Dominican order. Among his heretical beliefs is Bruno's defense of Copernicus's heliocentric theory on metaphysical grounds.   **ASTRO**

1574   Tycho, under the patronage of Danish king Frederick II, establishes an observatory on the Danish island of Ven. For twenty years he and his assistants carry out accurate, detailed naked-eye observations of the stars and planets.   **ASTRO**

1575   Spanish physician Juan Huarte recommends that ability tests be given and vocational counseling be used to match people with their occupations. He also claims that intelligence and higher culture are possible only in moderate climatic zones.   **PSYCH**

1575   Porcelain dinnerware is produced for the first time in Europe by Tuscan grand duke Francesco Maria de Medici.   **TECH**

1576   English explorer Martin Frobisher fails to find a northwest passage from Europe to Asia but does discover Baffin Island and, in 1578, rediscovers Greenland. *See* 982.   **EARTH**

1577   Using parallax theory, Tycho proves that a bright comet he is observing is at least three times as far away as the moon, contradicting the conventional belief that comets are luminous vapors in the atmosphere.   **ASTRO**

1577	During an expedition in 1577–1580, English mariner Francis Drake circumnavigates the globe for the first time since the voyage of Magellan in 1522. On the way he discovers the Drake Passage or Drake Strait south of Tierra del Fuego and sails up the California coast as far as San Francisco Bay. **EARTH**
1578	French physician Guillaume de Baillou is the first to describe whooping cough and coins the term *rheumatism* for soreness, stiffness, and inflammation of the joints and muscles. **MED**
1578	The first medical school on the North American continent is established, at the University of Mexico. **MED**
Apr. 1, 1578	English physician William Harvey (d. 1657) is born in Folkestone, Kent, England. He will be known for establishing that the heart is a muscle and that blood circulates. He will bring about the end of unquestioning acceptance of Galen and Greek medicine. Some will consider him the founder of modern physiology. **MED**
1580	Italian scientist Prospero Alpini discovers that plants have two sexes. **BIO**
1581	A Russian named Yermak Timofievich explores Siberia, conquering the Mongol kingdom of Sibir. **EARTH**
1581	While watching hanging lamps during a service in the cathedral of Pisa, the sixteen-year-old Galileo notes that the time of a pendulum's swing seems to be determined solely by its length, not by the width of its swing. This observation leads to the manufacture of accurate pendulum clocks by the late seventeenth century. **PHYS**
Oct. 15, 1582	Following the advice of Bavarian astronomer Cristoph Clavius, Pope Gregory XIII reforms the calendar. In his Gregorian calendar, still used today, century years not divisible by four hundred are not leap years. This change from the old Julian calendar, which had been in use in Europe since 46 B.C., results in ten days being dropped. Thus, the day after October 4 is proclaimed to be October 15. **ASTRO**
1583	Italian botanist Andrea Cesalpino proposes a plant classification system in his treatise *De plantis*. He classifies plants according to their roots and fruit organs, putting lichens and mushrooms at the bottom of the plant hierarchy. **BIO**
1583	Dutch mathematician Simon Stevinus founds the science of hydrostatics with discoveries about factors determining the pressure of liquids on surfaces. **PHYS**
1584	Sir Walter Raleigh brings the plant extract curare to England from South America. **MED**
1586	Potatoes imported from the Americas are planted in Ireland by explorer Sir Francis Drake. **BIO**

1586   Simon Stevinus works out a system of decimal fractions that allows fractions to be included in positional notation. He also discovers rules for locating the roots of equations.   **MATH**

1586   On dropping two objects of different weight, Simon Stevinus notes that they hit the ground at the same time, disproving Aristotle's long-held proposition that heavier bodies fall faster than lighter ones.   **PHYS**

1588   Italian botanist Giambattista della Porta tries to draw parallels between the medicinal properties of a plant and its external shape, arguing that plants resembling human organs can be useful in healing diseases of those organs.   **BIO**

c. 1589   William Lee of Cambridge, England, invents the stocking frame, the first knitting machine. It slowly gains popularity during the seventeenth century.   **TECH**

1590s   Galileo privately accepts the Copernican heliocentric explanation of the solar system.   **ASTRO**

1590   Galileo publishes his *De motu* (*On Motion*), showing how his experiments with falling bodies refute Aristotle's physics.   **PHYS**

1590   Rudolf Goeckel publishes a book of essays by different authors on human nature and the soul. This is the first book to have the word *psychology* (*Psychologia*) in its title.   **PSYCH**

1590   Dutch spectacle maker Zacharias Janssen invents the compound microscope. *See also* 1609, Lippershey.   **TECH**

1591   French mathematician François Viète introduces algebraic sign language using consonants for known quantities and vowels for unknown ones.   **MATH**

1592   Italian engineer Domenico Fontana discovers the ruins of the cities of Pompeii and Herculaneum, buried by the eruption of Mount Vesuvius in 79. Deliberate excavation will not occur until 1738, but this discovery marks the beginning of the science of archaeology.   **ARCH**

c. 1592   Galileo invents the thermoscope, a primitive thermometer.   **TECH**

1593   A shortage of lumber and firewood in England encourages the expansion of coal mining.   **TECH**

1594   Gerardus Mercator dies (*b.* 1512). His son publishes Mercator's great work, *Atlas sive cosmographicae*, posthumously.   **EARTH**

1595   The word *trigonometry* appears in print for what may be the first time, in a work by German mathematician Bartholomaeus Pitiscus.   **MATH**

1596   Dutch astronomer David Fabricius reports for the first time on the irregular variation of the star Omicron Ceti, or Mira. *See also* 1638, Holwarda.   **ASTRO**

1596   English botanist John Gerard's (*d.* 1612) *Herbal*, the greatest survey of botanical knowledge to date, is published.   **BIO**

1596   Dutch mathematician Ludolph van Ceulen calculates pi to twenty decimal places, later extending it to thirty-five places.   **MATH**

SIMIAN SHAKESPEARE

*A*bout the year 1601, English playwright William Shakespeare wrote the tragedy Hamlet, a masterpiece that sparked centuries of theatrical and literary interpretation. As an exemplar of the unique, unrepeatable nature of great art, the play also sparked a question that has become part of popular scientific lore: How long would it take for a monkey sitting at a typewriter to write Hamlet by randomly pounding on the keyboard?

This question has been raised in many contexts, sometimes by nihilists seeking to suggest the meaninglessness of human works, at other times by creationists arguing that random events could not have led to the evolution of intelligence. (The latter application is, however, misleading, since the natural selection of useful characteristics is, by definition, not random but selective.) Whatever its significance, the question itself is easily answered, not by setting a monkey in front of a typewriter and waiting, but with techniques drawn from probability theory. This area of mathematics was founded by French mathematicians Blaise Pascal and Pierre de Fermat around 1654, not long after Hamlet was written.

Assume that the number of symbols or characters in Hamlet—including all letters, punctuation, and spaces—equals 200,000. (Whether it is more or less, the basic idea will be the same.) There are 46 characters on a typewriter keyboard, not counting the shift key and such subtleties as tabs and returns (the monkey's editor will take care of those). Thus each time the monkey hits a key, he has a one in 46 ($\frac{1}{46}$) chance of hitting the right one, as for example the initial t in "to be or not to be." When he hits the next key, he again has a one in 46 chance of hitting the right key for the o in "to." The odds of his typing the complete word "to" are, then, $\frac{1}{46} \times \frac{1}{46}$, or $\left(\frac{1}{46}\right)^2$, $\frac{1}{2116}$. Similarly, the odds of his typing all 18 characters in "to be or not to be" in the correct sequence are $\left(\frac{1}{46}\right)^{18}$, equivalent to $\frac{1}{46}$ multiplied by itself 18 times. The odds of the monkey's typing all 200,000 characters therefore are $\left(\frac{1}{46}\right)^{200,000}$. This probability is so small as to be virtually zero, or, to put it another way, the time it would take is virtually infinite. The only known way for monkeys to write Hamlet is for them to evolve to be as intelligent as Shakespeare.

1596   Philosopher, mathematician, and scientist René Descartes is born in La Haye, France (*d.* 1650). Considered the founder of modern philosophy and analytic geometry, he will originate Cartesian coordinates and Cartesian curves. His contributions to science will include work in physiology, optics, and psychology.   **MISC**

1596   Korean admiral Visunsin builds the first ironclad warship.   **TECH**

1596   The water closet, meant to replace the chamber pot and privy, is developed by English poet Sir John Harington.   **TECH**

1597   After twenty years of research, Tycho is forced to leave his observatory at Ven when the new king of Denmark, Christian IV, cuts off his support. He then goes to Prague as court astronomer for Holy Roman Emperor Rudolph II.   **ASTRO**

1597   German alchemist Andreas Libau (Libavius) publishes his *Alchymia*, a landmark text in chemistry. Among other things, it explains how to prepare hydrochloric acid and ammonium sulfate.   **CHEM**

1597   Italian physician Gaspare Tagliacozzi publishes his studies on the reconstruction of the nose. He thus becomes established as the first modern plastic surgeon.   **MED**

1598   Italian aristocrat Carlo Ruini illustrates a work called *Dell' anatomia et dell' infirmita del cavallo*, the first comprehensive monograph on an animal's anatomy, in this case the horse.   **BIO**

1599   Italian naturalist Ulisse Aldrovandi publishes his classic studies in ornithology, the branch of zoology dealing with birds.   **BIO**

1600   Young mathematician Johannes Kepler becomes Tycho's assistant at Prague.   **ASTRO**

Feb. 17, 1600   The Italian philosopher Giordano Bruno (*b.* 1548), is burned at the stake in Rome for heresy, including his support for Copernican theory.   **ASTRO**

c. 1600   Johann Thölde, writing as Basil Valentine, is the probable discoverer of the elements antimony and bismuth.   **CHEM**

1600   English physician and scientist William Gilbert publishes *De magnete* (*On Magnetism*), the first work of physical science based completely on experimentation. In it he argues that the earth acts like a giant magnet with poles near the geographic poles.   **EARTH**

1600   William Gilbert is named president of the College of Physicians and personal physician to English queen Elizabeth I. She, and he, die three years later.   **MED**

Oct. 24, 1601   Danish astronomer Tycho Brahe (*b.* 1546) dies at Benatky, near Prague, Czechoslovakia. Johannes Kepler succeeds him as court astronomer to Emperor Rudolph II.   **ASTRO**

1601   French mathematician Pierre de Fermat is born (*d.* 1665). Not a professional mathematician, he publishes virtually nothing during his lifetime, but will eventually be regarded as the founder of number theory, a codiscoverer of analytic geometry, and a codiscoverer also of differential calculus. He will also be renowned for the theorems he scribbled in the margins of books, particularly one called Fermat's Last Theorem. *See* 1637, Fermat; c. 1810s.   **MATH**

1601   Fifty-three stations with overnight inns called *ryokans* and horse-changing stops are built in Edo and Osaka, Japan. Developed by a man named Ieyasa, regent of Tokugawa, these inns ease the burden of long-distance travel.   **TECH**

1601   Coffee, introduced to England by traveler Anthony Shirley, is sold for five pounds per ounce.   **TECH**

1601   Pepper is imported in large quantities to England by the East India Company, a trading concern.   **TECH**

1602   German astronomer Johann Bayer's celestial atlas *Uranometria* introduces a new system for naming and describing the locations of stars that is still in use today. In this system a star is named by a Greek letter and its constellation.   **ASTRO**

1602   Hugh Platt discovers coke, the residue left after distillation of coal, which later becomes an important fuel.   **TECH**

....

"[A] custome lothsome to the eye, hatefull to the nose, harmefull to the braine, dangerous to the lungs and in the blacke stinking fume thereof, nearest resembling the horrible, Stigian smoke of the pit that is bottomlesse."—James I of England on the newly introduced habit of tobacco smoking; in "Counterblaste to Tobacco"; published anonymously 1603

....

1604   Korean and Chinese astronomers, independently from Johannes Kepler at Prague, observe a supernova in the constellation Ophiuchus that lasts twelve months. Kepler's observations are published as *De stella nova* (*On the New Star*) in 1606.   **ASTRO**

1604   Galileo observes that a falling body increases its distance as the square of time.   **PHYS**

1605   English essayist Francis Bacon publishes his treatise *The Advancement of Learning*, which promotes experimentation and observation as the basis for knowledge.   **MISC**

1606   Spanish navigator Luis Vaez de Torres sails completely around New Guinea, showing it to be an island.   **EARTH**

THE MOONS OF JUPITER

*I*n 1609 Italian scientist Galileo Galilei received word that a Dutchman, Hans Lippershey, had invented a device "by the aid of which visible objects, although at a great distance from the eye of the observer, were seen distinctly as if near." Wasting no time, Galileo learned how to build his own telescope and constructed several models. In 1610 he discovered a startling fact about the planet Jupiter. In The Sidereal Messenger, published later that year, he reported his find.

On the 7th day of January in the present year, 1610, in the first hour of the following night, when I was viewing the constellations of the heavens through a telescope, the planet Jupiter presented itself to my view, and as I had prepared for myself a very excellent instrument, I noticed a circumstance which I had never been able to notice before, owing to want of power in my other telescope, namely, that three little stars, small but very bright, were near the planet....

I scarcely troubled at all about the distance between them and Jupiter, for, as I have said, at first I believed them to be fixed stars; but when on January 8th, led by some fatality, I turned again to look at the same part of the heavens, I found a very different state of things, for there were three little stars all west of Jupiter [where previously two had been east and one west], and nearer together than on the previous night....

[After more days of observation:]

I, therefore, concluded, and decided unhesitatingly, that there are three stars in the heavens moving about Jupiter, as Venus and Mercury around the Sun; which at length was established as clear as daylight by numerous other subsequent observations. These observations also established that there are not only three, but four, erratic sidereal bodies performing their revolutions round Jupiter....

[Galileo concludes:]

[W]e have a notable and splendid argument to remove the scruples of those who can tolerate the revolution of the planets round the sun in the Copernican system, yet are so disturbed by the motion of one Moon about the Earth, while both accomplish an orbit of a year's length about the sun, that they consider that this theory of the universe must be upset as impossible; for now we have not one planet only revolving about another, while both traverse a vast orbit about the Sun, but our sense of sight presents to us four satellites circling about Jupiter, like our Moon about the Earth, while the whole system travels over a mighty orbit about the Sun in the space of twelve years.

1608	Dutch spectacle maker Hans Lippershey invents the first telescope to attract public notice. Military telescopes had been used secretly by the Dutch for about twenty years. **ASTRO**
1609	Galileo builds his own telescope with three-power magnification, eventually making one with a magnification of thirty. **ASTRO**
1609	Johannes Kepler's *Astronomia nova* (*The New Astronomy*), published this year, contains both his first law (that the orbit of a planet around the sun is an ellipse) and second law (that these orbits sweep out equal areas in space in equal periods of time). **ASTRO**
1609	English mathematician Thomas Harriot uses a telescope to sketch the moon. **ASTRO**
1609	Italian anatomist Giulio Casserio finishes a series of five books on the hearing, sight, smell, taste, and touch organs of humans. This work, *Pentaestheseion*, will be noted for its literary style and illustrative plates. **BIO**
1609	Independently from Zacharias Janssen (*see* 1590) Dutch scientist Hans Lippershey invents the compound microscope, a central tube with lenses attached to both ends. **TECH**
1610	Italian scientist Galileo becomes the first to make significant astronomical observations using the telescope. He sees four of Jupiter's moons, the phases of Venus, and the individual stars of the Milky Way. He notes that Saturn has an odd appearance, later found to be rings. He publishes his discoveries in a work called *Sidereal Messenger*. **ASTRO**
c. 1610	Galileo uses the microscope to study insect anatomy. **BIO**
1610	Jean Beguin of France publishes his *Tyrocinium chymicum*, the first textbook on chemistry rather than alchemy. **CHEM**
1610	English navigator Henry Hudson, attempting to find the northwest passage, instead finds and enters the Canadian waterway now known as the Hudson Strait, leading to a large, landlocked body of water that will come to be called Hudson Bay. **EARTH**
1611	Galileo, Thomas Harriot, Johannes Fabricius, and German astronomer Father Christoph Scheiner independently discover sunspots. **ASTRO**
1611	English physician John Woodall recommends citrus fruit for protection against scurvy on long sea voyages. **MED**
1612	German astronomer Simon Marius (Simon Mayr) is the first to study the Andromeda galaxy. **ASTRO**

Petum Optimum Subter Solem

Le meilleur Tabac de sous le Soleil

The Best Tobacco under the Sun

Tobacco label, "The Best Tobacco under the Sun," seventeenth century. (*Arents Collection, New York Public Library*)

1612   Through advice from Native Americans, American colonists learn to grow and cure tobacco on a large scale and use it as a prime export commodity to England. Over fifteen hundred pounds per acre are grown in Virginia's James River Valley.   **BIO**

1613   In *The Sunspot Letters* Galileo supports the Copernican theory of heliocentrism in print for the first time.   **ASTRO**

1613　　　　Mathematician Pietro Cataldi develops techniques for handling continued fractions. **MATH**

1614　　　　Italian chemist Angelo Sala discovers that light darkens the white compound silver nitrate, a phenomenon relevant to the invention of photography two centuries later. **CHEM**

1614　　　　Scottish mathematician John Napier publishes a table of logarithms based on powers of 2. **MATH**

1614　　　　Italian physician Sanctorius (Santorio Santorio) publishes his studies on body weight, food, and excreta—the first metabolic balance studies. **MED**

1615　　　　Galileo travels to Rome to defend the Copernican theory. **ASTRO**

1615　　　　French explorer Samuel de Champlain reaches the eastward extension of Lake Huron, called Georgian Bay. He thus becomes the first European to sight the Great Lakes. **EARTH**

1615　　　　Rubber is introduced to Europe from South America, but its uses will not be fully developed for centuries. *See also* 1503. **TECH**

1615　　　　The use of coal in England grows in popularity, owing to rising timber costs. **TECH**

1616　　　　In a rebuff to Galileo, the Roman Catholic church issues a decree stating that the Copernican doctrine is "false and absurd" and should not be held or defended. Copernicus's *De revolutionibus* (1543) is placed on the church's *Index of Prohibited Books*, where it will remain until the nineteenth century. **ASTRO**

1616　　　　English explorer William Baffin reaches what is now Baffin Bay and travels to within eight hundred miles of the North Pole, a record held until the latter half of the nineteenth century. **EARTH**

1616　　　　English physician William Harvey lectures to the Royal College of Physicians about the circulation of the blood. **MED**

1617　　　　English mathematician Henry Briggs's *Logarithmorum chilias prima* (*Logarithms of Numbers from 1 to 10*) introduces logarithms based on powers of 10, or common logarithms. **MATH**

1617　　　　Dutch mathematician Willebrord Snell develops a technique for finding distances by trigonometric triangulation. **MATH**

1617　　　　French clergyman St. Vincent de Paul (1581–1660) organizes the Dames de Charité, women who visit the sick and dying, administering nursing services. With this organization St. Vincent introduces the modern principles of home health care and the idea that poverty should not keep people from giving or receiving medical care. **MED**

1617　　　　In London, King James I grants a charter to a newly formed society of pharmacists, allowing pharmacists to emerge as a distinct group of craftsmen separate from grocers. **MED**

1619   In his *Harmonice mundi* Johannes Kepler propounds his third law, that the squares of the times of revolution of any two planets are proportional to the cubes of their distances from the sun.   **ASTRO**

1619   Kepler publishes *Epitome astronomiae copernicae* (*Epitome of the Copernican Astronomy*), a defense of the Copernican doctrine. The Roman Catholic church places it on its *Index of Prohibited Books*. **ASTRO**

1619   From Ingulstadt, Germany, comes the first report of telescopic observations of a comet.   **ASTRO**

1620   English philosopher Francis Bacon points out that the outlines of Africa and South America generally mesh, an observation that will become important in the development of plate tectonics.   **EARTH**

1620   Francis Bacon publishes his *Novum organum*, a treatise outlining the scientific method based on the principles of experimentation and induction.   **MISC**

....

"The human understanding is of its own nature prone to abstractions and gives a substance and reality to things which are fleeting. But to resolve nature into abstractions is less to our purpose than to dissect her into parts.... Matter rather than forms should be the object of our attention, its configurations and changes of configuration, and simple action, and law of action or motion; for forms are figments of the human mind, unless you will call those laws of action forms."—Francis Bacon, English philosopher; in Novum organum, 1620

....

c. 1620   In London, Dutch inventor Cornelis Drebbel constructs the first submarine, using greased leather over a wooden form. Powered by rowers, the vessel cruises beneath the surface of the Thames.   **TECH**

1621   In his treatise *On the Formation of Eggs and Chickens*, Italian scientist Girolamo Fabrici gives detailed, sequential illustrations of chick embryo development. *See also* 1673, Malpighi.   **BIO**

c. 1621   English mathematician William Oughtred invents the slide rule. **MATH**

1621   Dutch mathematician Willebrord Snell formulates Snell's law, which concerns refraction of light. It states that the ratio of the sine of the angle of incidence to the sine of the angle of refraction is equal to the ratio of the refracting medium's index of refraction to the original medium's index of refraction.   **PHYS**

1622   Italian anatomist Gasparo Aselli discovers the lacteal vessels, an important intestinal lymph vessel.   **MED**

1623   Botanist Gaspard Bauhin of Switzerland classifies some six thousand plants and introduces the practice of using two names—one for the genus, another for the species—to classify living things.   **BIO**

1623   French mathematician, scientist, and religious philosopher Blaise Pascal is born (d. 1662). He will become the founder of probability theory, discover many properties of the cycloid, and lay the groundwork for the hydraulic press.   **MISC**

1624   Flemish physician Jan Baptista van Helmont studies the metabolism of the willow tree.   **BIO**

Sept. 10, 1624   Physician Thomas Sydenham is born in Wynford Eagle, England (d. 1689). Known as the English Hippocrates, he will be the first to describe measles and scarlet fever and will recommend such remedies as opium for pain and iron for anemia.   **MED**

1624   Jan Baptista van Helmont coins the word *gas* (from the Flemish word for *chaos*) to describe substances like air. One of the gases he identifies is carbon dioxide, which he calls *gas sylvestre* (wood gas).   **PHYS**

EXPERIMENT WITH A CHICKEN

*E*nglish philosopher, essayist, and statesman Francis Bacon (1561–1626) was not an expert in any one science but dabbled in many, doing things like stuffing a chicken with snow to test the idea that cold can preserve meat from decay. Much more valuable than such experiments was his development of a philosophy of knowledge that is one of the principal sources of the scientific method, and therefore of modern science.

In his works The Advancement of Learning (1605) and Novum organum (1620), Bacon laid out his belief that the Aristotelian method of deducing truth from a priori assumptions was not a valid way of uncovering truths about nature. He proposed instead what he called the inductive method: making numerous observations and experiments in order to build to general conclusions. Bacon perhaps overstated the case, since modern science uses both deduction (to frame theories, hypotheses, and predictions) and induction (to test predictions against the real world and provide evidence for the framing or reframing of theories). But he did provide philosophical underpinnings for science that served to increase the pace and rigor of scientific discovery.

As for Bacon's chicken and snow experiment, the outcome was never recorded. Bacon caught a severe chill while collecting the snow and died a few days later, a martyr, if an unglamorous one, to his own method.

1624   French philosopher Pierre Gassendi contributes to sensory psychology by being the first to measure sound velocity.   **PSYCH**

1625   German chemist Johann Glauber finds that hydrochloric acid can be formed with sulfuric acid and sodium chloride. The residue of this compound will gain popularity as the laxative known as sodium sulfate.   **MED**

1626   Sir Francis Bacon experiments with refrigerating food by placing snow in the cavities of chickens.   **TECH**

1627   Johannes Kepler publishes his *Rudolphine Tables*, planetary tables based on his theory of elliptical orbits.   **ASTRO**

1627   The auroch, or uru, the long-horned wild ox believed to be the ancestor of domestic cattle (*see* 6400 B.C.), becomes extinct when the last specimen dies in Poland.   **BIO**

1628   British physician William Harvey publishes a description of the circulation of blood that is largely correct, in contrast to the many erroneous ideas extant on blood movement. *See also* 1660, Malpighi.   **MED**

1628   A rudimentary version of the steam engine is developed by English engineer Edward Somerset.   **TECH**

c. 1629   French mathematician Pierre de Fermat discovers a method of finding maximum and minimum values for functions which represents the genesis of differential calculus.   **MATH**

1630   Pierre Vernier, a French military engineer, invents the Vernier scale, which measures angles and small distances with great precision. Though its original applications will be in navigation and astronomy, the Vernier scale will come into general use near the end of the seventeenth century.   **EARTH**

1630   Englishman Peter Chamberlen devises the first obstetrical forceps.   **MED**

1630   Italian natural philosopher Niccolò Cabeo observes that electrically charged bodies first attract, then repel each other. He is the first to use the term *lines of force* to describe the curves assumed by iron filings on a sheet of paper above a magnet.   **PHYS**

1631   Following Kepler's predictions, Pierre Gassendi observes the transit of Mercury across the sun.   **ASTRO**

1631   Mathematician Thomas Harriot's posthumously published work, *Artis analyticae praxis,* introduces a raised centered dot for multiplication and the symbols > and < for "greater than" and "less than."   **MATH**

1631   English mathematician William Oughtred introduces the × sign for multiplication.   **MATH**

1632   Galileo's *Dialogue on the Two Great World Systems* is published in Italian, not Latin, to reach a general audience. Using the conceit of a hypothetical debate among three philosophers, it makes a solid case for the Copernican theory. The Roman Catholic church promptly places a ban on it that will not be lifted until 1822. **ASTRO**

1632   In Delft, the Netherlands, microscopist and zoologist Anton van Leeuwenhoek is born (*d.* 1723). Although he will receive little scientific education, Leeuwenhoek will make pioneering discoveries regarding microbes, red blood cells, capillary systems, and insects' life cycles. After his invention of a double-convex microscope, he will describe three types of bacteria—bacilli, cocci, and spirilla—and discover protozoa and bacteria. **BIO**

1632   English philosopher John Locke is born (*d.* 1704). He will found British empiricism, the philosophical doctrine that all knowledge is derived from experience. Locke's views will be associated with the rise of experimental science in the eighteenth century. *See also* 1690. **MISC**

1633   Galileo, at age sixty-nine, is called before the Inquisition in Rome on charges of heresy. Pleading guilty, he recants his views and is sentenced to house arrest for the remainder of his life. **ASTRO**

1633   English physician Stephen Bradwell writes *Helps in Sudden Accidents*, the first book on first aid. **MED**

1635   English astronomer Henry Gellibrand presents evidence that the earth's magnetic poles shift position over time. **EARTH**

1635   Italian mathematician Francesco Bonaventura Cavalieri publishes the influential *Geometria indivisibilibus continuorum*, in which he develops the theory of indivisibles (infinite processes), an important stage in the development of the calculus. **MATH**

1635   Inland mail delivery by wheeled coaches is inaugurated between London and Edinburgh. **TECH**

1636   Sugar is first grown on Barbados. Introduced by the Dutch, it will become a mainstay crop in Barbados and other islands in the Caribbean. **TECH**

1637   King Christian IV of Denmark establishes a permanent astronomical observatory in Copenhagen. **ASTRO**

1637   In an appendix to his *Discourse on Method*, French mathematician René Descartes introduces analytic geometry, a branch of geometry in which all points are represented with respect to a coordinate system. (Pierre de Fermat had developed analytic geometry independently in 1636 or earlier, but his work was not published until 1670.) Descartes' work also introduces a system of exponential notation. **MATH**

1637   French mathematician Pierre de Fermat formulates, but does not prove, Fermat's Last Theorem, so called because for centuries it remains the last proposition of Fermat's to go unproven. It states that the expression $x^n + y^n = z^n$ has no positive integral solutions if n is an integer greater than 2. In 1993 British mathematician Andrew Wiles will finally prove it.   **MATH**

1637   Descartes explains the process of accommodation, in *Dioptrics*, his work on ophthalmology.   **MED**

1637   Descartes publishes his *Discourse on Method*, which begins from the premise of universal doubt, describes a mechanistic physical world divorced from the mind, and promotes the use of deduction in science.   **MISC**

1638   Dutch astronomer Phoclides Holwarda identifies the first known variable star, Omicron Ceti, or Mira, initially observed by David Fabricius in 1596.   **ASTRO**

1638   Galileo publishes *Mathematical Discourses and Demonstrations on Two New Sciences* in which he discusses the laws of motion and friction, refuting Aristotle on several points.   **PHYS**

c. 1639   English astronomer William Gascoigne invents the micrometer, a device placed in a telescope to measure the angular distance between stars.   **ASTRO**

1639   In his work known as *Brouillon project* (*Rough Draft*), French mathematician Girard Desargues develops projective geometry.   **MATH**

c. 1639   Descartes claims that the human body functions as a machine, a system of mechanical devices. He mistakenly believes the pineal gland to be the center of the human mind and soul.   **MED**

1640   French mathematician Pierre de Fermat develops modern number theory.   **MATH**

c. 1640   Italian matron Jeanne Biscot develops the abilities of the patients she cares for during the Thirty Years' War (1618–1648). Her hospitals become workshops where patients enrich their personal skills, marking the beginning of occupational therapy.   **MED**

1640   In *De motu gravium*, Evangelista Torricelli of Italy applies Galileo's laws of motion to fluids, thus founding the science of hydrodynamics.   **PHYS**

1640   Stagecoaches to transport people are introduced in England.   **TECH**

1641   The first living chimpanzee is brought out of the wild to the Netherlands.   **BIO**

1641   Using his father's theories, Galileo's son designs a clock with a pendulum.   **TECH**

1642	Sailing from Dutch outposts in Indonesia, mariner Abel Janszoon Tasman becomes the first European to reach what is now the island of Tasmania and the southern island of New Zealand. **EARTH**
1642	French scientist Blaise Pascal invents the adding machine and also contributes to the development of differential calculus. **MATH**
Dec. 25, 1642	On Christmas of the same year that Italian scientist Galileo Galilei dies (*b.* 1564), English mathematician and physicist Isaac Newton is born (*d.* 1727). He will found the field of celestial mechanics, co-invent calculus, and make revolutionary breakthroughs in the studies of optics, gravitation, and motion. In his most famous work, known as the *Principia* (1687), he will present his three laws of motion and the law of universal gravitation. **MISC**
1643	Italian mathematician Evangelista Torricelli invents the barometer. **TECH**
1644	Dutch explorer Abel Tasman becomes the first European to discover the continent of Australia. **EARTH**
1644	Evangelista Torricelli publishes discoveries about the cycloid, including methods of finding its area and constructing the tangent. Earlier and independently, French mathematician Gilles Personne de Roberval made similar discoveries but did not publish them. **MATH**
1644	Descartes explains reflex action, the involuntary response to a stimulus. **MED**
1644	Descartes publishes his *Principles of Philosophy*, which builds on the *Discourse on Method* (1637) in describing natural phenomena in mechanistic terms. **MISC**
1645	German physicist and engineer Otto von Guericke invents the first practical air pump. Vacuums created by this device allow von Guericke to carry out experiments revealing that in vacuums sound does not travel, fire is extinguished, and animals stop breathing. Von Guericke will also make the first measurement of the density of air. **PHYS**
1647	*Selenographia*, by German-Polish astronomer Johannes Hevelius, is the first map of the visible side of the moon. **ASTRO**
1647	In Italy, physician Georg Wirsung discovers the pancreatic duct, which passes pancreatic juice through into the small bowel, where the juice assists with food breakdown. **MED**
1648	Flemish physician Jan Baptista van Helmont claims that baby mice are produced either by spontaneous generation or through the joining of adult male and female mice. **BIO**
1648	Using barometers, French scientist Blaise Pascal demonstrates that air pressure decreases with altitude and shows that air has a finite height. **EARTH**

1648   Pascal formulates what is termed Pascal's law, that in a confined fluid, externally applied pressure is transmitted uniformly in all directions and pushes at right angles to any surface in or surrounding the fluid. This principle will be the basis for the hydraulic press. **PHYS**

....

"Man is only a reed, the weakest thing in nature; but he is a thinking reed."—Blaise Pascal, French mathematician, scientist, and philosopher; seventeenth century

....

1648   The Taj Mahal, a massive marble and sandstone mausoleum, is built in Agra, India, by Mughal leader Shāh Jahān. **TECH**

1648   Iron production flourishes in the Massachusetts colony, developed by John Winthrop Jr., son of the colony's first governor. **TECH**

1650   Belgian astronomer Godefroy Wendelin calculates the sun's distance from the earth as being 240 times the moon's distance. Though this is less than the actual value (400 times), it is still more accurate than Aristarchus's old value of 20 times. *See* 200s B.C. **ASTRO**

1650   Italian astronomer Giambattista Riccioli discovers the first known double star, Mizar. **ASTRO**

c. 1650   Anglican bishop James Ussher calculates from biblical genealogies that the creation of the world took place in 4004 B.C., a finding that will later be contradicted by geology. **EARTH**

1650   Between now and 1677, English anatomist and physiologist Francis Glisson is the first to prove that muscles contract when performing activity and to describe childhood rickets. He also lays the foundation for modern knowledge of the anatomy of the liver. **MED**

1650   French mathematician Pierre de Fermat articulates the principle of least time to describe the behavior of light, which he says travels from one point to another in such a way that the travel time is as short as possible. **PHYS**

1651   English physician William Harvey denounces what he sees as erroneous conceptions of animal generation, including the belief that embryos are miniature versions of adult organisms. Harvey claims instead that embryo growth involves the successive development of structures. He also rejects the currently popular idea that the primary generative agent of reproduction is the male, arguing rather that *"ex ovo omina"* (all creatures come from an egg). **BIO**

1651   The practice of whaling is popularized in Massachusetts by New Bedford developer Joseph Russell. **BIO**

1651   English physician Nathaniel Highmore discovers the maxillary sinus. **MED**

1651   English philosopher Thomas Hobbes publishes his *Leviathan*, which provides a rationalistic explanation for the existence of governments. In it he argues that humans voluntarily submit to absolute authority in order to protect themselves from each other's violent tendencies. Hobbes will be considered the father of political science. *See also* 1690, John Locke.   **SOC**

1654   French mathematicians Blaise Pascal and Pierre de Fermat found probability theory, developing methods for judging the likelihood of outcomes in games of dice.   **MATH**

1654   German physicist Otto von Guericke demonstrates the force of air pressure through experiments in which the muscle power of humans or animals competes with air pressure.   **PHYS**

1655   English mathematician John Wallis publishes his *Arithmetica infinitorum*, in which he applies algebra to the treatment of infinite processes. *See* 1635, Cavalieri.   **MATH**

1655   A book by Isaac de la Peyrère is publicly burned for hypothesizing that unusually chipped stones found in France were made by humans before the time of Adam.   **PALEO**

1656   Dutch scientist Christiaan Huygens discovers the rings of Saturn, explaining the oddness of the planet's shape identified by Galileo in 1610.   **ASTRO**

1656   German anatomist Werner Rolfink demonstrates that a cataract is a clouding of the eye lens, using executed criminals for his dissections.   **MED**

1656   English physician Sir Christopher Wren is the first to successfully inject drugs into veins.   **MED**

1656   Christiaan Huygens invents an accurate pendulum clock, ushering in a new era of precision in timekeeping. *See also* 1673, Huygens.   **TECH**

1657   English physicist Robert Hooke demonstrates that all bodies fall at equal rates in a vacuum.   **PHYS**

1658   Johann Rudolf Glauber publishes *Opera omnia chymica*, an important early work of chemistry.   **CHEM**

c. 1658   Further experimenting with pendulum clocks, Christian Huygens discovers that the cycloid curve is a tautochrone, a curve along which a mass point in a gravitational field reaches its lowest point in a time independent of the starting point. He also studies involutes and evolutes of cycloids and other curves.   **MATH**

1658   Dutch mathematician Jan de Witt devises kinematic and planimetric definitions of conic sections.   **MATH**

1658	Dutch naturalist Jan Swammerdam announces the discovery of the oxygen-carrying element of the blood, red blood corpuscles (red blood cells or erythrocytes). **MED**
1658	Moravian educator Jan Amos Komenský (Comenius) stresses the presentation of educational material in accordance with a child's developmental stages. He also introduces the planned school year and group instruction formats. **PSYCH**
1659	The modern sign for division (÷) is introduced by German mathematician Johann Heinrich Rahn. **MATH**
c. 1660	Dutch biologist Anton van Leeuwenhoek develops the single-lens microscope, able to magnify nearly two hundred times. Although not the first to invent microscopes, van Leeuwenhoek does more with microscopy than many other scientists. In 1677, for instance, he will discover the one-celled animals called protozoa as well as sperm cells. *See also* 1632, van Leeuwenhoek. **MED**
1660	Italian physician Marcello Malpighi discovers capillary circulation, an important missing link in William Harvey's 1628 discovery (q.v.) of blood circulation. **MED**
1660	Otto von Guericke designs a rotating sulfur globe that can be electrified by rubbing, demonstrating the large-scale existence of static electricity. **PHYS**
1661	Irish chemist Robert Boyle publishes *The Skeptical Chymist*, a work distinguishing scientific chemistry from medieval alchemy and defining elements as substances that cannot be converted into anything simpler. **CHEM**
1662	British mathematicians John Graunt and William Petty compile the first book on statistics, including the first mortality table (for London residents). **MATH**
1662	British king Charles II charters the scientific association known as the Royal Society. **MISC**
1662	Robert Boyle discovers Boyle's law, that the volume of a mass of gas at a constant temperature is inversely proportional to its pressure. This argument is also called Mariotte's law, after its independent discovery by French physicist Edme Mariotte in 1676. This principle supports the hypothesis that gases, and perhaps all other forms of matter, are made up of atoms that can be pressed closer together. **PHYS**
1663	Girolamo Cardano's *Book on Games of Chance* is the first known work on probability theory. **MATH**
1664	Italian astronomer Giovanni Alfonso Borelli discovers that a comet's orbit is a parabola. **ASTRO**
c. 1665	Isaac Newton discovers the general binomial theorem. **MATH**

1665   Italian-born French astronomer Giovanni Cassini determines the ro-
            tation rates of Mars and Jupiter.   **ASTRO**

1665   In his classic landmark book *Micrographia*, English biologist Robert
            Hooke publishes the first drawings of cells and is the first to use the
            word *cell* to describe the living fibers he sees under a compound
            microscope.   **BIO**

1665   Blaise Pascal's *Treatise on Figurative Numbers*, published posthu-
            mously this year, widely disseminates the process of mathematical
            induction.   **MATH**

1665–1666   English mathematician and scientist Isaac Newton has his two most
            fertile years of discovery. During this time he discovers the general
            method of the calculus, which he calls the "theory of fluxions," and
            achieves his most important insights into gravitation and the compo-
            sition of light. *See* 1666. Publication of his discoveries will await the
            Principia (1687) and later works of 1704 and 1736.   **MATH**

1665   Dutch anatomist Fredrick Ruyson is the first to demonstrate the ex-
            istence of valves in the lymphatics.   **MED**

1665   In a posthumous publication, Italian physicist Francesco Maria
            Grimaldi reveals his discovery of the diffraction of light, the bend-
            ing of light waves as they pass through an aperture or around a bar-
            rier. *See also* 1801, Young.   **PHYS**

1665   Parisian government official Pierre Petit invents the filar micrometer,
            a device for measuring very small distances, angles, or objects. **TECH**

1666   Italian-French astronomer Giovanni Cassini discovers the polar ice
            caps of Mars.   **ASTRO**

1666   English physician Thomas Sydenham uses Jesuits' bark, containing
            quinine, to treat malaria.   **MED**

1666   While working in his garden at Woolsthorpe, England, Isaac Newton
            observes an apple falling from a tree and begins the train of
            thought that will lead to his theory of universal gravitation, as ex-
            pounded two decades later in the *Principia* (1687).   **PHYS**

1666   Experimenting with a prism, Newton discovers that color is a prop-
            erty of light and that white light is composed of a spectrum of col-
            ors.   **PHYS**

1667   English naturalist John Ray classifies plants by the number of their
            seed leaves, establishing the categories of monocots and dicots. **BIO**

1667   Scottish mathematician James Gregory makes important advances
            in infinitesimal analysis, including the extension of the Archimedean
            algorithm to the quadrature of hyperbolas and ellipses.   **MATH**

Newton analyzing a ray of light. (*C. Horne,* Great Men and Famous Women, *Selmar Publishers, New York, 1894)*

1667   English physician and microscopist Robert Hooke demonstrates
             the function of the lungs by exhibiting the process of artificial
             respiration.   **MED**

June 15,   French physician Jean-Baptiste Denis carries out the first modern
1667   blood transfusion by infusing twelve ounces of lamb's blood into
             a fifteen-year-old boy. The boy's health improves after the
             procedure.   **MED**

1668   Isaac Newton invents the reflecting telescope.   **ASTRO**

1668   Italian naturalist and physician Francesco Redi experiments with
              meat, both uncovered and covered in jars, and disproves that mag-
              gots comes from decaying tissue. Although his results refute the
              theory of spontaneous generation, they go unacknowledged by his
              peers.   **BIO**

1668   James Gregory discovers what is later called Gregory's series, the
              series for arctan x.   **MATH**

1668   German mathematician Nicolaus Mercator publishes the logarith-
              mic approximation formula now known as Mercator's series.   **MATH**

1668   English mathematician John Wallis articulates the law of conserva-
              tion of momentum, stating that the total momentum (mass times
              velocity) of a closed system remains unchanged.   **PHYS**

1669   Italian anatomist Marcello Malpighi publishes his microscopic find-
              ings on the anatomy of a silkworm. He shows the insect to have no
              lungs, only a tracheal system distributing air through its body
              through holes in its sides.   **BIO**

1669   German chemist Hennig Brand discovers the element phosphorus. **CHEM**

1669   Isaac Newton writes *De analysi per aequationes numero terminorum
              infinitas*, first published in 1711. It contains his infinite analysis
              and the first systematic account of the calculus. Also for the first
              time, an area is found through the inverse of what is now called
              differentiation.   **MATH**

1669   English physician Thomas Sydenham advocates fresh air for
              sickrooms, activity for tuberculosis sufferers, and simplified pre-
              scriptions.   **MED**

1669   Danish geologist Nicolaus Steno proposes that fossils are the pet-
              rified remains of ancient creatures, a view that is eventually
              accepted.   **PALEO**

1669   While studying a crystal of Icelandic feldspar, Danish physician
              Erasmus Bartholin observes the phenomenon of double refraction,
              the apparent doubling of images when viewed through the crystal.
              See also 1808.   **PHYS**

1670s   Using a pendulum, French astronomer Jean Richer concludes that
              the diameter of the earth is greater around the equator than from
              pole to pole.   **EARTH**

1670   English mathematician Isaac Barrow develops a method of tangents
              quite similar to that used in the differential calculus.   **MATH**

1670   Clocks are built with minute hands for the first time.   **TECH**

1670   A decimal-based system for measurement is developed by French
              cleric Gabriel Mouton.   **TECH**

1671   The Paris Observatory, begun in 1667, is completed, under director Giovanni Cassini, an Italian-French astronomer.   **ASTRO**

1671   Cassini discovers Iapetus, a satellite of Saturn. He will later discover other satellites of Saturn: Rhea (1672) and Tethys and Dione (1684).   **ASTRO**

1671   Rice is cultivated in the colony of South Carolina.   **BIO**

c. 1671   Isaac Newton writes a second account of the calculus, titled *Method of Fluxions*. In it he also proposes eight new types of coordinate systems, including what are now called bipolar coordinates, and suggests what is known as Newton's method for approximate solutions of equations. This work will not be published until 1736.   **MATH**

1671   German mathematician Gottfried Wilhelm Leibniz invents a calculating machine that multiplies and divides.   **MATH**

1672   French scientist N. Cassegrain invents the Cassegrain type of reflecting telescope.   **ASTRO**

1673   Astronomer Giovanni Cassini of the Paris Observatory, assisted by Jean Richer, determines the distance of Mars from the earth and uses it to calculate the scale of the solar system. His figure of 86 million miles for the sun's distance from the earth is only 7 percent off.   **ASTRO**

1673   Italian Marcello Malpighi describes a chick embryo's development, contributing to the early science of embryology. *See also* 1621, Fabrici.   **BIO**

1673   In 1673–1676, working independently from Isaac Newton, German mathematician Gottfried Wilhelm Leibniz begins to develop the calculus.   **MATH**

1673   Dutch scientist Christiaan Huygens publishes *Horologium oscillatorium*, a work on pendulum clocks (*see* 1656) that contains several important laws of mechanics, including the law of centripetal force, Huygens's law for pendular motion, and the principle of conservation of kinetic energy.   **PHYS**

1674   British chemist John Mayow identifies the action of oxygen in burning, or oxidizing, metals and in respiration. Oxygen itself will not be isolated until Joseph Priestley's work in 1774.   **CHEM**

1674   Pierre Perrault, a lawyer and government official in Paris, solves the mystery of springs' origins by proving that rainfall is more than sufficient to supply the flow of springs and rivers. This analysis probably marks the beginning of the study of the hydrologic cycle.   **EARTH**

1674   The tourniquet is invented to arrest hemorrhage.   **MED**

1674   Between now and 1675, French philosopher and physicist Nicholas de Malebranche expresses the belief that the human soul has two kinds of faculties: the understanding and the will. The understanding is passive, including sensory impressions, imagination, and memory. The will consists of attitudes and inclinations.   **PSYCH**

1675   The Royal Observatory at Greenwich, England, is completed. Its director and first Astronomer Royal is John Flamsteed.   **ASTRO**

1675   Giovanni Cassini discovers the Cassini division, a gap in Saturn's rings.   **ASTRO**

1675   Danish astronomer Olaus Roemer makes the first reasonable estimate of the speed of light: 141,000 miles per second, about three-fourths of the actual value.   **PHYS**

1676   Isaac Newton writes a third account of the calculus, *De quadratura curvarum*, in which he introduces the concept of prime and ultimate ratios. This work will not be published for nearly thirty years. *See* 1704, Newton.   **MATH**

....

"If I have seen further, it is by standing on the shoulders of giants."—Sir Isaac Newton, English mathematician and physicist; 1676

....

1676   English physicist Robert Hooke articulates what has become known as Hooke's law, saying that within the limit of elasticity the stress applied to a material is proportional to the strain that results in its change in dimension or stretch.   **PHYS**

c. 1677   With the microscope he invented c. 1660, Dutch scientist Anton van Leeuwenhoek discovers microscopic organisms.   **BIO**

1677   Van Leeuwenhoek describes spermatozoa.   **BIO**

1678   After two years' work on the island of St. Helena in the South Atlantic, English astronomer Edmund Halley publishes the first catalog of the southern stars.   **ASTRO**

1678   Dutch astronomer Christiaan Huygens's *Treatise on Light* (published in 1690) maintains that light consists of waves, whereas Newton contends that light is made up of particles.   **PHYS**

1678   Brick, formerly used only for ovens and fireplaces, is used for an entire house in Boston.   **TECH**

1679   Italian naturalist Marcello Malpighi observes the detailed structure of plant cells and publishes his findings in *Anatomes plantarum*. At the same time, English naturalist Nehemiah Grew provides detailed, definitive descriptions of the sexual reproduction of plant cells in *The Anatomy of Plants* (1682). Their work sets a long-lasting standard for discussing cells as structural units and also shows the connection between microscopic exploration and cell study.   **BIO**

1679   Robert Hooke becomes the first to formulate the movement of planets as a mechanical problem, though his theory that gravitational attraction varies inversely with distance from the sun is later proven incorrect. *See* 1687, Newton.   **PHYS**

1679   French physicist Denis Papin invents the pressure cooker, the first practical application of steam power.   **TECH**

1680s   Swiss mathematicians Jakob (Jacques) and Johann (Jean) Bernoulli make a number of contributions to differential and integral calculus as well as to the integration of many ordinary differential equations. Jakob contributes the logarithmic spiral, the lemniscate, and the isochrone. He also contributes to the study of polar coordinates, the catenary, and isoperimetric figures. The two brothers and Gottfried Wilhelm Leibniz devise and solve the Bernoulli equation.   **MATH**

1680   The last dodo dies on the island of Mauritius in the Indian Ocean. This flightless bird was exterminated by Dutch settlers, who arrived in 1598.   **BIO**

1680   German biochemist Johann Joachim Becher proves that fermentation cannot happen without the presence of essential sugars.   **BIO**

1680   American entomologist John Banister classifies fifty-two American insect species.   **BIO**

1682   Edmund Halley observes the comet that will be named for him after his correct prediction, in 1705, that it will return in 1758.   **ASTRO**

1683   Dutch scientist Anton van Leeuwenhoek is the first to discover bacteria in the human mouth.   **BIO**

1684   In a posthumous publication, French astronomer Jean Picard (1620–1682) reports a fairly accurate figure for the circumference and diameter of the earth. These figures are the first real improvement on those proposed by Eratosthenes in 240 B.C.   **EARTH**

1684   German mathematician Gottfried Wilhelm Leibniz publishes his first paper on the calculus with a second following in 1686. He coins the terms *differential calculus* and (with Jacques Bernoulli) *integral calculus*.   **MATH**

| 1685 | English mathematician John Wallis devises methods for working with imaginary numbers. **MATH** |

1686　Edmund Halley produces the first meteorological world map showing the prevailing tropical winds, which are monsoons and trade winds. **EARTH**

1686　Sir Thomas Sydenham is first to describe chorea (dancing mania), a severe nerve disorder caused by the streptococcus responsible for rheumatic fever. **MED**

1687　Isaac Newton theorizes that the earth is an oblate spheroid slightly flattened at the poles and bulging at the equator. **EARTH**

Sept. 1687　Newton publishes his greatest work, *Philosophiae naturalis principia mathematica* (*Mathematical Principles of Natural Philosophy*), known as the *Principia*. This work outlines the law of universal gravitation and the three laws of motion. It also includes the first published documentation of Newton's discovery of the calculus (*see* 1665–1666) and several new theorems on conics. **PHYS**

1688　In France, large sheets of glass are being made for mirrors and windows, an innovation that will lead to the commonplace use of panes of glass. **TECH**

c. 1690s　Swiss mathematician Johann Bernoulli, often considered the inventor of the exponential calculus, studies exponential curves. **MATH**

1690　The oldest mathematical society still in existence, the Mathematische Gesellschaft, is founded in Germany. **MATH**

1690　In his *Essay Concerning Human Understanding*, English philosopher John Locke (*see* 1632) opposes the belief in innate ideas, arguing that the mind at birth is a blank slate that acquires all its knowledge from experience. Locke's ideas will influence philosophers David Hume (*see* 1739) and George Berkeley (*see* 1709) and will form the underlying basis for the twentieth-century American psychological school of behaviorism. **PSYCH**

1690　John Locke publishes *Two Treatises on Civil Government*, in which he offers an alternative to Thomas Hobbes's view of the origin of governments (*see* 1651). In it Locke argues that human nature is good, that people are born equal, free, and with certain inalienable rights, and that people form a "social contract" to guarantee those rights. Locke's views will influence centuries of political theory and practice, notably in the U.S. Declaration of Independence and Constitution. **SOC**

1691　English naturalist John Ray publishes a major classification of organic life, *The Wisdom of God Manifested in the Works of Creation*, bringing together information on the vast number of new plants and animals discovered around the world over the last few centuries. **BIO**

THE PRINCIPIA

A scientific work that contributes a small advance in knowledge may be considered worthwhile; a work that contributes a momentous advance may be considered great; but a work that contributes several momentous advances is in another league altogether. Such a work is Isaac Newton's Principia. Published in Latin late in 1687, it laid the basis for the science of mechanics (the study of the interaction between matter and forces) for over two centuries by defining the unifying principles known as the laws of motion and the law of gravitation.

The three laws of motion govern the way bodies move in almost all situations, from the fall of a leaf to the collision of automobiles, from the spinning of dancers to the orbits of planets. Although Albert Einstein showed in 1905 that Newton's laws of motion do not apply when objects move at relative speeds close to that of light, Newtonian mechanics still holds in most human-scale circumstances.

The three laws of motion are:

1. A body at rest remains at rest, and a moving body continues to move in a straight line at the same velocity unless acted upon by external forces.
2. When a force acts upon a moving body, the rate at which its momentum (mass times velocity) changes is proportional to, and in the same direction as, the force applied.
3. When a force acts upon a body, the body exerts an equal force, or reaction, in the opposite direction.

The Principia also presented Newton's law of gravitation, which states that the gravitational force between two bodies is proportional to their mass and inversely proportional to the square of the distance between them. Einstein's general theory of relativity (1916) brought new understanding to the study of gravitation, but Newton's law still holds well enough to serve as the basis for such tasks as analyzing orbits and planning space missions. In mathematical terms, Newton's law of gravitation states:

$$F = G \frac{m_1 m_2}{d^2}$$

Where F is the force of gravitation between two bodies, G the gravitational constant (a quantity equal to about 6.7×10^{-11} m^3 kg^{-1} s^{-2}), $m_1 m_2$ the masses of the two bodies, and d^2 the square of the distance between them.

1691   Like Nicolaus Steno in Denmark (*see* 1669), English naturalist John Ray argues that fossils are the remains of ancient creatures. **PALEO**

1693   John Ray continues to classify animals, sorting them on the basis of hoofs, toes, and teeth. **BIO**

1693   In unpublished letters, German mathematician Gottfried Wilhelm Leibniz makes the first Western reference to the method of determinants. **MATH**

1693   Edmund Halley prepares the first mortality tables, statistically relating human death rates to age. **MISC**

1694   Botany professor Joseph Pitton de Tournefort, considered at this time to be the leader of French botanical thought, publishes *Elemens de botanique*. It inventories and describes more than eight thousand plants and devises an artificial classification system that will be accepted until the work of Carolus Linnaeus in 1735. In 1719, this work is republished in English as *The Complete Herbal*. **BIO**

1695   English chemist Nehemiah Grew isolates magnesium sulfate, popularly known as epsom salts. **CHEM**

1696   Swiss mathematician Johann (Jean) Bernoulli discovers L'Hôpital's rule on indeterminate forms, named for French mathematician Guillaume François Antoine de L'Hôpital, who publishes it this year in the first printed textbook on the differential calculus, *Analyse des infiniment petits*. **MATH**

c. 1697   Swiss mathematicians Jakob (Jacques) and Johann (Jean) Bernoulli solve the problem of the brachistochrone, the curve of quickest descent for a mass point moving between two points in a gravitational field, proving that this curve is a cycloid. As a result, they are often considered the inventors of the calculus of variations. **MATH**

1698   Edmund Halley undertakes the first ocean voyage for a purely scientific purpose, to measure and map magnetic declinations all over the world, such as the distance between the direction of the compass needle and true north. **EARTH**

1698   English engineer Thomas Savery invents a steam-driven pump, the "miner's friend," for use in coal mining. **TECH**

1698   The London Stock Exchange opens. The New York Stock Exchange will follow in 1792. **TECH**

1698   Champagne is invented by French cellarer Dom Pierre Pérignon in the abbey of d'Hautvilliers. **TECH**

1699   French physicist Guillaume Amontons invents an air thermometer that measures temperature by the change in gas pressure. Using this device he shows that the volume of a fixed quantity of a gas increases as the temperature rises and decreases as the temperature falls, and that the rate of change in volume is the same for all gases. His breakthrough is forgotten, however, until rediscovered by Jacques-Alexandre-César Charles in 1787. *See also* 1802, Gay-Lussac.   **PHYS**

....

"I do not know what I may appear to the world, but to myself I seem to have been only like a boy playing on the sea-shore, and diverting myself in now and then finding a smoother pebble or a prettier shell than ordinary, whilst the great ocean of truth lay all undiscovered before me."—Sir Isaac Newton, English mathematician and physicist; c. 1700

....

1700s   Swiss naturalist and entomologist Charles Bonnet is the first to use the term *evolution* to describe the concept that periodic catastrophes result in increasingly higher life forms.   **BIO**

1700s   Eastern Native American tribes are observed to keep wounds clean. In clashes with European colonists this "primitive" treatment is often found to be effective. Native Americans also isolate the wounded for treatment, while white soldiers are kept together in infirmaries, where they often die of hospital-acquired infections.   **MED**

1700s   "Idiot cages" are used to confine and display mentally ill people, usually as a source of public entertainment.   **PSYCH**

Cages used to house the mentally ill in the eighteenth century. (*Germanisches National Museum, Nürnberg*)

1700s   In England the straitjacket is invented to restrain agitated asylum patients.   **PSYCH**

1700   Ole Rømer of Denmark invents the meridian telescope.   **ASTRO**

c. 1700   German chemist George Ernst Stahl proposes that objects burn or rust because they lose a combustible substance called phlogiston, a theory disproved by Antoine-Laurent Lavoisier in 1772.   **CHEM**

1700   Gottfried Wilhelm Leibniz explains that any base such as 10, 12, or 2 can be used for positional notation and that a system with a base of 2, the binary system, is particularly useful. This system, consisting of the symbols 1 and 0, will one day become the basis for digital computers.   **MATH**

c. 1700   Native American women have long been using quinine, sassafras, datura, ipecac, cascara, and witch hazel to treat minor illnesses and injuries. All of these substances will become part of modern pharmacopeia.   **MED**

1700   Italian physician Bernardino Ramazzini publishes a work describing forty occupational diseases. He is the first to write on the subject.   **MED**

1700   French physicist Joseph Sauveur coins the term *acoustics* for describing the relations of musical tones.   **PHYS**

1701   English farmer Jethro Tull invents a multirow machine drill for planting three lines of seeds simultaneously, which decreases waste and increases productivity.   **TECH**

1702   Dutch chemist William Homberg discovers boric acid.   **CHEM**

1702   David Gregory, Savilian Professor of Astronomy at Oxford, publishes *Astronomiae physicae & geometricae elementa*, the first textbook of astronomy based on Newtonian principles.   **EARTH**

1702   The *Daily Courant*, the first daily newspaper, begins publication in London. Three years later the first regular newspaper in the American colonies, the weekly *News-Letter*, is published in Boston.   **TECH**

1703   Isaac Newton, a member of the Royal Society since 1672, is elected president of that body, a post in which he will serve until his death in 1727.   **MISC**

1704   Newton publishes *De quadratura curvarum*, written in 1676. This is the first clear published account of Newton's version of the calculus, though hints of it had appeared in the *Principia* (1687).   **MATH**

1704   Newton publishes *Enumeration of Curves of [the] Third Degree*, the first work devoted solely to graphs of higher plane curves in algebra, written about 1676.   **MATH**

1704   In his *Optics* Newton theorizes that light is made up of particles called corpuscles, a view that conflicts with Christiaan Huygens's wave theory of light (*see* 1678). Newton also argues that white light is made up of the colors of the spectrum.   **PHYS**

1704   German mathematician Gottfried Wilhelm Leibniz finishes his *New Essays on Understanding*, in which he disputes John Locke's theory that empirical knowledge is humans' only source of truth. Leibniz says the human mind has innate intelligence, inborn ideas, truths, dispositions, habits, and potentials. This book, with its nativist views, goes unpublished until 1765.   **PSYCH**

1705   Edmund Halley theorizes that the comet of 1682 is a regular visitor, observed since antiquity (*see* 240 B.C., China), and correctly predicts it will return seventy-six years later, in December 1758.   **ASTRO**

1705   The Royal Observatory of Berlin is established.   **ASTRO**

1705   Queen Anne knights English scientist Isaac Newton.   **MISC**

1705   Experimenting with a clock inside a vacuum, English physicist Francis Hauksbee shows that sound can travel only in a fluid medium such as air.   **PHYS**

1706   The Greek letter *pi* is first used as the symbol for the ratio of a circle's circumference to its diameter.   **MATH**

1706   Francis Hauksbee invents a crank-operated glass sphere that can produce an intense charge of static electricity.   **PHYS**

1707   Swiss mathematician Leonhard Euler, one of the most productive mathematicians in history, is born (*d.* 1783). He will publish 560 books and papers during his lifetime and hundreds more will be published afterward. He will contribute to every mathematical field of his day as well as to such related areas as astronomy, hydraulics, artillery, shipbuilding, and optics. His systems of notation will remain standard to the present day.   **MATH**

1708   The United East India Company is formed in England from smaller trading companies, making it the premier shipping firm for importing fabrics, foods, and military materials like saltpeter.   **TECH**

1709   English empirical philosopher George Berkeley publishes his *Essay towards a New Theory of Vision*, in which he agrees with John Locke that all knowledge comes from experience and depends on human perception.   **PSYCH**

1709   English ironworks master Abraham Darby shows that coke, a derivative of coal, can be used instead of wood-based charcoal to smelt iron. This discovery greatly increases the market for coal and improves iron production. With the invention of the Newcomen engine (*see* 1712), this breakthrough marks one of the starting points of the industrial revolution in England.   **TECH**

c. 1710   The Pennsylvania rifle, invented in England's American colonies, is a substantial improvement on the preferred firearm of the day, the smooth-bore musket.   **TECH**

1712   English blacksmith Thomas Newcomen invents the steam engine that bears his name, which uses steam to drive a piston to generate power. This device is more efficient than Thomas Savery's steam-driven "miner's friend," of 1698.   **TECH**

1713   *Ars conjectandi* (*The Art of Conjecturing*), by Swiss mathematician Jakob Bernoulli, published this year posthumously, becomes the first substantial book on the theory of probability. It contains the first full proof of the binomial theorem for positive integral powers as well as the Bernoulli numbers, which will be useful in writing infinite series expansions.   **MATH**

1713   The first schooner is built, by Scottish-American captain Andrew Robinson in Massachusetts. Schooners will become important to the growing American fishing industry.   **TECH**

1714   German physicist Daniel Gabriel Fahrenheit invents the mercury thermometer and the Fahrenheit scale.   **TECH**

Apr. 22,   A total solar eclipse, visible in Britain and parts of Europe, is the
1715   first such eclipse to be so widely anticipated as to draw large numbers of astronomers as observers. Edmund Halley prepares maps charting the predicted path of totality.   **ASTRO**

1715   English mathematician Brook Taylor publishes the Taylor series, along with other components of the calculus, in his *Methodus incrementorum*.   **MATH**

1716   Boston preacher Cotton Mather writes that his Negro slaves practiced smallpox inoculation in Africa by applying serum from the pustule of an infected person into an incision made on a healthy individual. Greek physician Emmanuel Timoni draws attention to primitive smallpox vaccination techniques in such places as China and central Europe, where smallpox scabs are used to infect healthy people and produce immunity.   **MED**

1718   Edmund Halley discovers the "proper motion" (independent movement) of stars, contradicting the ancient theory that the stars are fixed.   **ASTRO**

1718   Potatoes, originally an Andean crop, are introduced to Boston, their first appearance in England's American colonies.   **BIO**

1718   French-born English mathematician Abraham de Moivre publishes his *Doctrine of Chances*, an important work on probability.   **MATH**

1723   M. A. Capeller publishes *Prodomus crystallographiae*, the earliest known treatise on crystallography.   **PHYS**

1724   The possibility of cross-fertilizing corn is established.   **BIO**

1724   German physicist Daniel Gabriel Fahrenheit describes the super-
            cooling of water.   **PHYS**

1725   John Flamsteed's three-volume *Historia coelestis Britannica*, pub-
            lished posthumously, catalogs some three thousand stars.   **ASTRO**

1725   Plaster of Paris is used to cast metal printing plates, reducing cost
            and improving the efficiency of printing by letterpress.   **TECH**

....

"Nature, and Nature's laws lay hid in night;
God said, Let Newton be! and all was light."
—Alexander Pope, English poet;
eighteenth century

"It did not last: the Devil howling 'Ho!
Let Einstein be!' restored the status quo."
—J. C. (Sir John) Squire; in a twentieth-
century answer to Pope

....

1727   In *Vegetable Staticks* English botanist Stephen Hales reports on his
            work with plant fluid flows and plant respiration. This book also de-
            scribes experiments determining the generation or depletion of air
            by various substances. These discoveries later reinforce the claim
            of Hales to be one of the founders of modern plant physiology. **BIO**

c. 1727   Swiss mathematician Leonhard Euler introduces the letter *e* to rep-
            resent the base of the system of natural logarithms. This notation
            will become standard.   **MATH**

Mar. 20,   Sir Isaac Newton, the first scientist to be buried in Westminster
1727   Abbey, dies in London.   **MISC**

1727   A basic property of photography is discovered by German chemist
            J. H. Schulze, who determines that light, not heat, activates the
            chemicals involved in the process of deriving silver salts from silver
            nitrate.   **TECH**

1728   English astronomer James Bradley discovers the aberration of
            starlight, the apparent displacement of a star's position due to the
            orbital motion of the earth. This finding gives the most definite
            proof to date that the earth moves in space.   **ASTRO**

1728   Danish navigator Vitus J. Bering, working for Czar Peter the Great,
            discovers the passage now called the Bering Strait, proving that
            North America is not connected by land to Asia.   **EARTH**

1728   British-educated physician John Hunter (*d.* 1793), considered the founder of experimental and surgical pathology, is born in Scotland. He will introduce a flexible tube passed into the stomach for artificial feeding, be first to study teeth scientifically, and argue that aneurysms from arterial disease should be tied off. Hunter will also posit that blood is alive and that the human embryo is, in each stage, a completed form of a lower order of the species.   **MED**

1729   French scientist Louis Bourget distinguishes between organic and inorganic growth.   **BIO**

1729   English scientist Stephen Gray theorizes that electricity is a fluid and discovers that some substances are electrical conductors but others are nonconductors, or insulators.   **PHYS**

1729   Dutch physicist Pieter van Musschenbroek is one of the first people in modern times to use the word "physics," a term dating back to Aristotle, to mean natural philosophy.   **PHYS**

c. 1730   English naturalist Henry Baker begins his essays on the microscope, introducing it to the lay public. One of his most significant finds will be his observation of various crystal shapes.   **BIO**

1730   In England, Lord Charles Townshend determines that livestock can be maintained throughout the year, most importantly in the winter, on turnips rather than on seasonally grown feed. This discovery allows beef to be available year-round.   **TECH**

1731   American mathematician Thomas Godfrey and English inventor John Hadley independently invent the reflecting quadrant, the precursor of the modern sextant.   **ASTRO**

1731   In a posthumous work, Swiss mathematician Jakob Bernoulli introduces Bernoulli numbers.   **MATH**

1731   French mathematician Alexis-Claude Clairaut identifies the Clairaut differential equation.   **MATH**

1731   British chemist and physicist Henry Cavendish, discoverer of hydrogen, is born (*d.* 1810). His studies on electricity, unpublished until 1879, anticipate the work of such later scientists as Charles de Coulomb, Michael Faraday, and Georg Ohm. He will also perform the first calculations of the gravitational constant and of the earth's mass and density.   **PHYS**

1731   American inventor and statesman Benjamin Franklin improves and enlarges the postal service by streamlining routes throughout the colonies.   **TECH**

1732–1734   German philosopher Baron Christian von Wolff develops the field of rational psychology, a subdivision of empirical psychology that depends more on reason than experience.   **PSYCH**

1733   Swiss mathematician Leonhard Euler publishes a seminal work of modern mathematical analysis.   **MATH**

1733   French physicist Charles-François de Cisternay du Fay distinguishes "vitreous" from "resinous" electricity, noting that each attracts the other but repels itself. This finding links electricity to magnetism, which exhibits similar patterns of attraction and repulsion.   **PHYS**

1733   English weaver John Kay invents the flying shuttle, which vastly improves on the hand loom and simplifies the industrialization of textile production.   **TECH**

1734   French entomologist René de Réaumur begins publishing the first of a six-volume work on insect history that was completed in 1742.   **BIO**

1734   English bishop George Berkeley publishes *The Analyst*, an attack on the intellectual basis of the calculus, the theory of fluxions. It spurs Scottish mathematician Colin Maclaurin to respond with a defense entitled *Treatise of Fluxions* (1742).   **MATH**

1735   Swedish naturalist Carolus Linnaeus presents his first system of plant classification, *Systema naturae*, sorting flora according to the number of their stamens and pistils. This will lead to further botanical classification, including Linnaeus's use of binomial nomenclature to record plant genera and species. Linnaeus's method of classification will persist to the present day.   **BIO**

1735   Swedish chemist Georg Brandt discovers the element cobalt.   **CHEM**

1735   Spanish scientist Antonio de Ulloa discovers the element platinum.   **CHEM**

1735   Geographic expeditions to equatorial and polar regions confirm Isaac Newton's 1687 theory that the earth is an oblate spheroid.   **EARTH**

1736   French chemist Henri-Louis Duhamel du Monceau is the first to distinguish potassium salts from sodium salts.   **CHEM**

1736   French surgeon Jean-Louis Petit distinguishes between cerebral compression and concussion, paving the way for different—and more successful—treatments of injury.   **MED**

1736   New York City's Bellevue Hospital has its beginnings as a room in the public workhouse for those who are physically sick or mentally ill. It will open officially as a hospital in 1812.   **MED**

1736   Swiss mathematician Leonhard Euler writes *Mechanics*, the first book to be devoted to that subject. With analytical methods it develops Newton's dynamics of the mass point.   **PHYS**

1736   The chronometer is introduced by British inventor John Harrison. Used in conjunction with a quadrant, it can aid a navigator in pinpointing his longitudinal position.   **TECH**

Eskimo parka made of birdskins from St. Lawrence Island area explored by Vitus Bering. (*National Museum of Natural History*)

1737   *Biblia naturae*, by Dutch naturalist Jan Swammerdam, is published posthumously. It introduces discoveries and conclusions drawn from Swammerdam's microscopic experiments with dissected insects.   **BIO**

1738   Planned excavation begins at Pompeii and Herculaneum in Italy. (*see* 79 and 1592).   **ARCH**

1738   Dutch diplomat Benoit de Maillet suggests an "ultra-Neptunian" theory, that the earth's surface was shaped by the action of a universal ocean.   **EARTH**

1738   Swiss physicist Daniel Bernoulli publishes what will be called the Bernoulli theorem, stating that at any point in a pipe of flowing fluid the sum of the pressure energy, kinetic energy, and potential energy is constant. Following Boyle (*see* 1662), Bernoulli makes his explanation in terms of the movement of atoms comprising the fluid. **PHYS**

1739   Swiss naturalist Abraham Trembley discovers the hydra, giving rise to speculation by some scientists that the freshwater polyp may represent a link between the animal and vegetable kingdoms.   **BIO**

1739   French explorers Pierre and Paul Mallet become the first Europeans to see the Rocky Mountains.   **EARTH**

1739   Physicist George Martine shows that the amount of heat in an object is not proportional to its volume.   **PHYS**

1739   Scottish philosopher and diplomat David Hume publishes *A Treatise on Human Nature*, claiming that complex ideas are formed from simple ones based on three laws of association: resemblance, continuity, and cause-and-effect relationships.   **PSYCH**

1739   Glass is manufactured in what will become the state of New Jersey in a factory set up by German-American businessman Caspar Wistar.   **TECH**

1740   Swiss entomologist Charles Bonnet discovers that female aphids can reproduce without fertilization.   **BIO**

1740   Antonio Moro publishes a significant study of marine fossils.   **PALEO**

1740   Sheffield steel, a superstrong cast steel produced in airless crucibles, is introduced by Englishman Benjamin Huntsman.   **TECH**

....

"Could not one say that since, in the accidental combination of Nature's productions, only those could survive which found themselves provided with certain appropriate relationships, it is no wonder that these relationships are present in all the species that actually exist? These species which we see today are only the smallest part of those which a blind destiny produced."—P.-L. M. de Maupertuis, French scientist, suggesting in Essai de cosmologi (1741) certain natural processes that were to be more fully expounded by Charles Darwin in The Origin of Species (1859)

....

1741   Indigo is harvested in South Carolina, beginning a dyestuffs industry in that region.   **BIO**

1741   Vitus J. Bering is the first European to reach Alaska, on his second voyage. Russia claims and explores the Aleutian Islands and Alaska until selling them to the United States in 1867.   **EARTH**

1741   Irish physician Fielding Ould draws attention to the benefits of cutting the female perineum during delivery to prevent the baby's head and shoulders from tearing the woman's pelvic floor. This procedure will become known as episiotomy.   **MED**

1742   Using the hydra, Swiss naturalist Abraham Trembley makes the first permanent tissue graft.   **BIO**

1742   German-Russian mathematician Christian Goldbach frames "Goldbach's conjecture"—that any even number greater than 2 can be expressed as the sum of two prime numbers. The conjecture has never been either proven or disproven.   **MATH**

1742   Swedish astronomer Anders Celsius invents the Centigrade or Celsius scale of temperature, which will eventually supersede the Fahrenheit scale (*see* 1714) except in the United States.   **TECH**

1742   Coal is mined in Virginia for the first time in the region.   **TECH**

1742   Benjamin Franklin invents the Franklin stove, which heats a room by circulating preheated air. Also known as a Pennsylvania fireplace, this lean-to-shaped stove contains an air box and is positioned inside a fireplace.   **TECH**

1743   French mathematician Alexis Claude Clairaut explains how to compute gravitational force at a given latitude.   **ASTRO**

1743   French physicist Jean Le Rond d'Alembert formulates d'Alembert's principle: In a closed system of moving bodies, actions and reactions are in equilibrium.   **PHYS**

1744   Swiss mathematician Leonhard Euler discovers transcendental numbers, numbers that can never be a solution to a polynomial algebraic equation (as distinguished from algebraic numbers).   **MATH**

1744   Leonhard Euler publishes the first exposition of the calculus of variations, including Euler's equations.   **MATH**

1744   Russian physicist Mikhail V. Lomonosov proposes correctly that heat is a form of motion.   **PHYS**

1744   French physicist Pierre-Louis de Maupertuis formulates the principle of least action: Nature operates in such a way that action—the product of force, distance, and time—is at a minimum.   **PHYS**

1745   Dutch physicist Pieter van Musschenbroek of the University of Leyden and German physicist Ewald Georg von Kleist independently invent the Leyden jar, the first practical device for storing static electricity.   **PHYS**

1746   Swiss mathematician Leonhard Euler uses the wave theory of light to develop a mathematics of the refraction of light.   **PHYS**

1746   American philosopher and theologian Jonathan Edwards writes on psychological questions in relation to religion. His *Treatise Concerning Religious Affections* will be considered one of the first books of psychology written by an American. Edwards believes that there is no free will; that all human choices are made by God.   **PSYCH**

1747   French mathematician Alexis-Claude Clairaut publishes the first approximate resolution of the three-body problem, examining how three celestial bodies interact.   **ASTRO**

1747   Scottish physician James Lind shows, in the first controlled dietary
              study, that citrus fruits cure scurvy.   **MED**

1747   American scientist and inventor Benjamin Franklin argues against
              du Fay's theory of 1733 that there are two electrical fluids, suggest-
              ing instead that there is only one, of which an excess could be
              called positive, a deficiency negative.   **PHYS**

1747   Theorizing about vibrating strings, French physicist Jean Le Rond
              d'Alembert publishes the general solution of the partial differential-
              wave equation in two dimensions.   **PHYS**

....

***"We are under obligation to the ancients for having
exhausted all the false theories that could be formed."
—Bernard Le Bovier, Sieur de Fontenelle,
French philosopher; eighteenth century***

....

1748   James Bradley discovers the nutation (wobbling) of the earth's axis,
              an irregular periodic oscillation of the earth's poles caused by per-
              turbation from the sun and moon.   **ASTRO**

1748   Swiss mathematician Leonhard Euler publishes *Introductio in
              analysin infinitorum*, which establishes the strictly analytic treat-
              ment of trigonometric functions. This book contains the Euler iden-
              tities, an algebraic theory of elimination, an exposition on infinite
              series, and a chapter on the Zeta function.   **MATH**

1748   Welsh Catholic priest Father John T. Needham claims to have
              proven spontaneous generation by cooking meat, cooling it, then
              reheating it. He claims to have identifed *animalcules* in the broth,
              which appear spontaneously. The erroneous belief that living or-
              ganisms can be generated directly from lifeless matter will persist
              for another century.   **MED**

1748   French physicist Jean-Antoine Nollet discovers osmosis, the pas-
              sage of a solvent such as water through a semipermeable mem-
              brane separating two solutions that have different concentrations.
              He also identifies osmotic pressure, the pressure required to stop
              the flow from a pure solvent into a solution. In osmosis the solvent
              tends to flow from the weaker to the stronger solution until the two
              are equal in concentration or osmotic pressure is applied. *See also*
              1877, Wilhelm Pfeffer.   **PHYS**

1748   French philosopher Julien Offroy de La Mettrie pioneers French ma-
              terialism. In his book *L'Homme-machine* (*Man as Machine*), he argues
              that the body and soul are mortal and that life and thought are noth-
              ing more than the nervous system's mechanical action.   **PSYCH**

1749   In the first volume of his book *Natural History*, French naturalist George-Louis de Buffon disagrees with earlier classifications by Andrea Cesalpino and Carolus Linnaeus, claiming that nature's life chain has small gradations from one type to another and that the discontinuous categories are artificially constructed. He also suggests that organic species are descended from a few primordial types in a process of evolution through degeneration from perfect to less perfect forms.   **BIO**

1749   Swedish naturalist Carolus Linnaeus describes how nature limits competition between species by allotting each its own geographical location and placement in the food chain. He claims that reproductive rates and predators maintain a species' proper numerical proportions.   **BIO**

1749   In his *Natural History*, French naturalist Georges-Louis Leclerc de Buffon speculates that the earth formed seventy-five thousand years ago through collision of the sun with a comet. Though incorrect, these speculations open the door to further study of the age of the earth.   **EARTH**

1749   French scientist Pierre Bouguer notes the "Bouguer correction," observing that the lessening of the pull of gravity with altitude is partially compensated for by the gravitational attraction of the intervening rock.   **EARTH**

1749   Scottish astronomer Alexander Wilson is the first to use kites for exploring the properties of the atmosphere, attaching thermometers to them to try to measure temperatures at a height.   **EARTH**

1749   British physician and biologist David Hartley describes positive afterimages for both auditory and visual stimuli, such as the glow from a flame after it goes out and the sound of a bell after it has stopped ringing. This theory of vibrations and his hypothesis that the mind and body always work together make Hartley the originator of physiological psychology.   **PSYCH**

1750   Swiss mathematician Gabriel Cramer publishes Cramer's rule (actually discovered by Scottish mathematician Colin Maclaurin as early as 1729) for solving simultaneous equations by determinants.   **MATH**

1751   Swedish mineralogist Baron Axel F. Cronstedt discovers the element nickel.   **CHEM**

1751   Paris physician Jean-Étienne Guettard discovers a region of extinct volcanoes in Auvergne, France.   **EARTH**

1751   The first public hospital in Britain's American colonies is organized in Philadelphia.   **MED**

1751–1752	French scientist Denis Diderot and physicist Jean Le Rond d'Alembert publish the first volume of the *Encyclopédie*. The first modern encyclopedia, it takes a rational approach to "the sciences, the arts, and customs." **MISC**

1751   Flying a kite attached to a metal key in a thunderstorm, Benjamin Franklin proves that lightning is electricity. **PHYS**

1752   French physician Jacques Daviel originates modern lens extraction as a cure for cataracts. **MED**

1752   French physicist Jean Le Rond d'Alembert formulates certain principles of hydrodynamics. **PHYS**

1752   Building on his studies of lightning and electricity, Benjamin Franklin invents the lightning rod. **TECH**

1752   Publicly funded globe streetlights are installed in Philadelphia, the first such lighting system in Britain's American colonies. **TECH**

1753   Chemist C. G. Junine demonstrates that the element bismuth is different from lead. **CHEM**

1753   The Conestoga wagon, a transport vehicle for persons and cargo, is popularized by the Pennsylvania Dutch. It is named for the town where it was developed. **TECH**

1754   French scientist Denis Diderot revives the theory of Empedocles of Acragas that, in the past, various animal organs thrived independently and random combinations of these organs were eventually joined to create modern animals. **BIO**

1754   Swiss naturalist Charles Bonnet details the nutritional value of plants. **BIO**

1754   Scottish chemist Joseph Black heats limestone (calcium carbonate), producing carbon dioxide and lime (calcium oxide). On finding that the process can be reversed by combining calcium oxide with carbon dioxide or simply leaving calcium oxide in the open air, he discovers that carbon dioxide must be a component of air. This experiment is important as the first to apply quantitative analysis to chemical reactions. **CHEM**

1754   Scottish physician William Smellie pioneers midwifery by men. **MED**

1754   Swiss-French philosopher Jean-Jacques Rousseau publishes his *Discourse on the Inequalities of Men*. In this and *The Social Contract* (1762), Rousseau expounds his influential views about the "noble" natural condition of humans, the corrupting influence of civilization, and the formation of the social contract to correct inequalities. **SOC**

1755   German philosopher Immanuel Kant speculates about the existence of distant collections of stars or "island universes." **ASTRO**

PIECES OF AIR

*S*ince the time of the ancient Greeks, air was considered to be a discrete element, impossible to break down further. Not until the eighteenth century did it become clear that air was made up of several different gases. In experiments beginning in 1754, Scottish chemist Joseph Black discovered that a lump of lime (calcium oxide) would gradually turn to limestone (calcium carbonate) if left in the open air. He had already established that this reaction required the addition of the gas we call carbon dioxide. Clearly, carbon dioxide was part of air, but experimentation showed that it could not support combustion or animal life. What was it living things breathed?

Black asked his student Daniel Rutherford to look into this question. In 1772, Rutherford burned a candle in a closed container until the flame went out. When Rutherford used chemicals to draw out the carbon dioxide in the container, he found that a large quantity of another gas was left over. It, too, failed to support life or combustion. Eventually this gas became known as nitrogen, because it was also found in niter (potassium nitrate).

The breathable component of air was discovered by English chemist Joseph Priestley in 1774. He found that mercury, heated in air, produced a red powder called mercuric oxide. When it was heated in a sealed container, it broke down into mercury and some sort of gas. Priestley found that this gas not only supported the processes of respiration and combustion but enhanced them.

It was French chemist Antoine-Laurent Lavoisier who determined the relative proportions of the known atmospheric gases. In experiments in the 1770s he found that after mercury was heated to produce mercuric oxide, about four-fifths of the air in the closed container still remained. He concluded that this gas, which did not support life, was Rutherford's gas nitrogen. Priestley's gas, which Lavoisier called oxygen (Greek for "acid producer"), represented the other fifth of the air. Black's gas, "fixed air" or carbon dioxide, was present in only marginal quantities.

Lavoisier's figures were roughly correct, though other components of air have since been found and more exact estimates made. It is now known that nitrogen and oxygen make up about 99 percent (nitrogen 78.08 percent, oxygen 20.95 percent) of the gases in earth's atmosphere. The rest is mostly argon (0.93 percent) and carbon dioxide (0.03 percent). Neon, helium, methane, krypton, hydrogen, xenon, and ozone are also present in minute traces.

Nov. 1, 1755	A disastrous earthquake befalls Lisbon, sparking increased interest in geological phenomena. **EARTH**
1755	Swiss mathematician Leonhard Euler publishes *Institutiones calculi differentialis*, an influential textbook on differential calculus, followed in 1768–1774 by *Institutiones calculi integralis*. **MATH**
1756	English physicist John Canton observes magnetic storms in the earth's magnetic field. **EARTH**
1756	In Berlin, physician and metallurgist Johann Gottlob Lehman publishes *Versuch einer Geschichte von Flotzgeburgen*, an important geologic account. He recognizes stratified rocks (*Flotzeburge*) as being of sedimentary origin, distinct from igneous (veined) rock. **EARTH**
1757	The modern sextant, used to chart navigation, is developed by British seaman John Campbell. **TECH**
Dec. 25, 1758	As predicted by Edmund Halley in 1705, the comet of 1682 returns, the first such return ever predicted. The object is named Halley's Comet in his honor. **ASTRO**
1758	French botanist Henri du Monceau describes tree structure and physiology. **BIO**
1758	German chemist Andreas Sigismund Marggraf invents a technique called the flame test for identifying different substances by noting the colors of their flames when heated. **CHEM**
1758	Swedish chemist Axel F. Cronstedt begins to classify minerals by their chemical structure as well as appearance when he distinguishes four classes of minerals: bitumens, earths, metals, and salts. **CHEM**
1760s	French mathematician Jean Le Rond d'Alembert formulates the limit concept in calculus. **MATH**
1760s	English researcher Arthur Young uses questionnaires to survey the population. Questionnaires and case studies, which are also developed in this century, will become basic tools of social science research. **SOC**
1760	In London, the Kew Botanical Gardens opens. **BIO**
1760	Scottish chemist Joseph Black shows that mercury has a greater heat capacity than water in that a quantity of mercury heats faster than an equal one of water does. This experiment marks the beginning of the scientific study of heat. **CHEM**
1760	German physicist Johann H. Lambert introduces the term *albedo* for the varying rates of reflection of the planets. **PHYS**
1760	Between now and 1762, Dutch anatomist Pieter Camper publishes *Demonstrationum anatomico-pathologicarum*, a two-volume work comparing anatomy in different human races. **SOC**

1761   Mikhail V. Lomonosov discovers the atmosphere of Venus while observing that planet's transit across the sun.   **ASTRO**

1761   Joseph-Nicolas Delisle of Paris organizes astronomers around the world to observe the transit of Venus across the sun. Jeremiah Horrocks and Edmund Halley had already promoted the idea that simultaneous observations of this rare event from different places on earth would allow scientists to determine the distance to Venus and the sun. Observations are made this year and at the transit of 1769. The next transits (which always come in pairs eight years apart) are not until 1874 and 1882.   **ASTRO**

1761   French evolutionist Jean-Baptiste Robinet publishes the first volume of a five-volume work in which he claims that the Creator made organic beings on a scale and that they all have the internal energy to move upward toward the top, where humans are. Robinet also posits that all matter contains life and even inorganic matter can evolve into a living organism.   **BIO**

1761   In France the first veterinary school is founded.   **BIO**

1761   German physician George Christian Fuschel publishes a lengthy article dealing with the stratigraphy of the area of Thuringa. Notably, it introduces the (still current) sense of formation as the primary unit of the study of rock strata. Fuschel correlates strata by means of index fossils.   **EARTH**

1761   German mathematician Johann H. Lambert proves that pi is an irrational number.   **MATH**

1761   Italian physician Giovanni Morgagni becomes the father of morbid anatomy after linking certain postmortem findings with disease symptoms experienced by the dying.   **MED**

1762   British astronomer James Bradley completes a catalog of 60,000 stars.   **ASTRO**

1762   Scottish chemist Joseph Black discovers latent heat, the quantity of heat absorbed or released when a substance changes its physical phase at constant temperature (e.g., from solid to liquid or liquid to gas).   **CHEM**

1763   German botanist J. G. Kölreuter publishes the results of his experiments on plants by animals carrying pollen.   **BIO**

c. 1764   Scottish philosopher Thomas Reid becomes the first member of the so-called Scottish School of psychology, objecting to empiricism and associationism. Reid disagrees with the principles of association which say that all human knowledge is experience. He proposes, in part, the theory now known as faculty psychology, that the mind is an organized unity with the ability to act on needs such as self-preservation, desire, self-esteem, pity, and gratitude.   **PSYCH**

1764	The first system for measuring and naming sizes of type is developed by French engraver Pierre Simon Fournier and outlined in his work *Manuel typographique*. **TECH**
1765	Geologist Nicolas Desmarest, the inspector-general of manufactures in France, discovers prismatic basalt to be of volcanic origin. **EARTH**
1765	Swiss scientist Horace Bénédict de Saussure invents the electrometer, a device for measuring voltage differences without drawing an appreciable amount of current from the source. **TECH**
1765	The steam engine is refined by Scottish engineer James Watt. With its separate chamber for condensing the steam, this engine supersedes the Newcomen engine of 1712 in its efficiency. It will be patented in 1769. *See also* 1698, Savery. **TECH**
1766	German astronomer Johann Daniel Titius or Tiety of Wittenberg discovers that the distances of the known planets from the sun are proportional to the terms of the series 0, 3, 6, 12 … Johann E. Bode, director of the Berlin Observatory, will publish this finding in 1772, hence its common name Bode's law. This "law" will later be found to apply to Uranus (discovered in 1781) but not Neptune (1846) and Pluto (1930). It is therefore not a universal law but an observation about certain planets of the solar system. **ASTRO**
1766	British chemist Henry Cavendish discovers an inflammable gas he calls fire air, produced by reaction between acid and certain metals. It is now known to be the element hydrogen. *See* 1784, Cavendish. **CHEM**
1766	The as-yet-unidentified element nitrogen, generated by an electrical charge, is used to enrich soil in experiments conducted by chemist Henry Cavendish. **TECH**
1767	Nevil Maskelyne, Astronomer Royal, begins annual publication of the *British Nautical Almanac*, describing the position of celestial bodies at specific times, for use in navigation. **ASTRO**
1767	British chemist Joseph Priestley publishes *The History and Present State of Electricity*, in which he suggests that electrical forces, like gravitational ones, increase or decrease in inverse proportion to the square of the distance. This book also contains the first detailed account of Benjamin Franklin's kite experiment. *See* 1751. **PHYS**
1768	Italian biologist Lazzaro Spallanzani determines that food can be protected from microorganisms by being sealed to prevent air penetration. **BIO**
1768–1771	During an around-the-world voyage on the H.M.S. *Endeavor*, British naturalist Joseph Banks collects 3,607 plant species, some 1,400 of which had not previously been identified. **BIO**

FIZZY WATER

*I*n addition to discovering ammonia, sulfur dioxide, and the gas now known as oxygen, eighteenth-century theologian and chemist Joseph Priestley also invented carbonated water. While living near a brewery in 1768 he appropriated some of its carbon dioxide and added it to household water. The carbon dioxide infused the water with a tartness and fizz now associated with refreshments like soda pop (when sugar and flavorings are added), quinine or tonic water (when quinine is added), or club soda or seltzer (in its unadulterated form).

1768   Chemist Joseph Priestley dissolves carbon dioxide in water to produce carbonated water, now called seltzer or soda water and the basis of all future carbonated soft drinks.   **CHEM**

1768   On an expedition from 1768 to 1771, British navigator James Cook charts the coasts of New Zealand and the eastern coast of what is then called New Holland. He realizes that the latter is large enough to be a continent; it comes to be called Australia.   **EARTH**

1768   French physicist Antoine Baumé invents the graduated hydrometer, which uses the Baumé scale for specific gravities of liquids.   **TECH**

1769   This year's transit of Venus (*see* 1761, Delisle) is observed from such far-flung places as Tahiti (visited by Captain James Cook), Siberia, and Ireland. Data from the transits of 1761 and 1769 will be used to determine the distance from the earth to the sun—and hence the scale of the solar system—with greater accuracy than ever before.   **ASTRO**

1769   Wine grapes are first planted in California.   **BIO**

1769   French chemist Antoine-Laurent Lavoisier develops methods of quantitative chemistry through which he disproves the ancient Greek theory that water boiled long enough will be partially converted into sediment.   **CHEM**

1769   British surgeon Percivall Pott publishes treatises on tuberculosis of the spine (Pott's disease) and a particular fracture of the leg with the dislocation of the foot outward and backward (Pott's fracture).   **MED**

1769   A spinning frame that can produce thread sturdy enough for apparel is invented by British manufacturer Richard Arkwright.   **TECH**

1769   Scottish engineer James Watt patents the steam engine he developed in 1765, which will play a major role in the industrial revolution.   **TECH**

c. 1770s   Danish biologist Otto F. Müller devises a dredge to collect samples of living organisms from the ocean's floor.   **EARTH**

1770   Swiss entomologist Charles Bonnet maintains his stand that the female of a species contains miniature forms of all future generations in her body, stating further that catastrophic evolution occurs occasionally, at which time these miniatures within the females evolve upward. Bonnet will later predict that this type of evolution will allow inorganic matter to live, animals to reason, and humans to become angels.   **BIO**

1770   British chemist Joseph Priestley collects and studies water-soluble gases, including ammonia, sulfur dioxide, and hydrogen chloride.   **CHEM**

1770   Swedish pharmacist Carl Wilhelm Scheele discovers tartaric acid.   **CHEM**

c. 1770   Italian physiologist Lazzaro Spallanzani experiments with artificial insemination in dogs and proves that sperm is necessary for fertilization of the ovum.   **MED**

1770   British inventor James Hargreaves patents the spinning jenny, which helps automate textile manufacturing.   **TECH**

1771   Some two hundred years after his death in 1565, *Opera botanica*, by Swiss naturalist Konrad von Gesner, is published in Nuremburg.   **BIO**

1771   Joseph Priestley discovers that plants produce a substance that supports combustion and animal breathing, a substance he will identify as oxygen three years later.   **CHEM**

1771   Fossils of ancient humans and extinct cave bears are found together in Germany.   **PALEO**

1771   British philologist Sir William Jones discovers relationships among Latin, Greek, and Sanskrit that will lead to reconstruction of Indo-European and the development of modern comparative philology.   **SOC**

1772   British chemist Daniel Rutherford discovers the element nitrogen.   **CHEM**

1772   French chemist Antoine-Laurent Lavoisier disproves Georg Ernst Stahl's 1700 theory that a loss of a combustible substance called phlogiston causes burning, discovering instead that burning or rusting objects combine with some substance in the air, later shown to be oxygen.   **CHEM**

Burning Glass designed for Antoine Lavoisier made to use sunlight for heat for experiments. (Oeuvres de Lavoisier, *Paris*)

1772   By burning a diamond and producing carbon dioxide, Lavoisier discovers that diamonds consist of carbon and are related to coal.   **CHEM**

1772   Austrian physician Franz Anton Mesmer claims that mental power (magnetism) exerts extraordinary influence on the human body. By 1775, he will be calling this healing power animal magnetism and claiming it has medicinal value. Mesmer will use this popular form of hypnotism to cure patients until the French government investigates his theory, finds against it, and mesmerizing falls into disrepute.   **PSYCH**

1772   Rubber is named by British scientist Joseph Priestley for its ability to erase penciled errors through rubbing.   **TECH**

1773   Through microscopic and chemical experiments, French scientist Hilaire-Marin Rouelle discovers potassium and sodium in human and animal blood.   **BIO**

1773   In Virginia, the Williamsburg Eastern Lunatic Asylum, the first official U.S. asylum for the mentally ill, is founded.   **PSYCH**

1774   The Shakers, a religious sect from England, settle in the American colonies. Among their accomplishments in animal husbandry will be the breeding of the Poland China hog, a hybrid of a U.S. domestic hog and the Big China hog. Versatile and hardy, it will become a staple of U.S. livestock.   **TECH**

1774   Joseph Priestley discovers the element oxygen. Swedish chemist
            Carl Wilhelm Scheele had independently discovered it in 1772, but
            he failed to publish before Priestley and forfeited the credit for the
            discovery.   **CHEM**

1774   The same year that he is scooped by Priestley, Scheele discovers
            the elements chlorine, manganese, and barium—but fails to get
            undisputed credit for any of them. Swedish mineralogist Johan
            Gottlieb Gahn completes his discovery of manganese this year and
            gets credit for it. Barium (found in 1808) and chlorine (1810) are
            usually credited to British chemist Humphry Davy, who first identi-
            fied them as elements rather than compounds.   **CHEM**

DIAMONDS ARE NOT FOREVER

*O*ne of the more expensive ways of producing carbon dioxide is to
burn a diamond. This is precisely what French chemist Antoine-
Laurent Lavoisier did in 1772. First he and some fellow chemists
pooled their funds to buy a diamond; then, they heated it to a high enough
temperature to burn it. The result was a container of very costly carbon
dioxide, demonstrating a link between diamonds and carbon. By the end of
the eighteenth century, British chemist Smithson Tennant and French
chemist Guyton de Morveau had shown that diamonds are a form of pure
carbon that can be converted to graphite. Graphite and carbon are al-
lotropes of carbon—two forms of the same element that differ only in their
crystal structures. A diamond's atoms bond to one another in a tightly
packed tetrahedral arrangement, making it very dense and very hard. But
the more stable form of the element is the lowly graphite, in which the
atoms are arranged in loosely stacked but durable layers. Over millions of
years, in fact, diamonds tend to turn into graphite. In geologic terms, then,
diamonds are not forever.

If diamonds can be turned into graphite, can graphite be turned into diamonds? Only by applying temperatures and pressures great enough to break
up the graphite and pack the carbon atoms into the dense tetrahedral shape.
Chemists tried to do this all through the nineteenth and early twentieth centuries but could not achieve the necessary conditions. Then, in 1955, scientists
at General Electric succeeded in reaching pressures of 100,000 atmospheres
and temperatures of 2,500° C. Using chromium as a catalyst, they succeeded
in turning graphite into diamonds. In 1962, at still higher temperatures and
pressures, they did the same thing without the aid of a catalyst. They had
shown that Lavoisier's conversion process of two hundred years earlier was
reversible, though considerably easier in one direction than the other.

1775   Danish entomologist Johan Christian Fabricius classifies insects by
            their mouth structure.   **BIO**

1775   Joseph Priestley identifies hydrochloric and sulfuric acid.   **CHEM**

1775   British surgeon Percivall Pott gives the first clear example of occu-
            pation-related cancer, in chimney sweeps who develop cancer of
            the scrotum from prolonged exposure to soot and ashes.   **MED**

1775   Italian physicist Alessandro Volta invents a device that can both
            generate and store static electricity. *See also* 1800, Volta. **PHYS**

1775   The first patent for a flush toilet is issued to British inventor
            Alexander Cummings, though such toilets will not become com-
            mon until the nineteenth century.   **TECH**

1776   Swedish chemists Carl W. Scheele and Torbern Olof Bergman inde-
            pendently discover uric acid.   **CHEM**

1776   American physician and statesman Benjamin Rush signs the
            Declaration of Independence. He will become surgeon general of
            the Continental Army, on the staff at Pennsylvania Hospital (where
            he will found the first free dispensary in the United States), and be
            treasurer of the U.S. Mint from 1797 to 1813. In 1812 he will pub-
            lish the first U.S. treatise on psychiatry.   **MED**

1776   Chemist Matthew Dobson proves that the sweetness in diabetic
            blood and urine is due to sugar and suggests that diabetes is not a
            kidney problem but rather a malfunction of metabolism and di-
            gestion.   **MED**

1776   British social philosopher Adam Smith publishes *An Inquiry into the
            Nature and Causes of the Wealth of Nations*, the founding work of
            classical economics. In it Smith argues for a laissez-faire approach
            to the market in which individuals pursuing their own interests im-
            prove the condition of society as a whole.   **SOC**

1776   German anatomist and natural historian Johann Friedrich
            Blumenbach publishes *On the Natural Varieties of Mankind*, which
            divides the human race into American Indian, Caucasian,
            Ethiopian, Malayan, and Mongolian branches. He also postulates
            that Caucasians were the original human race which then "degen-
            erated" into the other divisions under different environmental de-
            mands.   **SOC**

1776   The submarine is first used in combat, during the American
            Revolution. This seven-foot vessel, called the *Connecticut Turtle*, is
            designed by David Bushnell of wood, iron, and pitch. Driven by a
            hand-cranked propeller, it attempts unsuccessfully to sink British
            warships in New York harbor.   **TECH**

1777	French naturalist Georges-Louis Leclerc de Buffon introduces what is referred to as the needle problem, the first example of a geometric probability. **MATH**
1777	French physicist Charles-Augustin de Coulomb invents the torsion balance, a weight scale that relies on the force required to twist, or apply torsion to, a wire or fiber. **TECH**
1778	Swedish chemist Carl Wilhelm Scheele discovers the element molybdenum, though he often loses credit for the discovery to Swedish mineralogist Peter Jacob Hjelm. **CHEM**
1779	Dutch botanist Jan Ingenhousz proves that green plants give off oxygen in the presence of sunlight and that their roots, flowers, and fruits exude carbon dioxide in the absence of light. He also shows that plants get carbon from the atmosphere, not from the soil. **BIO**
1779	Swiss geologist Horace-Bénédict de Saussure coins the term *geology* and correctly describes the movement of glaciers. **EARTH**
1780	Italian anatomist Luigi Galvani observes that dissected frog legs twitch when electricity is applied and when making contact with two different metals. Though he is wrong in concluding that animal tissue is the source of electricity, his experiments will spur further research into electricity, including that of Alessandro Volta in 1800. **BIO**
1780	German geologist Abraham Gottlob Werner, who will come to be known as the father of historic geology, publishes the influential article *Kurze Klassification und Beschreibung de verschiedenen Gebirgsatzen*. Although he is a neptunist (*see* 1738, de Maillet), believing that the earth's lands precipitated out of a universal ocean, Werner will be renowned for his careful definitions, classification of minerals, and application of chronology to rock formations. **EARTH**
c. 1780	British physician David Pitcairn is first to note that rheumatic fever can damage the heart. **MED**
1780	Italian physiologist Lazzaro Spallanzani proves that digestion is a chemical reaction to gastric juice. **MED**
1780	Scottish physician John Brown develops the Brownian (Brunonian) system of medicine, which sees all body tissues as excitable and life as the result of stimuli acting on tissues. Disease, Brown believes, is caused by either excessive or insufficient stimulation. His preferred treatments for disease are opium and alcohol. **MED**
1780	In London, British physician James Graham establishes the Temple of Health and Hymen for the treatment of fertility. After paying Graham fifty guineas, infertile and impotent couples use the elaborate "temple" and "grand celestial bed" in hopes of conceiving children of unusual beauty and physique. **MED**

1780   Geologists in central Germany study the Buntsandstein and Muschelkalk fossil beds, which date respectively from the early and middle Triassic periods. *See* 1834, von Alberti.   **PALEO**

1780   An automated flour mill is developed by American merchant Oliver Evans. It operates by a water-powered conveyor belt.   **TECH**

1781   French astronomer Charles Messier catalogs 103 nebulae, or patches of luminous cloud that later turn out to be galaxies.   **ASTRO**

Mar. 13, 1781   German-English astronomer William Herschel discovers Uranus, the seventh planet from the sun and the first to be discovered by telescope.   **ASTRO**

1781   French mineralogist René-Just Haüy founds the modern science of crystallography when he discovers that crystals are built on successive additions of a unit cell with a constant geometric shape, which he believes may be determined by its chemical composition.   **CHEM**

1781   Czechoslovakian mathematician and priest Bernhard Bolzano makes numerous discoveries that do not become widely known and are later rediscovered by others, including the arithmetization of the calculus and the recognition of pathological functions.   **MATH**

1781   A smallpox outbreak among Spanish settlers in Texas spreads north to Canada. More than 130,000 Native Americans die, halving the populations of the Blackfoot, Cree, Arapaho, Shoshoni, and Crow peoples.   **MED**

1781   Physicist Johan Carl Wilcke introduces the idea of specific heat, the quantity of heat required to raise the temperature of a given substance by a given amount.   **PHYS**

1781   German philosopher Immanuel Kant argues against the empiricist viewpoint that all human beings are born with equal potential and are the product of education and environment. In his *Critique of Pure Reason* Kant takes instead the nativist viewpoint, stressing that inherited characteristics and inborn intuitions frame human experience but are not dependent on it.   **PSYCH**

1781   After three months of construction, the first all-iron bridge is put into operation, in Shropshire, England. The 378-ton bridge spans 100 feet. The iron for the bridge was cast by Abraham Darby III, grandson of ironworks master Abraham Darby. *See* 1709.   **TECH**

1782   British astronomer John Goodricke suggests that the star Algol has a dark companion that circles and periodically eclipses it. *See* 1889, Vogel.   **ASTRO**

1782   While investigating a badger intestine, German zoologist Johann Melchior Goeze identifies the hookworm.   **BIO**

1782   Scottish engineer James Watt patents a double-acting rotary steam engine, which improves significantly on his steam engine of 1769.   **TECH**

THE GEORGIAN PLANET

*F*ive planets, all of them visible to the naked eye, have been known since ancient times: Mercury, Venus, Mars, Jupiter, and Saturn. By the eighteenth century, it was understood that the earth itself is a planet orbiting the sun, bringing the tally to six. Not until 1781 was a seventh planet discovered: Uranus.

Ironically, Uranus had been visible all along. On a clear, dark night it can be seen dimly—dimly enough that the ancients never noticed it. It took amateur astronomer William Herschel (1738–1822), using a telescope of his own invention, to discover this object. Born in Germany, Herschel was a musician by trade, working as a chapel organist in Bath, England. However, he had a taste for astronomy and a talent for optics that allowed him to build telescopes with far better resolution than those used by the professionals of the time. On a Tuesday night, March 13, 1781, watching the skies with such a telescope, he noted a "curious either nebulous Star or perhaps a Comet." By its disklike shape and characteristic orbit it was proven to be a planet, the first to be discovered since antiquity.

The name of the new planet was uncertain for some time. Herschel wanted to call it the Georgian Planet after George III, then king of Britain; for his loyalty, Herschel was appointed private astronomer to the king in 1782. Others suggested Planet Herschel, while others pressed for a name drawn from Greco-Roman mythology, in keeping with the names of the other known planets. The latter tradition finally won out and the planet was named for Uranus, the mythological father of Saturn. The precedent was maintained when the eighth and ninth planets were discovered: Neptune in 1846 (named for a brother of Jupiter) and Pluto (a son of Saturn) in 1930.

June 1783	Jacques and Joseph Montgolfier of France send up the first flying balloon, filled with smoke. **TECH**
1783	Spanish mineralogists Juan José and Fausto d'Elhuyar y de Suvisa discover the element tungsten. **CHEM**
1783	Swedish chemist Carl W. Scheele discovers the compound glycerine. **CHEM**
1783	British ironworks master Henry Cort improves wrought-iron production by developing a system for puddling iron. **TECH**
Nov. 21, 1783	Frenchmen Jean Pilâtre de Rozier and the Marquis François d'Arlandes make the first manned free-balloon flight, reaching a height of about 500 feet and traveling about 5.5 miles during their twenty-minute flight. **TECH**

THE FIRST LOCOMOTIVE

*T*he first working steam locomotive did not run on rails and carried no passengers. It was a model 14 inches high and 19¼ inches long, built in England in 1784 by William Murdoch, an employee of Scottish inventor James Watt. The terrier-sized steam-driven model ran through the streets at six to eight miles an hour, and, according to legend, scared the village parson half to death. A concerned Watt asked Murdoch not to conduct any more such experiments.

Twenty years later, in 1804, British inventor Richard Trevithick was the first to put a full-sized steam locomotive on rails. The result was far more influential.

1784   German-English astronomer William Herschel observes distorting mists or clouds on Mars. **ASTRO**

1784   Austrian mineralogist Franz Joseph Müller discovers the element tellurium. **CHEM**

1784   British chemist Henry Cavendish discovers that water is composed of hydrogen and oxygen, from which he gives hydrogen its name (from the Greek for "water former"). **CHEM**

1784   Swedish chemist Carl W. Scheele identifies citric acid. **CHEM**

1784   French chemist Gaspard Monge liquefies sulfur dioxide, the first substance normally known as a gas to be liquefied. **CHEM**

1784   American physician John Jeffries flies a balloon over London to collect air samples at various heights. **EARTH**

1784   French aeronaut Jean-Pierre-François Blanchard invents the parachute and he makes and survives the first jump. **EARTH**

1784   American inventor and statesman Benjamin Franklin invents bifocal lenses. **MED**

1784   Italian physician Domenico Cotugno discovers cerebrospinal fluid, the water cushion that protects the brain and spinal cord from shock. **MED**

1784   British physicist George Atwood determines the acceleration of a free-falling body. **PHYS**

1784   Jean-Baptiste Meusnier designs the first powered balloon with a crew cranking three propellers on a single shaft to enable the elliptically shaped balloon to reach speeds of about 3 mph. **TECH**

1785   William Herschel theorizes that the Milky Way is a flattened system of stars, or a galaxy. His estimates of the galaxy's diameter and thickness are overly conservative.   **ASTRO**

1785   Pierre Simon de Laplace publishes his *Theory on the Attraction of Spheroids and the Shape of Planets*, which contains what is now known as the Laplace equation. This partial differential equation describes electromagnetic, gravitational, and other potentials.   **ASTRO**

1785   British physician William Withering describes the correct use of digitalis to treat heart failure.   **MED**

1785   French scientist Charles de Coulomb defines Coulomb's law: The force between two stationary electric charges is proportional to the product of the charges and inversely proportional to the square of the distance between them.   **PHYS**

1785   For the first time, in Nottinghamshire, England, a textile plant is powered by steam.   **TECH**

1786–1802   William Herschel will publish three catalogs listing 2,500 nebulae. These will become the basis for the *New General Catalogue* (NGC) of 1864 and 1888.   **ASTRO**

1786   Frenchmen Michel-Gabriel Paccard and Jacques Balmat become the first to climb to the summit of Mont Blanc, the highest peak in the Alps. This feat wins them a prize and inaugurates the modern sport of mountain climbing.   **EARTH**

1786   The durable linen-wool fabric called linsey-woolsey is developed and popularized by American tradesmen.   **TECH**

1786   A nail-making machine is invented and patented by Massachusetts inventor Ezekiel Reed.   **TECH**

1786   The first grain thresher that works by sandwiching grain between a moving cylinder and a curved metal sheet is invented by Scottish agricultural engineer Andrew Meikle.   **TECH**

1786   English gunsmith Henry Nock invents a breech-loading musket.   **TECH**

1787   William Herschel discovers Titania and Oberon, two moons of Uranus.   **ASTRO**

1787   French scientists Jacques-Alexandre-César Charles (in 1787) and Joseph-Louis Gay-Lussac (in 1802) rediscover Guillaume Amontons's forgotten 1699 law that at constant pressure, all gases expand by the same amount for a given rise in temperature. This principle is now sometimes called Charles's law.   **CHEM**

1787   French chemist Antoine-Laurent Lavoisier and colleagues publish *The Method of Chemical Nomenclature*, a systematic approach to naming chemical substances and processes. This system soon gains universal acceptance among chemists.   **CHEM**

1787   French chemist Claude-Louis Berthollet identifies the composition of ammonia, hydrogen sulfide, and prussic acid.   **CHEM**

1787   A large fossil bone discovered in New Jersey and reported on by Caspar Wistar and Timothy Matlack (though the find goes unpublished and unverified) may be the first dinosaur bone ever collected.   **PALEO**

....

"The indifferent state of agriculture among us does not proceed from a want of knowledge merely. It is from our having such quantities of land to waste as we please. In Europe the object is to make the most of their land, labor being abundant; here it is to make the most of our labor, land being abundant."—**Thomas Jefferson, commenting on America; in** Notes on Virginia, **1782**

....

1787   Danish philologist Rasmus Christian Rask is born (*d.* 1832). In addition to compiling the first usable Anglo-Saxon and Icelandic grammars, he will publish important work on the relationships of the Indo-European languages.   **SOC**

1787   In two separate events, the first steamboats are demonstrated by U.S. inventors, one on the Potomac River, by James Rumsey, the other on the Delaware, by John Fitch.   **TECH**

1787   The processes of grinding grain and sifting flour are automated by a system developed by U.S. inventor Oliver Evans, simplifying the labor and time needed to produce bread.   **TECH**

1788   In a posthumous publication, Swedish mineralogist Torbern Olof Bergman (*d.* 1784) presents tables of affinities marking the extent to which given chemicals interact, including predictions about reactions as yet unobserved.   **CHEM**

1788   French mathematician Joseph-Louis Lagrange formulates the function now called Lagrangian that expresses the difference between kinetic and potential energy for every point in an object's path.   **PHYS**

1788   In his *Analytical Mechanics*, Joseph-Louis Lagrange works out general equations through which algebra and calculus, rather than geometry, can be used to solve mechanical problems.   **PHYS**

1789   German-English astronomer William Herschel discovers the Saturnian moons Mimas and Enceladus.   **ASTRO**

1789   Herschel completes the world's then-largest telescope, a reflecting telescope with a 48-inch mirror.   **ASTRO**

1789	French botanist Antoine-Laurent de Jussieu is one of the first to attempt sorting and assigning plants under a "natural" classification system when he classifies them into natural families like grasses, lilies, and palms. **BIO**
1789	German chemist Martin Heinrich Klaproth discovers the elements uranium and zirconium. **CHEM**
1789	French chemist Claude-Louis Berthollet shows that, contrary to the accepted belief, not all acids contain oxygen. **CHEM**
1789	In a textbook on chemistry, Antoine-Laurent Lavoisier states the principle of conservation of mass: In a closed system, the total amount of mass remains the same regardless of physical or chemical changes. This law will eventually be revised by Einstein in his 1905 law of the conservation of mass-energy. **CHEM**
1789	Corn-based bourbon whiskey is first produced in the Kentucky territory, by a minister named Elijah Craig. **TECH**
1790	American engineer and entrepreneur Samuel Slater (1768–1835) opens the first working U.S. cotton mill. With ironmaster David Wilkinson, Slater builds a mill from plans used for similar plants in England. This event marks the beginning of the industrial revolution in the United States. **TECH**

1790 model of the 48-spindle water frame used by Samuel Slater in Rhode Island. (*Smithsonian Institution*)

1790   William Herschel discovers planetary nebulae, shells of gas sur-
              rounding certain stars.   **ASTRO**

....

*"Seeing is in some respect an art, which must be learnt. To
make a person see with such a power is nearly the same as if
I were to make him play one of Handel's fugues upon the
organ."—William Herschel, German-English astronomer and
organist, on seeing through a telescope; eighteenth century*

....

1790   A French government commission including such scientists as
              Lagrange, Laplace, and Lavoisier begins to define the metric system
              of measurement.   **MISC**

1790   British archaeologist John Frere finds stone tools and the fossil re-
              mains of extinct animals at Hoxne, Suffolk, England.   **PALEO**

1791   British minister William Gregor discovers the element titanium. **CHEM**

1791   German chemist Jeremias Richter defines the principle of stoi-
              chiometry, specifying the fixed relative proportions in which chem-
              ical substances react.   **CHEM**

1791   From Freiberg, German mineralogist A. G. Werner publishes *Neue
              Theorie von den Enstehung der Gänge*, dealing with the formation of
              ore deposits, an extension of his theory on the origin of rocks. **EARTH**

1791   French physicist Pierre Prévost shows that cold is the absence of
              heat and that all bodies radiate heat continuously.   **PHYS**

1791   French author Donatien-Alphonse-François de Sade, better known
              as the Marquis de Sade, publishes the novel *Justine*, in which he de-
              scribes the sexual gratification derived from inflicting pain on a
              loved one, an abnormal sexual practice later called "sadism." **PSYCH**

1791   The French National Assembly recommends making an attempt to
              standardize measurements for the meter and quadrant. They sug-
              gest that the meter represent one ten-millionth part of a quadrant
              of the surface of the earth and the gram one cubic centimeter of
              water at 4° C.   **TECH**

1792   The Mint of the United States opens, to produce coins based on a
              decimal system.   **TECH**

1792   American Eli Whitney invents the cotton gin, a cylindrical machine
              that quickly separates cotton fibers from seeds, a task that is slow
              and laborious by hand. The new invention vastly increases cotton
              production and increases the South's dependence on slaves to pick
              the cotton to be processed by the gin.   **TECH**

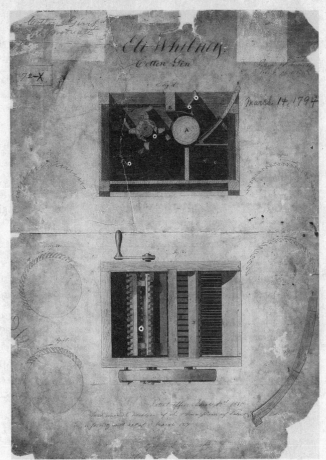

Eli Whitney's patent for the cotton gin, 1794. (*National Archives*)

1793   German botanist Christian Sprengel (1750–1816) describes the
            plant pollination process, emphasizing the influence of winds and
            insects in cross-pollination.   **BIO**

1793   Irish barrister and scientist Richard Kirwan attacks Scottish geolo-
            gist James Hutton's uniformitarian (*see* 1795, Hutton) and vulcanist
            ideas. Vulcanists, who also included Scottish philosopher William
            Hamilton (1788–1856) and French geologist Nicolas Desmarest
            (1725–1815), believed that basaltic rocks were the product of vol-
            canic lava flow.   **EARTH**

1794   German physicist Ernst Chladni argues that meteorites are extrater-
            restrial in origin.   **ASTRO**

1794   Finnish chemist Johan Gadolin discovers yttrium, the first known rare earth element. It will not be completely isolated from other elements until Swedish chemist Carl Gustaf Mosander does so about 1843.   **CHEM**

1794   British chemist Elizabeth Fulhame publishes her *Essay on Combustion*, in which she develops a theory of combustion as a process combining oxygenation (combination with oxygen) and reduction (restoration of oxygenated bodies).   **CHEM**

1794   French mathematician Adrien-Marie Legendre publishes his highly influential textbook *Elements of Geometry*.   **MATH**

c. 1794   Italian surgeon and anatomist Antonio Scarpa describes certain vital parts of the human anatomy which will be named for him: Scarpa's fascia, Scarpa's fluid, Scarpa's femoral triangle, and Scarpa's membrane and ganglion.   **MED**

1794   In the first military use of a balloon, Frenchman Jean-Marie Coutelle makes two observation flights over the enemy's camp.   **TECH**

1794   In Pennsylvania the Lancaster Road, a toll road, opens to join Lancaster and its surrounding areas with the Philadelphia area. **TECH**

1795   German poet Johann Wolfgang von Goethe claims two archetype plans exist for living beings. One archetype is for the animal world and one is for the plant world.   **BIO**

1795   In his *Theory of the Earth* Scottish naturalist James Hutton elaborates the "uniformitarian principle" that geological processes, such as erosion, work at a more or less uniform rate. The principle implies that the earth is much older than previously believed. **EARTH**

1795   Between now and 1797, Mungo Park becomes the first European to explore the Niger River.   **EARTH**

1795   French mathematician Gaspard Monge publishes *Feuilles d'analyse*. In this and his 1802 memoir with Jean-N.-P. Hachette, he systematizes solid analytic geometry and elementary differential geometry in what approximates their present state. These works include the two Monge theorems.   **MATH**

1795   German mathematician Carl Friedrich Gauss discovers, independently of Leonhard Euler, the law of quadratic reciprocity in number theory.   **MATH**

c. 1795   German-Austrian physician Franz Joseph Gall begins writing on phrenology, the science of the mind. He claims that personality can be judged by physical appearances, especially skull characteristics, and argues that qualities such as honesty and depravity are directly associated with bumps and ridges of the skull over specific brain regions.   **PSYCH**

1795   Sensory psychophysiologist Ernst Heinrich Weber is born in Wittenberg, Germany (*d.* 1878). He will be the first to study touch and kinesthesis, in elaborate experiments. He will also discover a major psychophysical principle, which Gustav Fechner will identify as Weber's law, that the just-noticeable increment in stimulus intensity is a constant fraction of the intensity already present.   **PSYCH**

1795   The Springfield flintlock musket is developed and named the first official piece of U.S. weaponry. The musket derives its name from its town of origin, Springfield, Massachusetts, the site of the first American arsenal in 1794.   **TECH**

1796   French astronomer Pierre Simon de Laplace publishes his theory that the solar system formed by condensation from a cloud of gas. This "nebular hypothesis" is the basis of present-day theories of the solar system's origin.   **ASTRO**

1796   Chemist J. T. Lowitz isolates pure ethyl alcohol.   **CHEM**

1796   German mathematician Carl Friedrich Gauss invents a method for constructing a heptadecagon (a polygon with seventeen sides of equal lengths) with compass and straight edge, and shows that an equilateral heptagon (a polygon with seven equal sides) could not be built the same way. His discoveries, which mark the first notable advance in geometry since ancient Greece, show the value in mathematics of proving impossibility.   **MATH**

May 14,   British physician Edward Jenner inoculates the arm of eight-year-
1796   old James Phipp with pus from a cowpox sore on a milkmaid's arm. The boy develops a similar sore, but does not get sick. Then in July Jenner inoculates Phipp with smallpox, proving that the mild cowpox infection had protected him from smallpox. By 1823 Jenner's treatment will be practiced throughout the world, making smallpox the first disease to be conquered by vaccination.   **MED**

1797   German astronomer Heinrich Wilhelm Olbers devises new methods for calculating the parabolic orbits of comets.   **ASTRO**

1797   French naturalist Georges Dagobert, Baron Cuvier, publishes his *Tableau élémentaire de l'histoire naturelle des animaux*, the founding work of comparative anatomy.   **BIO**

1797   Baron Cuvier adopts the term *phylum* (from the Greek for *tribe*) for a taxonomic category more general than the class but more specific than the kingdom. Phylums represent the basic body plans of organisms.   **BIO**

1797   French chemist Louis-Nicolas Vauquelin discovers the element chromium.   **CHEM**

1797   Scottish geologist Sir James Hall pioneers work in high-pressure, high-temperature mineralogy (later called experimental petrology).   **EARTH**

1797   British physician William Hyde Wollaston discovers uric acid, the end product of purine metabolism, in gouty joints, linking the cause and effect of gout.   **MED**

1797   While studying blood pressure, physician Jean Poiseuille formulates laws governing the passage of fluids through narrow tubes.   **PHYS**

1797   Cigarettes, small cigars in paper wrappers, are produced in Cuba.   **TECH**

1798   French astronomer Pierre Simon de Laplace proposes the existence of the objects later known as black holes.   **ASTRO**

1798   French chemist Vauquelin discovers the element beryllium.   **CHEM**

....

"Population, when unchecked, increases in geometrical ratio. Subsistence increases only in an arithmetical ratio."
—Thomas Robert Malthus, English economist, explaining why unchecked population growth should lead to famine; in An Essay on the Principle of Population, 1798

....

1798   French chemist Louis-Bernard Guyton de Morveau succeeds in liquefying ammonia, until then known only as a gas.   **CHEM**

1798   British chemist Henry Cavendish determines the gravitational constant, the only unknown to date in Newton's law of gravitation, and the mass and density of the earth.   **PHYS**

1798   British physicist Benjamin Thompson demonstrates that heat should be understood as the increased motion of particles when heated, not as a type of fluid (caloric), as previously believed.   **PHYS**

1798   British economist Thomas Robert Malthus publishes his *Essay on the Principle of Population*, in which he argues that population tends to increase in geometric progression but food supply in arithmetic progression, so that population will tend to outstrip food supply until it is reduced by famine, disease, or war.   **SOC**

1798   Eli Whitney refines mass production through the development of jigs, metal patterns that allow for consistent duplication of parts. This development will help to form the American system of mass production.   **TECH**

1798   The printing process of lithography is developed by Bavarian printer Aloys Senefelder. Operating through the incompatibility of oil and water, this technique uses oil-based ink to print images, while paper not meant to accept images is water treated, thus rejecting the ink.   **TECH**

1799   A French soldier in Napoleon's army invading Egypt discovers an inscribed black stone near the town of Rosetta. The inscription on this, the Rosetta Stone, is found to date to 197 B.C. and is written in three languages: Greek and two forms of Egyptian hieroglyphics. The stone enables scholars (*see* 1822) to learn to read ancient Egyptian texts.   **ARCH**

....

"Soldiers! Forty centuries gaze down upon you."
—Napoleon Bonaparte, French emperor and general;
on seeing the Great Pyramids of Giza, 1799

....

1799   Wilhelm von Humboldt observes the Leonid meteor shower, a periodic event that will later (*see* 1866) be found to be associated with a comet.   **ASTRO**

1799   From now to 1825, Pierre Simon de Laplace's five-volume work *Celestial Mechanics* is published, summarizing and extending current knowledge. Laplace shows that the solar system is stable, despite periodic perturbations.   **ASTRO**

1799   French chemist Joseph-Louis Proust articulates Proust's law or the law of definite (constant) proportions: The proportions of the elements in a compound are always the same, no matter how the compound is made.   **CHEM**

1799   The British Mineralogical Society is founded.   **EARTH**

1799   In his dissertation at Helmstedt, German mathematician Carl Friedrich Gauss gives the first rigorous proof of what he calls the "fundamental theorem of algebra."   **MATH**

1799   English geologist William Smith suggests that rock strata can be identified by their characteristic fossils. This system of classification will become basic to paleontology. *See also* 1815.   **PALEO**

1799   In Siberia a mammoth is found preserved in ice.   **PALEO**

1799   British paleontologist Mary Anning is born (*d.* 1847). She will become a professional fossil collector whose dramatic finds will create a sensation in London geological circles. Among her finds will be remains of an ichthyosaur (1811), a plesiosaur, and a pterodactyl.   **PALEO**

1799   French chemist Philippe Lebon pioneers the theory and practice of gas lighting, using flammable gas derived from wood.   **TECH**

1799   The first suspension bridge using iron chains for support is built by U.S. engineer James Finley.   **TECH**

THE GEOLOGIC TIME CHART

*I*n 1799, English geologist William Smith noted that different strata, or
layers, of rock had their own characteristic fossils, which turned up in
those layers and nowhere else. He suggested that the various strata of
rock, even when bent and interrupted by geologic pressures, could be identified by their typical fossils. This insight, coupled with the inference that
higher strata are more recent and lower strata older, meant that the layers
of the earth's crust offered a guide to the history of life. Paleontologists
have since named the intervals of prehistoric time, with their contempora-
neous life forms, for the rock strata associated with them.

In the following chart, the intervals of geologic time are arranged in de-
scending order from most recent (top) to earliest (bottom). The columns
from left to right indicate increasingly subordinate units of time. Thus, the
Pleistocene epoch is one stage of the Quaternary period, which in turn is a
phase of the Cenozoic era. The dates in the column at the far right indicate
in millions of years how long ago the interval began. These intervals are
not of equal length. The earliest stage, the Precambrian era, lasted about 4
billion years, more than 85 percent of the earth's history to date.

Era	Period	Epoch	MYA (Millions of years ago)
Cenozoic	Quaternary	Holocene	.01
		Pleistocene	1.8
	Tertiary	Pliocene	7
		Miocene	23
		Oligocene	38
		Eocene	53
		Paleocene	65
Mesozoic	Cretaceous		136
	Jurassic		190
	Triassic		225
Paleozoic	Permian		280
	Carboniferous		345
	Devonian		395
	Silurian		440
	Ordovician		500
	Cambrian		570
Precambrian			4,600

1800	German scientist Karl Friedrich Burdach introduces the word *biology* for the study of the morphology, physiology, and psychology of humans. In 1882 a broader definition is proposed by Gottfried Treviranus and Jean-Baptiste de Lamarck to include the study of life in general. **BIO**
1800	French biologist Marie-François-Xavier Bichat publishes a treatise on membranes in which he classifies tissues into twenty-one types. **BIO**
1800	English chemist William Nicholson constructs his own electric battery and electrolyzes water, breaking it into its components hydrogen and oxygen. **CHEM**
1800	German physicist Johann Wilhelm Ritter invents electroplating when he passes a current through a copper sulfate solution. He also discovers that water consists of two parts hydrogen to one part oxygen. **CHEM**
1800	British chemist Humphry Davy discovers nitrous oxide and its intoxicating effects. As laughing gas it will become the first chemical anesthetic. **CHEM**
1800	British chemist William H. Wollaston develops a method for making platinum malleable. **CHEM**
1800	Robert Fulton, who will gain fame as the constructor of the first successful steamship, is the first to use metal to build a submarine. **EARTH**
1800	German physician Johann A. W. Hedenus is the first to perform a thyroidectomy (remove a thyroid) for goiter treatment. **MED**
1800	French and English chemists learn to purify water by chlorination. **MED**
c. 1800	In Germany the Keuper fossil beds, dating from the late Triassic, are described. **PALEO**
1800	In the Connecticut Valley, Pliny Moody finds fossil footprints of Triassic dinosaurs. For many years they will be thought to belong to extinct birds. *See* 1848, Hitchcock; 1915, Lull. **PALEO**
1800	Studying the spectrum of sunlight, German-English astronomer William Herschel discovers infrared radiation, the first known form of radiation other than visible light. **PHYS**
c. 1800	German physician Ferdinand Autenreith invents the "padded room" for use with mental patients. **PSYCH**
1800	Italian physicist Alessandro Volta invents the voltaic cell, or electric battery, consisting of alternating disks of copper and zinc and of cardboard soaked in a salt solution. **TECH**
Jan. 1, 1801	Italian astronomer Giuseppe Piazzi discovers Ceres, the first known asteroid. Carl Friedrich Gauss soon calculates its orbit. **ASTRO**

1801   French naturalist Jean-Baptiste de Lamarck begins to classify inver-
        tebrates, constructing such divisions as crustaceans and echino-
        derms. *See also* 1815, Lamarck.   **BIO**

1801   English chemist Charles Hatchett discovers the element niobium,
        which he calls columbium.   **CHEM**

1801   German mathematician Carl Friedrich Gauss publishes work on the
        law of quadratic reciprocity and the theory of congruences.   **MATH**

1801   Gauss's *Disquisitiones arithmeticae* represents the beginning of
        modern number theory. It contains the theory of quadratic congru-
        ences, forms, and residues.   **MATH**

1801   English physician Thomas Young gives the first description of visual
        astigmatism, or eye surface discrepancy.   **MED**

1801   Noting the phenomenon of diffraction of light (*see* 1665, Grimaldi),
        and interference patterns, English physicist Thomas Young argues
        that light is wavelike rather than particlelike. He speculates that the
        waves are longitudinal, like sound, rather than transverse, like wa-
        ter. Seventeen years later he will be proven wrong. *See* 1818,
        Fresnel.   **PHYS**

WHO'S IN A NAME

*I*talian physicist Alessandro Volta, inventor of the voltaic cell (1800),
is one of a select group of scientists whose names have been memo-
rialized in units of measurement. Here are some other members of
that group.

Scientist	Unit (abbreviation)	Physical Quantity
André M. Ampère (1775–1836)	ampere (A)	Electric current
A. J. Ångstrom (1814–1874)	angstrom (Å)	Small distance
A. H. Becquerel (1852–1908)	becquerel (Bq)	Radioactivity
Charles A. de Coulomb (1736–1806)	coulomb (C)	Electric charge
Heinrich Hertz (1857–1894)	hertz (Hz)	Frequency
James P. Joule (1818–1889)	joule (J)	Energy
Isaac Newton (1642–1727)	newton (N)	Force
Georg S. Ohm (1789–1854)	ohm (Ω)	Electric resistance
Blaise Pascal (1623-1662)	pascal (Pa)	Pressure
Alessandro Volta (1745–1827)	volt (V)	Electric potential difference
James Watt (1736–1819)	watt (W)	Power

1801	German physicist Johann Wilhelm Ritter discovers ultraviolet radiation. **PHYS**
1801	British chemist and physicist William Henry discovers Henry's law, that the mass of gas dissolved in a liquid at equilibrium and constant temperature is proportional to the pressure of the gas. **PHYS**
1801	French physician and humanitarian Philippe Pinel strives to make the treatment of the mentally ill more humane. **PSYCH**
1801	The usual treatment for the mentally ill in asylums includes bloodletting, bathing, and purging. **PSYCH**
1801	Frenchman Joseph-Marie Jacquard invents the Jacquard loom, which uses punched cards to guide needle motions so as to produce patterned textiles. Later in the century (*see* 1834), Charles Babbage will realize that punched cards can control calculator processes, preparing the way for the digital computer in the twentieth century. **TECH**
1802	German-English astronomer William Herschel discovers that the two brightest stars in Castor are a binary star system. **ASTRO**
1802	German astronomer Heinrich Wilhelm Olbers discovers Pallas, the second asteroid to be identified. **ASTRO**
1802	Swedish chemist Anders G. Ekeberg discovers the element tantalum. **CHEM**
c. 1802	Scottish physician Sir Charles Bell diagnoses Bell's palsy, a one-sided facial weakness or paralysis caused by compression of the facial nerve. **MED**
1802	French scientist Joseph-Louis Gay-Lussac demonstrates that the volume of a fixed mass of gas at constant pressure changes by a constant fraction for each degree of temperature change. First noted by Guillaume Amontons in 1699, this is now known as Charles's law (*see* 1787) or Gay-Lussac's law. *See also* 1808, Gay-Lussac. **PHYS**
1802	Italian scientist Gian Domenico Romagnosi discovers that electricity passing through a wire will cause a magnetic needle to orient itself perpendicular to the wire. **TECH**
1802	The first photograph is produced by British physician Thomas Wedgwood but fades quickly. He treats paper with silver nitrate to hold the photographic impression. **TECH**
1802	The first icebox, the progenitor of the refrigerator, is developed by U.S. farmer Thomas Moore. It consists of two wooden boxes, one within the other, with the space between them insulated by charcoal or ashes. A third box, made of tin, sits atop the smaller box. **TECH**

Apr. 26, 1803   Witnesses at Orne, France, observe a bolide, or meteor in the form of an explosive fireball. Meteoritic stones are then found in the area. Physicist Jean-Baptiste Biot describes the event and determines that the meteorites did not originate on earth.   **ASTRO**

1803   Swedish chemist Jöns Jakob Berzelius, Swedish mineralogist Wilhelm Hisinger, and German chemist Martin H. Klaproth discover the element cerium.   **CHEM**

1803   British chemist Smithson Tennant discovers the element osmium. **CHEM**

1803   British chemist William H. Wollaston discovers the elements palladium and rhodium.   **CHEM**

1803   In his *Essay on Static Chemistry*, French chemist Claude-Louis Berthollet shows that reaction rates depend on the quantities of the reacting substances as well as their affinities.   **CHEM**

1803   British meteorologist Luke Howard coins names for types of clouds, including cumulus, cirrus, nimbus, and stratus.   **EARTH**

1803   French mathematician Lazare Carnot publishes *Géométrie de position*, a work establishing him as cofounder (with Gaspard Monge; *see* 1795) of modern pure geometry.   **MATH**

1803   American physician James Conrad Otto describes the first clear account of hemophilia.   **MED**

1803   English chemist John Dalton draws on existing evidence to argue that matter is made up of tiny particles called atoms, a word coined by Democritus in 460 B.C. He establishes the concept of atomic weight—different masses for the atoms of different elements—though his preliminary table of atomic weights contains many errors. *See* 1818, Berzelius.   **PHYS**

1803   U.S. engineer Robert Fulton builds his first steam-powered ship. **TECH**

1804   Swiss botanist Nicolas-Théodore de Saussure stresses the importance of soil nitrogen and carbon dioxide to green plants. He also demonstrates plants' capacity to absorb water.   **BIO**

1804   British chemist Smithson Tennant discovers the element iridium. **CHEM**

1804   In the first high-altitude research flight, French scientists Jean-Baptiste Biot and Joseph-Louis Gay-Lussac ascend four miles in a balloon to study the atmosphere and the earth's magnetic field.   **EARTH**

1804–1806   Americans Meriwether Lewis and William Clark explore the region known as the Louisiana Purchase, from the Mississippi River to the Rocky Mountains, and push on west to the Pacific Ocean.   **EARTH**

1804   Italian physician Antonio Scarpa describes arteriosclerosis as lesions coating the lining of arteries.   **MED**

1804   French surgeon René Laënnec describes peritonitis, an inflammation of the membranes lining the abdomen.   **MED**

Simia Ursina, illustration from Alexander von Humboldt's *Observations of Zoology and Comparative Zoology*. (*Bibliothéque Nationale, Paris*)

1804   The first steam locomotive to operate on a railroad, constructed by British inventor Richard Trevithick, travels nearly ten miles and achieves speeds of almost five miles per hour.   **TECH**

1804   The first foods to be vacuum packed are packaged by Nicolas Appert at his factory in France.   **TECH**

1805   After twenty years of analyzing the proper motion of stars, William Herschel shows that the sun, together with its planets, is moving through the galaxy.   **ASTRO**

1805   German explorer and botanist Alexander von Humboldt publishes his *Essai sur la géographie des plantes*, about his five-year voyage to the Americas, thus introducing plant geography.   **BIO**

Nov. 15, 1805   The Lewis and Clark expedition reaches the Pacific Ocean, completing the first overland trip by settlers across what is now the United States of America.   **EARTH**

1805   German mathematician Peter Gustav Lejeune Dirichlet is born (*d.* 1859). He will show the value of applying analysis to number theory and introduce Dirichlet's theorem and the Dirichlet series. He will also contribute the Dirichlet principle to the calculus of variations.   **MATH**

"Organic chemistry just now is enough to drive one mad. It gives me the impression of a primeval tropical forest full of the most remarkable things, a monstrous and boundless thicket with no way of escape, and into which one may well dread to enter."—Baron Jöns Jakob Berzelius, Swedish chemist; early nineteenth century

1805   German pharmacist Friedrich Sertürner extracts morphine from opium and uses it to relieve pain.   **MED**

1805   French scientist Pierre Simon de Laplace proposes his theory of capillary forces.   **PHYS**

1805   German naturalist Johann Friedrich Blumenbach founds the science of physical anthropology.   **SOC**

1805   The first covered bridge in America opens, over the Schuylkill River in Pennsylvania.   **TECH**

1806   Italian botanist Giovanni Amici determines the importance of intercellular space for gas conduction in plants.   **BIO**

1806   French chemist Louis-Nicolas Vauquelin discovers the compound asparagine, which will turn out to be the first known amino acid.   **CHEM**

1806   Scotsman Patrick Clark develops a cotton thread that rivals silk thread in strength. With his brother James, Clark opens a thread-making factory. Eventually, cotton thread will become the thread of choice.   **TECH**

1807   British chemist Humphry Davy discovers the elements sodium and potassium.   **CHEM**

1807   Swedish chemist Jöns Jakob Berzelius distinguishes organic from inorganic compounds, defining organic compounds as those obtained from living or dead organisms or related to such compounds and inorganic compounds as all others.   **CHEM**

1807   Humphry Davy develops the science of electrochemistry, following the discovery in 1800 by William Nicholson that an electric current can decompose water into oxygen and hydrogen.   **CHEM**

1807   Swiss geodesist Ferdinand R. Hassler convinces American President Thomas Jefferson and Treasury Secretary Albert Gallatin to establish a Survey of the Coast. **EARTH**

Nov. 13, 1807   The Geological Society of London is founded. This scientific organization will maintain a library and study collection, discuss and disseminate geological observations, and adopt a single nomenclature. **EARTH**

1807   French mathematician Jean-Baptiste-Joseph Fourier, demonstrates Fourier's theorem, that any periodic oscillation can be expressed as a series of trigonometric functions known as a Fourier series. *See also* 1822, Fourier. **MATH**

1807   English physicist Thomas Young introduces the physical concept of energy. **PHYS**

1807   Thomas Young develops the coefficients of elasticity of materials. **PHYS**

1807   The 133-foot S.S. *Clermont* begins regular cargo service between New York and Albany, becoming the first commercially successful steamship. Designed by Robert Fulton, it uses a Boulton and Watt engine and paddlewheels, which will become a distinguishing feature of steamboats for years to come. **TECH**

1808   British chemist Humphry Davy discovers the elements barium, calcium, magnesium, and strontium. **CHEM**

1808   Davy and French chemists Joseph-Louis Gay-Lussac and Louis-Jacques Thénard discover the element boron. **CHEM**

1808   French scientist Joseph-Louis Gay-Lussac shows that when gases combine chemically, the volume of the reactants and of the product (if gaseous) bear simple relationships to one another, given constant temperature and pressure. This principle is the one usually known as Gay-Lussac's law, though his discovery in 1803 concerning the relationship of volume and temperature change in gases sometimes also goes by the same name. **PHYS**

1808   Studying sunlight that has passed through a crystal of Icelandic feldspar (*see* 1669, Bartholin), French physicist Étienne-Louis Malus (1775–1812) discovers the polarization of light. **PHYS**

1808   English chemist John Dalton publishes his *New System of Chemical Philosophy*, formalizing arguments for atomic theory he advanced as early as 1803. **PHYS**

1809   French zoologist Jean-Baptiste de Lamarck introduces the first scientific theory on how evolution occurs, now known as Lamarckism. According to him, offspring can inherit characteristics or traits that their parents have acquired during the parents' lifetime. This concept will later be discredited by Charles Darwin and August Weissman. **BIO**

1809 English naturalist Charles Darwin is born (*d*. 1882). In his 1859 book *On the Origin of Species*, he will explain the theory of evolution by natural selection, which will revolutionize the life sciences and humanity's understanding of its own origins. He will acquire much of his evidence during his voyage on the H.M.S. *Beagle* (1831–1836). He will also discuss human evolution (in *The Descent of Man*, 1871) and write on the origin of coral reefs. **BIO**

1809 American physician Ephraim McDowell successfully, without anesthesia, removes a twenty-two-pound ovarian tumor. He will be considered the father of ovariotomy. **MED**

1809 The first ocean voyage by steamboat is completed, by U.S. seaman Moses Rogers traveling from New York City to the Delaware River by way of Cape May, New Jersey. **TECH**

1810s The term *morphology* is introduced to describe the study of organic form. It particularly concerns the unity underlying plant and animal diversity. German naturalist and poet Johann Wolfgang von Goethe is among those to popularize the term. **BIO**

c. 1810s French mathematician Sophie Germain formulates Germain's theorem. A step toward proving Fermat's Last Theorem (*see* 1601), it shows the impossibility of positive integral solutions to $x^n + y^n = z^n$ if x, y, and z are prime to each other and to n, where n is any prime less than 100. **MATH**

1810 British chemist Humphry Davy is the first to identify chlorine as an element. *See also* 1774, Priestley and Scheele. **CHEM**

1810 French mathematician Joseph-Diez Gergonne begins publication of the first private mathematical journal, *Annales de mathématiques pures et appliquées*. **MATH**

1810 Between now and 1819, Austrian physician Franz Joseph Gall and his student Johann Spurzheim publish a five-volume work on phrenology, which attempts to develop a perfect knowledge of human nature based on measurements of multiple species' skulls and brains. They theorize that brain functions are localized in the cerebral cortex and that the brain is a bundle of individual organs governing the moral, sexual, and intellectual traits of human behavior. **PSYCH**

1810 The differential gear, used to steer and turn carriages, is developed by a German publisher, Rudolph Ackermann. **TECH**

1810 British inventor Peter Durand is issued a patent for an early version of a tin-plated receptacle that proves to be the precursor to the can. **TECH**

1811 German-English astronomer William Herschel theorizes that stars originate in nebulae. **ASTRO**

1811 French chemist Bernard Courtois discovers the element iodine. **CHEM**

1811   Italian physicist Amedeo Avogadro formulates Avogadro's hypothesis, or Avogadro's law, that equal volumes of all gases contain equal numbers of particles at the same temperature and pressure. The term he uses to describe these particles, which he believes to be combinations of atoms, is *molecules*.   **PHYS**

1811   Massachusetts General Hospital is established in Boston.   **MED**

1811   Scottish physician Charles Bell discovers spinal nerve functions, which convey impulses to and from the spinal cord.   **MED**

1811   British paleontologist Mary Anning discovers the first complete ichthyosaur skeleton.   **PALEO**

1811   Scottish physicist Sir David Brewster discovers Brewster's law, which says that the extent of the polarization of light reflected from a transparent surface is greatest when the reflected ray is at right angles to the refracted ray.   **PHYS**

1811   The S.S. *New Orleans* becomes the first steamship to traverse the Mississippi River Valley, on a fourteen-day trip from Pittsburgh to New Orleans.   **TECH**

1811   New York City planning officials adopt the so-called Commissioners' Plan, requiring streets north of Union Square to be aligned by a grid system, as in older Spanish cities.   **TECH**

1812   French botanist Augustin-Pyrame de Candolle is the first to use the word *taxonomy* for classification of species.   **BIO**

1812   Boiling starch in water and sulfuric acid, German-Russian chemist Gottlieb Sigismund Constantin Kirchhoff discovers glucose. He notes that starch is made up of glucose units and that the sulfuric acid was not consumed in the chemical reaction but made the reaction possible. Swedish chemist Jöns Jakob Berzelius will call the latter phenomenon *catalysis*.   **CHEM**

1812   French scientist and mathematician Pierre Simon de Laplace publishes significant work on analytic probability theory.   **MATH**

1812   French mathematician Siméon-Denis Poisson discovers the Poisson equation in potential theory.   **MATH**

1812   French mathematician Jean-Victor Poncelet formulates the principle of continuity, or the principle of permanence of mathematical relations, although it is not published until 1862–1864.   **MATH**

1812   New York City's Bellevue Hospital is formally established. *See also* 1736.   **MED**

1812   French anatomist Baron Cuvier discovers the first known fossil remains of a pterodactyl, a flying reptile. He also publishes his *Inquiry into Fossil Remains*, the first major work of paleontology. Although he describes extinct forms of life in detail and classifies them according to the Linnaean scheme, he does not consider them ancestors of living things but products of earlier, separate creations, each ending catastrophically. This view will become known as catastrophism.   **PALEO**

1812   French scientist Pierre Simon de Laplace posits a mechanistic model of the universe—one in which the entire history of the universe could theoretically be derived by knowing the mass, position, and velocity of every particle. This idea will prevail until Werner Heisenberg's uncertainty principle (*see* 1927) articulates the limits of human knowledge of the physical universe.   **PHYS**

1812   English chemist and physicist William H. Wollaston invents the camera lucida, a device that projects the image of an object onto a flat surface, such as a piece of paper, where a drawing of it can be traced.   **TECH**

1813   Swedish chemist Jöns Jakob Berzelius proposes a system of chemical symbols that will be widely adopted: capital letters for atoms—with lowercase letters to distinguish elements such as Ca (Calcium) from Cl (Chlorine)—and, for compounds, combinations of these symbols with appropriate lowercase numerals representing the number of atoms in molecules (e.g., H_2O for water).   **CHEM**

1813   London author Robert Bakewell publishes his influential English geology textbook *Introduction to Geology*. It basically adheres to Abraham G. Werner's ideas but reveals some of James Hutton's influence.   **EARTH**

1813   German physician Johann Peter Frank publishes the first comprehensive treatise on public health. His credo is "to prevent evils through wise ordinances." Frank's suggestions, including food inspection, sanitation, prenatal care, and vital statistics on infectious diseases, are thought to be radical and are not accepted in many areas of Europe.   **MED**

1813   American physician Thomas Sutton distinguishes between hallucinations caused by organic brain inflammation and delirium tremens, caused by alcohol addiction and withdrawal.   **PSYCH**

1814   While observing sunlight that has passed through a slit and then a prism, German physicist Joseph von Fraunhofer discovers spectral lines. He maps many of the lines produced by sunlight (now called Fraunhofer lines).   **ASTRO**

1814   French scientists J. J. Colin and H. G. de Claubry discover the starch-iodine reaction. French scientist F. V. Raspail applies it microscopically, founding the study of cells' chemical components, histochemistry.   **BIO**

1814   Swedish chemist Jöns Jakob Berzelius theorizes that compounds consist of positively charged and negatively charged components.   **CHEM**

1814   A gas lighting works is erected in London. In it the gas filters out from a central location to local gas mains.   **TECH**

1814   The first steam locomotive, developed by George Stephenson, to transport coal through England, inaugurates the mass use of railroad transportation. The design is based on the 1804 one of Richard Trevithick.   **TECH**

1814   The first commercially sold tinned food is produced, at the Donkin-Hall factory in England. Tinned food had earlier been produced in England but only for the military.   **TECH**

1815   German astronomer Heinrich Wilhelm Olbers discovers a comet, which he names for himself. He proposes that a comet's tail is a cloud of matter expelled from the nucleus, which always points away from the sun, due to a repulsion effect.   **ASTRO**

1815   Between now and 1822, French naturalist Jean-Baptiste de Lamarck becomes the first to use the terms *vertebrate* and *invertebrate*. With his seven-volume work, the *Natural History of Invertebrates*, Lamarck founds modern invertebrate biology.   **BIO**

1815   French physicist Jean-Baptiste Biot discovers that the plane of polarized light is twisted in different directions by different organic liquids. He speculates that this difference is caused by asymmetry in organic molecules.   **CHEM**

1815   French scientist Joseph-Louis Gay-Lussac discovers the poisonous gas cyanogen (C_2N_2), noting the extreme stability of the cyano group, the carbon-nitrogen combination, which is the first known organic radical.   **CHEM**

1815   English chemist William Prout advances Prout's hypothesis, that hydrogen is the fundamental atom out of which all other atoms are made. This hypothesis will appear to be disproven by the subsequent discovery of atomic weights that are not exact multiples of hydrogen's, though the later discovery of thermonuclear fusion will show that Prout was partly right.   **CHEM**

1815   English mathematicians Charles Babbage, John Herschel, and George Peacock found the Analytic Society to emphasize the abstract nature of algebra and bring new continental developments in mathematics to Britain.   **MATH**

1815   During the Napoleonic wars, French surgeon Dominique-Jean Larrey introduces "flying ambulances," man-powered litters to pick up the wounded during battle instead of leaving them unattended until the fighting ends.   **MED**

1815   William Smith publishes *The Geological Map of England*, the first book to classify rock strata on the basis of characteristic fossils. *See also* 1799.   **PALEO**

1815   French physicist Baron Augustin Louis Cauchy develops mathematical formulas for describing turbulence.   **PHYS**

1815   Macadam, a moisture-resistant road covering made of bits of stone, is developed by Scottish surveyor John McAdam.   **TECH**

1816   French mathematician Sophie Germain develops a mathematical model to calculate the vibration of elastic surfaces.   **MATH**

1816   French physician René Laënnec invents the modern stethoscope. He uses the term *rales* for the air sound in bronchii when they contain secretions or are tightened by spasms.   **MED**

1816   The celeripede, a two-wheeled forerunner of the modern bicycle, is developed by French physicist Joseph Nicéphore Niepce.   **TECH**

1817   French chemists Pierre-Joseph Pelletier and Joseph-Bienaimé Caventou isolate and name chlorophyll.   **BIO**

1817   Hereford cattle are imported to America for the first time. The hardy breed will become the most popular cattle in the western United States.   **BIO**

1817   German chemist Friedrich Strohmeyer discovers the element cadmium.   **CHEM**

1817   Swedish chemist Johan August Arfwedson discovers the element lithium.   **CHEM**

1817   British physician James Parkinson describes the shaking palsy now called Parkinson's disease that is characterized by a slowly spreading fine muscle tremor.   **MED**

1817   Between now and 1818, American dentist Anthony Plantson introduces the dental plate.   **MED**

1817   In *The Principles of Political Economy and Taxation*, British economist David Ricardo advances influential theories on the determination of wages and value.   **SOC**

1818   French astronomer Jean-Louis Pons discovers the comet with the shortest known period (3.29 years), now called Encke's comet for German astronomer Johann Encke, who analyzes its orbit.   **ASTRO**

1818   Swedish chemist Jöns Jakob Berzelius discovers the element selenium.   **CHEM**

FRANKENSTEIN'S TEACHER

When Mary Shelley's novel Frankenstein was published in 1818, chemistry seemed the most powerful of sciences. New elements were being discovered, the atomic and molecular structure of matter was being analyzed, and the stuff of life itself, organic compounds, was yielding to the scientist. It was Shelley's inspiration that a young person might be lured by the glamour of scientific conquest to try things he would wish he had left alone. So she invented Victor Frankenstein, who brought a nonliving creature of his own design to life, providing grist for future horror stories and a metaphor that still haunts our conceptions of science. Here Frankenstein, a university student, is transfixed by a lecture from his chemistry teacher, Professor Waldman:

> "The ancient teachers of this science," said he [Waldman], "promised impossibilities and performed nothing. The modern masters promise very little; they know that metals cannot be transmuted and that the elixir of life is a chimera. But these philosophers, whose hands seem only made to dabble in dirt, and their eyes to pore over the microscope or crucible, have indeed performed miracles. They penetrate into the recesses of nature and show how she works in her hiding-places. They ascend into the heavens; they have discovered how the blood circulates, and the nature of the air we breathe. They have acquired new and almost unlimited powers; they can command the thunders of heaven, mimic the earthquake, and even mock the invisible world with its own shadows."

> Such were the professor's words—rather let me say such the words of the fate—enounced to destroy me. As he went on I felt as if my soul were grappling with a palpable enemy; one by one the various keys were touched which formed the mechanism of my being; chord after chord was sounded, and soon my mind was filled with one thought, one conception, one purpose. So much has been done, exclaimed the soul of Frankenstein—more, far more, will I achieve; treading in the steps already marked, I will pioneer a new way, explore unknown powers, and unfold to the world the deepest mysteries of creation.

1818   Berzelius publishes a table of atomic and molecular weights based on some two thousand analyses of chemicals performed over ten years. His tables are considerably more accurate than those of John Dalton. *See* 1803.   **CHEM**

1818   American geologist Benjamin Silliman establishes the *American Journal of Science*, through which he will gain an international reputation.   **EARTH**

1818   French chemist Louis-Jacques Thénard discovers hydrogen peroxide, a mild antiseptic and germicide.   **MED**

1818   French chemists Joseph Caventou and Pierre Pelletier isolate strychnine.   **MED**

1818   Scottish physician John Cheyne and Irish physician William Stokes describe a breathing pattern often associated with impending death: periods of no breathing (apnea), followed by increased respiration.   **MED**

1818   In the Connecticut Valley, Solomon Ellsworth Jr. and Nathan Smith discover fossil bones of the dinosaur *Anchisaurus*, but the significance of this find is not initially understood.   **PALEO**

1818   French physicist Augustin-Jean Fresnel argues that light is a transverse, not longitudinal, wave, as Thomas Young (*see* 1801) had thought.   **PHYS**

1819   French chemists Pierre-Louis Dulong and Alexis-Thérèse Petit show that the specific heat of an element, the amount of heat required to raise its temperature 1° C, is inversely proportional to its atomic weight.   **CHEM**

1819   German chemist Eilhardt Mitscherlich states Mitscherlich's law, or the law of isomorphism, that substances with the same crystal structure have similar chemical formulae.   **CHEM**

1819   Paris author J. F. d'Aubuisson de Voisins publishes the first successful French geology textbook, which mainly follows Abraham Werner's theories.   **EARTH**

1819   In New Haven, Connecticut, the American Geological Society is founded.   **EARTH**

1819   In works published now and in 1832, French mathematican Adrien-Marie Legendre develops several important tools of analysis, including the Legendre functions, which are solutions of the Legendre differential equation.   **MATH**

1819   French chemists Joseph Caventou and Pierre Pelletier isolate the antimalarial substance quinine.   **MED**

1819	Rome and Utica, New York, are joined in the opening of the first part of the Erie Canal. The canal was two years in construction, mainly by thousands of immigrants. **TECH**
1819	The first transatlantic trip by sail/steamship is completed as the U.S.S. *Savannah* travels from Georgia to Liverpool, England. **TECH**
1820s	French·biologist Baron Cuvier makes a major contribution to morphology with his arrangement of animals into four groups: vertebrates, articulates, mollusks, and radiates. **BIO**
1820s	French mathematician Augustin Louis Cauchy develops the foundation of the calculus as it is now generally known. Using d'Alembert's limit concept (*see* 1760s) to define the derivative of a function, he takes significant steps toward the arithmetization of analysis. **MATH**
1820s	Between now and the 1840s, during the age of reform in the United States, many poorhouses (almshouses) are built, filled with the poor and mentally ill. They are used as clinical laboratories for medical students. **MED**
c. 1820	The statue *Venus de Milo* is discovered on the Greek island of Melos. **ARCH**
1820	English scientists John Herschel and Charles Babbage are among the founding members of the Royal Astronomical Society. **ASTRO**
1820	The Royal Observatory at Cape Town is established to make observations in the Southern Hemisphere comparable with those made at Greenwich. **ASTRO**
1820	French naturalist Henri Braconnot uses hydrolysis to obtain glucose from materials such as linen, bark, and sawdust. He is also the first to isolate, from gelatin, the amino acid glycine. **CHEM**
1820	Twenty-one-year-old American sealer Nathaniel Brown Palmer is the first to explore the Antarctic Peninsula. **EARTH**
1820	French chemists and physicians demonstrate the value of iodine in treating goiter. **MED**
1820	The United States's first pharmacopeia is published. **MED**
1820	Danish physicist Hans Christian Oersted shows that electricity and magnetism are related, noting that a magnetic needle moves when electricity flows through a nearby wire. Experiments by French physicists André-Marie Ampère and François Arago support Oersted's finding, establishing the concept of electromagnetism. **PHYS**
1820	German physicist Joseph von Fraunhofer invents the diffraction grating, a device composed of fine, closely spaced wires used in producing light spectra. **PHYS**

1820   French physicist André-Marie Ampère shows that a wire helix or
          solenoid acts like a bar magnet when electric current flows through
          it. He also states the right-hand rule for the action of an electric cur-
          rent on a magnet.   **PHYS**

1820   Physicist Dominique-François Arago shows that iron is not the only
          magnetic substance when he magnetizes a copper wire by passing
          electricity through it.   **PHYS**

1820   German physicist Johann Salomo Christoph Schweigger
          (1779–1857) invents the galvanometer, an instrument for measur-
          ing electric current.   **TECH**

1821   Austrian chemist Johann Joseph Loschmidt is born (d. 1895). He
          will develop the practice of using single lines for single bonds, dou-
          ble lines for double bonds, and so on. He will also calculate
          Avogadro's number (see 1865) and determine that the structures of
          aromatic compounds contain a benzene ring.   **CHEM**

1821   Anthropologist Gabriel de Mortillet is born in France (d. 1898). He
          will be the first to distinguish the subdivisions of the Paleolithic
          (Old Stone) Age, which lasted from about 2.5 million to 9,000 years
          ago. These periods, identified on the basis of their characteristic
          stone tools, will include the Acheulian and the Mousterian.   **PALEO**

1821   British physicist Michael Faraday is the first to speak about electro-
          magnetism as a field in which particles generate lines of force. In
          an experiment with magnets and electrified wires he shows that
          electricity can produce motion.   **PHYS**

1821   Russian-German physicist Thomas Johann Seebeck notes the
          Seebeck effect, which states that two different metals will generate
          electricity if their points of juncture are maintained at different
          temperatures. This is the first known example of thermoelectricity,
          or electricity generated by temperature difference.   **PHYS**

1822   French linguist Jean-François Champollion founds modern
          Egyptology when he deciphers the ancient Egyptian hieroglyphics
          inscribed on the Rosetta Stone (see 1799).   **ARCH**

1822   English antiquarian William Bullock recovers relics and casts of
          Aztec artifacts from Teotihuacán and other sites in the Valley of
          Mexico.   **ARCH**

1822   After two centuries, the Roman Catholic church lifts its ban on the
          works of Copernicus, Galileo, and Kepler. See also 1835.   **ASTRO**

1822   William Daniel Congbeare and William Phillips publish a textbook
          of stratigraphy that becomes a basic field manual for geologists.
          Congbeare and Phillips are the first to identify the Carboniferous
          period.   **EARTH**

1822   Mineralogist Alexandre Brongniart and zoologist A. G. Desmarest publish the first extensive study of trilobites. Their work will influence future investigations of Paleozoic stratigraphy.   **EARTH**

1822   French mathematician Jean-Victor Poncelet begins the study of projective geometry, which analyzes the shadows cast by geometric figures, as a field separate from analytical and algebraic geometry. **MATH**

1822   Chemist Georges-Simon Serulas discovers iodoform and its antibacterial action.   **MED**

1822   Jean-Baptiste-Julien d'Halloy identifies the Cretaceous period of earth's history.   **PALEO**

1822   In his *Analytical Theory of Heat*, French mathematician Jean-Baptiste-Joseph, Baron Fourier, applies his Fourier theorem (*see* 1807) to the study of heat flow. This work also introduces the mathematical technique of dimensional analysis, in which an equation or solution is checked by analyzing the consistency of the dimensions in which it is expressed.   **PHYS**

1822   German philologist and folklorist Jakob Grimm formulates Grimm's law, a principle of relationships in Indo-European languages dealing with shifts in consonants in the development of English and the other Germanic languages.   **SOC**

1822   British engineer George Stephenson builds the first iron railroad bridge in the world.   **TECH**

1822   In England, American inventor William Church patents the first typesetting machine, which combines automatic composition with manual activity to set words and line length.   **TECH**

1822   The first lasting photograph is produced by French physicist Joseph Niepce. The photograph is made permanent through the use of asphaltum.   **TECH**

1823   German astronomer Joseph von Fraunhofer invents the first lensed telescope to be mounted equatorially with a clock drive.   **ASTRO**

1823   German chemist Johann Wolfgang Döbereiner discovers that powdered platinum is an effective catalyst for hydrogen reactions. **CHEM**

1823   British physicist Michael Faraday systematically uses cold and pressure to liquefy gases, beginning with chlorine.   **CHEM**

1823   Exploring Nigeria overland, Scotsman Hugh Clapperton becomes the first European to sight Lake Chad.   **EARTH**

1823   British physicist William Sturgeon invents the electromagnet, a magnet powered by an electric current.   **TECH**

1823   British inventor Francis Ronalds offers his electric telegraph system to the military but is rejected.   **TECH**

1823   A rubber-treated fabric is developed by Scottish scientist Charles Macintosh. It is a predecessor to the fabric used in the raincoat that will take this inventor's name.   **TECH**

c. 1824   Swedish chemist Jöns Jakob Berzelius discovers the element silicon.   **CHEM**

1824   Berzelius and French scientist Joseph-Louis Gay-Lussac identify the first known isomers, chemical compounds with the same molecular formulas but different molecular structures or arrangements of atoms, resulting in different properties. The formulas of the compounds are determined by German chemists Justus von Liebig and Friedrich Wöhler. *See also* 1830, Berzelius.   **CHEM**

1824   Norwegian mathematician Niels Henrik Abel shows that a general algebraic solution for equations of the fifth degree (quintic equations, those involving x^5) is impossible. *See also* 1830, Galois.   **MATH**

1824   English cleric and geologist William Buckland publishes a description of the Cretaceous carnivore *Megalosaurus*, identified from fossils in Stonesfield, England. It is the first dinosaur to be described, though the term *dinosaur* will not be introduced until the time of Richard Owen (*see* 1841).   **PALEO**

1824   Irish mathematician William Rowan Hamilton states the physical principle that an object or collection of objects always moves in such a way that the action has the least possible value.   **PHYS**

1824   French physicist Nicolas-Léonard-Sadi Carnot publishes *Reflections on the Motive Power of Fire*, the first scientific analysis of steam engine efficiency. Carnot will be considered the founder of thermodynamics, the study of the laws governing the conversion of energy from one form to another.   **PHYS**

1824   The Hartford (Connecticut) Retreat is founded for the humane treatment of mental illness. By the end of the century it will shift from being an innovative curative institution to a custodial one.   **PSYCH**

1824   Portland cement, a resilient water-resistant compound made from a heated mixture of chalk and clay, is patented by British bricklayer Joseph Aspdin.   **TECH**

1824   The first round barn is built, by the Shakers in Hancock, New York. Its design, with dividers that form feeding stations, will make it popular with farmers of dairy livestock.   **TECH**

1825   Danish physicist Hans Christian Oersted discovers the element aluminum.   **CHEM**

1825   British scientist Michael Faraday isolates benzene from whale oil. **CHEM**

1825   The full length of the 363-mile Erie Canal opens in New York State, providing a link between the Hudson River and the Great Lakes and sparking other canal projects.   **EARTH**

Excavation of the Erie Canal at Lockport, 1825. (*Library of Congress*)

1825   French mathematician Augustin Louis Cauchy develops complex
             function theory and introduces Cauchy's integral theorem with
             residues.   **MATH**

c. 1825   French physician François Broussais (1772–1838) believes that the
             body's vital functions depend on inflammation or irritation. He
             claims nature has no healing power and it is necessary to stop dis-
             ease by taking active measures—notably bloodletting and leeching.
             He prescribes applying up to one hundred leeches a day to control
             a patient's inflammation and disease.   **MED**

1825   French physician Jean-Baptiste Bouillaud is the first to describe
             aphasia, an inability or difficulty speaking, and link it to trauma in
             the brain's anterior lobe.   **MED**

1825   British physician and paleontologist Gideon Mantell claims that
             fossil teeth discovered in Tilgate Forest, England, belong to an ex-
             tinct reptile, which he calls *Iguanodon*, the second dinosaur to be
             discovered.   **PALEO**

1825   On a 27-mile line the first steam train passenger service is offered,
             by the Stockton & Darlington Railway in England. The first U.S.
             passenger line, the Baltimore & Ohio, will begin to be built in
             Maryland in 1828.   **TECH**

1826   German astronomer Heinrich Wilhelm Olbers poses Olbers's para-
              dox: if the stars are distributed uniformly through infinite, unchang-
              ing space, why is the sky dark at night? Everywhere one looks,
              there should be a star. The Big Bang theory in the twentieth centu-
              ry will explain this paradox by showing that the universe is lumpy,
              finite, and changing.   **ASTRO**

1826   German-Russian embryologist Karl Ernst von Baer discovers the
              eggs of mammals and states that "every animal which springs from
              the coition of male and female is developed from an ovum, and
              none from a simple formative fluid." His later two-volume *History
              of the Development of Animals* is one of the founding works of mod-
              ern embryology. His studies in comparative embryology will offer
              ways of demonstrating the likeness of various animal forms.   **BIO**

1826   French chemist Antoine-Jérôme Balard discovers bromine.   **CHEM**

1826   French chemist Jean-Baptiste-André Dumas invents a technique for
              measuring the vapor densities of substances that are not gases at
              normal temperatures.   **CHEM**

AN IGUANODON PROPER

*D*inosaurs have been part of popular culture since life-sized models
of Mesozoic animals were first exhibited at the Crystal Palace in
Sydenham, England, in 1854. The audiences flocking to see the
movie Jurassic Park in 1993 were only the latest in a long tradition of dinosaur admirers. But few have taken dinosaur mania closer to heart than the
British town fathers who embedded a dinosaur in their civic coat of arms.

The dinosaur was the iguanodon, a large, bipedal herbivore of the
Cretaceous period (136–65 million years ago). The second dinosaur to be
discovered (after the megalosaurus, in 1824), it was identified in 1825 by
English physician and amateur paleontologist Gideon Mantell on the basis
of fossil teeth discovered in Tilgate Forest by his wife, Mary Ann. Then in
1834 Mantell identified a partial skeleton of the creature, which W. H.
Bensted had dug out of his quarry in Maidstone, Kent. Mantell acquired the
skeleton for his collection, but the town of Maidstone continued to feel a
sense of ownership. In 1949 the town fathers persuaded the Royal College
of Arms to let them show the dinosaur as a part of their civic shield. In the
words of the official citation, the coat of arms now reads, "On the dexter
side an Iguanodon proper Collared Gules suspended therefrom by a chain
Or a scroll of Parchment."

Aug. 18, 1826	Scottish explorer Gordon Laing is the first European to visit Timbuktu in Africa. **EARTH**
1826	Russian mathematician Nikolai Ivanovich Lobachevsky publishes the first non-Euclidean geometry, which includes this axiom: "Through a given point, not on a given line, any number of lines can be drawn parallel to a given line." Hungarian mathematician János Bolyai will independently publish the same geometry in 1832. **MATH**
1826	German engineer August Leopold Crelle begins publication of the influential periodical *Journal für die reine und angewandte Mathematik*. **MATH**
1826	French mathematicians Jean-Victor Poncelet and Joseph-Diez Gergonne independently discover the principle of duality in geometry. **MATH**
1826	Norwegian mathematician Niels Henrik Abel and German mathematician Carl Gustav Jacobi begin to develop the theory of elliptic functions. (German mathematician Carl Friedrich Gauss had earlier made some of the same discoveries but not published them.) **MATH**
1826	Between now and 1837 cholera is pandemic—that is, epidemic at the same time in many different parts of the world. **MED**
1826	The first commercially workable gas stove is developed by British businessman James Sharp, who will begin to mass produce it twelve years later. **TECH**
1827	Between now and 1839, American ornithologist and naturalist John James Audubon (1785–1851) publishes his multivolume ornithology collection, *Birds of America*, containing more than one thousand paintings of bird life. **BIO**
1827	British scientist Michael Faraday publishes *Chemical Manipulation*, a manual concerning distillation and other forms of chemical processing. **CHEM**
1827	German mathematicians A. F. Möbius, Julius Plücker, and Karl Wilhelm Feuerbach develop homogeneous coordinates. **MATH**
1827	British physician Richard Bright describes nephritis, a kidney disease which will be named for him. **MED**
1827	Irish physicians Robert Adams and William Stokes discover a form of altered consciousness (now called the Stokes-Adams syndrome) caused by decreased blood flow to the brain as the result of a heart block. **MED**
1827	German physicist Georg Simon Ohm defines Ohm's law, that the flow of current through a conductor is directly proportional to the potential difference and inversely proportional to the resistance. **PHYS**

Great Horned Owls by John James Audubon. (*New-York Historical Society*)

1827   Scottish botanist Robert Brown discovers the phenomenon called Brownian motion, the continuous random movement of microscopic solid particles when suspended in a fluid.   **PHYS**

1827   Irish mathematician and physicist William Hamilton unifies the study of optics and correctly predicts conical refraction in his *Theory of Systems of Rays.* **PHYS**

1827   Public transportation begins in New York City with the inauguration by Abraham Bower of a twelve-seat horsedrawn bus. **TECH**

....

"Research gave the unexpected result that, by combination of cyanic acid with ammonia, urea is formed. A noteworthy fact since it furnishes an example of the artificial production of an organic—indeed, a so-called animal—substance from inorganic materials!"—Friedrich Wöhler, German chemist; on his synthesis of urea, 1828

....

1828   After classifying four major vegetation periods from the Carboniferous to the Tertiary, French botanist Adolphe Brongniart (1801–1876) sorts the plant kingdom into six classes: agamae, cellular cryptogams, vascular cryptogams, gymnosperms, monocotyledonous angiosperms, and dicotyledonous angiosperms. **BIO**

1828   Swedish chemist Jöns Jakob Berzelius discovers the·element thorium. **CHEM**

1828   German chemist Friedrich Wöhler is the first to synthesize an organic compound from inorganic chemicals in the laboratory when he synthesizes urea, the principal waste product found in urine. This experiment shows that organic compounds do not occur only in living things. **CHEM**

1828   English mathematician George Green publishes the first attempt at a mathematical theory of electromagnetism, his *Essay on the Application of Mathematical Analysis to Theories of Electricity and Magnetism.* **PHYS**

1828   The *Cherokee Phoenix*, the first Native American newspaper, is published. It is written and printed in the Cherokee alphabet, which was developed in 1824 by Cherokee linguist Sequoia. **TECH**

1828   The blast furnace is developed for use in iron production by Scottish inventor James Beaumont Neilson. **TECH**

1828   An inexpensive process for making chocolate candy is patented by Dutch chocolatier Conrad van Houten. The solid form of chocolate is made possible by an extraction process that yields the cocoa butter needed to bind the dry ingredients (sugar and cocoa powder) together. **TECH**

1829   French geologist Alexandre Brongniart gives the name Jurassic to the period lasting from 190 to 139 million years ago, following the Triassic. This second period of the Mesozoic era was named for the Jura Mountains of France and Switzerland.   **EARTH**

1829   Searching for Noah's ark in eastern Turkey, German Johann Jacob von Parrot scales Mount Ararat.   **EARTH**

1829   Scottish physicist William Nicol invents the Nicol prism, a device for producing plane-polarized light (*see* 1815, Biot), that makes possible the technique of polarimetry.   **PHYS**

1829   Scottish scientist Thomas Graham, one of the founders of physical chemistry, formulates Graham's law (the law of gaseous diffusion), which says that the rate at which a gas diffuses is inversely proportional to the square root of its density.   **PHYS**

1829   French physicist Gaspard-Gustave de Coriolis coins the term *kinetic energy*.   **PHYS**

1829   Scottish philosopher James Mill publishes his *Analysis of the Phenomena of the Human Mind*, adding muscle sensation (kinesthesis), disorganized sensation (itching or tickling), and gastrointestinal tract sensations to Aristotle's classic five senses. Mill argues that the sensations from these eight senses are the basic elements of consciousness and ideas.   **PSYCH**

1829   American physicist Joseph Henry improves upon the electromagnet invented by William Sturgeon in 1823. By 1831 Henry's electromagnet can lift a ton of iron.   **TECH**

1829   The *Tom Thumb*, developed by American entrepreneur Peter Cooper, becomes the first U.S.-built locomotive.   **TECH**

1829   Through an accidental discovery by French photographer Louis Daguerre, silver iodide is found to be light sensitive.   **TECH**

1829   The Tremont House, the first modern hotel, with private sleeping quarters, opens in Boston.   **TECH**

1830s   British scholar William Whewell coins the word *scientist*.   **MISC**

c. 1830 British geologist Charles Lyell dismisses the idea of the comparative stability of the earth when he shows that a given fauna may be older than the land it inhabits. His evidence will be important in the development of biogeography, the study of the distribution of organisms through space and time.   **BIO**

1830   British optician Joseph Jackson Lister invents the achromatic microscope, which eliminates chromatic aberration, allowing the study of fine detail in cells and bacteria.   **BIO**

1830   Swedish chemist Nils G. Sefström discovers the element vanadium. **CHEM**

1830   Swedish chemist Jöns Jakob Berzelius coins the term *isomerism* to
              describe compounds with identical chemical composition but dif-
              ferent molecular structures and properties. The phenomenon was
              first noted by Berzelius and Joseph Gay-Lussac in 1824.   **CHEM**

c. 1830   Élie de Beaumont develops his influential doctrines on the origin of
              mountain ranges, including the basic ideas of tectonic upheaval
              and stratigraphical methods. In 1852 he will sum up his work in
              the three-volume *Notice sur les systèmes de montagnes*.   **EARTH**

....

**"Nowadays all is looked for at shops. To buy the thing ready
made is the taste of the day: thousands who are housekeepers
buy their dinners ready cooked."—William Cobbett, political
writer, on the loss of domestic skills encouraged by the
industrial revolution; in Rural Rides, 1830**

....

1830   British geologist Charles Lyell begins the publication of his
              Principles of Geology (three volumes, 1830–1833), which establish-
              es the principle of uniformitarianism in place of the popular theory
              of catastrophism. This work lays the foundations of modern dy-
              namic geology but also has broad public appeal and helps to make
              geology a popular science.   **EARTH**

1830   Alexander Dallas Barche sets up the first U.S. magnetic observato-
              ry, in the garden of his home in Philadelphia.   **EARTH**

1830   French mathematician Évariste Galois invents group theory and
              shows that no equation of any degree higher than the fourth can be
              solved by algebraic methods. His work goes unpublished until
              1846. *See also* 1824, Abel.   **MATH**

1830   Charles Babbage publishes his *Reflections on the Decline of Science
              in England*, a critique of British science that results in the formation
              of the British Association for the Advancement of Science.   **MISC**

1830   P. C. Schmerling finds stone tools, human skulls, and mammoth
              bones buried together at a site in Belgium.   **PALEO**

1830   French tailor Barthélemy Thimmonier invents the first single-thread
              sewing machine.   **TECH**

1830   The T-rail, which will become standard equipment for rail lines, is
              invented by Robert Livingston Stevens.   **TECH**

1830   The world's first platform scale, the Fairbanks scale, is developed
              by American inventor Thaddeus Fairbanks. It operates through a
              system of levers and sliding weights as counterbalances.   **TECH**

1831   British botanist Robert Brown discovers the cell nucleus in plants. **BIO**

Cyrus Hall McCormick's reaper. (*International Harvester*)

1831   British naturalist Charles Darwin embarks on a five-year voyage
            aboard the H.M.S. *Beagle*. The ship's principal mission is to chart
            South America's coasts, but Darwin will take the opportunity to
            study the flora and fauna of many regions. These researches will
            form the basis for his theory of evolution by natural selection pub-
            lished in 1859.   **BIO**

1831   American chemist Samuel Guthrie discovers the compound chloro-
            form, which will gain wide use as an anesthetic.   **CHEM**

c. 1831   English geologist Adam Sedgwick engages in field work studying rock
            succession and the structure of the mountains in North Wales. **EARTH**

1831   American meteorologist William Redfield publishes a chart of the
            hurricane of 1821, establishing the rotary motion of tropical storms
            and identifying their region of origin and paths.   **EARTH**

1831   English physicist Michael Faraday and American physicist Joseph
            Henry independently discover that a changing magnetic force can
            generate electricity, a process called electromagnetic induction. **PHYS**

1831   Michael Faraday invents the dynamo, or electric generator, capable
            of producing electricity indefinitely by the turning of a copper
            wheel across magnetic lines of force.   **TECH**

1831   Joseph Henry invents the electric motor, in which electric current is
            used to turn a wheel.   **TECH**

1831   French chemist Charles Sauria invents the first practical phosphorus
            match, which lights by friction when struck on a rough surface. **TECH**

1831   The new London Bridge, which replaces the 900-year-old original,
            is opened to traffic across the Thames River.   **TECH**

1831   Cast iron that can be molded into a variety of shapes is patented by U.S. inventor Seth Boyden.   **TECH**

1831   American farmer Cyrus Hall McCormick develops and demonstrates his horse-drawn reaper. Operating through a series of mechanical knives, claws, and a metal receptacle, it vastly improves the efficiency of farming and will be used widely.   **TECH**

1832   British physicist Michael Faraday studies electrolysis, the production of a chemical reaction by passing electric current through a liquid or solution (an electrolyte), and describes the basic laws of electrolysis.   **CHEM**

1832   Irish physician Dominic Corrigan describes a full bounding pulse, now known to be Corrigan's pulse, associated with heart disease.   **MED**

1832   British physician Thomas Hodgkin describes a disease that enlarges the lymph tissue, spleen, and liver. Now known as Hodgkin's disease, it comes to be classified under general lymphomas.   **MED**

1832   The first cholera outbreak in the United States is initially considered to be the plight of the sinful, from its concentration among immigrants and in impoverished big cities.   **MED**

THE ROMANTIC MATHEMATICIAN

French mathematical genius Évariste Galois (1811–1832) had a short, tragic life befitting the age of romanticism. The son of a mayor of a small town near Paris, he participated on the republican side in the Revolution of 1830, was arrested for alleged threats against King Louis Philippe, tried without success to get papers published by the Academy, and finally died at age twenty in a duel over a woman. The night before the duel, fearing the worst, he wrote a letter to a friend summarizing his discoveries in the theory of equations and asking that they be submitted for comment to the era's leading mathematicians. "After this," he wrote, "there will be, I hope, some people who will find it to their advantage to decipher all this mess."

As it turned out, Galois's "mess" contained a unifying theory of groups that would prove crucial to modern algebra, geometry, and physics. This work did not reach a wide audience until 1846, when most of Galois's papers were finally published in the Journal de mathématiques. Now considered a major figure in nineteenth-century mathematics, Galois fulfilled the romantic destiny of the hero who burns brightly but briefly.

1832   Scottish phrenologist George Combe continues the earlier work of Franz Joseph Gall and Johann Spurzheim, but turns phrenology into more of a faddish cult than a science. He will help form more than forty-five regional phrenological societies that will flourish in the early twentieth century.   **PSYCH**

1832   The first fully fashioned clipper ship, the *Ann McKim*, is built in Baltimore for local businessman Isaac McKim.   **TECH**

1833   German astronomer Friedrich Wilhelm Bessel completes a catalog of fifty thousand stars begun in 1821.   **ASTRO**

· ·

"The whole of the developments and operations of analysis are now capable of being executed by machinery....As soon as an Analytical Engine exists, it will necessarily guide the future course of science."—Charles Babbage, English mathematician and inventor; on his early nineteenth-century unrealized vision of what we now call the computer

· ·

1833   The first European magnetic observatory is established, at Göttingen, Germany.   **ASTRO**

1833   French chemist Anselme Payen isolates diastase, a plant enzyme that speeds the conversion of starch into glucose. It is the first known organic catalyst that is not itself an organism.   **CHEM**

1833   British mathematician Charles Babbage publishes *On the Economy of Machinery and Manufactures*, which presents an early form of operations research.   **MATH**

1833   American physician William Beaumont studies the reaction of the stomach to food, liquid, and emotions through an unhealed abdominal gunshot wound. The wounded man had lived, but the open gastric fistula left a window into the digestion process.   **MED**

1833   British geologist Charles Lyell identifies new epochs to earth's history: the Recent, Pliocene, Miocene, and Eocene.   **PALEO**

1833   English physicists Michael Faraday and William Whewell coin a number of terms related to electricity, including *electrode, cathode, anode, ion, cation, anion, electrolyte,* and *electrolysis*.   **PHYS**

1833   American house construction is revolutionized by the development of the balloon frame house by U.S. builder Augustus Deodat Taylor. Its simple wood frame, made of two-by-fours, is sturdier and easier to build than previous designs.   **TECH**

1833   For the first time, rollers rather than millstones are used to grind grain in a practice introduced by a Swiss miller.   **TECH**

1834   Danish scholar Christian Jorgensen Thomsen divides the history of humanity into the Stone Age, the Bronze Age, and the Iron Age. **ARCH**

1834   British mathematician and astronomer John Herschel begins the first thorough survey of the southern stars. He notes that the Magellanic clouds discovered by Ferdinand Magellan in 1519–1521 are composed of many individual stars. **ASTRO**

1834   French chemist Anselme Payen discovers cellulose, the main constituent of the cell walls of higher plants. **CHEM**

1834   Mining engineer and geologist J. Charpentier advances the geological understanding of glaciers with his paper *Notice sur la cause probable du transport des blocs erratiques de la Suisse.* **EARTH**

1834   W. H. Bensted and Gideon Mantell discover a partial skeleton of *Iguanodon* in Maidstone, England (*see also* 1825). During this decade five other dinosaur genera are discovered: *Hylaeosaurus*, *Macrodontophion*, *Thecodontosaurus*, *Paleosaurus*, and *Plateosaurus*. **PALEO**

1834   German geologist Friedrich von Alberti introduces the Triassic (threefold) system of dating fossils. The oldest and lowest rocks are the Buntsandstein, with Muschelkalk rocks intermediate and Keuper rocks the highest and youngest. *See also* 1780 and c. 1800. **PALEO**

1834   French physicist Jean-Charles-Athanase Peltier discovers the so-called Peltier effect, the change in temperature produced when an electric current passes through a juncture between two different metals or semiconductors. **PHYS**

1834   German scholar J. F. Herbert describes *psychology*, a term originally introduced in 1734 by Christian von Wolff, as a science based on experience, mathematics, metaphysics, and possible experimentation. **PSYCH**

1834   English mathematician and inventor Charles Babbage begins work on an "analytical engine" to perform arithmetic operations on the basis of instructions from punched cards. Now regarded as the forerunner of the modern digital computer, this engine was never completed. **TECH**

1834   Hansom cabs, designed by British architect Joseph Aloysius Hansom, are used for passenger trade in London. **TECH**

1834   Braille, a system of raised print for the blind, is developed by French teacher Louis Braille, a blind man himself. **TECH**

1834   A compression machine that cools water through a process of heat absorption is introduced by American inventor Jacob Perkins. His invention promotes further study of gas refrigeration. **TECH**

1835   This year's edition of the Roman Catholic church's *Index of Prohibited Books* is the first since the seventeenth century not to include the heliocentric works of Copernicus, Galileo, and Kepler. The decision to lift the ban was actually made in 1822. **ASTRO**

1835	English naturalist Charles Darwin visits the Galapagos Islands off Ecuador. This island chain's distinctive life forms, particularly its finches, provide him with evidence for the evolution of species. **BIO**
1835	French chemist C. S. A. Thilorier creates dry ice when he succeeds in freezing carbon dioxide into a solid form. During his experiments he induces temperatures as low as −110° C, the lowest temperature yet reached on the earth's surface. **CHEM**
1835	Swedish chemist Jöns Jakob Berzelius coins the term *catalysis* for the action of agents that aid a chemical reaction but are not affected by it. **CHEM**
1835	French physicist Gaspard-Gustave de Coriolis describes the Coriolis force, which is the apparent deflection of a moving body caused by unequal rates of rotation between two rotating systems, such as the earth and the air. The Coriolis force will become important later in understanding winds and ocean currents. **EARTH**
1835	Irish physician Robert Graves describes the thyroid condition called Graves's disease. **MED**
1835	German physician Theodor Schwann discovers pepsin, the chief enzyme in gastric juice. **MED**
1835	English geologist Adam Sedgwick names the Cambrian period. **PALEO**
1835	Scottish geologist Roderick I. Murchison identifies the Silurian period. **PALEO**
1835	Physicist Heinrich Lenz formulates Lenz's law, that an induced electric current always flows in such a direction as to oppose the change producing it. **PHYS**
1835	Zinc-coated galvanized iron is developed in France. **TECH**
1836	British astronomer Francis Baily notes Baily's beads, the bright spots along the moon's edge visible during a total eclipse. **ASTRO**
1836	By use of a microscope, yeast is found to be a living organism. **BIO**
1836	French chemist Auguste Laurent shows that a chlorine atom can be substituted for a hydrogen atom in a compound without great change in the compound's properties. **CHEM**
1836	French mathematician Joseph Liouville founds the influential *Journal de Mathématiques Pures et Appliquées*. **MATH**
1836	British chemist John Frederic Daniell invents the Daniell cell, a battery that uses copper and zinc electrodes and is more reliable than the voltaic cell of 1800. **TECH**
1836	U.S. inventor Samuel Colt develops the Colt six-shooter revolver, which in many incarnations over the years becomes a popular firearm. **TECH**

1837	French mathematician Pierre Wantsel proves that doubling the cube and trisecting the angle are impossible using the ancient Greek rules of employing only a straightedge and compass for geometric constructions. Similarly, squaring the circle is later shown to be impossible. **MATH**

1837   French mathematician Siméon Poisson discovers Poisson's law, part of the theory of probability.   **MATH**

1837   The *Cambridge Mathematical Journal* is founded in England.   **MATH**

1837   Smallpox again ravages Native Americans, this time carried by whiskey peddlers on the Missouri River. Recourse to the traditional Native American remedy of sweat baths only makes the fever worse. Many Native Americans drown themselves in the river or cut their own throats to escape the pain and suffering of the disease.   **MED**

1837   French surgeon Marie-Jean-Pierre Flourens discovers that the lower portion of the brain stem, the medulla oblongata, is the body's respiratory center.   **MED**

1837   In England an electric telegraph is patented by scientists Charles Wheatstone and William Fothergill Cooke. In the United States a magnetic telegraph is patented by American inventor Samuel F. B. Morse. A Morse code to translate the English alphabet and Arabic numerals into dots and dashes is developed by Morse and his assistant Alfred Vail.   **TECH**

1837   The Pitman shorthand system, which translates phonetic sounds and common phrases into stylized page markings, is developed by Englishman Isaac Pitman.   **TECH**

1837   The first steam-powered thresher, more efficient than earlier versions, is patented by American inventors John and Hiram Pitts.   **TECH**

1838   German astronomer Friedrich Wilhelm Bessel is the first to correctly calculate the distance of a star. He uses a heliometer, a device for measuring distances in the sky, to measure the parallax of the star 61 Cygni and deduce its distance, about eleven light-years.   **ASTRO**

1838   Dutch chemist Gerardus Johannes Mulder coins the word *protein* (from the Greek for "first") to describe the molecule that is the basic building block of albuminous substances and, as is later found, of all living things.   **CHEM**

1838–1839   French archaeologist Jacques Boucher de Perthes presents his theory that unusual stone objects found near Abbeville, France, are tools made by humans sometime before the Great Flood.   **PALEO**

1838   British physicist Michael Faraday discovers a phosphorescent glow produced by electric discharges in low-pressure gases.   **PHYS**

1838   British physician Robert Gerdiner Hill, while serving as a surgeon at the Lincoln Asylum, institutes nonrestraint policies for mental patients, insisting that restraints are "never justifiable and always injurious."   **PSYCH**

1838   American psychiatrist J. Esquirol recommends applying leeches to the anus of mentally ill patients suffering from depression, then, after the leeches have formed hemorrhoids, removing the leeches and draining the hemorrhoids. This bloodletting is thought to draw the mental malady away from the patient's brain.   **PSYCH**

1838   French philosopher Auguste Comte coins the term *sociology*. He is considered the founder of this discipline as well as of the philosophical school known as positivism, which holds that the only real ("positive") knowledge is that which is gained by observation and experiment.   **SOC**

1838   The first transatlantic crossing by ships powered entirely by steam is completed by British ships the S.S. *Sirius* and S.S. *Great Western*, which travel from England to New York.   **TECH**

1839   John Lloyd Stephens and Frederick Catherwood begin an expedition in which they will discover Mayan ruins in Copán and other sites in Central America.   **ARCH**

1839   British astronomer Thomas Henderson makes a nearly correct estimate of the distance of the star Alpha Centauri at 4.3 light-years away.   **ASTRO**

1839   British naturalist Charles Darwin publishes the journal of his 1831–1836 voyage on the H.M.S. *Beagle. See also* 1831 and 1835.   **BIO**

1839   Swedish chemist Carl Gustaf Mosander discovers the rare earth element lanthanum.   **CHEM**

1839   In a joint paper titled "On the Physical Structure of Devonshire" Adam Sedgwick and Roderick Murchison name the Devonian period.   **PALEO**

1839   French inventor Louis Daguerre introduces the first commercially viable photographic process, the daguerreotype, in which a direct positive image is made on a silver-coated plate.   **TECH**

1839   British physicist William Robert Grove invents the fuel cell, an electric cell that runs on hydrogen and oxygen fuel, but the device is never made economical enough for general use.   **TECH**

1839   U.S. inventor Isaac Babbitt invents the group of alloys known as Babbitt metals used in making bearings.   **TECH**

1839   The first full-fledged bicycle is built in Scotland by blacksmith Kirkpatrick MacMillan. *See also* 1861, velocipede.   **TECH**

1839   American hardware buyer Charles Goodyear discovers a process to "vulcanize" rubber, by which it retains its elasticity in all weather. Previously, rubber became sticky in warm weather and brittle in cold.   **TECH**

1840s   At Nineveh, Iraq, British archaeologist Sir Austen Henry Layard begins to excavate the remains of the clay tablet library of King Assurbanipal of Assyria (669–663 B.C.). Later excavations in 1852–1854 uncover parts of the *Epic of Gilgamesh,* among other texts. *See* 1872.   **ARCH**

1840s   British naturalist Charles Darwin earns a reputation as a geologist, especially for his explanation of the formation of coral atolls.   **EARTH**

1840   German-born Russian astronomer Friedrich Wilhelm von Struve calculates the parallax of the star Vega, twenty-seven light-years away.   **ASTRO**

1840   Swiss-Russian chemist Germain Henri Hess formulates Hess's law, or the law of constant heat summation, which states that the amount of heat developed or absorbed in a chemical reaction is fixed, regardless of the route taken. This discovery marks the beginning of thermochemistry, the study of the interrelationship of heat and chemical reactions.   **CHEM**

ONLY THE NAME WAS GOODYEAR

*I*n 1839, when a combination of rubber, sulfur, and white lead overheated in shopkeeper Charles Goodyear's kitchen, a temperature-resistant rubber was created that would revolutionize transportation, public health, and everyday life. But credit for the material that lined a raincoat or formed the hose that brought water to a burning building would not go to Goodyear, who had depleted his savings and could not develop his findings in time to obtain the first patent.

Instead, the spoils for inventing vulcanized rubber went to scientists and entrepreneurs who used Goodyear's experimental findings. These included Englishman Thomas Hancock, who refined Goodyear's work and received the first British patent for durable rubber; and American surgeon Benjamin Franklin Goodrich, who foresaw the myriad uses of rubber, beginning with the rubber hose, and founded his own rubber-manufacturing business, the B. F. Goodrich Co., in 1870.

Even when the Goodyear Tire and Rubber Co. was founded in 1898 by Frank Sieberling, it was in no way affiliated with the inventor, a regular in debtors' prison who had died in 1860 nearly one-half million dollars in debt. In the case of the Goodyear Tire and Rubber Co., only the name was Goodyear.

1840   German-Swiss chemist Christian Friedrich Schönbein discovers ozone, later identified as a form of oxygen by Irish physical chemist Thomas Andrews.   **CHEM**

1840   Philadelphia physicist A. D. Bache sets up an elaborate magnetic observatory in a specially designed nonmagnetic building at Girard College.   **EARTH**

1840   Swiss zoologist and geologist Louis Agassiz advances his theory of ice ages in his *Études sur les glaciers*, using evidence of glaciation in Switzerland and other parts of Europe.   **EARTH**

1840   American explorer Charles Wilkes concludes that the South Polar land mass is continental in size. Twice as large as Australia, it lies almost completely within the Antarctic Circle.   **EARTH**

1840   In Philadelphia the Association of American Geologists is formally organized.   **EARTH**

1840   British physicist James P. Joule formulates the first of Joule's laws, describing the heat produced when an electric current flows through resistance for a given time. Joule's second law states that, for ideal gases, the internal energy of a given mass of gas is a function of temperature alone, not of volume or pressure.   **PHYS**

1840   French chemist Alexandre-Edmond Becquerel discovers that light can stimulate chemical reactions that result in an electric discharge.   **PHYS**

1840   The term *negative,* referring to the reverse image created during the photographic process, is coined by astronomer Sir F. W. Herschel.   **TECH**

1841   German astronomer Friedrich Wilhelm Bessel discovers that the star Sirius has a dark companion, Sirius B, which will later become the first known white dwarf star.   **ASTRO**

1841   Swiss embryologist Rudolf Albert von Kölliker describes spermatozoa and provides evidence to support neuron theory.   **BIO**

1841   Swedish chemist Jöns Jakob Berzelius discovers allotropy, the existence of two or more different forms of an element, when he converts charcoal into graphite.   **CHEM**

1841   Scottish missionary David Livingstone reaches Cape Town, then moves northward, attempting to convert Africans, becoming the first Westerner to explore the Kalahari Desert.   **EARTH**

1841   English anatomist and paleontologist Richard Owen describes two new genera of dinosaurs, *Cladeidon* and *Cetiosaurus*.   **PALEO**

1841   Richard Owen coins the name *Dinosauria* ("terrible lizard") for the group of reptiles that includes *Megalosaurus* and *Iguanodon*.   **PALEO**

1841   The first professional psychiatric association in the world, the Association of Medical Officers of Asylums and Hospitals for the Insane, is founded in England. In 1971 it will become known as the Royal College of Psychiatrists.   **PSYCH**

1841   American schoolteacher Dorothea Dix begins campaigning to reform the care of the mentally ill and poor in almshouses. Between 1841 and 1880 Dix is directly responsible for the creation of thirty-two new state insane asylums.   **PSYCH**

1841   Scottish surgeon James Braid witnesses demonstrations of mesmerism. Initially skeptical, he eventually proves that this "nervous sleep" can be induced by having a patient fixate on an object placed above the line of vision. Braid will later realize that suggestion is of primary importance to hypnosis. He will be considered the discoverer of hypnosis and credited with taking the phenomenon out of a magical, mystical arena and applying it to the physiological realm.   **PSYCH**

1841   British inventor William Henry Fox Talbot patents a new photographic process, which involves the making of a paper negative (the calotype) from which any number of paper positives can be printed. Talbot's calotype method, forerunner of modern photographic processes, will eventually supersede that of Louis Daguerre in 1839.   **TECH**

1841   In Paris, arc lights for streets are demonstrated.   **TECH**

1841   The first usable breech-loading (rather than muzzle-loading) rifle, the needle gun, is developed by Prussian gunmaker Johann Nikolaus von Dreyse.   **TECH**

1842   Austrian physicist Christian Johann Doppler discovers the Doppler effect: an apparent shift in wavelengths toward higher frequency as a source of light or sound approaches, and toward lower frequency as it recedes. *See also* 1848, Fizeau.   **PHYS**

1842   American psychologist and philosopher William James is born in Massachusetts (*d.* 1910). Known as the dean of American psychologists, he will develop the school of functionalism, which seeks to understand the conscious aspects of mental life. James will advocate a pragmatic viewpoint on life and theology and struggle with the issues of mental and emotional freedom. Two of his most important works will be *Principles of Psychology* (1890) and *Varieties of Religious Experience* (1902).   **PSYCH**

1843   Heinrich Samuel Schwabe discovers the sunspot cycle, a semiregular fluctuation in sunspot activity, later found to occur in periods of eleven years.   **ASTRO**

1843	England's Rothamsted Experimental Station is established by English agriculturalist John Lawes and chemist Joseph Henry Gilbert for the study of wheat and other grains. **BIO**
1843	Swedish chemist Carl Gustaf Mosander discovers the rare earth elements erbium and terbium. About this time he also chemically isolates the rare earth element yttrium, first discovered by Johan Gadolin in 1794. **CHEM**
1843	Irish mathematician William Hamilton invents a self-consistent algebra of hypercomplex numbers, which he calls quaternions. **MATH**
1843	British mathematician Arthur Cayley works out the analytic geometry of three or more dimensions, which will be called n-dimensional analytic geometry. **MATH**
1843	American physician and author Oliver Wendell Holmes reports that childbed fever is contagious, but his peers scoff at the idea. **MED**
1843	British physicist James P. Joule formulates the mechanical equivalent of heat, the ratio of a unit of mechanical energy to the equivalent unit of thermal energy. Symbolized as J, it has an approximate value of 41,800,000 ergs (4.18 joules) per calorie. This discovery shows a fixed quantity of work results in a fixed amount of heat. **PHYS**
1843	German physicist Julius Robert von Mayer discovers that heat and mechanical work have a direct relationship and are different forms of energy. **PHYS**
1843	In England, the House of Lords decides that an individual is not responsible for a crime he has committed if the person is "laboring under a defect of reason" and has a diseased mind. The M'Naghten rule, as it will be called, will not have a U.S. counterpart until the issuance of the Durham rule in 1954. **PSYCH**
1843	French physiologist Marie-Jean Baptiste Flourens refutes phrenologists' claims by proving that the skull's contours do not correspond to those of the brain, thus disproving the basic assumption of phrenology. Despite this evidence, phrenology long persists as a fad. **PSYCH**
1843	British engineer Sir George Cayley designs, on paper, the first practical helicopter. **TECH**
1843	British inventor Charles Wheatstone popularizes, though he does not invent, the Wheatstone bridge, an electrical circuit that precisely measures the value of a resistance. **TECH**
1843	American farmer Jerome Increase Case develops the Case threshing machine, more efficient than earlier thresher designs. **TECH**
1843	U.S. shop apprentice Elias Howe, Jr., invents the interlocking-stitch Howe sewing machine. **TECH**

Howe's sewing machine, the first patented lockstitch machine, 1846. (*Smithsonian Institution*)

1844   French scientists Jean-Baptiste Boussingault and Jean-Baptiste Dumas, experimenting with plant decomposition, prove that as plants decompose their carbonic acid is reduced to carbon, water to hydrogen, ammonium hydroxide to ammonium, and nitric acid to nitrogen.   **BIO**

1844   British writer Robert Chambers anonymously publishes *Vestiges of the Natural History of Creation*, a controversial work that promotes the idea of biological evolution, influencing Charles Darwin and Alfred Wallace (*see* 1859, Darwin).   **BIO**

1844   Russian chemist Karl K. Klaus discovers the element ruthenium. **CHEM**

1844   German mathematician Hermann Grassmann publishes his *Theory of Extension*, in which he gives a detailed exposition of n-dimensional vector space.   **MATH**

1844   Amyl nitrite, a drug later used to dilate blood vessels, is discovered. **MED**

1844   The American Psychiatric Association is founded.   **PSYCH**

1844   U.S. entrepreneur Henry Wells begins an express delivery service between Buffalo and Detroit, beginning a company called Wells & Co., which eventually develops into Wells, Fargo & Co.   **TECH**

1844   German engineer Gottlob Keller pioneers the wood-pulp paper process, which creates an inexpensive paper for periodicals.   **TECH**

May 24,   The first telegraph message, from Washington, D.C., to Baltimore,
1844   Maryland, is transmitted. Sent by Samuel F. B. Morse to his assistant Alfred Vail, it reads, "What hath God wrought!"   **TECH**

....

"What hath God wrought!"—Samuel F. B. Morse to assistant Alfred L. Vail, quoting the Bible (Numbers 23.23) in the first telegraph message, sent from the Supreme Court Room of the U.S. Capitol to the Mount Claire Station of the Baltimore & Ohio Railroad; Baltimore, Maryland; May 24, 1844

....

1845   English chemist Michael Faraday identifies six "permanent gases" that cannot be liquefied with the then-current technology: hydrogen, oxygen, nitrogen, carbon monoxide, methane, and nitric oxide.   **CHEM**

1845   German chemist Christian Friedrich Schönbein discovers the explosive nitrocellulose, or gun cotton.   **CHEM**

1845   British geologist Charles Lyell publishes *Travels in North America*, on his recent investigations there.   **EARTH**

1845   American gynecologist James Marion Sims (1813–1883) is the first to surgically relieve a woman suffering from vesicovaginal fistula, an opening from the bladder into the vagina. Sims will later invent the vaginal speculum.   **MED**

1845   American dentist Claudius Ash originates the single porcelain tooth, which can be set individually into plates for false teeth. This technique eventually replaces older methods like jamming teeth gathered from the dead into a socket prepared in the recipient's gums and wearing dentures made of celluloid, cloth, and ivory.   **MED**

1845   British physicist Michael Faraday discovers paramagnetism and diamagnetism, and suggests that light is a form of electromagnetism, from his observations of the effects of a magnetic field on light polarization in crystals.   **PHYS**

1845   German psychiatrist Wilhelm Griesinger publishes his textbook *Mental Pathology and Therapeutics*, a turning point in psychiatry that shifts the center of the science from France to Germany.   **PSYCH**

1845   The hydraulic crane is patented by British inventor William Armstrong.   **TECH**

1845   The first cable suspension aqueduct bridge, spanning the Allegheny
              River in Pittsburgh, Pennsylvania, is opened to traffic. The 162-foot
              bridge is constructed by German-American engineer John Augustus
              Roebling.   **TECH**

1846   British archaeologist Henry Creswicke Rawlinson deciphers
              cuneiform, an ancient Mesopotamian script, from an inscription in
              three languages carved into a cliff in Persia during the reign of
              Darius the Great (521–486 B.C.). He works without knowing the
              studies of German Georg F. Grotefend, whose 1802 translation of
              cuneiform went unnoticed.   **ARCH**

1846   Mounds built by Native Americans in the Mississippi River Valley,
              including the Serpent Mound in what is now Ohio, are excavated
              by E. George Squier and Edward H. Davis.   **ARCH**

Sept. 23,   German astronomer Johann Gottfried Galle and his assistant
1846   Heinrich d'Arrest are the first to sight Neptune, the eighth planet
              from the sun, corroborating predictions by French mathematician
              Urbain-Jean-Joseph Leverrier and British mathematician John
              Couch Adams, who are credited with the discovery.   **ASTRO**

....

*"The animal frame, though destined to fulfill so many other
ends, is as a machine more perfect than the best contrived
steam-engine—that is, is capable of more work with the
same expenditure of fuel."—James Prescott Joule,
British physicist; mid-nineteenth century*

....

Oct. 10,   British astronomer William Lassell discovers Triton, a satellite of
1846   Neptune.   **ASTRO**

1846   American explorer and scientist James Dana publishes *Zoophytes*,
              in which he classifies and describes the physiology and ecology of
              hundreds of these invertebrate animals. Zoophytes include sea
              anemones and sponges.   **BIO**

1846   New York professor Elias Loomis publishes the first synoptic weath-
              er map.   **EARTH**

1846   British naturalist Edward Forbes, a pioneer in biogeography, main-
              tains that most of the plants and animals of the British Isles migrat-
              ed there from the European continent over land connections before
              and after the glacial epoch.   **EARTH**

1846   The Smithsonian Institution is founded in Washington, D.C., with a
              bequest from British chemist and mineralogist James Smithson. **MISC**

1846   American dentist William Thomas Morton (1819–1868) introduces ether anesthesia. After success with nitrous oxide in tooth removal, Morton collaborates with Massachusetts General Hospital surgeon John Warren to use ether during an operation to remove a neck tumor. The surgery is a success, and when the patient recovers he says he felt no pain.   **MED**

1846   French chemist Louis Pasteur studies the phenomenon of optical activity, the ability of certain substances with asymmetric molecules to rotate the plane of plane-polarized light as it passes through a crystal or solution. He discovers that molecules of these substances exist in two different forms that are mirror images of each other.   **PHYS**

1846   German physicist Wilhelm Eduard Weber develops a system of fundamental units for electricity and a method for deducing the magnetic force on a charged particle.   **PHYS**

1846   German philosopher Theodor Waitz writes a fundamental psychology book, *Foundations of Psychology*.   **PSYCH**

1846   Boston machinist Elias Howe patents the first modern sewing machine. Powered by a hand-driven wheel, it has a double-thread, lockstitch system.   **TECH**

1846   The Pennsylvania Railroad, eventually one of the nation's largest, is chartered.   **TECH**

1846   A standard gauge for railroads is adopted in Britain.   **TECH**

1847   U.S. manufacturer Richard Hoe patents his rotary, or "lightning," press, which prints more efficiently by being cylinder- rather than flatbed-driven.   **TECH**

Oct. 1,   American astronomer Maria Mitchell discovers a comet. She will
1847   become the first woman member of the American Academy of Arts and Sciences (1848) and the American Association for the Advancement of Science (1850).   **ASTRO**

1847   German botanist Matthias Jakob Schleiden and German zoologist and botanist Theodor Schwann publish in *Beiträge zur Phytogenesis* what will become the basis for modern cell theory. These scientists argue that cells are the fundamental organic units common to all living beings and develop by "free formation" out of formless cytoblastemic substances in the same basic way. German zoologist Robert Remak and pathologist Rudolf Virchow will further develop the Schleiden-Schwann cell theory.   **BIO**

1847   Italian chemist Ascanio Sobrero first produces the explosive nitroglycerin.   **CHEM**

1847   German chemist Lambert Babo states Babo's law, that the vapor pressure of a liquid decreases with the addition of a solute, the amount of the decrease being proportional to the quantity of solute dissolved. **CHEM**

1847   The Association of American Geologists changes its name to the American Association for the Advancement of Science, holding regular annual meetings from this year forward. Unlike its European counterparts, the AAAS becomes a forum for the exchange of scientific information without regard to social status, and spends little money on formal activities. **EARTH**

··

*"All the varied forms in the animal tissues are
nothing but transformed cells."—Theodor Schwann,
German physiologist, outlining the underlying principle
of the cell theory he developed with Jakob Matthias
Schleiden; nineteenth century*

··

1847   English mathematician George Boole publishes *The Mathematical Analysis of Logic*, the founding work of Boolean algebra or symbolic logic. In it Boole develops a set of symbols and algebraic manipulations that express logical arguments. **MATH**

1847   English inventor Charles Babbage designs the first ophthalmoscope with which to study the retina, but his invention is neglected and Hermann von Helmholtz later receives the credit. *See* 1851. **MED**

1847   The American Medical Association is established and holds its first meeting in Philadelphia. **MED**

1847   Hungarian physician Ignaz P. Semmelweis discovers that puerperal sepsis (childbed fever) occurs when medical students fail to wash their hands before delivering babies. After he requires students to wash their hands with soap and chlorinated lime, the death rate in that maternity ward drops significantly. Semmelweiss and Oliver Wendell Holmes will be ridiculed for their views on childbed fever but eventually will be proven correct. **MED**

1847   German physicist Hermann Ludwig Ferdinand von Helmholtz states the law of conservation of energy, the first law of thermodynamics: In an isolated system, the total amount of energy does not change. Fellow German Julius Robert von Mayer (in 1842) and English physicist James P. Joule (in 1847) also contribute to the development of this law. **PHYS**

NO SUCH THING AS A FREE LUNCH

*T*he first and second laws of thermodynamics (the study of the in-
terrelation of energy, heat, and work) are the bane of wishful
thinkers in all walks of life. They can be expressed mathematical-
ly as physical principles, but from their initial formulation in the nineteenth century they have carried philosophical implications as well.

The first law, credited to German physicist Hermann von Helmholtz in
1847, states that the total amount of energy in an isolated system does not
change. Also known as the law of the conservation of energy, it implies that
if you build a machine to turn a wheel, cool a room, or cook a hamburger
you must draw off the energy from somewhere else. Put simply, there is no
such thing as a free lunch.

The second law, formulated by German physicist Rudolf Clausius in
1850, states that the disorder of an isolated system (the unavailability of
energy to do useful work) increases with time or, at best, remains constant.
This law is also known as the law of entropy, after a term Clausius coined
for a measure of a system's disorder. Another way of stating it is that
whenever work takes place, some energy is converted into waste heat. This
means that having a perpetual motion machine—such as a steamship that
would run eternally by using the heat from its own pipes to heat more water and make more steam—is in principle impossible. It also means that
the total disorder of the universe will inevitably become greater, not less.

A third law of thermodynamics, the law of absolute zero, was formulated by German physical chemist Walther H. Nernst in 1906. It states that all
bodies at absolute zero would have the same entropy, though absolute zero,
the state at which all molecular motion stops, can never be completely attained. This law is important to physicists because it provides an absolute
scale of values for measuring entropy. But because it is less easy than the
other two laws to translate into everyday terms, it has never been as popular among armchair philosophers.

1847   English-born American scientist John W. Draper discovers that all
         materials begin to glow red at about 525° C (977° F) and change
         color as the temperature rises until they finally glow white.   **PHYS**

1847   A process for cutting dressmaker patterns for use with the newly
         invented sewing machine is developed by American tailor
         Ebenezer Butterick.   **TECH**

1847   The first adhesive postage stamps are used, in the United States.   **TECH**

1848   In the industrial regions of England a dark-colored variety of pepper moth replaces light-colored ones after industrial air pollution begins blackening trees, making the light-colored moths visible to insect-eating birds. This example of an adapted organism reproducing in greater numbers than a competing strain becomes a classic instance of natural adaptation by a process of differential reproduction.   **BIO**

1848   French chemist Louis Pasteur notes that one form of tartaric acid bends light to the left, the other to the right. This discovery will be important in the development of stereochemistry, the branch of chemistry concerned with molecular structure and its impact on chemical properties. *See* 1874, van't Hoff.   **CHEM**

1848   New England theologian and geologist Edward B. Hitchcock publishes a study of fossil tracks he has collected in the Connecticut Valley. He proposes that the tracks are those of extinct birds, but they will turn out to be those of dinosaurs. *See also* 1800, Moody, and 1915, Lull.   **PALEO**

1848   French physicist Armand Hippolyte Louis Fizeau notes that the Doppler effect in light (*see* 1842) is best observed by monitoring the changing positions of spectral lines, known as the Doppler-Fizeau effect.   **PHYS**

1848   British physicist William Thomson, later Lord Kelvin, theorizes that there is an absolute temperature, absolute zero, below which no further energy loss is possible, and that this temperature should be the starting point of a new absolute scale of temperature. With absolute zero at $-273.15°$ C, this scale is henceforth called the Kelvin scale.   **PHYS**

1849   French astronomer Edouard-Albert Roche formulates Roche's limit, specifiying the distance from a planet within which tidal forces will tend to break a satellite apart. The concept is later advanced to explain Saturn's rings, which are within Roche's limit.   **ASTRO**

1849   British physician Thomas Addison describes pernicious anemia. **MED**

1849   Elizabeth Blackwell, America's first female physician, graduates from Geneva College of Medicine in upstate New York.   **MED**

1849   British physicist William Thomson introduces the term *thermodynamics*.   **PHYS**

1849   A safety pin is patented by American inventor Walter Hunt.   **TECH**

1849   In New York City, American inventor James Bogardus completes a commission to build the first prefabricated homes. His iron-and-glass constructions start a trend that extends to several American cities.   **TECH**

c. 1850s   Beginning now, British mathematician James Joseph Sylvester coins numerous mathematical terms that will become accepted, such as *syzygy, cogredient, invariant, covariant,* and *contravariant.*   **MATH**

1850s   A generation of social theorists who will be known as legalists, including Léon Duguit, Maurice Hauriou, and Georg Jellinek, is born. Near the end of the century they will help establish political science as a separate academic discipline.   **SOC**

1850   The first photographic plates are used to record images of stars and the moon, foreshadowing the later importance of photography as a tool of astronomy.   **ASTRO**

c. 1850   Irish engineer Robert Mallet coins the term *seismology* to refer to the study of earthquakes and the earth's mechanical properties.   **EARTH**

1850   British sanitarian Sir Edwin Chadwick establishes that poverty and sickness are linked. In his report on the "labouring poor" to England's Poor Law Commission, Chadwick says eradicating disease is hopeless unless poverty is also eradicated.   **MED**

1850   Epidemiology, the study of the causes, distribution, and control of disease, becomes a branch of medical science as physicians seeking to prevent disease form the London Epidemiological Society.   **MED**

1850   Building on experiments the previous year by French physicist Armand-Hippolyte-Louis Fizeau, his assistant, Jean-Bernard-Léon Foucault, determines the speed of light to within less than 1 percent of its actual value.   **PHYS**

1850   German physicist Rudolf Julius Emanuel Clausius formulates the second law of thermodynamics, which states that the disorder of a closed system increases with time, or that some energy is always lost as heat in any energy conversion. Clausius later coins the word *entropy* for the ratio of a system's heat content to its absolute temperature, which serves as a measure of its disorder.   **PHYS**

1850   Using the thermopile he has invented, Italian physicist Macedonio Melloni studies infrared radiation, showing that it consists of waves of the same structure as light but longer.   **PHYS**

July 20, 1850   In Grimma, Saxony, German experimental psychologist Georg Elias Müller is born (*d.* 1934). His 1873 doctoral dissertation will be the first empirical study on attention. An expert on vision and memory, he will codiscover Jost's law, the law which states that when two associations are of equal strength, a repetition strengthens the older one more than the newer one. Müller will also introduce the memory drum, a device for verbal recall used in learning experiments.   **PSYCH**

1850   Boston machinist Isaac Singer patents a foot-operated sewing machine that becomes a commercial success. Elias Howe (*see* 1846) later sues him, successfully, for patent infringement. **TECH**

1850   The Illinois Central becomes the first U.S. railroad to receive a government land grant. Eventually it will be the leading north–south line in the United States. **TECH**

1851   British astronomer William Lassell discovers Ariel and Umbriel, two satellites of Uranus. **ASTRO**

1851   French physicist Jean-Bernard-Léon Foucault constructs a pendulum experiment that demonstrates the rotation of the earth. **EARTH**

1851   German mathematician Georg Friedrich Bernhard Riemann writes his doctoral thesis on the theory of complex functions, introducing the Cauchy-Riemann equations and laying the basis for the concept of the Riemann surface, an important step in the development of topology. **MATH**

1851   German surgeon Hermann von Helmholtz invents the ophthalmoscope, an instrument for examining the interior of the eye, independently of Charles Babbage's version (*see* 1847). **MED**

1851   Irish-born British physicist George Gabriel Stokes introduces a mathematical formula for the fall of a small body, such as a droplet, through a fluid, like air. **PHYS**

1851   English philosopher and economist John Stuart Mill publishes his *Principles of Political Economy*, which will be a basic economic text for decades. **SOC**

1851   The Crystal Palace, assembled from prefabricated elements, is built to house the Great Exhibition of 1851 in London. This huge enclosure of glass and iron is a precursor to the glass and steel buildings of modern architecture. **TECH**

1851   The wet collodion process for developing photographs, which will replace the Daguerreotype process, is developed by English architect Scott Archer. **TECH**

1852   German scientist Hermann von Helmholtz determines the speed at which messages travel along nerves. **BIO**

1852   English chemist Edward Frankland formulates the theory of valence, stating that an atom of a given element is able to combine with a fixed number of other kinds of atoms according to certain basic rules. An atom's valence will later be found to be related to its atomic weight. **CHEM**

1852   French physicist Jean-Bernard-Léon Foucault invents the gyro-
          scope.   **EARTH**

1852   French mathematician Michel Chasles publishes *Traité de géométrie
          supérieure*, which establishes the use of directed line segments in
          pure geometry.   **MATH**

1852   The American Pharmacy Association is founded.   **MED**

1852   German physician and physiologist Robert Remak shows that tis-
          sue growth is due to cell division.   **MED**

1852   British physicists James P. Joule and William Thomson, Lord Kelvin,
          demonstrate the Joule-Thomson effect, the temperature change
          (usually a drop) that occurs when a gas expands through a porous
          plug into a region of lower pressure.   **PHYS**

1852   British physicist George Stokes gives the name *fluorescence* to the glow
          observed when an electric current passes through a partially evacuated
          tube. This term will later be used for any visible light resulting from a
          collision of matter and radiation rather than a rise in temperature. **PHYS**

1852   An oil distilled from coal tar, developed and sold by Boston drug
          makers as coal oil, will eventually be known instead by the name
          given it in 1855 by New York physician Abraham Gesner, *kerosene*.
          Among its uses are as a patent medicine and lamp oil.   **TECH**

1852   On the Michigan Southern Railway, the first train successfully trav-
          els from the East Coast to Chicago.   **TECH**

1852   American mechanic Elisha Graves Otis patents the safety elevator,
          also known as the safety hoister. This cagelike apparatus, which op-
          erates by a combination of rope, grips, and ratchets, will become a
          key factor in the proliferation of multistory buildings. **TECH**

Sept. 24, French engineer Henri Giffard takes the first dirigible for a
1852   flight.   **TECH**

....

***"[W]ithin half a century, machinery will perform all work—
automata will direct them. The only tasks of the human race
will be to make love, study, and be happy."***
—The United States Review, 1853

....

1853   Italian chemist Stanislao Cannizzaro discovers the Cannizzaro reaction,
          a reaction of aldehydes to yield carboxylic acids and alcohols. **CHEM**

1853   *On Coral Reefs and Islands*, published in New York by J. D. Dana,
          confirms Darwin's subsistence theory of the formation of coral
          atolls and offers new insight on corals and reefbuilding. **EARTH**

1853   Mathematician William Shanks calculates pi to 707 decimal places,
          though only the value to 527 places is correct.   **MATH**

1853   French physicist Jean-Bernard-Léon Foucault shows that light travels faster in air than in water, a discovery that lends support to the wave theory of light.   **PHYS**

1853   Scottish physicist William J. M. Rankine develops the concept of potential energy, or the energy stored in a body due to its position or shape.   **PHYS**

1853   British engineer George Cayley designs and builds the first successful manned glider.   **TECH**

1853   Swedish inventor J. E. Lundstrom patents the safety match.   **TECH**

....

"All safe. All safe, ladies and gentlemen."—Elisha Otis,
stepping from his newly invented elevator; after a
demonstration at the New York Industrial Fair; 1854

....

1854   German scientist Hermann von Helmholtz predicts the "heat death" of the universe, which he argues will result when the universe reaches a state of uniform temperature.   **ASTRO**

1854   Von Helmholtz posits that gravitational contraction is the source of the sun's heat. From this hypothesis British physicist William Thomson calculates that the sun's age is about 25 million years, which conflicts with geology's estimate of a much older age for the earth. The conflict is not resolved until 1938, when thermonuclear fusion is proposed as the principal source of the sun's energy. **ASTRO**

1854   British chemist Alexander W. Williamson explains how a catalyst works. *See also* 1835, Berzelius.   **CHEM**

1854   While searching for an undersea path for the transatlantic cable, U.S. oceanographer Matthew F. Maury discovers Telegraph Plateau, a shallow section of the Atlantic Ocean. This is the first important physical discovery about the ocean floor.   **EARTH**

1854   German mathematician Georg Riemann develops a non-Euclidean geometry that resembles the geometry for the surface of a sphere. In his system all lines intersect and are finite in length, and no two lines are parallel.   **MATH**

1854   Between now and the 1870s, English mathematicians Arthur Cayley and James Joseph Sylvester develop the algebra of forms, or *quantics,* representing the beginning of the theory of algebraic invariants.   **MATH**

1854   German obstetrician Karl S. F. Credé devises a means of excising the placenta and uterine clots to reduce the risk of hemorrhage following childbirth.   **MED**

1854   Spanish vocal instructor Manuel García invents the modern laryngoscope, making otolaryngology—the sciences of the ear, nose, and larynx—possible.   **MED**

1854   British physician John Snow advises the vestrymen of St. James's parish in London to remove the handle of the Broad Street well pump in Soho. Its removal brings the 1854 London cholera epidemic to an abrupt halt, proving Snow's 1849 theory that cholera is a water-borne disease.   **MED**

1854   German bacteriologist Paul Ehrlich is born in Strehlen, Silesia (d. 1915). Ehrlich, considered the founder of modern chemotherapy, will become known for his methylene-blue cell-staining method and his classification of white blood cells.   **MED**

1854   British philanthropist Florence Nightingale arrives in Scutari, Constantinople, with thirty-eight nurses to administer to the sick and injured soldiers of the Crimean War (1854–1856). She will become known as the founder of modern nursing and hospital sanitary reforms.   **MED**

1854   German ophthalmologist Albrecht von Graefe (1828–1870) introduces iridectomy, the surgical removal of a portion of the iris, in glaucoma treatment. Von Graefe will be considered the father of modern eye surgery.   **MED**

1854   Life-sized models of dinosaurs are displayed publicly for the first time, at the Crystal Palace, which has been moved from London (*see* 1851) to Sydenham, England.   **PALEO**

1854   English anatomist Richard Owen describes the first dinosaur found in the Southern Hemisphere: *Massospondylus*, discovered in Triassic deposits in the Red Beds of South Africa.   **PALEO**

1854   French psychopathologist Jules Baillarger is credited with the first significant description of bipolar disorder, which he calls *la folie à double forme*. For decades this disorder will be known as "circular insanity" in English.   **PSYCH**

1854   American professor Benjamin Silliman effects a fractional distillation of crude petroleum, which creates a clean-burning Pennsylvania "rock-oil." The oil company Silliman forms with a co-partner will be one of many such formed over the next few decades.   **TECH**

1855   French astronomer Urbain Leverrier posits the existence of a planet he designates Vulcan to account for irregularities in Mercury's orbit. These variations will later be accounted for by the general theory of relativity.   **ASTRO**

1855   Irish astronomer William Parsons observes the spiral structure of galaxies.   **ASTRO**

A RIVER IN THE OCEAN

*T*he first modern oceanographer was American naval officer Matthew Fontaine Maury (1806–1873), who was assigned to the depot of charts and instruments after being disabled in an accident. Maury made the most of his post, developing charts of the Atlantic Ocean's winds and currents to reduce nautical travel time. In 1855 he published the first textbook of oceanography, Physical Geography of the Sea.

Maury is best known for his charting of the Gulf Stream. Fifty miles wide at its start and moving at an average speed of four miles per hour, this powerful current annually propels warm water from the Gulf of Mexico to the North Atlantic. In Maury's words, "There is a river in the ocean."

Impressive as it is, the Gulf Stream is actually one part of a larger circular movement of water generated by the Coriolis effect. From the North Atlantic the current continues to flow clockwise in the eastward movement known as the North Atlantic drift. Part of the current, deflected by the European land mass, strays up past Britain to Norway. The rest, the Canaries current, moves south along the Canary Islands, then, as the north equatorial current, is deflected westward back to the Caribbean, where the cycle begins again.

1855	U.S. oceanographer Matthew Maury publishes *Physical Geography of the Sea*, the first textbook on oceanography.	**EARTH**
1855	British physician Thomas Addison describes Addison's disease, a syndrome resulting from a deficiency in adrenocortical hormone secretion.	**MED**
1855	Scottish mathematician James Clerk Maxwell gives mathematical expression to the physical concept of lines of force originated by Michael Faraday in 1821.	**PHYS**
1855	German physicist Heinrich Daniel Ruhmkorff invents the induction coil that now bears his name.	**PHYS**
1855	British physicist William Thomson proposes a theory for transmitting electrical signals through undersea cables, which will be applied in constructing the first transatlantic cable.	**PHYS**
c. 1855	German chemist Robert Bunsen begins using the gas burner that bears his name, the Bunsen burner. It was actually invented by a technician named C. Desaga and earlier was independently invented by Michael Faraday.	**TECH**
1855	German inventor Johann Heinrich Wilhelm Geissler invents the Geissler tube, an improved device for producing vacuums.	**TECH**

1855	Aluminum is produced for commercial use by French chemist Henri-Étienne Sainte-Claire Deville. **TECH**

1855   Aluminum is produced for commercial use by French chemist Henri-Étienne Sainte-Claire Deville.   **TECH**

1855   Celluloid, the first man-made plastic, made from gun cotton and camphor, is patented by British chemist Alexander Parkes.   **TECH**

1855   A process for condensing milk is patented by an American, Gail Borden.   **TECH**

1856   British astronomer Norman Robert Pogson quantifies the old stellar magnitude system devised by Hipparchus (*see* 100s B.C.), constructing ratios for the relative brightnesses of stars.   **ASTRO**

c. 1856   French physiologist Claude Bernard discovers glycogen and its function in the liver, and coins the term *internal secretion*.   **BIO**

1856   German mathematician Karl Weierstrass becomes professor of mathematics at the University of Berlin. Among his many contributions will be the discovery of analytic continuation and uniform convergence.   **MATH**

c. 1856   English epidemiologist William Budd proves that typhoid is a waterborne disease.   **MED**

1856   Austrian neurologist Sigmund Freud is born in Moravia (*d.* 1939, London). One of the best-known names in early psychiatry, Freud will become recognized as the founder of psychoanalysis. Freud's theories on the unconscious and infantile sexuality will dominate twentieth-century psychiatry.   **MED**

1856   American paleontologist Joseph Leidy becomes the first person in the Western Hemisphere to identify dinosaur fossils. The fossils he describes include teeth of the *Trachodon* and *Deinodon*, found in what is now Montana.   **PALEO**

1856   Johann C. Fuhrott discovers the first known skull of Neanderthal man, in the Neander Valley near Düsseldorf, Germany. Experts disagree on whether its heavy brow ridge and retreating forehead represent the features of an early form of human or of a diseased individual. *See also* c. 1880s.   **PALEO**

1856   British engineer Henry Bessemer patents the Bessemer converter, which uses cold air to convert pig iron to steel, a method that becomes known as the Bessemer process.   **TECH**

1856   Mauve, the first chemical dye, is accidentally discovered by British chemistry student William Henry Perkin. This dye is coal-tar-based.   **TECH**

1856   The American telegraph company Western Union is chartered by businessman Hiram Sibley and financier Ezra Cornell. It proceeds to unite several smaller telegraph companies to become the largest in the United States.   **TECH**

THE BOWLEGGED COSSACK

*I*t is now accepted that the fossils discovered in a cave in the Neander Valley (Neander Thal in Old German) near Düsseldorf, Germany, in 1856 represent an extinct form of early humanity. But that consensus was not reached for decades. Neanderthal (or Neandertal) man first came to light in a storm of controversy.

The fossil remains—a partial skull and some limb bones—were clearly human, but they exhibited such unusual features as a heavy brow ridge, a receding forehead and chin, large teeth, and bowed limb bones. Because reliable methods of dating were not then available, it was anyone's guess how old the bones were. Some suggested that the fossils represented an early race of subhumans, but others believed they were those of a much more recent but diseased individual. A contemporary German anatomist, F. Mayer, proposed a specific date—1814, less than fifty years earlier. He theorized that the bones were those of a Cossack cavalryman who had deserted the Russian army as it forced Napoleon to retreat across the Rhine that year. The bowed legs supposedly came from years of sitting in the saddle, complicated by a childhood case of rickets.

Charles Darwin's The Origin of Species, published three years later in 1859, intensified the controversy by supplying theoretical grounds for arguing that humans had evolved from earlier forms of life. English biologist Thomas H. Huxley and French anthropologist Pierre-Paul Broca both advanced the view that Neanderthal man represented an extinct human form. As late as the 1870s, however, the German pathologist Rudolf Virchow was still claiming that the bones were those of a hapless, relatively recent individual who had been afflicted with rickets, head injuries, and severe arthritis.

It took the discovery of several fairly complete Neanderthal skeletons in Spy, Belgium (1887), and La Chapelle-aux-Saints, France (1908), to make it clear that the Neanderthals were a distinct people who had lived in Europe from about 150,000 years ago to 35,000 years ago. Later discoveries showed that they had also lived in the Middle East, in such sites as Israel and Iraq. However, controversy has followed the Neanderthals even to the present day. Though it is generally held that they were a subspecies (Homo sapiens neanderthalensis) of modern humanity, some scientists argue that they were a distinct species (Homo neanderthalensis). And the mechanism of their extinction remains an open question: whether they evolved into modern humans (a view not widely held), interbred with modern humans, or were wiped out by modern humans, either passively by competition or actively by warfare.

1857　　Scottish physicist James Clerk Maxwell shows that Saturn's rings are not solid but are made up of discrete particles.　**ASTRO**

1857　　German mathematician Georg Riemann makes a conjecture that becomes known as the Riemann hypothesis, stating that the non-real zeroes of the zeta function are complex numbers whose real part is always equal to one half. The conjecture will remain unconfirmed to the present day, though a generalized version of it is proven by Belgian mathematician Pierre Deligne in 1974.　**MATH**

1857　　German physiologist Wilhelm Petters discovers acetone in diabetic urine, implying that the pathology and treatment of diabetes are purely chemical problems.　**MED**

1857　　German physicist Rudolf Clausius proposes a mathematical foundation for the kinetic theory of heat.　**PHYS**

1857　　The first passenger elevator in a commercial building is put in use in the E. G. Haughwort Store in downtown New York City.　**TECH**

1858　　Warren de la Rue of England invents the photoheliograph, a device for photographing the sun.　**ASTRO**

1858　　French physiologist Claude Bernard discovers the vasodilator and vasoconstrictor nerves, which are responsible for constricting and dilating the blood vessels.　**BIO**

1858　　German chemist Friedrich August Kekule von Stradonitz works out the basic structure of organic molecules, showing how they are made up of chains of carbon atoms attached to other atoms.　**CHEM**

1858　　Kekule von Stradonitz and British chemist Archibald Scott Couper, working independently, develop a system of chemical notation in which the valence of each atom is indicated by dashes.　**CHEM**

1858　　American geologist Antonio Snider-Pellegrini is an early advocate of the theory of continental drift, which will be fully developed by Alfred Wegener in the twentieth century. Snider-Pellegrini proposes that the atlantic continents broke up and drifted apart in the distant past.　**EARTH**

1858　　British explorer John Hanning Speke reaches the largest lake in Africa, Lake Victoria Nyanza. In 1862 Speke will prove it to be one of the principal sources of the Nile.　**EARTH**

1858　　*The Geology of Pennsylvania*, the finest geologic map of an American state thus far, appears in print.　**EARTH**

1858　　English mathematician Arthur Cayley publishes an analysis of the theory of transformations, representing the beginning of his study of matrices.　**MATH**

1858   The United Kingdom passes the Medical Act of 1858, establishing the General Council of Medical Education to regulate and register the medical profession and protect the public from unqualified physicians. *See also* 1878, Dentists Act.   **MED**

....

"I no longer felt any doubt that the lake at my feet gave birth to that interesting river, the source of which has been the subject of so much speculation, and the object of so many explorers."—John Hanning Speke, British explorer, on being the first European, in 1858, to see Lake Victoria Nyanza, East Africa. In 1862 he showed this lake to be one of the principal sources of the Nile.

....

1858   British surgeon Henry Gray publishes *Gray's Anatomy*, which becomes the standard anatomy textbook for more than a century. **MED**

1858   American Joseph Leidy describes a partial skeleton of the dinosaur *Hadrosaurus foulkii*, discovered by W. P. Foulke at Haddonfield, New Jersey.   **PALEO**

WHY DID GRAY MATTER?

*B*ritish anatomist Henry Gray's 1858 book Anatomy, Descriptive and Surgical *wasn't the only anatomy book on the market in the mid-nineteenth century. Ever since Andreas Vesalius established the modern subject of anatomy with* De humani corporis fabrica *in 1543 there had been numerous texts in the field. But the completeness, clarity, and intelligibility of Gray's* Anatomy *have made it a lasting resource for physicians and medical students.*

The Philadelphia publishers Blancard and Lea, purchasers of the American rights to Gray's book in 1859, were right in believing they had their hands on the most understandable anatomy book to date. Colleagues praised Gray for the thoroughness of his dissections, the coherent literary style of the text, and the innovative use of 363 illustrations drawn by Henry Van Dyke Carter.

Despite Gray's other writings on the development of the optic nerve and retina, the human spleen, and the ductless (endocrine) glands, this fellow of the Royal College of Surgeons will probably always be remembered best for the work that begins, "The entire skeleton in the adult consists of 200 distinct bones."

1858   German pathologist Rudolf Virchow publishes what will be his most famous work, *Die Cellularpathologie*, establishing the foundation of cellular pathology, which studies the effect of disease on cells. He determines that there are "no specific cells in disease, only modifications of physiological types." Virchow was the first to describe not only leukemia and the doctrine of embolism (blood vessel obstruction by a clot or foreign substance) but leukocytosis (marked by increased numbers of white blood cells in the blood).   **MED**

1858   German physicist Julius Plücker observes the flow of an electric current through the vacuum of a Geissler tube and notes that the position of the resulting fluorescence shifts when an electromagnetic field is applied.   **PHYS**

1858   The first usable two-tiered sleeping car is developed, by American cabinetmaker George M. Pullman for the Chicago & Alton Railroad.   **TECH**

1858   Central Park, designed by Frederick Law Olmsted and landscape designer Calvert Vaux, opens in New York but is not fully completed for five years.   **TECH**

1858   The first mechanically operated refrigerator, which cools through the use of liquid ammonia, is invented by Frenchman Ferdinand P. A. Carré.   **TECH**

1858   The zinc-lidded Mason jar, which revolutionizes home canning, is devised by American craftsman John Mason.   **TECH**

Aug. 16,   The first transatlantic cable message is sent, from Queen Victoria to
1858   U.S. President James Buchanan. The queen's message reads, "Glory to God in the Highest, peace on earth, goodwill to men." The cable will fail in a few weeks and the first permanent one not be láid until 1866.   **TECH**

1859   British astronomer Richard Christopher Carrington discovers the differential rotation of the sun's equator and poles.   **ASTRO**

1859   British naturalist Charles Darwin explains his theory of evolution by natural selection in *The Origin of Species*. He amasses evidence to show that species are modified and new species emerge as individuals better adapted to their environment outreproduce those less well adapted. About the same time, British naturalist Alfred Russel Wallace develops a similar theory. Though controversial, Darwin's theory eventually will be accepted by scientists.   **BIO**

1859   German chemists Robert Wilhelm Bunsen and Gustav Robert Kirchhoff invent the spectroscope, a device to chemically analyze elements heated to incandescence. The spectroscope will be used to discover new elements and study the chemical composition of the sun and stars.   **CHEM**

THE ORIGIN OF SPECIES

*I*n *1859, British naturalist Charles Darwin published* The Origin of Species by Means of Natural Selection, *the controversial book that introduced the theory of evolution by natural selection as an explanation for the history of life. Meticulously documented and argued, the book was scientifically rigorous but aimed at the general reader. Though sometimes hard to follow through the thicket of supporting examples drawn from plant and animal life, its calm, reasoned prose occasionally approaches quiet grandeur. Nowhere is this more true than in its famous closing paragraph:*

> *It is interesting to contemplate an entangled bank, clothed with many plants of many kinds, with birds singing on the bushes, with various insects flitting about, and with worms crawling through the damp earth, and to reflect that these elaborately constructed forms, so different from each other, and dependent on each other in so complex a manner, have all been produced by laws acting around us. These laws, taken in the largest sense, being Growth with Reproduction; Inheritance which is almost implied by reproduction; Variability from the indirect and direct action of the external conditions of life, and from use and disuse; a Ratio of Increase so high as to lead to a Struggle for Life, and as a consequence to Natural Selection, entailing Divergence of Character and the Extinction of less-improved forms. Thus, from the war of nature, from famine and death, the most exalted object which we are capable of conceiving, namely, the production of the higher animals, directly follows. There is grandeur in this view of life, with its several powers, having been originally breathed into a few forms or into one; and that, whilst this planet has gone cycling on according to the fixed law of gravity, from so simple a beginning endless forms most beautiful and most wonderful have been, and are being, evolved.*

1859   British physician Alfred Garrod (1819–1907) is the first to clearly distinguish between osteoarthritis (marked by cartilage destruction in joints, and spur formation), and rheumatoid arthritis, which is characterized by joints swelling, deformity, and inflammation.   **MED**

1859   German psychologist Moritz Lazarus and German philologist Heymann Steinthal found the first comparative psychology journal. **PSYCH**

1859   Scottish mathematician James Clerk Maxwell develops the kinetic theory of gases, which explains the physical properties of gases in terms of the random movement of particles. Existing laws concerning gases, such as Boyle's law (1662), can be deduced from Maxwell's theory.   **PHYS**

1859   American businessmen Orson Fowler and Lorenzo and Samuel Wells establish a firm to sell phrenological equipment and related devices. They write a best-selling book entitled the *Phrenological Self-Instructor*. Phrenology becomes widely accepted as businesses require phrenological exams before hiring, people considering marriage are advised first to consult a phrenologist, and the 1860 presidential candidates are phrenologically analyzed for their leadership abilities.   **PSYCH**

1859   Scottish physician Lockhart Robinson begins using wet sheets to treat mental illness. In this method a cold, wet sheet is wrapped around a patient's naked body to control agitation. This "wet pack" will be used into the twentieth century, until the advent of antipsychotic drugs in the 1950s.   **PSYCH**

1859   French anthropologist and surgeon Pierre-Paul Broca founds the Société d'Anthropologie.   **SOC**

1859   English philosopher John Stuart Mill publishes *On Liberty*, a classic statement of utilitarian political theory, in which he argues that public action should aim to promote the greatest happiness of the greatest number of people.   **SOC**

Aug. 28, 1859   American railway conductor Edwin L. Drake drills sixty-nine feet under the ground at Titusville, Pennsylvania, to produce the first petroleum oil well.   **TECH**

1860s   In the early part of the decade, American experimenter L. M. Rutherford devises a telescopic lens system optically designed to take photos—in effect a camera with a telescope as a lens.   **ASTRO**

1860s   Glass goggles first come into use for underwater exploration.   **TECH**

1860   French physicist Gaston Planté invents a rechargeable storage battery. At this time he also invents the first workable electric storage battery.   **TECH**

1860   Many notable scientists, including especially the Swiss-American Louis Agassiz, criticize Charles Darwin and the evolutionary theory he presented in his *Origin of Species*. Agassiz claims, for instance, that each species has been separately—and divinely—created.   **BIO**

1860   German chemist Robert Bunsen and German physicist Gustav Kirchhoff discover the elements cesium and rubidium.   **CHEM**

Oil Derricks at Pit Hole, Pennsylvania. (*American Petroleum Institute*)

1860   By now, French chemist Pierre-Eugène-Marcelin Berthelot has synthesized a number of organic compounds in the laboratory, including some that do not occur in living tissue, disproving the idea that only living tissue can produce organic compounds.   **CHEM**

1860   A conference in Karlsruhe, Germany, on the structure of organic molecules is the first international scientific meeting, organized chiefly by German chemist Friedrich August Kekule von Stradonitz. At the conference, Italian chemist Stanislao Cannizzaro urges his fellow colleagues to accept Amedeo Avogadro's 1811 hypothesis that all gases at a given temperature contain the same number of molecules. The acceptance that is eventually given permits the determination of the molecular weight of different gases.   **CHEM**

1860   French physician Georges Hayes begins his studies on platelets, the smallest cellular elements of the blood, and is the first to accurately count them. Platelets will prove important in the diagnosis and treatment of many immunological diseases.   **MED**

1860   Dutch ophthalmologist Frans Donders introduces the use of glasses to correct visual astigmatism.   **MED**

1860	The first nurse-training school is established by Florence Nightingale at London's St. Thomas Hospital. **MED**
1860	German physicist Gustav Kirchhoff hypothesizes that a black body, or a body that absorbs all incoming light, will emit all wavelengths of light when heated. **PHYS**
1860	Scottish physicist James Clerk Maxwell and Austrian physicist Ludwig Eduard Boltzmann independently develop the Maxwell-Boltzmann statistics analyzing the statistical behavior of molecules in a gas. **PHYS**
1860	Samuel Archer King and William Black become the first aerial photographers when they take two photographs of Boston from a balloon. **TECH**
1860	Belgian inventor Jean-Joseph Étienne Lenoir patents an early internal combustion engine. A more efficient engine will be created by Nikolaus Otto in 1876. **TECH**
1860	The first Winchester repeating rifle is put into production in the United States. **TECH**
1860	The Pony Express begins operation transporting mail by relay teams on horseback between Missouri and California. **TECH**
1860	Linoleum, a linseed-oil-based hard floor covering, is developed by British inventor Frederick Walton. **TECH**
1861	German physicist Gustav Kirchhoff shows that the composition of the sun can be determined by spectral analysis. **ASTRO**
1861	German cytologist Max Schultze develops the theory of protoplasm (cell substance), based on his own work and on earlier cell studies by Casper Friedrich Wolff, Félix Dujardin, Jan Purkinje, and Hugo von Mohl. According to Schultze, a cell's most basic components are its nucleus and protoplasm. **BIO**
1861	British physicist Sir William Crookes discovers the element thallium. **CHEM**
1861	German chemist Friedrich August Kekule von Stradonitz publishes a textbook on organic chemistry that defines its subject as the chemistry of carbon compounds, not living things. **CHEM**
1861	Scottish physical chemist Thomas Graham distinguishes colloids from crystalloids. The former are substances such as gelatin and starch that will not dissolve through a membrane, whereas the latter will. **CHEM**
1861	American surgeon Gordon Buck introduces the weight-and-pulley apparatus since called Buck's traction to use with orthopedic patients. **MED**

1861   American gynecologist James Marion Sims develops a method for the surgical removal of the cervix and describes vaginismus, or painful vaginal spasms.   **MED**

1861   French physician Prosper Ménière describes the type of vertigo and progressive deafness associated with the ear that is now known as Menière's disease.   **MED**

1861   Quarry workers in Solnhofen, Germany, unearth a fossil of *Archaeopteryx*. With both reptilian and avian features, this creature appears to represent an intermediate phase in the evolution of birds, thus lending support to Darwin's theories. *Archaeopteryx* flourished during the Jurassic period, about 150 million years ago.   **PALEO**

1861   French surgeon Pierre-Paul Broca discovers the speech center in the brain, which leads to his theory of the localization of function. His work will initiate systematic mapping of areas of the brain and their functions, a fundamental concept in brain surgery.   **PSYCH**

1861   The velocipede, or bicycle, is developed by Parisian transportation designer Pierre Michaux. *See also* 1839, MacMillan.   **TECH**

1861   The multiround, rapid-firing Gatling gun is developed by American engineer Richard Jordan Gatling.   **TECH**

1861   Steelmaking is streamlined with the development of the open-hearth process, invented independently by French engineer Pierre Émile Martin and German-born British inventor William Siemens.   **TECH**

1862   German biochemist Ernst Felix Hoppe-Seyler is first to crystallize and name the protein called hemoglobin that is responsible for the blood's red color. He also establishes the first biochemistry laboratory, at the University of Tübingen.   **BIO**

1862   Charles Darwin writes in detail on cross-fertilization, including insects' role in the process, in his *Fertilization of Orchids*.   **BIO**

1862   German botanist Julius von Sachs establishes that plant starch results from photosynthesis with carbon dioxide absorbed from the air.   **BIO**

c. 1862   British physicist William Thomson launches an attack on uniformitarianism and Darwinian evolution, arguing from the present temperature of the earth and the presumed rate of its past cooling that the earth is not as old as supposed. This argument will seem incontrovertible until the discovery of radioactivity in 1898 shows that the earth possesses a source of internal heat unknown to Thomson.   **EARTH**

1862   French chemist Louis Pasteur publishes a paper supporting the germ theory of disease. His own discoveries will later provide further evidence (*see* 1880).   **MED**

1863   British astronomer William Huggins argues from stellar spectra that stars are composed of the same elements that exist on earth.   **ASTRO**

1863	German mineralogists Ferdinand Reich and Theodor Richter discover the element indium. **CHEM**
1863	British chemist John Alexander Reina Newlands makes a list of elements in order of their atomic weight, claiming to find a law of octaves governing the properties of the elements, a claim later discredited. **CHEM**
1863	German chemist Adolf von Baeyer discovers barbituric acid, the parent compound of barbiturates. **CHEM**
1863	Irish physicist John Tyndall discovers the greenhouse effect: gases such as carbon dioxide and water vapor in the atmosphere permit visible light to enter but tend to hold in the infrared radiation emitted by the earth's surface. As a result, the earth's surface is warmer than it would be without these gases. **EARTH**
1863	British scientist Francis Galton publishes *Meteorographica*, which introduces modern weather-mapping techniques and the concept of anticyclones, or high-pressure areas of the atmosphere. **EARTH**
1863	British geophysicist Augustus Love discovers the phenomenon called the Love wave, a type of earthquake. His subsequent research allows geologists to measure the thickness of the earth's crust. **EARTH**
1863	J. D. Dana writes his *Manual of Geology*, an essential text of American geology for four decades. **EARTH**
c. 1863	Dutch ophthalmologist Herman Snellen develops the Snellen eye chart to test sharpness of vision. **MED**
1863	French bacteriologist Louis Pasteur develops the process of partial heat sterilization now called pasteurization that prevents wine spoilage. It will later be used with milk and beer. **MED**
Oct. 26, 1863	Swiss humanitarian Jean-Henri Dunant establishes a relief society in Geneva that will eventually evolve into the International Red Cross. **MED**
1863	The U.S. Congress gives the National Academy of Sciences in Washington, D.C., its charter to advise the government on issues concerning science and technology. **MISC**
1863	English scientist Thomas Henry Huxley publishes *Man's Place in Nature*, the first book to take a scientific approach to human evolution. Using comparative anatomy, Huxley deduces that the chimpanzee and the gorilla are the closest relatives of humans and all evolved according to the same principles. **PALEO**
1863	The London Underground, the first subsurface public railway, is opened. **TECH**

1863   Granula (not Granola), the first cold breakfast food, made of baked graham, is introduced to the public by American sanitarium operator James Caleb Jackson.   **TECH**

....

"Science is nothing but trained and organized common sense, differing from the latter only as a veteran may differ from a raw recruit: and its methods differ from those of common sense only as far as the guardsman's cut and thrust differ from the manner in which a savage wields his club."
—Thomas H. Huxley, English biologist;
late nineteenth century

....

1864   The distance of the earth from the sun is calculated as 91 million miles, close to the actual value of 92.96 million miles.   **ASTRO**

1864–1867   In his *Principles of Biology* (1864, 1867), English philosopher Herbert Spencer coins the term *survival of the fittest* to describe a way of understanding Darwin's theory of natural selection. Spencer will also suggest that the concept implies that the weakest, most useless members of society should be allowed to die off.   **BIO**

1864   Louis Pasteur proves that microorganisms exist in the atmosphere and are not spontaneously generated.   **MED**

1864   In an effort to cut down the spread of syphilis, England passes the Contagious Diseases Act, requiring compulsory medical exams and registration of all prostitutes in towns and seaports where military personnel are housed.   **MED**

1864   Influential German sociologist Max Weber is born (*d.* 1920). He will develop methodologies for cross-cultural studies and argue that sociology should be value free. *See* 1904.   **SOC**

1864   Americans George M. Pullman and Benjamin Field patent the design for a sleeping car, the *Pioneer*, with convertible berths.   **TECH**

1865   While daydreaming about a snake coiling in on itself, German chemist Friedrich August Kekule von Stradonitz discovers the ring structure of the benzene molecule.   **CHEM**

1865   Austrian chemist Johann Joseph Loschmidt calculates the number of molecules in one mole of a gas. The number, which has the approximate value 6×10^{23}, is called Avogadro's number or, later, the Avogadro constant. From this number the mass of molecules and atoms can be calculated.   **CHEM**

1865   Construction of the Union Pacific Railroad begins in the United States.   **EARTH**

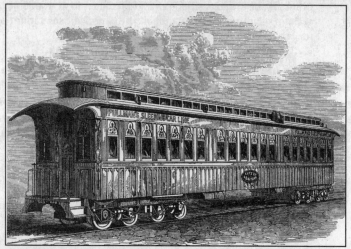

Pullman car, 1876, exterior and interior. (*New York Public Library*)

July 14, 1865	British artist turned mountaineer Edward Whymper reaches the top of the Matterhorn in the Alps. **EARTH**
1865	German mathematician August Ferdinand Möbius invents the Möbius strip, a ribbon of paper with only one edge and one side. This invention is one of the founding events of topology, the branch of geometry concerned with the properties of objects that are not changed by continuous deformations such as stretching and twisting. **MATH**
1865	French physiologist Claude Bernard marks a medical ethics milestone when he concludes that medical experiments can be permissible and even obligatory. He displays no interest in the informed consent issue. **MED**
Aug. 12, 1865	After studying Louis Pasteur's theories on bacteria, English physician Joseph Lister successfully uses carbolic acid as a surgical antiseptic. This antiseptic will forever change the survival rate and safety of surgery, as gangrene and suppuration (pus formation) are remarkably reduced. **MED**
1865	Scottish mathematician and physicist James Clerk Maxwell formulates Maxwell's equations, which describe the behavior of electric and magnetic fields and show that a changing field of one type will generate a field of the other type. The value Maxwell calculates for the speed of electromagnetic radiation closely matches the measured speed of light, leading him to propose that light is electromagnetic in nature. These equations represent the first theoretical unification of physical phenomena. **PHYS**
1865	British anthropologist Edward B. Tylor publishes his *Early History of Mankind*. **SOC**
1865	A design and production system to manufacture the interchangeable parts of rifles is developed by American machinists Francis Asbury Pratt and Amos Whitney. The two found their industrial factory, Pratt & Whitney, this year. **TECH**
1865	American inventor Linus Yale patents the type of cylinder lock called the Yale lock that will become popular for both commercial and residential use. **TECH**
1865	A compression ice-making machine is devised by American inventor Thaddeus Sobieski Coulincourt Lowe. It will be useful in developing refrigeration technology. **TECH**
1866	U.S. astronomer Daniel Kirkwood discovers the gaps now known as Kirkwood gaps in the distribution of asteroids. The uneven spacing is caused by the influence of Jupiter's gravity. **ASTRO**

THE ELECTROMAGNETIC SPECTRUM

*S*ince the publication of James Clerk Maxwell's equations describing electromagnetism in 1865, scientists have come to understand the full range of wavelengths over which electromagnetic radiation extends. Visible light is only one narrow part of this electromagnetic spectrum. The spectrum of radiation, from longest to shortest wavelengths, is as follows:

Type	Wavelength (Meters)
Radio	10^5–10^{-3}
Infrared	10^{-3}–10^{-6}
Visible light	10^{-7}
Ultraviolet	10^{-7}–10^{-9}
X-ray	10^{-9}–10^{-11}
Gamma rays	10^{-11}–10^{-14}

These varieties of radiation share a common wave structure of crests (high points) and troughs (low points). They differ only in the length of their waves or, to put it another way, their frequency, the number of times per second a wave passes a given point. Wavelength and frequency are inversely proportional; that is, long waves have low frequencies, short waves high frequencies. Frequency is also a reflection of energy level. The highest-frequency (shortest) waves, gamma rays and X-rays, are the most energetic and most potentially damaging to delicate systems like living tissue. The lowest-frequency, or longest, waves (infrared and radio) are the weakest waves.

Despite the explanatory power of the wave theory of electromagnetic radiation, it would become clear in the twentieth century (see 1900, Planck) that such rays could also be usefully regarded as particles, or quanta.

1866   After experimenting with the crossbreeding of sweet peas and making a statistical analysis of the results, Austrian monk Gregor J. Mendel concludes that each of an organism's inherited traits is determined by two heredity units called genes, one from each parent organism. Forgotten until the twentieth century, Mendel's laws of inheritance will form the basis of classical genetics. It is later understood that Mendel's genes are the material acted upon by natural selection in Darwin's theory of evolution. **BIO**

1866   German biologist Ernst Haeckel is first to use the word *ecology*. **BIO**

1866   Haeckel popularizes the idea that ontology recapitulates phylogeny, meaning that an embryo's stages of development mirror the evolutionary history of that species. Haeckel calls this the biogenetic law, but the doctrine will later be considered overstated, for embryonic development is far more complex.   **BIO**

1866   French geologist Gabriel-Auguste Daubrée proposes the existence of an iron and nickel core at the center of the earth.   **EARTH**

1866   F. Zirkel publishes *Lerbuch der Petrography*, a textbook on petrology notable for including an account of H. C. Sorby's technique for examining thin sections of rock with a polarizing microscope.   **EARTH**

1866–1867   British scientist Thomas H. Huxley names two Triassic dinosaurs from South Africa, *Euskelosaurus* and *Orosaurus*.   **PALEO**

1866   German physicist August Kundt designs Kundt's tube, a device to measure the speed of sound in different fluids.   **TECH**

CHOLERA AND GOD'S WILL

*T*he U.S. cholera epidemics of 1832, 1849, and 1866 killed tens of thousands of Americans in several cities. It is now known that cholera is spread through contaminated food, contact with afflicted persons, and, particularly, impure drinking water. It is also recognized that education about disease prevention and a supply of safe drinking water is the best deterrent to the spread of the disease.

But it was not until 1866 that public health agencies like New York City's Metropolitan Board of Health began to use new sanitation standards and education to stem the spread of the disease.

It was not until 1883 that the Vibrio comma *bacterium that causes cholera was discovered.*

Before then, most Americans saw cholera as a God-given retribution for moral failure. It was divine punishment for a life not lived in adherence to religious beliefs and upright behavior. Comments in newspapers like this August 1849 Scioto Gazette *from Chillicothe, Ohio, are representative of that belief in divine force as a cause of the spread of the disease.*

The Almighty conducts the order of Providence by rule—rules that are alike at all times and abiding. Who however shall set bounds to the physical and the moral—and pretend to tell where one ends and the other begins? Who can say whether it is from chemical or moral causes that this community is scourged, while that is spared?

1866   The first usable dynamo-electrical machine or dynamo, which allows for the mass generation of electricity, is developed by Ernst Werner von Siemens.   **TECH**

1866   Dynamite is developed by Swedish engineer Alfred Bernhard Nobel. The new compound is a mixture of nitroglycerin and diatomaceous earth.   **TECH**

1866   American merchant Cyrus West Field lays the first permanent transatlantic telegraph cable. *See also* 1854, Maury.   **TECH**

1867   The International Botanical Congress establishes the rules for botanical nomenclature known as the Paris Code. However, not until 1930 will a botanical code with worldwide acceptance be adopted.   **BIO**

1867   Norwegian chemists Cato Maximilian Guldberg and Peter Waage formulate the law of mass action, which states that the rate at which a chemical reaction occurs is proportional to the product of the active masses of the reactants. The active masses are defined by their concentration, the quantity of mass in a given volume.   **CHEM**

1867   British gynecologist John Braxton Hicks describes the painless uterine contractions in pregnancy that come to be called false labor.   **MED**

1867   British physician Sir Thomas Allbutt introduces the modern clinical thermometer.   **MED**

1867–1894   German social philosopher Karl Marx publishes *Das Kapital*, which his colleague Friedrich Engels finishes editing after Marx's death in 1883. The work is a systematic exposition of the economic and political philosophy now known as Marxism, which places class struggle at the center of history and predicts the overthrow of the capitalist class by the exploited working class. Marx's work strongly influences economics, political science, and sociology among other fields.   **SOC**

1867   French engineer Georges Leclanché invents the dry cell, an electric battery employing a chemical paste rather than fluids.   **TECH**

1867   The safety boiler, which reduces explosions, is patented by American engineers George Babcock and Stephen Wilcox. In the same year the two found the company Babcock & Wilcox.   **TECH**

1867   The first U.S. steam-operated elevated railway opens in New York City.   **TECH**

1868   British astronomer Sir William Huggins uses the Doppler-Fizeau effect (*see* 1848) to calculate that the star Sirius is moving away from us at twenty-nine miles per second, a relatively close estimate.   **ASTRO**

1868   Italian astronomer Pietro Angelo Secchi completes the first spectroscopic catalog, of about four thousand stars.   **ASTRO**

| 1868 | German botanist Julius von Sachs publishes his textbook *Lehrbuch der Botanik*, which will have a major influence on botany's emergence as a comprehensive discipline.   **BIO** |

| 1868 | French astronomer Pierre-Jules-César Janssen and British astronomer Joseph Norman Lockyer discover the element helium. *See also* 1895, Ramsay.   **CHEM** |

| 1868 | French paleontologist Édouard-Armand-Isidore-Hippolyte Lartet discovers four prehistoric human skeletons in Cro-Magnon, France. This Cro-Magnon man, some forty thousand years old, will be considered the first anatomically modern human ancestor.   **PALEO** |

| 1868 | British physician Sir William Gull becomes the first to describe anorexia nervosa, an eating disorder characterized by self-starvation.   **PSYCH** |

| 1868 | American George Westinghouse invents the Westinghouse air brake, which will be crucial to more efficient train travel. In 1872 he will introduce the automatic air brake.   **TECH** |

| 1868 | The knuckle coupler, a safer alternative to the old standard link-and-pin system of joining rail cars, is patented by former American military officer Eli Hamilton Janney.   **TECH** |

| 1868 | Tungsten steel, harder than other types, is developed by English metallurgist Robert Forester Mushet.   **TECH** |

| 1868 | The typewriter is patented by American inventors Christopher Sholes, Carlos G. Glidden, and Samuel W. Soule. In 1874, it will be produced in quantity by the Remington Fire Arms Co.   **TECH** |

| 1869 | English naturalist and zoologist Alfred Russel Wallace publishes *The Malay Archipelago: The Land of the Orangutan and the Bird of Paradise*. In it, he points out that Malay animal life is divided into two distinct types. The animal life in the western half is like that in India, that in the eastern half more like Australia's. The line dividing the two regions is still called Wallace's line. This discovery marks the foundation of biogeography.   **BIO** |

| 1869 | French botanist Jules Raulin proves that zinc is crucial to the growth of the plant *Aspergillus*.   **BIO** |

| Mar. 6, 1869 | Russian chemist Dmitry Ivanovich Mendeleyev publishes the periodic table of the elements.   **CHEM** |

| Dec. 1869 | Modern medicine's first demonstration of free skin grafting is done in Paris.   **MED** |

| 1869 | Irish physical chemist Thomas Andrews suggests that every gas has a critical temperature above which it cannot be turned into liquid by an increase in pressure alone.   **PHYS** |

1869   Irish physicist John Tyndall discovers the Tyndall effect, a characteristic scattering of light through a medium containing small particles. The effect accounts for the blueness of the sky and the redness of sunsets.   **PHYS**

1869   British scientist Francis Galton publishes *Hereditary Genius*, concerning the familial tendency to inherit brilliance. He will pioneer the use of statistics in psychological measurement.   **PSYCH**

1869   The 103-mile-long Suez Canal opens for use, uniting the Gulf of Suez on the south with the Mediterranean Sea via the Red Sea. Trade and travel become far less onerous.   **TECH**

1869   Margarine, an oil-based butter substitute, is produced commercially for the first time by Frenchman Hippolyte Mége-Mouries.   **TECH**

1869   The U.S. transcontinental railroad is completed on May 10 at Promontory Point, Utah. There 1,006 miles of line built by the Union Pacific Railway from Omaha, Nebraska, joins 680 miles built by the Central Pacific Railway from Sacramento, California.   **TECH**

1870s   German mathematician Georg Ferdinand Cantor establishes the theory of sets (or *Mengenlehre*, aggregates) as a distinct field of research and develops an arithmetic of transfinite numbers.   **MATH**

1870s   At mid-decade American paleontologist O. C. Marsh makes a number of major contributions to vertebrate paleontology. In addition to clarifying the evolutionary history of the horse, Marsh discovers many dinosaur species and offers evidence of a link between reptiles and birds. *See also* 1877, March and Cope.   **PALEO**

1870s   Austrian physicist Ernst Mach states Mach's principle, that a body's inertia can be attributed to the interaction between that body and the rest of the universe and a body in isolation will have an inertia equal to zero.   **PHYS**

1870   German archaeologist Alexander Conze classifies chronological styles of pottery, providing a key to dating of strata.   **ARCH**

1870   English biologist Alfred Wallace publishes *Contributions to the Theory of Natural Selection* and American biologist Edward Cope publishes *Systematic Arrangement of the Extinct Bactrachia, Reptilia, and Aves of North America*. Both publications provide additional support for the theory of evolution.   **BIO**

1870   The U.S. Weather Bureau is established, largely due to the efforts of meteorologist Cleveland Abbe.   **EARTH**

c. 1870   German surgeon Friedrich Trendelenburg begins positioning surgery patients on their backs with the pelvis elevated and the head downward at an angle. This Trendelenburg's position will come into common use in abdominal surgery and to combat shock.   **MED**

c. 1870   The passage of pure food laws in western Europe advances the cause of preventive medicine.   **MED**

1870   Drawing on his studies of the Seneca people, American anthropologist Lewis Henry Morgan correlates kinship terminology with cultural traditions of marriage and descent.   **SOC**

1870   English machinists William Hillman and James Kemp Starley patent a light, all-metal bicycle. *See also* 1839, MacMillan.   **TECH**

1870   A rotary press capable of printing two sides of a page at once is developed by U.S. inventor Richard Hoe.   **TECH**

1870   The first personal mechanical can opener, using a moving wheel to cut metal, is developed by American inventor William Lyman.   **TECH**

1871   German archaeologist Heinrich Schliemann begins excavating a hill called Hissarlik in Turkey and discovers the ruins of ancient Troy, the legendary site of Homer's *Iliad*.   **ARCH**

1871   Russian chemist Dmitry Mendeleyev predicts the properties of three elements missing from his periodic table—eka-boron, eka-aluminum, and eka-silicon. His predictions later prove to be correct.   **CHEM**

1871   German chemist Max Bodenstein develops the concept of a chemical chain reaction, a reaction whose products cause further reactions of the same kind and is therefore self-sustaining.   **CHEM**

1871   Harvard University supports American physiologist Henry Pickering Bowditch in establishing the first U.S. physiology laboratory. He will become known for childhood-growth investigations that will determine that growth is dependent on good nutrition and arrested development can be a signal of disease.   **MED**

1871   Charles Darwin publishes *The Descent of Man, and Selection in Relation to Sex*, in which he extends his theory of natural selection to human evolution and invents the concept of sexual selection. He also suggests that humans evolved from apelike ancestors in Africa millions of years ago.   **PALEO**

1871–1893   British scientist William Crawford Williamson publishes a series of papers describing fossil plants found in coal deposits in northern England. This work proves a major contribution to paleobotany research.   **PALEO**

1871   British anthropologist Edward B. Tylor publishes *Primitive Culture*, in which he discusses animistic religion and develops methods for making cultural comparisons.   **SOC**

1872   From clay tablets discovered at Nineveh (*see* 1840s), English archaeologist George Smith deciphers the *Epic of Gilgamesh*, a Sumerian story that may date back to as early as 2500 B.C.   **ARCH**

1872   The Ebers papyrus (*see* 1600 B.C.) is discovered in the ruins of Thebes, Egypt. It becomes important for its documentation of ancient Egyptian medicine.   **ARCH**

1872   Studying the star Vega, U.S. astronomer Henry Draper becomes the first to photograph a stellar spectrum.   **ASTRO**

1872   German botanist Ferdinand J. Cohn founds the science of bacteriology.   **BIO**

1872   French biology professor Henri de Lacaze-Duthiers establishes a "Laboratory of Experimental Zoology," the Roscoff Biological Station, at Roscoff, Brittany.   **BIO**

1872   A U.S. government survey of the fortieth parallel, led by geologist Clarence King, exposes a mining stock fraud in what will come to be known as "the diamond hoax."   **EARTH**

....

"It is the customary fate of new truths to begin as heresies and to end as superstitions."—Thomas H. Huxley, English biologist; late nineteenth century

....

1872–1876   The *Challenger* expedition, a cooperative effort of the Admiralty and the Royal Society, voyages a total of 68,890 miles, making 492 deep soundings and 133 dredgings. The scope and thoroughness of this research makes the expedition a milestone in the history of oceanography.   **EARTH**

1872   American Ferdinand Hayden has the Yellowstone region declared the first U.S. national park, marking the beginning of the national park movement.   **EARTH**

1872   American geologist John Wesley Powell begins systematically surveying the canyon country of Colorado.   **EARTH**

1872   Contributions are made to the arithmetization of analysis by several mathematicians, including Frenchman H. C. R. Méray and Germans Karl Weierstrass, H. E. Heine, Georg Cantor, and J. W. R. Dedekind.   **MATH**

1872   German mathematician J. W. R. Dedekind introduces the so-called Dedekind cut, with which irrational numbers can be defined.   **MATH**

1872   German mathematician Felix Klein gives an address known as the Erlanger Program, in which he describes geometry as the study of invariant properties under a particular transformation group.   **MATH**

c. 1872   The first U.S. nursing school is founded, at New York City's Bellevue Hospital.   **MED**

1872	Austrian dermatologist Moritz K. Kaposi describes the skin disease called Kaposi's sarcoma that will become associated with acquired immune deficiency syndrome (AIDS) in the late twentieth century. **MED**
1872	American physician George Sumner Huntington describes the hereditary neurological disease characterized by grotesque grimaces and dementia that is now known as Huntington's chorea. **PSYCH**
1872	German aviator Paul Haenlein flies in the first dirigible to be powered by an internal combustion engine, fueled by coal gas from the supporting bag. **TECH**
1873	British astronomer Richard Anthony Proctor argues that lunar craters were formed by meteoric impact. **ASTRO**
1873	The occurrence of mitosis—mitotic nuclear division—in cells is recognized for the first time. **BIO**
1873	Italian histologist Camillo Golgi introduces cellular staining with silver salts. The network of membranous vesicles in the cell known as the Golgi apparatus is revealed for the first time with this staining. **BIO**
1873	British scientist Walter Bagehot publishes *Physics and Politics*, applying the theory of natural selection to the rise and fall of human customs and institutions. **BIO**
1873	The International Meteorological Organization is founded. **EARTH**
1873	German mineralologist Ferdinand Zirkel and German geologist Karl Rosenbusch simultaneously but independently publish similar treatises on microscopical petrography, thus laying the foundations of the field. **EARTH**
1873	French mathematician Charles Hermite identifies the first proven transcendental number: *e*, equal to 2.71828... Transcendental numbers are those that are not algebraic, meaning they cannot serve as solutions to any conceivable polynomial equation. **MATH**
1873	Dutch physicist Johannes Diderik van der Waals modifies existing gas laws, observing that only perfect gases (those with zero-volume molecules and no attraction between molecules, which exist only in theory) obey the unmodified laws. Most real gases under most conditions approximately follow the existing laws, but van der Waals introduces the more accurate van der Waals equation of state that is especially useful at extremes of temperature and pressure. **PHYS**
1873	The magnetic effect of electric convection is observed by U.S. physicist Henry Augustus Rowland. **TECH**
1873	The world's first cable-car streetcar begins operation, in San Francisco. **TECH**
1873	In France the perfume industry is simplified with discoveries of a process to extract floral essences. **TECH**

JUST YOU WAIT, HENRY SWEET

*T*he insufferable Henry Higgins in George Bernard Shaw's 1912 play Pygmalion, the basis for the 1956 musical My Fair Lady, was based on an actual professor of phonetics and Old English, Henry Sweet (1845–1912). This British scholar invented his own system of phonetics and published such influential works as History of English Sounds *(1874) and* Handbook of Phonetics *(1877).*

1873   Barbed wire, or the devil's rope, is demonstrated for fencing off farmers' crops and ranchers' stock by American Henry Rose. Machines to produce barbed wire are subsequently patented by Americans Jacob Haish and Joseph Farwell Glidden.   **TECH**

1874   American photographer William Henry Jackson explores the ancient Native American cliff dwellings of Mesa Verde, Colorado.   **ARCH**

1874   German zoologist Anton Dohrn founds the Naples, Italy, Zoological Station, the model for many biological stations in the future.   **BIO**

1874   Dutch chemist Jacobus Hendricus van't Hoff (and, independently, French chemist Joseph-Achille Le Bel) advances the tetrahedral carbon atom as a three-dimensional representation of organic molecules. This model proves useful in explaining optical activity, the ability of some substances to rotate the plane of polarized light *(see* 1815 and 1846), and creates interest in stereochemistry, the study of how the structural arrangement of atoms in molecules affects a substance's chemical properties.   **CHEM**

1874   German mathematician Georg Ferdinand Cantor investigates transfinite numbers.   **MATH**

1874   British physician and feminist Sophia Louisa Jex-Blake founds the London School of Medicine for Women, to ensure the availability of medical education for women.   **MED**

1874   German physicist Karl Ferdinand Braun notes that in certain crystals an electric current will flow in one direction but not in the opposite one.   **PHYS**

1874   German novelist Leopold von Sacher-Masoch writes *Die Messalinen Weins*, in which he describes sexual gratification derived from pain. His name is the origin of the term *masochism*.   **PSYCH**

Aug. 31, 1874	American psychologist Edward Lee Thorndike is born in Williamsburg, Massachusetts (*d.* 1949). He will be the first psychologist to study animal behavior in laboratory experiments. At Columbia University he will teach that psychology should study behavior, not conscious experience or mental conditions. He will apply work with animals to human education, leading to his pioneering work in the field of mental measurement. **PSYCH**
1874	The steel-arched Eads Bridge at St. Louis, Missouri, becomes the first bridge to span the Mississippi River. **TECH**
1874	Chilled ridged rollers are used, along with millstones, to produce flour more efficiently at the C. C. Washburn mill in Wisconsin. **TECH**
1875	In California, Luther Burbank establishes a plant nursery for the study and cultivation of grasses, grains, fruits, and vegetables. **BIO**
1875	Pathologist Oscar Hertwig demonstrates that sperm enters the ovum, at which point fertilization takes place. **BIO**
1875	French chemist Paul-Émile Lecoq de Boisbaudran discovers the element gallium, which corresponds to Mendeleyev's eka-aluminum and thus supports the validity of the periodic table. *See* 1869 and 1871. **CHEM**
1875	V. V. Dokudaev begins field studies of Russian soils from which he evolves the basic principles of the new science of pedology, or soil science. **EARTH**
1875	Russian mathematician Sonya (Sofya) Vasilyevna Kovalevskaya furthers the work of Augustin Louis Cauchy in solving partial differential equations; the result is called the Cauchy-Kovalevskaya theorem. **MATH**
1875	German pathologist Rudolf Virchow becomes the first to describe congenital spina bifida, a defect in the spinal canal walls that allows the spine to protrude in the form of a tumor. **MED**
1875	Scottish physicist John Kerr discovers the Kerr effect, or the ability of some substances, when placed in an electric field, to differentially refract light waves whose vibrations occur in two directions. **PHYS**
1875	British physicist William Crookes invents the radiometer, a set of pivoted vanes whose spontaneous motion in sunlight in a partial vacuum lends support to the kinetic theory of gases. **PHYS**
1875	Swiss psychiatrist Carl Gustav Jung is born in Zurich (*d.* 1961). He will be best known for his theories on the collective unconscious, the interpretation of dreams, and the division of personalities into introvert and extrovert. He will form his own school of analytical psychology after breaking with his teacher and colleague Sigmund Freud. **PSYCH**

1875   French neurologist Guillaume Duchenne (b. 1806) dies. Duchenne, a pioneer of neurology, was the founder of electrotherapy and described numerous neurological disorders. The spinal cord and brain stem degeneration which develops in untreated syphilis, Duchenne's disease, was named for him.   **PSYCH**

1875   British philosopher and scientist John Stuart Mill proposes post-hoc analysis: the examination of different childhood experiences to discover the effect they have on moral character development. In the twentieth century, developmental psychologists will use this procedure in longitudinal studies of children.   **PSYCH**

c. 1875   American sociologist William Graham Sumner, a follower of British scholar Herbert Spencer, teaches the first American course in sociology, at Yale University.   **SOC**

1875   British engineer Thomas Moy demonstrates the "Aerial Steamer," at the Crystal Palace in London. This steam-powered pilotless monoplane lifts itself six inches off the ground while attached to a tether on a circular track.   **TECH**

1875   British physicist William Crookes invents an improved vacuum tube called the Crookes tube.   **TECH**

1875   Blasting gelatin is developed by Swedish inventor Alfred Nobel. **TECH**

1875   The telephone is invented by Scottish-American teacher Alexander Graham Bell. It comes about as a result of trying to develop a system of electric speech for the deaf students Bell teaches.   **TECH**

1875   A wax-stencil duplicating process that is developed now will be patented next year by American inventor Thomas Alva Edison. These machines will be improved by both Edison and the machine's authorized licensee, American Albert Blake Dick, who will eventually develop the A. B. Dick Diaphragm Mimeograph.   **TECH**

1875   Synthetic vanillin, which in its natural form is an ingredient of vanilla beans, is patented by British scientist Ferdinand Tiemann.   **TECH**

1875   The first milk chocolate for public consumption, made by mixing chocolate and sweetened condensed milk, is pioneered in Vevey, Switzerland, by staff members of the Nestlé and Daniel Peter chocolate factories.   **TECH**

1876–1878   German archaeologist Heinrich Schliemann excavates ancient Mycenae, the legendary city of the Greek leader Agamemnon.   **ARCH**

1876   English naturalist Alfred Wallace systematizes the science of biogeography. In his *Geographical Distribution of Animals*, Wallace discusses extinct fauna and their geographical movement or relocation over the years.   **BIO**

1876   British evolutionist Charles Darwin publishes *The Effects of Cross and Self Fertilization in the Vegetable Kingdom*, in which he claims that cross-fertilization increases the strength and vigor of offspring.   **BIO**

1876   American physicist Josiah Willard Gibbs begins publishing a two-year series of papers outlining the laws of chemical thermodynamics. In discussing the basic forces that operate in chemical reactions he defines the concepts of free energy, chemical potential, equilibrium between phases of matter, degrees of freedom, and the equation called the phase rule.   **CHEM**

c. 1876   Between now and 1880 Henrik Mohn and Cato Maximilian Guldberg develop the field of dynamical meteorology, with the results known as the Mohn-Guldberg equations.   **EARTH**

1876   British explorer Henry M. Stanley circumnavigates Africa's Lake Victoria and charts the course of the Congo River.   **EARTH**

1876   German bacteriologist Robert Koch isolates the anthrax bacillus, the cause of an infectious disease that attacks cattle, sheep, horses, and goats and is passed to humans by these animals.   **MED**

1876   American librarian Melvil Dewey invents the Dewey decimal system for classifying and organizing books in libraries.   **MISC**

1876   American paleontologists Edward D. Cope and Charles H. Sternberg explore the Judith River formation in Montana, discovering fossils of Cretaceous dinosaurs.   **PALEO**

1876   Near his home in Trenton Falls, New York, geologist Charles Doolittle Walcott discovers the first U.S. trilobite with its appendages preserved.   **PALEO**

1876   German physicist Eugen Goldstein discovers cathode rays, streams of fluorescence flowing from the cathode, or negatively charged electrode, in an evacuated tube.   **PHYS**

1876   Scottish psychologist Alexander Bain founds the periodical *Mind*, the first general psychological journal. At this time psychology begins to develop as a discipline apart from philosophy and physiology.   **PSYCH**

1876–1896   English sociologist Herbert Spencer applies evolution concepts to human sociology. In his three-volume *Principles of Sociology*, Spencer writes about the process of individual differentiation from a group and its effect on individual freedom.   **SOC**

1876   German inventor Nikolaus August Otto constructs the first practical internal-combustion engine, in which the piston makes four strokes (a four-cycle engine).   **TECH**

1876   The Corliss 160-horsepower engine or dynamo, named for American designer George Henry Corliss, is used to run exhibits at Machinery Hall in the U.S. Centennial Exposition. It is immortalized as a nineteenth-century icon in the essay "The Virgin and the Dynamo" by American author Henry Adams.   **TECH**

1876   American shopowner Henry Sherwin, cofounder of the Sherwin-Williams Co., develops a process for grinding and dispersing pigments into linseed oil and popularizes ready-to-use paint.   **TECH**

1876   On an improved, patented version of his telephone, Scottish-American inventor Alexander Graham Bell utters to his assistant Thomas Watson the first complete sentences transmitted over the telephone: "Mr. Watson, come here. I want you." The call takes place at Bell's residence in Boston, Massachusetts. The first telephone is sold in May 1877.   **TECH**

....

"Mr. Watson, come here. I want you."—Alexander Graham Bell to assistant Thomas A. Watson, in the first complete sentences relayed over telephone wire, Boston; March 10, 1876

....

1876   The Howe floater, which distributes melted solder onto can tops and bottoms, mechanizes the soldering process and speeds it 100-fold.   **TECH**

1877   U.S. astronomer Asaph Hall discovers Phobos and Deimos, the two satellites of Mars.   **ASTRO**

1877   Italian astronomer Giovanni Schiaparelli observes lines on Mars that he calls *canali*, or channels. U.S. astronomer Percival Lowell will misinterpret these to be canals, considering them evidence of waterworks constructed by intelligent beings.   **ASTRO**

1877   German botanist Wilhelm Pfeffer explains osmosis (*see* 1748, Jean-Antoine Nollet) by relating it to movement of molecules across a membrane. As a result of his studies, Pfeffer is able to calculate the molecular weight of proteins involved in osmosis.   **BIO**

1877   German biochemist F. Hoppe-Seyler coins the term *biochemistry* for the study of the chemistry of living organisms, which will emerge as a full-fledged discipline early in the twentieth century.   **BIO**

1877   French physicist Louis-Paul Cailletet (and, independently, Swiss chemist Raoul-Pierre Pictet) liquefies oxygen, nitrogen, and carbon monoxide.   **CHEM**

1877   British anesthesiologist Joseph Clover invents equipment now called Clover's apparatus to more safely administer anesthesia.   **MED**

Building the Secrettown trestle in the Sierras, 1877. (*National Park Service*)

1877   American paleontologists and lifelong rivals Othniel Charles Marsh and Edward Drinker Cope make the first of several separate collections of late Jurassic dinosaur skeletons in the Morrison formation in Colorado and at Como Bluff, Wyoming. The dinosaurs they discover in the next few years will include *Allosaurus*, *Apatosaurus*, (*Brontosaurus*), *Diplodocus*, *Camarasaurus*, and *Stegosaurus*.   **PALEO**

1877   Russian physiologist Ivan Pavlov begins his studies on conditioned response in relation to dog's digestion.   **PSYCH**

1877   American anthropologist Lewis Henry Morgan publishes his *Ancient Society*, which proposes that human societies go through stages of evolution from savagery to barbarism to civilization.   **SOC**

1877   Swiss physician A. E. Fick invents the first practical contact lenses, but as they are made of glass and cover the entire eyeball, they are not widely used.   **TECH**

1877   The first telephone switchboard is put into operation, in Boston.   **TECH**

1877   The first phonograph is tested by its inventor, American Thomas Alva Edison, who sings and hears played back "Mary Had a Little Lamb." His phonograph operates by recording sounds on indented metal cylinders.   **TECH**

1878	German archaeologist Heinrich Schliemann discovers ancient Ithaca, the legendary home of Greek hero Odysseus. **ARCH**
1878	Jacques L. Soret and Marc Delafontaine discover the element holmium. **CHEM**
1878	The United Kingdom passes the Dentists Act, requiring dentists to be registered. Like the earlier Medical Act (*see* 1858), it is an attempt to protect the public from unqualified practitioners. **MED**
1878	A large group of well-preserved *Iguanodon* skeletons is discovered in a coal mine at Bernissart, Belgium. *See* 1882, Dollo. **PALEO**
1878	German neurologist Wilhelm Erb discovers a disease marked by muscular weakness and fatigability, now called myasthenia gravis. **PSYCH**
1878	The Japanese term *shinrigaku,* later formally adopted as the Japanese word for *psychology,* is first used in Japanese literature. **PSYCH**
Jan. 9, 1878	In Greenville, South Carolina, John Broadus Watson, the founder of behavioral psychology, is born (*d.* 1958). This area of work restricts the field to the study of objectively observable behavior, which it then explains in stimulus-response terms. His writings will include *Animal Education* (1903), *Behavior* (1914), and *Psychological Care of the Infant and Child* (1928). **PSYCH**
1878	U.S. inventor Thomas Alva Edison discovers that, by subdividing or stepping down electrical current, electric power can be supplied for mechanical use in the home. **TECH**
1878	British chemist Joseph Swan demonstrates the first carbon filament incandescent bulb, in London. **TECH**
1878	At the Remington Arms Co., in Connecticut, a shift key is developed for the Remington typewriter, for the first time allowing the production of upper- and lower-case letters. **TECH**
1878	By accidentally injecting air into the mixture, the first floating soap is invented, by a factory worker at the Procter & Gamble Co. in Cincinnati, Ohio. The product is named Ivory Soap by company owner Harley Procter, noting the word in a psalm in church. **TECH**
1879	The first known prehistoric paintings, done by Cro-Magnon man some fourteen thousand years ago, are discovered on cave walls in Altamira, Spain. **ARCH**
1879	English astronomer George H. Darwin suggests a now-discredited theory of lunar formation, that the moon formed from material ejected from the earth's crust during an early period of rapid rotation. **ASTRO**
1879	French chemist Paul-Émile Lecoq de Boisbaudran discovers the element samarium. **CHEM**

1879   Swedish chemist Lars Fredrik Nilson discovers the element scandium, Mendeleyev's predicted eka-boron (see 1871). Swedish chemist Per Teodor Cleve discovers the element thulium.   **CHEM**

1879   American chemists Ira Remsen and Constantine Fahlberg synthesize orthobenzoyl sulfimide, or saccharin. This sweet organic compound will become the first commercial sugar substitute.   **CHEM**

1879   Russian chemist Vladimir Markovnikov shows that carbon rings with four atoms, rather than the more commonly known six, can be formed.   **CHEM**

1879   American astronomer E. C. Pickering invents the meridian photometer and lays the foundations of exact stellar photometry.   **EARTH**

1879   Clarence King heads the newly organized U.S. Geological Survey. After two years, he will resign and John Wesley Powell will take his place.   **EARTH**

1879   French mathematician Jules-Henri Poincaré writes a doctoral thesis on differential equations that leads him to discover the properties of automorphic functions, one of his many contributions to the theory of differential equations and other areas of mathematics (including topology; see 1895).   **MATH**

1879   German physician Albert Neisser identifies the bacteria that cause gonorrhea and meningococcal meningitis, inflammation of the brain or spinal cord.   **MED**

1879   French dermatologists coin the term biopsy for the process of taking skin for microscopic examination.   **MED**

1879   Austrian physicist Josef Stefan formulates Stefan's law (derived theoretically later by Ludwig Boltzmann; see 1884), which states that the total energy radiated per unit surface area of a blackbody in unit time is proportional to its absolute temperature raised to the fourth power.   **PHYS**

1879   Edwin H. Hall discovers the Hall effect, the production of an electromotive force within a conductor or semiconductor carrying current in the presence of a strong transverse magnetic field.   **PHYS**

1879   American physicist Albert Einstein is born in Germany (d. 1955). With his theories of special relativity (1905) and general relativity (1916), he will do away with the concept of absolute space and time that had dominated physics since Newton in the seventeenth century. He will develop new understandings of gravity and matter-energy, contribute to quantum theory and atomic physics, and attempt (unsuccessfully) to develop a unified field theory. He will emigrate to the United States in 1933.   **PHYS**

1879   Wilhelm Wundt founds the world's first psychological research laboratory, at the University of Leipzig in Germany.   **PSYCH**

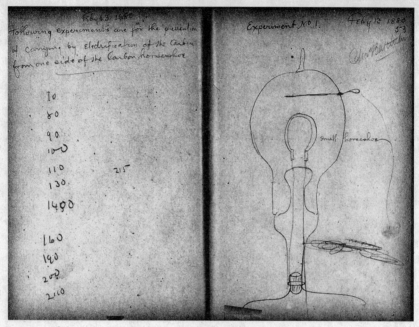

Drawing of the light bulb by Thomas Edison. (*Edison National Historic Site, National Park Service*)

1879   U.S. inventor Thomas Alva Edison demonstrates an incandescent vacuum light bulb that burns for nearly fifty hours and is still not extinguished.   **TECH**

1879   English-American photographer Miles Ainscoe Seed introduces the portable Seed Dry-Plate for taking photographs, which is more stable and less dependent on chemicals than the wet plate.   **TECH**

1879   Milk bottles are developed to replace household pitchers. The first bottles are used by a Brooklyn dairy. Within two decades they are commonplace nationally.   **TECH**

1880s   American mathematician Josiah W. Gibbs develops a system of vector analysis.   **MATH**

1880s   Two skeletons of Neanderthal man (*see* 1856) are found in a cave at Spy, Belgium, buried with stone tools and bones of extinct mammals. This discovery, excavated according to scientific methods, helps convince scientists that Neanderthal man represents an earlier variety of human being.   **PALEO**

A BETTER LIGHT BULB

*B*y the 1870s, the streets of Paris and other cities were lit by electric arc lamps that worked by forcing a continuous discharge of current across the air space between two conductors. These lights were harsh, flickering, and hazardous. A better electric light was needed, and inventors set out to make one.

Scientists had noted that a wire or filament heated by electricity would sometimes glow. Unfortunately, filaments never survived long enough to be practical as a light source, because oxygen in the air quickly oxidized and destroyed them. By 1875, English physicist William Crookes had invented a method for removing much of the air from a tube. It was found that a wire filament placed in a vacuum tube glowed longer, but it still disintegrated too soon to make it useful in a lamp.

American inventor Thomas Alva Edison came on the case. He tried hundreds of different materials until, on October 21, 1879, he found his filament: an ordinary scorched cotton thread. A bulb with this carbon filament burned for forty hours. Edison quickly registered a patent and on New Year's Eve 1879 lit up the main street of Menlo Park, New Jersey. Three years later, his Pearl Street Power Station provided electric power to 203 Manhattan customers enjoying the light of more than three thousand electric lamps.

There was one shower on Edison's parade. A rival English inventor, Joseph Swan, had also discovered the carbon filament and patented his own lamp in 1878. However, Swan was slower in setting up a system to distribute public electricity, so that Edison received the fame. The two men initially sued each other for patent violations but eventually settled their claims and became partners.

The electric bulb continued to improve. In 1910 the heat-resisting element tungsten replaced cotton as the filament of choice. In 1913 the inert gas nitrogen replaced the vacuum as the preferred environment for filaments. Today's incandescent bulbs burn for about two thousand hours.

c. 1880s   American psychologist William James and Danish scientist Karl Lange independently develop the theory that emotion is a consequence of physiological stimulus. For example, the sight of an oncoming train produces a physical response followed by an emotion, fear. This theory is the reverse of the then-popular view of emotion.   **PSYCH**

1880   Archaeologist M. Kalokairinos discovers the walls of the labyrinth at the palace of King Minos at Knossos, Crete.   **ARCH**

1880   Russian chemist Friedrich K. Beilstein begins publication of his classic *Handbook of Organic Chemistry*.   **CHEM**

1880   American schoolteacher and autodidact William Ferrel designs an analog machine to predict tidal maxima and minima.   **EARTH**

1880   In Ecuador, Edward Whymper climbs the Andean peak Chimborazo—twice.   **EARTH**

1880   British geologist John Milne becomes a leading figure in modern seismology by inventing, then progressively improving, the seismograph, a device to measure the strength of earthquakes.   **EARTH**

1880   Louis Pasteur discovers streptococcus, staphylococcus, and pneumococcus bacteria and develops a vaccine for anthrax and chicken cholera.   **MED**

1880   English ophthalmologist Warren Tay describes the cherry-red spots at the backs of the eyes that are characteristic of the fatal inherited metabolic disorder called Tay-Sachs disease, causing physical and mental retardation.   **MED**

1880   Paleontologist O. C. Marsh learns to protect fossils by encasing them in a jacket of burlap and plaster of Paris. This method will become standard practice for fossil hunters.   **PALEO**

1880   British physicist William Crookes shows that cathode rays are not electromagnetic waves like light but streams of electrically charged particles.   **PHYS**

1880   French physicist Émile Hilaire Amagat begins experiments in inducing and studying high pressure conditions, reaching a pressure equal to three thousand atmospheres.   **PHYS**

1880   French chemist Pierre Curie discovers piezoelectricity, arising from the interaction of pressure and electric potential in certain crystals, which can be manipulated to produce ultrasonic vibrations. This phenomenon will prove important to the development of microphones and other electronic sound instruments.   **PHYS**

1880   Austrian physician Josef Breuer begins treating the hysterical patient he calls Anna O. Her case study will be essential in the development of psychoanalysis. *See also* 1895, Breuer and Freud.   **PSYCH**

1880   In Britain, parcel post service begins. It will begin in the United States in 1913.   **TECH**

1881   Heinrich Karl Brugsch and Gaston Maspero discover mummies of over thirty members of Egyptian royalty, including Ramses the Great, in a cave at Dier el-Bahri near Luxor, Egypt.   **ARCH**

1881   U.S. astronomer Edward Emerson Barnard makes the first photographic discovery of a comet.   **ASTRO**

1881   Charles Darwin writes about how earthworms shape the landscape by creating an upper layer of soil through loosening soil and grinding down rock particles. His point is once again to show the great effects that occur through the accumulation of small changes over time.   **BIO**

1881   British mathematician John Venn invents the Venn diagram, in which intersecting circles are used to represent logical statements.   **MATH**

1881   German-born American physicist Albert Abraham Michelson invents the interferometer, which he uses to attempt to measure the speed of the Earth's absolute motion through the luminiferous ether, a light-carrying substance then thought to fill all of space. The experiment fails to detect any motion through the ether. Michelson then refines his procedure and repeats the experiment, definitively, with Edward W. Morley (*see* 1887).   **PHYS**

1881   British physicist Joseph John Thomson discovers electromagnetic mass when he deduces that the mass of an object changes with the addition of an electric charge.   **PHYS**

1881   German psychologist Georg Elias Müller founds a psychophysic laboratory in Göttingen, Germany, a rival of Wilhelm Wundt's at Leipzig.   **PSYCH**

1881   English anthropologist A. R. Radcliffe-Brown is born (*d.* 1955). His structural-functional analyses of the interdependent parts of social systems will help build social anthropology as a science. *See* 1952.   **SOC**

1881   The Savoy Theatre in London becomes the first public building in Britain to be electrically lighted.   **TECH**

1881   Roll film for photographs is invented by U.S. inventor David Henderson Houston.   **TECH**

1881   The refrigerator car for transporting fresh meat is developed by U.S. meat merchant Gustavus Swift. This car speeds transport time to the East Coast, increasing the national availability of meat and lowering prices.   **TECH**

1882   U.S. scientist Henry Augustus Rowland invents a machine to make precision diffraction gratings for spectroscopic use. In 1886 he will use it to create an improved map of the solar spectrum incorporating some fourteen thousand lines.   **ASTRO**

1882   German botanist Eduard Adolf Strasburger observes changes in plant cells during division. He proceeds to sort protoplasm into its nucleoplasm (inside the nucleus) and cytoplasm (outside the nucleus).   **BIO**

1882   American geologist Clarence Edward Dutton shows that a relatively short geological time is enough for a river to cut through rock, creating a valley. His work strengthens geologists' acceptance that landforms are principally a result of surface denudation, the exposure of rock strata by erosion.   **EARTH**

1882   German mathematician Ferdinand von Lindemann determines that pi is a transcendental number, like *e* (*see* 1873, Hermite), and that the ancient Greek problem of squaring the circle with straightedge and compass in a finite number of steps is impossible.   **MATH**

1882   German bacteriologist Robert Koch discovers mycobacterius tuberculosis, the bacteria causing tuberculosis in mammals. He also establishes Koch's postulates or laws, the criteria to prove that a given disease is caused by a specific microorganism.   **MED**

1882   French paleontologist Louis Dollo publishes the first of a series of papers on the *Iguanodon* skeletons of Bernissart, Belgium (*see* 1878). He becomes the founder of ethological paleontology, the study of the relationships of ancient animals to their environment.   **PALEO**

1882   Argentine paleontologist Florentino Ameghino identifies fossils of late Cretaceous dinosaurs from Neuquén, Argentina, in Patagonia.   **PALEO**

1882   German-American physicist Albert A. Michelson attains a more accurate figure than Foucault did in 1849 for the speed of light: 186,320 miles per second, very close to the currently accepted value.   **PHYS**

1882   American psychologist G. Stanley Hall (1844–1924) founds the first formal psychological laboratory in the United States, at Johns Hopkins University in Baltimore.   **PSYCH**

Mar. 30, 1882   German-English psychoanalyst Melanie Klein is born (*d.* 1960). A pioneer of child psychoanalysis who will focus on early infantile stages, she will contribute to the understanding and psychoanalytic treatment of psychosis.   **PSYCH**

1883   Russian-born French bacteriologist Ilya Ilich Mechnikov demonstrates that certain cells called leukocytes move to damaged areas in the body, where they ingest bacteria.   **BIO**

1883   British anthropologist Francis Galton coins the term *eugenics* for the study of improving human qualities by selective, careful breeding.   **BIO**

Aug. 27, 1883   The volcano Krakatau (Krakatoa) in the Netherlands Indies erupts, destroying most of its island, killing nearly 40,000 people, and sending ocean waves as far away as Cape Horn.   **EARTH**

1883   On a trip to Egypt, German bacteriologist Robert Koch discovers the cholera bacillus.   **MED**

1883   German chemist Ludwig Knorr compiles the compound antipyrine, which reduces fever and pain. It is the first significant entirely man-made drug and its invention will begin the synthetic drug industry.   **MED**

1883   Birth control leader and American feminist Margaret Sanger is born
            (*d.* 1960). She will educate working-class women on issues con-
            cerning reproduction.   **MED**

1883   The *Journal of the American Medical Association* (JAMA) is estab-
            lished as a weekly magazine.   **MED**

1883   American inventor Thomas Alva Edison discovers the Edison effect,
            the flow of electric current from a hot carbon filament to a cold
            metal wire across a gap inside a light bulb. Useless as it was to
            Edison, this discovery nevertheless will become important in the
            development of electronics.   **PHYS**

1883   German-American anthropologist Franz Boas begins his field work
            with observations of Eskimos. He will become the most influential
            voice in American anthropology, training or inspiring such scholars as
            Ruth Benedict, Alfred Kroeber, Margaret Mead, and Edward Sapir. He
            and his followers will stress the importance of culture and language in
            shaping human behavior. Boas's strict methodology and painstaking
            research will build the credibility of cultural anthropology.   **SOC**

....

*"Economics has no near kinship with any physical science. It is
a branch of biology broadly interpreted."—Alfred Marshall,
British economist; late nineteenth century*

....

1883   Croatian electrical engineer Nikola Tesla constructs an induction
            motor that can make use of alternating current, which can be more
            easily obtained from generators than can direct current.   **TECH**

1883   French chemist Louis-Marie-Hilaire Bernigaud de Chardonnet in-
            vents rayon, the first synthetic fiber.   **TECH**

1883   The 1,595.5-foot Brooklyn Bridge, also known as the Great East
            River Bridge, opens to pedestrian traffic. Featuring a steel web
            truss for stabilization, it is designed by German-American John
            Augustus Roebling. Following Roebling's death in 1869, the bridge
            is completed by his son, Washington Augustus Roebling.   **TECH**

1883   The Maxim/Vickers gun, the first completely automatic machine
            gun, is developed by English engineer Hiram Maxim.   **TECH**

1884   At an international meeting in Washington, D.C., the prime meridi-
            an is established as running through Greenwich, England.   **ASTRO**

1884   Danish bacteriologist Hans Christian J. Gram stains bacteria with
            dye and finds that when it is washed with iodine and alcohol the
            dye stain is removed from some bacteria but not from others. The
            bacteria retaining the dye he calls Gram-positive, the bacteria free
            of the dye Gram-negative. This identification will become crucial
            once antibacterial agents are developed.   **BIO**

1884   Swedish chemist Svante Arrhenius advances the theory of ionic dissociation, which describes the breakdown of electrolytes, when in solution, into positively and negatively charged particles called ions.   **CHEM**

1884   German chemist Emil Hermann Fischer analyzes the structure of sugars and studies the compounds called purines.   **CHEM**

1884   German chemist Otto Wallach begins to isolate terpenes from essential oils in a process that will become invaluable to the perfume industry.   **CHEM**

1884   Russian mathematician Sonya (Sofya) Vasilyevna Kovalevskaya demonstrates the possibility of expressing certain kinds of Abelian integrals in terms of simpler elliptic integrals.   **MATH**

1884   German mathematician Gottlob Frege provides an influential definition of cardinal numbers in his *Die Grundlagen der Arithmetik* (*The Foundations of Arithmetic*).   **MATH**

1884   German gynecologist Karl S. Credé introduces the use of 1 percent silver nitrate solution in the eyes of newborn infants to prevent blindness from gonorrheal infection.   **MED**

1884   German bacteriologist Arthur Nicolaier discovers the tetanus (lockjaw) bacillus.   **MED**

1884   The first U.S. tuberculosis sanitarium is founded, in New York's Adirondack Mountains, by physician Edward Trudeau, whose studies on tuberculosis make him an authority on this lung disease.   **MED**

1884   German bacteriologist Friedrich Loeffler discovers the diphtheria bacillus.   **MED**

1884   Canadian paleontologist Joseph Burr Tyrrell discovers the partial skull of a Cretaceous carnivorous dinosaur, *Albertosaurus sarcophagus*, at the Red Deer River in Alberta, Canada.   **PALEO**

1884   Austrian physicist Ludwig Eduard Boltzmann, the founder of statistical mechanics, shows how Stefan's law (*see* 1879) can be derived from thermodynamic rules. As a result, this principle is sometimes known as the Stefan-Boltzmann law.   **PHYS**

1884   American psychologist William James founds the U.S. branch of the Society for Psychical Research.   **PSYCH**

1884   In Vienna, Austrian psychologist and psychotherapist Otto Rosenfeld (later Rank) is born (*d.* 1939). A specialist in the psychology of myth and dreams, Rank will become Sigmund Freud's assistant, and both men will profit from the other's intuitions and ideas. Many in the field will later say that Freud groomed Rank to take over as the leader in psychoanalysis, but Rank will break from Freud in 1923. Rank's early work *Myth of the Birth of a Hero* (1909) will become a psychoanalytic classic.   **PSYCH**

1884	British inventor and physicist Hertha Marks (later Marks Ayrton) invents an instrument for dividing a line into equal parts, since used by architects, artists, and engineers. **TECH**
1884	The compound steam turbine is developed by British engineer Charles Algernon Parsons. **TECH**
1884	German-American mechanic Ottmar Mergenthaler patents the Linotype typesetting machine. By its mechanizing of parts of the typesetting process, it becomes an extremely popular choice for printing daily periodicals. **TECH**
1884	German archaeologist Heinrich Schliemann excavates Tiryns. **ARCH**
1885	A supernova appears in the Andromeda galaxy (M31), the only extragalactic supernova visible to the naked eye until 1987. **ASTRO**
1885	Austrian chemist Carl Auer discovers the elements neodymium and praseodymium. **CHEM**
1885	German biochemist Albrecht Kossel studies the molecular structure of nucleic acids, isolating two purines, three pyrimidines, and a sugar molecule. **CHEM**
1885	Chemist Jacobus van't Hoff proposes the van't Hoff factor, which appears in equations for osmotic pressure and other colligative properties. **CHEM**
c. 1885	Austrian geologist Eduard Suess begins publication of *The Face of the Earth* (1885–1909), a five-volume work based on the premise that the earth contracted while cooling, and that this contraction can explain the earth's geological features. **EARTH**
1885	*Snow Cover: Its Effect on Climate and Weather,* by A. I. Voeykov, considered the first important work on the subject, is published in St. Petersburg. **EARTH**
1885	German bacteriologist Paul Ehrlich expounds his side-chain theory stating that there is a special affinity between certain drugs and specific cells. This theory lays the foundation for Ehrlich's development of arsenic as a treatment for syphilis. **MED**
1885	Swiss physicist Johann Jakob Balmer develops an equation to interrelate the wavelengths of the hydrogen spectrum. This principle yields the so-called Balmer series of lines in the visible hydrogen spectrum. **PHYS**
1885	German psychologist Herman Ebbinghaus (1850–1909) publishes the first experimental research on memory. In it he asserts that learning and practice are linked in that if the time spent learning is doubled, then the amount learned will be doubled also. Ebbinghaus is later considered the father of memory research. **PSYCH**

1885   Between now and 1905, Ebbinghaus works on developing a sentence completion test (the first successful test of higher mental abilities) and the nonsense syllable, the latter of which will revolutionize the study of learning and association.   **PSYCH**

1885   British anthropologist Francis Galton notes the uniqueness of each individual's fingerprints and works out a system for classifying them. His work will become important in law enforcement.   **SOC**

1885   American electrical engineer William Stanley invents the transformer, to shift the voltage and amperage of alternating current and direct current.   **TECH**

1885   The first skyscraper, built for the Home Insurance Co., goes up in Chicago. Designed by American architect William LeBaron Jenney, it is a ten-story steel-framed marble building.   **TECH**

1885   A workable transmitter for dispersing mass electrical power is refined by American inventor and manufacturer George Westinghouse and electrical engineer William Stanley. It employs alternating current.   **TECH**

1885   German engineer Carl Friedrich Benz develops the first working motor car powered by gasoline.   **TECH**

1885   The safety bicycle, with two wheels of equal size, is developed by English inventor J. K. Stanley. Previously (*see* 1861), bicycles were built with large front wheels.   **TECH**

1886   French chemist Paul-Émile Lecoq de Boisbaudran discovers the element dysprosium. Boisbaudran and Swiss chemist Jean-Charles de Marignac discover the element gadolinium. French chemist Henri Moissan discovers the element fluorine. German chemist Clemens Alexander Winkler discovers the element germanium, Mendeleyev's predicted eka-silicon (*see* 1871).   **CHEM**

1886   French physical chemist François-Marie Raoult discovers Raoult's law, that the partial pressure of solvent vapors in equilibrium with a solution is proportional to the ratio of the number of solvent molecules to solute (dissolved) molecules. This law provides a new way of determining the molecular weight of solutes.   **CHEM**

1886   S. Ziesel develops the Ziesel reaction to determine how many methoxy groups are in an organic compound.   **CHEM**

1886   Two Englishmen build the first electric submarine, the *Nautilus*, which can cruise for 130 kilometers between recharges.   **EARTH**

1886   German physicist Eugen Goldstein discovers channel rays or canal rays, streams of positive ions produced by boring holes in the cathode of an evacuated tube.   **PHYS**

1886   American chemist Charles Martin Hall and French metallurgist
            Paul-Louis-Toussaint Héroult independently invent a cheap way of
            isolating aluminum. This Hall-Héroult process will make the once-
            precious metal a common structural material.   **TECH**

1886   A halftone photo-engraving process, using multi-sized dots on the
            page, is devised by U.S. printer Frederick Eugene Ives.   **TECH**

1887   The Lick refracting telescope, on Mount Hamilton near San
            Francisco, becomes the world's first mountaintop telescope. Its
            lens is 36 inches (91 cm) across.   **ASTRO**

1887   British scientist William Abney invents a way to photograph infrared
            radiation, a technique he uses to observe the solar spectrum.   **ASTRO**

1887   French physiologist Raphael Dubois is the first to show the chemi-
            cal nature of bioluminescence, the technique of producing light by
            living organisms such as glowworms, some bacteria, certain fungi,
            and various deep-sea creatures.   **BIO**

1887   English paleontologist Harry Govier Seeley divides dinosaurs into
            two orders, based primarily on the structure of their pelvic girdle:
            the *Ornithischia* (bird hipped) and the *Saurischia* (lizard hipped).
            This classification will become standard, as will his grouping of di-
            nosaurs into one category with crocodiles, birds, and the extinct
            reptiles known as thecodonts. (The reptiles in this group are now
            known as archosaurs.)   **PALEO**

1887   German-American physicist A. A. Michelson and American chemist
            Edward Morley perform a definitive version of an earlier Michelson
            experiment (*see* 1881) demonstrating that the earth has no dis-
            cernible motion through the luminiferous ether postulated by scien-
            tists. These puzzling results will not be completely explained until
            Einstein does so in 1905.   **PHYS**

1887   German physicist Heinrich Rudolph Hertz discovers the photoelec-
            tric effect, later defined as caused by the liberation of electrons
            from matter exposed to electromagnetic radiation.   **PHYS**

1887   Austrian physicist Ernst Mach studies what happens when solid ob-
            jects move rapidly through the air, particularly above the speed of
            sound. The standard measurement for the speed of a body relative
            to the speed of sound is now called a Mach number, with Mach 1
            being a speed equal to that of sound.   **PHYS**

1887   *The New York World* publishes a series of articles chronicling the
            treatment and abuse of the mentally ill in the New York City
            Lunatic Asylum on Blackwell's (later Roosevelt) Island. U.S. journal-
            ist Nellie Bly fakes insanity, is admitted under a pseudonym, and
            writes of her ordeal in *Ten Days in a Mad-House* (1888).   **PSYCH**

1887   French sociologist Émile Durkheim teaches the first course in sociology, at the University of Bordeaux. He develops scientific methods for sociology and emphasizes the importance of collective beliefs and values for social cohesion.   **SOC**

1887   The first Daimler motorized vehicle appears on the market.   **TECH**

1887   The first multicolumn adding machine, the Comptometer, is manufactured by the Felt & Tarrant Manufacturing Co. Its inventor is the business's cofounder Dorr Eugene Felt.   **TECH**

1887   The first motorized phonograph, playing recordings imprinted on wax cylinders, is invented by American inventor Thomas Alva Edison.   **TECH**

....

"I know a trade name must be short, vigorous, incapable of being misspelled to an extent that will destroy its identity, and, in order to satisfy the trademark laws, it must mean nothing."
—George Eastman, American inventor, on how he arrived at the trade name Kodak for his new camera; 1888

....

1888   British astronomer Joseph Lockyer outlines the evolutionary cycle of a star from birth to death.   **ASTRO**

1888   Johann L. E. Dreyer publishes *A New General Catalog of Nebulas and Clusters of Stars*, known simply as *NGC*, which revises John Herschel's 1864 catalog and now includes nearly eight thousand items. An *NGC* number becomes a standard designation for celestial objects.   **ASTRO**

1888   The Marine Biological Laboratory at Woods Hole, Massachusetts, holds its first classes.   **BIO**

1888   German anatomist Heinrich Wilhelm Gottfried von Waldeyer-Hartz suggests the name *chromosomes* for the chromatin threads that appear during cell division.   **BIO**

1888   French chemist Henri-Louis Le Châtelier states Le Châtelier's principle, that in a system in equilibrium any change in one of the factors tends to shift the equilibrium so as to minimize the original change.   **CHEM**

1888   Chemist Friedrich Wilhelm Ostwald discovers that catalysts affect reactions' speed, but not their equilibrium.   **CHEM**

1888   The American Mathematical Society is established.   **MATH**

1888   In the Judith River beds of Montana, John Bell Hatcher and O. C. Marsh discover the first known skull of *Triceratops*, a three-horned Cretaceous dinosaur.   **PALEO**

George Eastman peers though the viewfinder of the Kodak box camera.
(*International Museum of Photography, George Eastman House*)

1888   German physicist Heinrich Hertz verifies James Clerk Maxwell's
        equations (*see* 1865), using an oscillating current to produce radio
        waves that are electromagnetic in nature and behave as light does.
        Hertz's experiments confirm Maxwell's theory that light is an elec-
        tromagnetic phenomenon and represent the first known detection
        of radio waves.   **PHYS**

1888   Electric trolley cars, designed by American engineer Frank Julian
        Sprague, run successfully in Virginia.   **TECH**

1888   American inventor George Eastman markets the first low-cost,
        easy-to-use camera, the Kodak. This twenty-five-dollar device holds
        a roll of stripping paper for up to one hundred photographs.   **TECH**

| 1888 | A new shorthand system, called Light Line Phonography, is developed by American inventor John Robert Gregg.   **TECH** |

1888   A new shorthand system, called Light Line Phonography, is developed by American inventor John Robert Gregg.   **TECH**

1888   Construction is completed on the Washington Monument, the tallest masonry building in the world, rising 553 feet.   **TECH**

1889   German astronomer Hermann Carl Vogel, analyzing the Doppler shift of the star Algol, demonstrates that it is an eclipsing binary star.   **ASTRO**

1889   Working with Italian histologist Camillo Golgi, Spanish histologist Santiago Ramón y Cajal improves Golgi's cell stain and works out the cellular structure of the brain and spinal cord, further establishing neuron theory as a field on its own.   **BIO**

1889   Swedish chemist Svante Arrhenius analyzes the concepts of activation energy (i.e., the minimum energy required for chemical reactions to occur) and chain reactions.   **CHEM**

1889   German mountaineers Hans Meyer and Ludwig Purtscheller succeed in climbing Mount Kilimanjaro, at 5,895 meters the tallest peak in Africa.   **EARTH**

1889   American geologist William Morris Davis introduces a new method of landscape analysis using a concept of the cycle of erosion by which rivers contribute to the shaping of landscapes. Davis systematizes this field of study as geomorphology, the study of the development of landforms.   **EARTH**

1889   Between Uganda and Zaire, British explorer Henry Stanley discovers the Ruwenzori mountain range, flanked by Lakes Albert and Edward.   **EARTH**

1889   American geologist Clarence Edward Dutton introduces the term *isostasy* for the equilibrium that tends to exist in the earth's crust between the forces that elevate land masses and those that depress them. Dutton argues that the continents are made from lighter rock than the ocean floor.   **EARTH**

1889   Russian mathematician Sonya (Sofya) Vasilyevna Kovalevskaya publishes a significant paper on the rotation of asymmetric bodies about a fixed point.   **MATH**

1889   Italian mathematician Giuseppe Peano publishes *A Logical Exposition of the Principles of Geometry*, which applies symbolic logic to the task of building up the fundamental axioms of mathematics.   **MATH**

1889   At the Sorbonne, French psychologist Alfred Binet founds the first French psychological laboratory.   **PSYCH**

1889   British chemists Frederick Augustus Abel and James Dewar invent the smokeless explosive called cordite.   **TECH**

1889	The first electric sewing machines are introduced to the market by the I. M. Singer Co. **TECH**
1889	The coin-operated telephone, patented by American inventor William Gray, is first used in a Connecticut bank. **TECH**
c. 1890s	In the United States, geology is put to widespread practical use, particularly in assessing the lands of the newly acquired western territories and developing the mining industry. Universities such as Harvard, Columbia, and Yale develop research groups in economic geology whose work will rival that of the U.S. Geological Survey. **EARTH**
1890s	By now, Americans O. C. Marsh and Edward Drinker Cope have discovered 136 species of dinosaurs, although some of these will later be disallowed. As bitter personal enemies, these paleontologists have spent their careers trying to outdo each other. **PALEO**
1890	German astronomer Hermann Carl Vogel discovers spectroscopic binary stars. **ASTRO**
1890	U.S. astronomers Edward C. Pickering and Williamina Paton Fleming introduce the alphabetical Harvard Classification System for classifying stars according to their spectral characteristics. *See also* 1901, Annie Jump Cannon. **ASTRO**
c. 1890	Biometrics, the branch of science jointly studying biology and mathematics, begins when statistical methods to analyze human and biological evolution are developed. **BIO**
1890	Swiss cytologist Richard Altmann reports the discovery of bioblasts within cells. In 1898 German biologist C. Benda will name these organisms *mitochondria,* mistakenly believing them threads of cartilage. **BIO**
1890	Acetylene chemistry is discovered. **CHEM**
c. 1890	During the next two decades the theoretical foundations are established for measuring geological time by analyzing the products of radioactive decay. **EARTH**
1890	At Kedung Brebus, Java, in the Dutch East Indies, Dutch paleontologist Marie Eugène Dubois discovers fossils of Java man, now considered a variety of *Homo erectus,* a prehistoric ancestor of humans. *Homo erectus* evolved in Africa about 1.8 million years ago. **PALEO**
1890	American psychologist William James publishes his classic text *The Principles of Psychology.* **PSYCH**
1890	The U.S. Congress passes legislation dividing each state into districts, mandating a state hospital for each one. *Hospital,* not *asylum,* is from now on the preferred term for such institutions. **PSYCH**
1890	Scottish anthropologist James George Frazer publishes *The Golden Bough,* a monumental comparative study of folklore and religion. **SOC**

IMAGINARY EVIL

T *he most common phobia (persistent, irrational fear) for which people seek psychiatric treatment was also the first to be diagnosed: agoraphobia. The term was coined in the late 1800s by the German neurologist Alexander Karl Otto Westphal. From the Greek for "fear of the marketplace," it signifies an abnormal fear of open or public places.*

Westphal observed that this phobia keeps its sufferers away from such places as streets, stores, tunnels, public transportation, churches, theaters, and the post office at noon. Most agoraphobics were, and continue to be, women. Onset is usually between eighteen and thirty-five years of age and often begins with an unexpected, spontaneous panic attack that cannot be easily controlled, creating a generalized fear in future and similar situations.

People with agoraphobia are often emotionally repressed. Their parents may have been fearful and overprotective or may have forced the child to take on too much responsibility too soon. Though many agoraphobics eventually seek treatment, they usually do not pursue it for as long as ten years after the disorder arises.

1890	British economist Alfred Marshall, founder of the neoclassical school of economics, publishes the landmark work *Principles of Economics*. **SOC**
1890	French physicist Édouard-Eugène Branly invents a radiowave detector that improves on Hertz's of 1888. **TECH**
1890	An electromechanical punch-card system for recording data is refined by American engineer Herman Hollerith. Eventually patented, this Hollerith system is first used to record U.S. census findings. Hollerith's company will ultimately develop into International Business Machines (IBM). **TECH**
1891	German astronomer Maximilian Wolf makes the first photographic discovery of an asteroid. He will go on to discover some five hundred other asteroids. **ASTRO**
1891	German zoologist Karl Gottfried Semper introduces the idea of a food chain, claiming that an ecosystem maintains its energy flow by passing along materials through the process of eating and being eaten. **BIO**
1891	American inventor Edward Goodrich Acheson produces silicon carbide, or carborundum, a useful abrasive. **CHEM**

VICTORIAN BOTANISTS

*I*n the nineteenth century, most fields of scientific study were closed to women. One partial exception was botany, which, according to a 1980 article in the British Journal for the History of Science, was exempt because it reinforced "both of the contemporary alternative ideals of femininity"—the "unintense intellectualism" of the upper class and the "sentimentalized womanhood" of the middle class.

Given these restraints and others imposed by academic and professional institutions like the Linnean Society, which would not admit women, female botanists demonstrated their talents primarily as illustrators, researchers, and writers of popular works on botany. During the Victorian era hundreds of such works were written, many limited by the prevailing science of the era but some, though now relatively forgotten, still vivid. Among the more diligent female nature writers of the nineteenth and early twentieth centuries are:

- Elizabeth Knight Britton (1858–1934). U.S. botanist and early conservationist active in the founding of the Wild Flower Preservation Society of America and unofficial curator of the moss collection at Columbia University. She was the author of 346 scientific papers and is said to have provided the idea for establishing the New York Botanical Garden, which opened in 1891.

- Mary Agnes Meara Chase (1869–1963). U.S. botanist. After working as a meat inspector in the Chicago stockyards (1901–1903), she became a botanical artist and botanist specializing in agrostology, the study of grasses, for the U.S. Department of Agriculture (1903–1939).

- Alice Eastwood (1859–1953). U.S. botanist. Researched flowering plants of the Rocky Mountains. Author of A Popular Flora of Denver, Colorado (1893), she was also the curator of botany for the California Academy of Sciences (1892–1949), and was noted during her lifetime in American Men of Science.

- Ethel Sargant (1863–1918). British botanist. Specialist in the cytology and morphology of plants. Her work in plant embryology led to scientific papers on the life cycle of monocotyledons.

1891   German aeronautical engineer Otto Lilienthal successfully launches himself on the first flight of a glider, of his own design.   **EARTH**

1891   Hungarian physicist Roland Eötvös detects no significant difference between inertial and gravitational mass.   **PHYS**

1891   Irish physicist George Johnstone Stoney suggests the name *electron* for the as-yet-undiscovered fundamental unit of electricity. *See* 1897, Thomson.   **PHYS**

1891   American inventors Thomas Alva Edison and W. K. L. Dickson patent the Kinetograph camera and Kinetoscope viewer, the world's first motion picture system.   **TECH**

1891   The Carpenter Electric Heating Manufacturing Co. in the United States offers the first commercially available electric ovens.   **TECH**

1892   Photographer and self-taught U.S. astronomer Edward Barnard discovers Amalthea, a fifth satellite of Jupiter and the first to be found since the work of Galileo in 1610.   **ASTRO**

1892   Barnard presents evidence that novae are exploding stars.   **ASTRO**

1892   French physician and physicist Jaques-Arsène d'Arsonval applies an electromagnetic field to himself and finds that it produces warmth without muscle contraction. Thus begins the study of the interaction of electromagnetic energies with biological systems, or bioelectromagnetics.   **BIO**

1892   British geneticist and biologist J. B. S. Haldane is born in Oxford (*d.* 1964). He will formulate a mathematical approach to the study of natural selection that leads the way in establishing the rates of genetic change in populations. His writings will include *The Inequality of Man* (1932), *New Paths in Genetics* (1941), and *The Biochemistry of Genetics* (1954). Haldane will predict human cloning and acclaim its potential uses.   **BIO**

1892   German biologist August Weismann introduces the germ plasm theory of heredity, that a special hereditary substance embodies the only organic continuity between generations. He also claims that in germ cell formation, the process of meiosis, the nuclei undergo a halving of the chromosomes. Weismann repudiates Lamarckism, which argues that organisms inherit physical characteristics acquired by their parents during the latter's lifetime.   **BIO**

1892   Russian physicist Pyotr Nikolayevich Lebedev shows that light exerts pressure.   **PHYS**

1892   Irish physicist George Francis FitzGerald derives an equation now called the FitzGerald contraction (modified by Hendrik Lorentz in 1895) that accounts for the negative result of the 1887 Michelson-Morley experiment by predicting the contraction of a moving body in the direction of its motion. *See also* 1905, Einstein.   **PHYS**

Alexander Graham Bell makes the first New York to Chicago telephone call, 1892. (*AT&T Archives*)

1892   German physicist Philipp Eduard Lenard studies open-air cathode rays.   **PHYS**

1892   Czechoslovakian psychiatrist Arnold Pick (1851–1924) is the first to describe a presenile disorder marked by a deterioration in functional intelligence. This degenerative malody, Pick's disease, is characterized by mood swings, lack of social restraint, fatigue, confusion, and memory difficulties.   **PSYCH**

1892   British chemist James Dewar invents the Dewar flask, a double-walled container with a vacuum between the walls to slow temperature changes in its contents. It will achieve commercial use as a thermos bottle.   **TECH**

1892   The tin-plated bottle cap with a cork seal for beverage bottles is patented by Baltimore shop foreman William Painter.   **TECH**

1892   The cultured pearl, grown by implanting a small foreign object as an irritant in an oyster shell, is grown successfully by Japanese businessman Kokichi Mikimoto.   **TECH**

1893   English astronomer Edward Walter Maunder discovers the Maunder minimum, a seventy-year period from 1645 to 1715 when there were virtually no reports of sunspot activity. Not until the 1970s (*see* John A. Eddy) will Maunder's findings be corroborated.   **ASTRO**

1893   German physicist Wilhelm Wien shows that the peak wavelength at which an object radiates electromagnetic energy is inversely proportional to the object's absolute temperature. Hotter bodies radiate at shorter, more energetic, wavelengths.   **PHYS**

1893   The journal *Physical Review* begins publication.   **PHYS**

1893   French sociologist Émile Durkheim, one of the founders of sociology, publishes *The Division of Labor.*   **SOC**

1893   The first U.S. department of sociology is founded, at the University of Chicago. Chicago will be the center of American sociological studies in the period between the two world wars.   **SOC**

1893   German-American electrical engineer Charles Proteus Steinmetz develops the mathematics of alternating current (AC) circuitry, thus making AC equipment more useful and ensuring the demise of then-standard direct current.   **TECH**

1893   The first Ford motor vehicle, or gasoline buggy, is test driven by its inventor, American machinist Henry Ford.   **TECH**

1893   American inventor Whitcomb L. Judson introduces the clasp locker, forerunner to the zipper (*see* 1923).   **TECH**

1894   British physicist John William Strutt and British chemist William Ramsay discover the element argon.   **CHEM**

1894   British neurologist John Jackson publishes his paper "The Factors of Insanity," in which he defines the difference between positive and negative symptoms and describes their relationship to the nervous system.   **PSYCH**

1894   British physicist Oliver Joseph Lodge invents the device called the coherer, for detecting radio waves from a distance of half a mile. He is the first to send and receive radio-wave messages in the Morse code used in telegraphy.   **TECH**

YE OLDE MEDICAL DICTIONARY

*W*hen Victorian novelists consign their characters to the mountains to cure consumption or to their boudoirs to treat la grippe, *they refer to medical conditions now known by more modern names. Someday, commonly known modern medical conditions like the flu, tendinitis, or cancer may be either diminished as public health problems or designated by other names. Here are a few medical terms common in their time but now remembered only through literature and long-lived relatives.*

Catarrh. Marked inflammation of the mucus membranes of humans or animals.

Chilblains. Inflammation and swelling of the body, particularly feet and hands, through exposure to cold.

Consumption. Process of the diminution or wasting away of the human body, usually through tuberculosis.

Croup. An intermittent laryngitis, marked by a raspy cough and labored breathing, usually affecting infants.

Dropsy. Edema, the excess accumulation of liquid in human tissue or a bodily cavity.

Grippe. A contagious, feverish viral infection similar to influenza.

Halitosis. Bad breath.

Lumbago. Severe muscular inflammation in the lumbar region.

Melancholia. An emotional state marked by depression, perceived medical problems, and, at times, hallucinations.

Neurasthenia. An emotional or psychological state marked by feelings of fatigue, lethargy, and low self-worth.

St. Vitus' dance. Colloquial name for chorea or Sydenham's chorea. A group of diseases of humans and dogs marked by uncontrollable body and facial movements. The name is derived from St. Vitus, a Christian martyr tortured by Roman emperor Diocletian by immersion in a vat of molten lead and pitch.

Trench mouth. Also known as Vincent's angina or Vincent's infection. A contagious disease marked by ulceration of the mucus membrane of the mouth or respiratory system. The disease was discovered to be generated in the presence of the fusiform bacillus and spirillum, two germs active in hospital gangrene, by French bacteriologist Jean-Hyacinthe Vincent (1862–1950).

Vapors. A nervous condition marked by depression and hysteria.

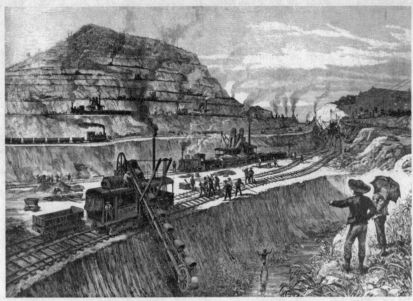

Cutting the canal at Panama. (*C. Horne,* Great Men and Famous Women, *Selmar Publishers, New York, 1894*)

1894	While drilling for water, oil is accidentally discovered in Texas for the first time. **TECH**
1894	The Hershey chocolate bar, created from sugar, milk, cocoa beans, and chocolate liqueur, is marketed. It sells for five cents, a price that will not rise for seventy-four years. **TECH**
1894	The diesel engine, mechanically simpler than a gasoline engine, is developed by German engineer Rudolf Diesel. **TECH**
1894	Pneumatic tires for automobiles are introduced in France by André and Édouard Michelin. In America pneumatic tires are manufactured by the Hartford Rubber Works. **TECH**
1895	In his work *Astronomical Constants*, Canadian-American astronomer Simon Newcomb calculates such constants as nutation, precession, and solar parallax. **ASTRO**
1895	In Germany the first germfree isolator, a sterilized glass chamber, is built. **BIO**
1895	British chemist William Ramsay is the first to discover helium on earth rather than in the solar spectrum. *See* 1868, Janssen. **CHEM**
1895	German chemist Carl Paul Gottfried von Linde develops a system for liquefying gases in quantities that are commercially useful. **CHEM**
1895	Coal-tar chemistry undergoes new developments. **CHEM**

1895   French mathematician Jules-Henri Poincaré publishes his *Analysis situ*, the first systematic treatment of topology.   **MATH**

c. 1895   German mathematician Georg Cantor proposes his continuum hypothesis, that there are no cardinal numbers between aleph-null (the smallest transfinite cardinal number) and the cardinal number of the points on a line. American mathematician Paul Cohen will revisit this hypothesis in 1963.   **MATH**

1895   German physicist Wilhelm Conrad Röntgen discovers X rays.   **PHYS**

1895   French physicist Jean-Baptiste Perrin performs experiments proving that cathode rays are streams, not waves, of negatively charged particles.   **PHYS**

1895   Dutch physicist Hendrik Antoon Lorentz independently derives George FitzGerald's equation (*see* 1892) and proposes also that mass increases with velocity, becoming infinite at the speed of light. The resulting formulation becomes known as the Lorentz-FitzGerald contraction.   **PHYS**

1895   French physicist Pierre Curie discovers that each ferromagnetic metal, such as iron or nickel, has a specific point during heating at which it loses its magnetism, an interval now known as the Curie point or Curie temperature.   **PHYS**

1895   Dutch physicist Hendrik Lorentz discovers the Lorentz force, a perpendicular force exerted by electric and magnetic fields on a moving, charged particle.   **PHYS**

1895–1896   Sigmund Freud identifies the phenomenon of projection, a defense mechanism in which a person projects feelings or wishes onto another person, group, or thing.   **PSYCH**

1895   American psychologist Gardner Murphy is born (*d.* 1979). He will create the biosocial theory of personality, which emphasizes that personality observation is possible only when a patient is interacting in a social environment. Gardner will also underscore the importance of developmental and environmental factors in determining personality.   **PSYCH**

1895   Austrian physician Josef Breuer and psychiatrist Sigmund Freud publish *Studies on Hysteria*, the first book on psychoanalysis. This work contains Breuer's case history of Anna O. (*see* 1880), often considered the founding case of psychoanalysis.   **PSYCH**

1895   French inventors Louis and Auguste Lumière patent and demonstrate the Cinématographe, a motion picture system that, unlike Edison's Kinetoscope (*see* 1891), allows film to be projected on a screen rather than viewed peep-show style.   **TECH**

Sigmund Freud's couch. (*The Freud Museum, London*)

1895	Italian electrical engineer Guglielmo Marconi and Russian physicist Aleksandr Stepanovich Popov invent the radio antenna, a device for strengthening radio signals. **TECH**
1896	American biologist Edmund Beecher Wilson publishes *The Cell in Development and Inheritance*. In this landmark work Wilson claims that higher life forms, whether animal or plant, consist of the structural units known as cells. **BIO**
1896	French mathematicians Jacques Hadamard and C. J. de la Vallée-Poussin independently prove the prime number theorem. **MATH**
1896	French physicist Antoine-Henri Becquerel discovers radiation from potassium uranyl sulfate, a uranium compound. *See* 1897, Marie Curie. **PHYS**
1896	Dutch physicist Pieter Zeeman discovers the Zeeman effect, the splitting of lines in a spectrum when the spectrum's source is exposed to a magnetic field. **PHYS**
1896	American physicist Wallace Clement Ware Sabine founds the science of architectural acoustics when he develops mathematical equations to aid in designing lecture and concert halls. **PHYS**
1896	Scottish physicist Charles Thomson Rees Wilson succeeds in producing an artificial cloud of water droplets. He now determines that dust and electrically charged ions in the atmosphere encourage the formation of clouds. **PHYS**

1896   American psychologist David Wechsler is born (*d.* 1981). He will de-
        vise the widely used individual intelligence scales that bear his
        name: the Wechsler Bellevue, the Wechsler Adult Intelligence, the
        Wechsler Intelligence Scale for Children, and the Wechsler
        Preschool and Primary Scale of Intelligence tests. He will be the first
        to combine verbal and nonverbal tests into a composite scale and to
        introduce the concept of nonintellective factors of intelligence. **PSYCH**

1896   U.S. inventor Edward Goodrich Acheson patents the Acheson
        process for manufacturing graphite by heating a mixture of coke
        and clay.   **TECH**

1896   The first U.S. motorized car to be put on the market is the Haynes-
        Duryea, made by the Duryea Motor Wagon Co. of Massachusetts.
        Also this year another American motorcar will be introduced, the
        Stanley Steamer, invented by brothers Francis Edgar and Freelan
        O. Stanley.   **TECH**

1897   With the support of U.S. astronomer George Ellery Hale, the
        world's largest refracting telescope to this day begins operation at
        the Yerkes Observatory in Williams Bay, Wisconsin. Its lens is 40
        inches (102 cm) in diameter. *See also* 1917 and 1948, Hale. **ASTRO**

NOBEL'S SECOND THOUGHTS

*B*y the age of thirty-three in 1866, Swedish engineer Alfred Nobel
had secured a place in technological history by combining nitroglycerin and diatomaceous earth to produce dynamite. Over the
next thirty years of his life Nobel would see his new substance, a safer alternative to the then-common blasting powder, used to tunnel through rock
for construction and to detonate explosives in the many wars of the late
nineteenth century.

Dismayed at the violence generated by his invention as well as believing
that "[i]nherited wealth is a misfortune which merely serves to dull a man's
faculties," Nobel willed shortly before his death in 1896 that much of his
fortune be used to establish annual prizes for science, literature, and peace.
In 1901 the first Nobel prizes were awarded: in physics, to Wilhelm
Röntgen of Germany for the discovery of Roentgen rays; in medicine, to
Emil von Behring for the development of a diphtheria antitoxin; in chemistry, to Jacobus van't Hoff of the Netherlands for his presentation of laws
of chemical dynamics and osmotic pressure in solutions; in literature, to
René-François-Armand "Sully" Prudhomme of France; and in peace, to
Henri Dunant of Switzerland and Frédéric Passy of France.

1897	German scientist Eduard Buchner (1860–1917) finds the chemical zymase to be the cause of alcohol's fermentation. **BIO**
1897	French chemist Paul Sabatier shows that nickel can be used as a catalyst. **CHEM**
1897	Henry F. Osborn and the American Museum of Natural History collect dinosaur skeletons in the first of several expeditions to the Morrison beds of Wyoming. **PALEO**
1897	Polish-French physicist and chemist Marie Sklodowska Curie publishes her first paper on the magnetism of tempered steel. **PHYS**
1897	British physicist Joseph John Thomson calculates the mass of the electron (named by Stoney; *see* 1891), the fundamental particle that carries the electric charge responsible for electricity. Thomson is considered the discoverer of the electron, the first known subatomic particle. *See also* 1899, Thomson. **PHYS**
1897	Marie Curie demonstrates that the radiation Antoine Becquerel discovered in a uranium compound in 1896 emanates from the uranium atom. **PHYS**
1897	British physicist Ernest Rutherford distinguishes two types of uranium radiation, the massive and positively charged alpha rays and the lighter and negatively charged beta rays. **PHYS**
1897	German psychiatrist Sigbert Ganser is first to describe a rare psychotic syndrome that seems to occur as a response to severe stress. Ganser's syndrome is characterized by incorrect, absurd, and silly responses to questions requiring only a factual answer, hallucinations, delusions, amnesia, and clouded consciousness. Some war veterans will be diagnosed as having Ganser's syndrome before posttraumatic stress disorder is documented in the late twentieth century. **PSYCH**
1897	With his work *Suicide: A Study in Sociology*, French sociologist Émile Durkheim becomes one of the first to present a rigorous statistical study. **SOC**
1897	German physicist Karl Ferdinand Braun invents the oscilloscope, a modification of the cathode-ray tube that is a predecessor to the television set. **TECH**
1897	U.S. engineer Simon Lake builds the *Argonaut*, which sails from Norfolk, Virginia, to New York under its own power, the first submarine to succeed in the open sea. **TECH**
Nov. 13, 1897	The first initially successful all-metal dirigible, designed by Hungarian David Schwarz, travels several miles from Berlin before crashing. **TECH**

Madame Marie Curie with her daughter, Irene. (*New York Daily News*)

1898	Russian engineer Konstantin Tsiolkovsky states a group of mathematical laws that form the basis for the field of astronautics, or space flight. **ASTRO**
1898	U.S. astronomer William Pickering discovers Phoebe, a satellite of Saturn. **ASTRO**
1898	German scientists Friedrich Loeffler (1852–1915) and Paul Frosch (1860–1928) prove that foot-and-mouth disease in livestock is caused by organisms small enough to pass through bacteriological filters. **BIO**
1898	The International Congress of Zoology organizes an International Commission on Zoological Nomenclature to set up guidelines for naming animals. In 1981 an extensively revised edition is published. **BIO**
1898	British chemists William Ramsay and Morris William Travers discover the elements krypton, neon, and xenon. **CHEM**
1898	French physicist Pierre Curie and Polish-French chemist Marie Sklodowska Curie discover radium and polonium. **CHEM**
1898	Scottish chemist James Dewar liquefies hydrogen. **CHEM**

1898   Heroin is synthesized from morphine. At first deemed a useful painkiller, it proves to be more dangerous and addictive than morphine.   **CHEM**

1898   German chemist Johann Goldschmidt invents thermite, which proves useful in welding because it burns at high temperatures and leaves a residue of iron or chromium.   **CHEM**

1898   Polish-French chemist and physicist Marie Curie coins the word *radioactivity* for the radiation produced by uranium, noting that thorium is also radioactive.   **PHYS**

1898   American psychologist William James introduces the term *pragmatism* to audiences at the University of California.   **PSYCH**

1898   English psychologist Havelock Ellis publishes the first of his seven volumes on sexuality collectively entitled *Studies in the Psychology of Sex*. He is the first to discuss sex in psychological terms, and his work will be subject to controversy and litigation.   **PSYCH**

1898   The first magnetic wire recording device, called the Telegraphone, is patented by Danish engineer Valdemar Paulsen.   **TECH**

....

"The interpretation of dreams is the royal road to the knowledge of the unconscious in mental life."
—Sigmund Freud, The Interpretation of Dreams; 1899

....

1899   German art historian Robert Koldewy begins excavating in Babylon. For the next eighteen years, these digs will uncover the remains of Nebuchadnezzar's palace, the Tower of Babel, and the Gate of Ishtar.   **ARCH**

1899   Using a spectroscope, astronomer William Wallace Campbell discovers that Polaris is a system of three stars.   **ASTRO**

1899   French chemist André-Louis Debierne discovers the element actinium.   **CHEM**

1899   Scottish chemist James Dewar produces solid hydrogen, reaching the lowest temperature yet attained: $-14°$ K.   **CHEM**

1899   German mathematician David Hilbert publishes his *Foundations of Geometry*, proposing an improved set of axioms for geometry.   **MATH**

1899   British physicist Joseph John Thomson calculates the charge of the electron, the particle he discovered in 1897. He also argues that ionization represents the splitting of electrons from the rest of the atom.   **PHYS**

1899   Franz Boas becomes the first professor of anthropology at Columbia University. He will found the "American historical school," which will stress the importance of historical research into folklore and belief.   **SOC**

1900   British archaeologist Arthur John Evans excavates the palace of Knossos, the capital of Crete in the time of the legendary King Minos of the Minoan civilization.   **ARCH**

....

"Science is always wrong. It never solves a problem without creating ten more."—George Bernard Shaw, Irish playwright and critic; c. 1900

....

1900   German biologist Cal Correns, Dutch botanist Hugo de Vries, and Austrian botanist Erich Tachermak independently rediscover the significance of Gregor Mendel's 1866 work in pea pods. These scientists, reexamining this information in the light of Darwin's theory of evolution, decide that the units of heredity found by Mendel provide a mechanism through which natural selection operates.   **BIO**

1900   German physicist Friedrich Ernst Dorn discovers the element radon.   **CHEM**

1900   Russian-born American chemist Moses Gomberg produces triphenylmethyl, the first known free radical, a molecule with an unattached carbon bond that can persist for an appreciable time.   **CHEM**

1900   German mathematician David Hilbert poses Hilbert's second problem: Whether it can be proved that the axioms of arithmetic are consistent (i.e., will not lead to contradictions). Subsequent attempts to prove this problem are doomed by Gödel's theorem (*see* 1931). The problem is one of several in an address by Hilbert entitled "Mathematical Problems." *See also* 1934, Gelfond.   **MATH**

....

"Every living thing is a sort of imperialist, seeking to transform as much as possible of its environment into itself and its seed."—Bertrand Russell, English philosopher and mathematician; c. 1900

....

1900   German physicist Max Karl Ernst Ludwig Planck states Planck's radiation law, giving the distribution of energy radiated by a blackbody. This law, the foundation of quantum theory, introduces the concept that energy is radiated in discrete packets called quanta. With this law Planck also introduces the Planck formula and the Planck constant.   **PHYS**

1900   British physicists John William Strutt, 3rd Baron Raleigh, and James Hopwood Jeans develop the Rayleigh-Jeans formula for predicting the distribution of energy radiated across long wavelengths by a blackbody. German physicist Wilhelm Wien works out the Wien formula for short wavelengths. Both are limiting cases of the Planck formula. **PHYS**

1900   Physicists measure the increase in the mass of electrons moving at speeds close to the speed of light, which confirms the Lorentz-FitzGerald contraction of 1895. **PHYS**

1900   French physicist Antoine-Henri Becquerel determines beta rays isolated in uranium radiation by Rutherford in 1897 are electrons. **PHYS**

....

"If all that survives of our fatally flawed civilization is the humble paper clip, archaeologists from some galaxy far, far away may give us more credit than we deserve. In our vast catalog of material innovation, no more perfectly conceived object exists."—Owen Edwards (in Elegant Solutions, 1989) on the Gem paper clip; invented c. 1900

....

1900   French physicist Paul Ulrich Villard detects gamma rays—electromagnetic radiation of very short wavelength and high energy—in uranium radiation. **PHYS**

1900   English physicist William Crookes discovers that a purified uranium compound in solution is only slightly radioactive but increases in radioactive intensity over time, suggesting that radioactivity is a form of change within the uranium atom. **PHYS**

1900   British physicist Owen Willans Richardson investigates the Edison effect of 1883 and discovers that heated metals tend to emit electrons. **PHYS**

1900   Sociologist Herbert Blumer is born. A student of American philosopher George Herbert Mead, he will found the sociological approach known as symbolic interactionism. **SOC**

1900   American Benjamin Holt invents the tractor. **TECH**

1900   The Trans-Siberian Railway opens, linking Moscow and Irkutsk. **TECH**

1900   Irish-American engineer John Phillip Holland designs the first modern submarine to be bought by the U.S. Navy. Named the *Holland*, it uses an internal combustion engine and an electric motor. **TECH**

1900   Eastman Kodak's one-dollar, six-exposure Brownie camera is introduced, to great success. **TECH**

1900   The hamburger (ground lean beef) on toast is introduced by American businessman Louis Lassen, in Connecticut. **TECH**

July 2, 1900	Count Ferdinand von Zeppelin of Germany flies the first of his series of rigid-frame airships. **TECH**
1901	U.S. astronomer Annie Jump Cannon introduces spectral subclasses into the Harvard Classification System for stars. *See* 1890. **ASTRO**
1901	Dutch botanist Hugo de Vries is the first to report gene mutations in plants. **BIO**
1901	French chemist Eugène-Anatole Demarçay discovers the element europium. **CHEM**
1901	French chemist Victor Grignard discovers Grignard reagents, a group of organometallic compounds of magnesium used as catalysts in organic synthesis reactions. **CHEM**
1901	Indanthrene blue, the first synthetic vat dye, is produced. **CHEM**
1901	F. A. Forel presents the first textbook on limnology, the intensive study of the physical and biological features of lakes. **EARTH**
1901	French physicist Pierre Curie measures the heat emitted by radium as 140 calories per hour. This energy flow becomes known as atomic energy because it is presumed to result from inside the atom rather than being caused by changes in chemical bonds to other atoms, as in the burning of wood. **PHYS**
1901	The U.S. National Bureau of Standards is founded. **PHYS**
1901–1920	French pioneer of the unconscious Pierre Marie Felix Janet does work on ego states via hypnosis. He is able to produce dissociative states, as are found in multiple personality disorder, and create a deeper understanding of the ego's role in personality. **PSYCH**
1901	American Alfred Louis Kroeber founds the anthropology department at the University of California–Berkeley. **SOC**

PRAIRIE DOG CITY

*T*he largest grouping of one animal species was the nearly one-half billion inhabitant colony of black-tailed prairie dogs (Cynomys ludovicianus), discovered in 1901, which spanned twenty-four thousand miles across the western United States. With its population of 400 million prairie dogs, this colony was fifty-five times greater than today's largest U.S. human metropolitan area, New York City, which boasts a mere 7.3 million residents.

1901   U.S. businessman Patillo Higgins strikes oil at the Spindletop gusher in Beaumont, Texas, which becomes one of the nation's most productive oil sources. In a short time, Texas becomes the dominant petroleum-yielding state.   **TECH**

1901   The mercury-vapor electric lamp is developed, by American engineer Peter Cooper Hewitt.   **TECH**

1901   German auto maker Gottlieb Daimler introduces a new motor vehicle to the public. The car is named by its distributor, Austrian statesman Emil Jellinek, for his young daughter Mercedes.   **TECH**

1901   Polyunsaturated and unsaturated fatty acids are hydrogenated for the first time by English chemist William Normann. The process, used to extend the shelf life of food, is later found to increase the risk of heart disease.   **TECH**

1901   The Multigraph, which prints by reproducing the written page, is produced by the American Multigraph Co.   **TECH**

1901   A usable electric vacuum cleaner is developed by British inventor Hubert Booth.   **TECH**

Dec. 21, 1901   Italian electrical engineer Guglielmo Marconi broadcasts radio waves from England to Newfoundland, marking the invention of the radio.   **TECH**

1902   The Code of Hammurabi, the oldest known legal code, from Mesopotamia in 1775 B.C., is discovered at Susa, Iran, by French archaeologists.   **ARCH**

c. 1902   While studying blood, American biochemist Lawrence Joseph Henderson introduces the nomogram (a chart of scaled lines for facilitating the calculating of variables) into biology.   **BIO**

1902   While studying beans, British geneticist William Bateson determines that variations in the beans caused by nutrition factors and the environment are not inherited by their offspring.   **BIO**

1902 •   Polish-French chemist and physicist Marie Sklodowska Curie makes a first determination of the atomic weight of radium as 225.93.   **CHEM**

1902   British physicist Ernest Rutherford and British chemist Frederick Soddy demonstrate that uranium and thorium break down in the course of radioactivity into a series of radioactive intermediate elements.   **CHEM**

1902   German-American chemist Herman Frasch perfects a method of removing sulfur from deep deposits by using superheated water to melt the substance.   **CHEM**

1902   British-American engineer Arthur Edwin Kennelly and, independently, Oliver Heaviside discover the Heaviside-Kennelly layer (or E-layer), a layer of the ionosphere (a part of earth's atmosphere) that reflects medium-frequency radio waves.   **EARTH**

1902   French meteorologist Léon-Philippe Teisserenc de Bort identifies the troposphere and stratosphere as two distinct layers of the earth's atmosphere.   **EARTH**

1902   Denmark, Sweden, Norway, England, the Netherlands, and Russia establish the International Council for the Exploration of the Seas, a still-functioning body.   **EARTH**

1902   German mathematician Gottlob Frege refines and extends Boole's 1847 system of symbolic logic but is unable to account for an apparent self-contradiction noted by British mathematician Bertrand Russell.   **MATH**

1902   French mathematician Henri Lebesgue redefines the theory of integration, introducing the Lebesgue measure.   **MATH**

1902   German physicist Philipp Lenard, investigating the photoelectric effect (*see* 1887, Hertz), discovers that it results from the emission of electrons by certain metals in response to specific wavelengths of light.   **PHYS**

1902   American psychologist Carl Ranson Rogers is born (*d.* 1987). He will take the focus off the psychoanalyst's couch and remove any authority the therapist has over an individual seeking help. Preferring the term *client* to *patient,* he will develop client-centered therapy, an introspective psychotherapy that concentrates on an individual's personal growth potential and self-healing capacity. Rogers will align with Abraham Maslow's later, related ideas of self-actualization.   **PSYCH**

1902   The American Anthropological Association is founded.   **SOC**

1902   Austrian-born German chemist Richard Adolf Zsigmondy devises the ultramicroscope, a microscope that makes use of the Tyndall effect (*see* 1869) to view colloidal particles.   **TECH**

1902   The first automat, operated by the Horn & Hardart Baking Co., opens in Philadelphia. It dispenses food from a series of glass-walled compartments that open when money is deposited.   **TECH**

1903   American geneticist Walter Sutton publishes a paper called "The Chromosomes Theory of Heredity," claiming that hereditary factors are located in chromosomes.   **BIO**

1903   Norwegian chemists Kristian Birkeland and Samuel Eyde introduce the Birkeland-Eyde process for the fixation of nitrogen by passing air through an electric arc.   **CHEM**

| 1903 | Norwegian explorer Roald Amundsen becomes the first to sail through the Northwest Passage, thus reaching the Pacific Ocean from the Atlantic. He will also be the first to reach the South Pole. *See* December 16, 1911. **EARTH** |

| 1903 | In his *History of Mechanics*, German physicist Ernst Mach critiques the concepts of absolute space and time in Newtonian physics in a work that influences Albert Einstein in 1905. **PHYS** |

| 1903 | French mathematician Jules-Henri Poincaré argues that small discrepancies in initial conditions can result in large differences within a short period. This observation will become important to chaos theory in the 1970s and later. **PHYS** |

| 1903 | Phenobarbital, a barbiturate and potent sedative, is first used. **PSYCH** |

| 1903 | Russian engineer Konstantin Tsiolkovsky publishes "The Investigation of Universal Space by Means of Reactive Devices," a seminal article in astronautics in which he suggests liquid hydrogen and liquid oxygen for use as propellants. **TECH** |

| 1903 | Henry Ford and twelve inventors found and incorporate the Ford Motor Co. in Detroit, Michigan, introducing their first automobile, the eight-horsepower, two- cylinder Model A. **TECH** |

| 1903 | The Harley-Davidson motorcycle is developed in Milwaukee, Wisconsin, by William Harley, Arthur Davidson, Walter Davidson, and others. **TECH** |

| 1903 | The Springfield rifle, which will be used widely in the armed forces, is developed at the U.S. arsenal in Springfield, Massachusetts. **TECH** |

| Dec. 17, 1903 | At Kitty Hawk, North Carolina, Orville Wright flies 120 feet in twelve seconds, in a twelve-horsepower biplane built by him and his brother Wilbur. It is the first successful flight of a heavier-than-air machine. **TECH** |

| 1904 | American-Argentine astronomer Charles D. Perrine discovers the sixth satellite of Jupiter. By the end of this century, the total of Jovian moons known will be brought to sixteen. **ASTRO** |

| 1904 | German astronomer Johannes Franz Hartmann discovers spectral absorption lines that indicate the existence of interstellar clouds of gas and dust. **ASTRO** |

| 1904 | German biologist Theodor Boveri, experimenting with sea urchins, decides on the necessity of a full set of chromosomes for an embryo's normal development. This discovery, coupled with Walter Sutton's discovery (*see* 1903), will form the basis for the Sutton-Boveri chromosome theory of inheritance. **BIO** |

| 1904 | The local anesthetic novocaine, or procaine, is synthesized. **CHEM** |

The Wright Brothers' famous flight at Kitty Hawk, North Carolina. (*Wright State University*)

1904   German chemist Richard Abegg suggests that chemical reactions occur when electrons transfer from one atom to another.   **CHEM**

1904   English chemist Frederick Stanley Kipping discovers silicones.   **CHEM**

1904   Norwegian-American meteorologist Jacob Bjerknes publishes *Weather Forecasting as a Problem in Mechanics and Physics,* an influential study that takes a scientific approach to weather forecasting.   **EARTH**

1904   German mathematician Ernst Zermelo formulates Zermelo's axiom of choice, which states that in any set of mutually exclusive non-empty sets there exists at least one set that contains one, and only one, element in common with each nonempty set. Paul J. Cohen will show (*see* 1963) that the axiom of choice cannot be proved within set theory.   **MATH**

1904   Rockefeller Institute scientists, including Austrian-American pathologist Karl Landsteiner, discover the Rhesus factor in blood. This subgrouping of blood types, which determines if a person is Rh positive or Rh negative, will make blood transfusions safer.   **MED**

1904 and 1911   Scottish paleontologist Robert Broom publishes papers on the Cretaceous and Triassic dinosaurs of South Africa which mark the beginning of sustained studies of dinosaurs in that region.   **PALEO**

1904 | British physicist Hertha Marks Ayrton becomes the first woman ever to address the Royal Society, reading a paper on the origin and growth of ripple marks in sand. She also becomes known about this time for her research on electric arcs. **PHYS**

1904 | British physicist Joseph Thomson proposes a model for atomic structure in which electrons are embedded in a positively charged atom like raisins in a pound cake. **PHYS**

1904 | Experimenting with the scattering of X rays, British physicist Charles Glover Barkla discovers that the number of charged particles in an atom varies according to its mass. He also shows that X-rays are transverse waves like light, confirming their electromagnetic nature. **PHYS**

1904 | British physicist William Henry Bragg shows that the energies of alpha particles are emitted only within certain sharply defined ranges. **PHYS**

1904 | American psychologist Edward B. Titchener establishes an organization of experimental psychologists who espouse the psychological viewpoint that will be referred to as existential psychology, or existentialism, which emphasizes subjectivity, personal decision, free will, and individuality. It will serve as a counterbalance to theories that stress the role of society and social groups. **PSYCH**

1904–1905 | German sociologist Max Weber publishes *The Protestant Ethic and the Spirit of Capitalism*, which relates Protestant ideals to the development of capitalism. **SOC**

1904 | The first electron radio tube, the diode thermionic valve, is developed by British engineer John Ambrose Fleming. **TECH**

1904 | Using hand-crafted muslin pouches, U.S. shop proprietor Thomas Sullivan invents the teabag. **TECH**

Sept. 15, 1904 | American aviator Orville Wright accomplishes the first airplane maneuvers when he makes a turn with an airplane. On September 20 his brother Wilbur makes the first complete circle. **TECH**

1905 | U.S. astronomers Thomas Chrowder Chamberlin and Forest Ray Moulton formulate an early version of the planetesimal hypothesis, which states that the solar system was formed by accretion from smaller particles called planetesimals. This part of their theory will come to be accepted (*see* 1944, Weizsäcker), though their belief that the solar system resulted from gaseous matter being pulled out of two stars as a result of a near collision will be discredited (*see* 1935, Russell). **ASTRO**

1905 | German chemist Richard Willstätter discovers the structure of chlorophyll. **CHEM**

1905   German physicist Albert Einstein proposes the theory of special rela-
             tivity, which accounts for physical phenomena at constant (nonaccel-
             erated) velocities close to the speed of light. This theory assumes that
             the speed of light is a constant and shows that velocity has meaning
             only in that it is relative to the observer. It upholds the validity of
             Newton's laws of motion for subrelativistic speeds, or speeds far be-
             low the speed of light, and accounts for the Lorentz-FitzGerald con-
             traction (*see* 1895). *See also* 1916, general relativity.   **PHYS**

1905   Einstein deduces as a consequence of his theory of special relativity
             (*see* above) that the mass of a body is a measure of its energy con-
             tent, according to the equation $E = mc^2$, where E is energy, m is
             mass, and c is the velocity of light. This means that previous con-
             servation laws (*see* 1769, Lavoisier, and 1847, Helmholtz) can be
             unified into a single law of the conservation of mass-energy.   **PHYS**

1905   Einstein explains the photoelectric effect (*see* 1902, Lenard) as a
             consequence of quantum theory (*see* 1900, Planck). Einstein's
             treatment shows that light, then regarded solely as a wave, can
             also be seen as a particle in some respects. A unit of light regarded
             as a particle, or a quantum of electromagnetic radiation, will be-
             come known as a photon.   **PHYS**

1905   Einstein formulates an equation to describe Brownian or Brunonian
             motion (*see* 1827) that will permit scientists to deduce the size of
             molecules and atoms.   **PHYS**

1905   American physicist Percy Williams Bridgman attains high-pressure
             conditions equal to 20,000 atmospheres.   **PHYS**

1905   French psychologist Alfred Binet publishes his first batteries of tests
             intended to measure intelligence, and introduces the term *intelli-
             gence quotient* or *IQ* for a score representing an individual's intelli-
             gence as measured against a standard.   **PSYCH**

1906   Dutch astronomer Jacobus Cornelis Kapteyn begins a survey of the
             Milky Way in which he will calculate the galaxy's diameter as
             23,000 light-years and its thickness as 6,000 light-years, closer to
             the truth than the 1785 results by William Herschel but still too
             small.   **ASTRO**

1906   U.S. astronomer Percival Lowell begins searching for a planet be-
             yond Neptune that would account for irregularities in the orbit of
             Uranus, but no such planet is discovered until after his death in
             1916. *See* February 18, 1930, Tombaugh.   **ASTRO**

1906   German astronomer Karl Schwarzschild theorizes that radiation is
             the principal cause of heat transmission within stars.   **ASTRO**

1906	British naturalist Henry Guppy publishes *Plant Dispersal*, the second volume of *Observations of a Naturalist in the Pacific Between 1896 and 1899*. In it Guppy tries to account for the current geographical distribution of plants and writes extensively about plant dispersal by flotation in seawater. **BIO**
1906	German chemist Richard Willstätter shows that chlorophyll molecules contain magnesium. **BIO**
1906	British biologist William Bateson coins the word *genetics* for the study of how physical, biochemical, and behavioral traits are transmitted from parents to children. **BIO**
1906	Austrian chemist Carl Auer von Welsbach and French chemist Georges Urbain discover the element lutetium. **CHEM**
1906	Russian botanist Mikhail Semenovich Tsvett develops the technique of chromatography for separating complex mixtures. **CHEM**
1906	American millionaire Andrew Carnegie finances the foundation of the Geophysical Laboratory in Washington, D.C., for the experimental study of minerogenesis and petrogenesis. **EARTH**
1906	John William Strutt discovers radioactivity in seawater. **EARTH**
Apr. 18, 1906	The most deadly earthquake in U.S. history strikes San Francisco, devastating more than 4 square miles and killing more than 500 people. The earthquake will later be estimated to have measured 8.3 on the Richter scale (*see* 1935, Charles Richter). **EARTH**
1906	French mathematician Maurice Fréchet develops functional calculus. **MATH**
1906	Russian mathematician A. A. Markov develops Markov chains, or strings of linked probabilities. **MATH**
c. 1906	West German physician Josef Schrudde develops a way to scrape fat off the body through small incisions in the skin. In the 1970s, Swiss physician Ulrich Kesselring will add suction to the process of fat scraping, creating liposuction (suction lipectomy). **MED**
1906	British physicist William Thomson disputes the developing theory of radioactive disintegration of atoms, suggesting that radium (discovered in 1898) is not an element but a molecular compound of lead and helium. Marie Curie will later prove him wrong. *See* 1911. **PHYS**
1906	British physicist Ernest Rutherford and German physicist Johannes Hans Wilhelm Geiger discover that alpha particles are related to helium atoms. **PHYS**
1906	British physicist Charles Barkla discovers a phenomenon characteristic of X rays: when they are scattered by diverse elements, more massive elements produce more penetrating X rays. **PHYS**

1906	German physical chemist Walther Hermann Nernst states the third law of thermodynamics, that all bodies at absolute zero would have the same entropy, though absolute zero can never be perfectly attained. **PHYS**

1906   Upon the death of her husband Pierre Curie, Marie Curie takes his place at the Sorbonne, becoming the university's first woman professor.   **PHYS**

1906   British physicist Joseph John Thomson shows that a hydrogen atom has only one electron, contrary to other theories that had been predicting many more.   **PHYS**

1906   American psychiatrist Morton Prince is the key individual behind the establishment of the *Journal of Abnormal Psychology*.   **PSYCH**

1906   British anthropologist W. H. R. Rivers introduces the genealogical method into social science research in his work *The Todas*.   **SOC**

1906   The Audion, or three-electrode vacuum tube amplifier, is invented by American Lee De Forest. This device makes the further development of radio possible.   **TECH**

1907   Biological productivity studies, measuring the amount and rate of production occurring in a given ecosystem in a certain time period, become popular. Biological productivity may apply to single organisms, populations, or entire communities and ecosystems. The concept helps scientists better understand food and fiber production, in addition to giving information about nonharvestable organisms.   **BIO**

1907   American zoologist Ross Granville Harrison becomes the first to culture tissues successfully.   **BIO**

1907   Dutch botanist Hugo de Vries publishes *Plant Breeding*, providing additional support for the importance of mutations in plant evolution.   **BIO**

1907   Swiss chemist Jean-Charles de Marignac discovers the element ytterbium.   **CHEM**

1907   At Mauer, near Heidelberg, Germany, quarry workers discover a hominid mandible. Whether it represents *Homo erectus*, Neanderthal man, or some other intermediate form remains unclear.   **EARTH**

1907   Russian-born German mathematician Hermann Minkowski publishes *Time and Space*, in which he sets forth a mathematical treatment of a four-dimensional universe in which time is the fourth dimension. Einstein will make use of Minkowski's model in his 1916 general theory of relativity.   **MATH**

1907   American chemist Bertram Borden Boltwood proposes that lead is the final product of the radioactive decay of uranium and thorium, arguing that knowing the rate of decay will make radioactive dating possible.   **PHYS**

1907   French physicist Pierre Weiss develops the theory that ferromag-
            netic substances consist of small magnetized regions called do-
            mains and that in strongly magnetized pieces the poles of the do-
            mains are aligned.   **PHYS**

1907   American sociologist William Graham Sumner publishes *Folkways*,
            in which he analyzes the lasting impact of folkways and mores. He
            here originates the concept of ethnocentrism, or the belief in the
            superiority of one's own culture.   **SOC**

1907   Nearly frictionless chrome and manganese-alloy ball bearings are
            developed by Swedish engineer Sven Gustav Wingquist.   **TECH**

1907   The first all-in-one electric clothes washer, the Thor, is developed
            by the Hurley Machine Co. in Chicago. The Maytag washer is intro-
            duced in Iowa later this year.   **TECH**

1908   The Archaeological Institute of America acknowledges the impor-
            tance of conducting investigations in the New World when it estab-
            lishes the School of American Archaeology in Santa Fe, New
            Mexico.   **ARCH**

1908   U.S. astronomer George Ellery Hale identifies magnetic fields in
            sunspots, leading to the discovery of the largely magnetic nature of
            sunspots.   **ASTRO**

1908   A mysterious event near Tunguska, Siberia, creates huge craters,
            destroys a herd of deer, and levels trees for twenty miles. Later it
            will seem probable that the site was hit by a meteorite, possibly a
            small comet or a chunk of one.   **ASTRO**

1908   Danish astronomer Ejnar Hertzsprung describes both the giant and
            dwarf stellar categories, also proposing the concept of absolute
            magnitude, or how to identify what the brightness of a star would
            be if all stars were seen at a standard distance.   **ASTRO**

1908   The first biological autoradiograph is taken when a frog is made ra-
            dioactive and placed on a photographic plate, so that an image of
            the entire animal is formed.   **BIO**

1908   American zoologist Joseph Grinnell suggests that competition be-
            tween species is a force that results in their adopting similar, yet
            separate habitats—distinct ecological niches.   **BIO**

1908   English scientist William Bayliss publishes his research on hor-
            mones in *The Nature of Enzyme Action*.   **BIO**

1908   English mathematician Godfrey H. Hardy and German obstetrician Wilhelm Weinberg independently formulate the now-designated Hardy-Weinberg law, which states that population gene and genotype frequencies remain constant from generation to generation if mating is random and if mutation, selection, immigration, and emigration do not occur. This law is now a fundamental principle of population genetics.   **BIO**

1908   Dutch physicist Heike Kamerlingh Onnes liquefies helium at 4° K, reaching temperatures as low as 0.8° K, although he is unable to solidify helium.   **CHEM**

1908   German chemist Fritz Haber devises the so-called Haber process for producing ammonia by the reaction of nitrogen with hydrogen. It has become valuable in fixating nitrogen for fertilizers and explosives.   **CHEM**

1908   French mathematician Maurice Fréchet introduces abstract spaces.   **MATH**

1908   French physician Charles Mantoux invents a skin test to detect tuberculosis.   **MED**

1908   German paleontologist Friedrich von Huene publishes a thorough monograph on the Triassic dinosaurs of Europe, those dating from the earliest period of dinosaur evolution.   **PALEO**

1908   In Wyoming, paleontologists Charles H. Sternberg and his sons Charles M., George, and Levi discover the first known fossilized dinosaur skin, an impression of the skin of a duck-billed dinosaur.   **PALEO**

1908   Neanderthal remains are recovered in France at Le Mustier and La Chapelle-aux-Saints.   **PALEO**

1908   Using Einstein's equation based on Brownian motion (*see* 1905), French physicist Jean-Baptiste Perrin calculates the approximate size of an atom as one hundred-millionth of a centimeter.   **PHYS**

1908   The International Conference on Electric Units and Standards adopts the international ampere as the basic unit of electric current.   **PHYS**

1908   Physicist Louis Paschen discovers the Paschen series of lines, in the far-infrared region of the hydrogen spectrum.   **PHYS**

1908   British-American psychologist William McDougall writes a pioneering book on social psychology containing a controversial theory of instincts. This purposive psychology claims that instincts, like hunger, sex, escape, curiosity, and self-assertion, are the impetus to all behavior.   **PSYCH**

1908   Austrian psychoanalyst Abraham Arden Brill becomes Sigmund Freud's translator into English. Brill coins the psychoanalytic term *id* from Freud's German word for the unconscious, *Es* (*it*), by adopting the Latin word for *it*.   **PSYCH**

1908 — American political scientist Arthur F. Bentley publishes *The Process of Government,* in which the concept of the group rather than the state is central. **SOC**

1908 — German physicist Johannes Geiger invents the Geiger counter, a device to detect and measure the ionizing particles emitted by radioactive substances. *See also* 1928, Müller. **TECH**

....

"Nothing has spread socialistic feeling in this country more than the use of the automobile."—Woodrow Wilson, Princeton University president and U.S. president-to-be; 1908

....

1908 — Henry Ford introduces the only-in-black Model T, which at $850.50 becomes a nationally best-selling automobile. **TECH**

1908 — The gyrocompass, which determines direction by the rotation of the earth, is developed by German engineer Hermann Anschutz-Kampfe. **TECH**

1909 — Dutch botanist Wilhelm L. Johannsen (1857–1927) suggests the term *genes* for the units of inheritance inside chromosomes. **BIO**

1909 — Austrian chemist Fritz Pregl develops techniques for analyzing minute amounts of organic chemicals. **CHEM**

1909 — The system of pH numbers for quantifying acidity and alkalinity is developed by Danish chemist Søren Peter Lauritz. **CHEM**

1909 — Croatian geologist Andrija Mohorovičić notes a change in properties thirty-two kilometers (20 miles) beneath the earth's surface. The Mohorovicic discontinuity, or Moho, marks the junction between the earth's mantle and its crust. **EARTH**

1909 — Florence Bascom, the first female Ph.D. from Johns Hopkins University, edits the U.S. Geological Survey's Philadelphia Folio, which will remain one of the most comprehensive geological descriptions of the area from Maine to Maryland. **EARTH**

Apr. 6, 1909 — U.S. Navy engineer Robert R. Peary, his African-American dogsled driver Matthew Hansen, and three Eskimos and their dogs are the first to reach the North Pole. **EARTH**

1909 — American neurosurgeon Harvey Cushing (1869–1939) discovers that acromegaly, a form of giantism, is due to an overproduction of the growth hormone in the pituitary gland. When Cushing surgically removes a portion of the oversized gland, the patient's symptoms disappear. This proves to have been an important step in understanding hormone activity. **MED**

1909 — French physician Charles Nicolle (1866–1936) discovers that the body louse is responsible for transmitting epidemic typhus. **MED**

Robert Peary. (*National Archives*)

1909   Paleontologist Earl Douglass of the Carnegie Museum in Pittsburgh
            discovers an almost complete skeleton of an *Apatosaurus*
            (*Brontosaurus*) at the Carnegie Quarry in what is now Dinosaur
            National Monument, Utah. Excavations from now through 1923
            will uncover the largest known concentration of Jurassic dinosaurs,
            including the *Diplodocus*, *Stegosaurus*, *Antrodemus* (*Allosaurus*), and
            Camptosaurus.   **PALEO**

1909–1912   German paleontologists begin expeditions in Tendaguru, East Africa
            (now Tanzania). Among the finds in the quarry of Jurassic dinosaurs
            is a skeleton of the largest known sauropod, *Brachiosaurus*.   **PALEO**

1909   In the Canadian Rockies, American paleontologist Charles Doolittle
            Walcott discovers the rich fossil site known as the Burgess Shale.
            This site contains the soft-bodied remains of creatures that lived
            530 million years ago, just after the Cambrian explosion of multi-
            cellular organisms.   **PALEO**

1909   With the founding of Chicago's Juvenile Psychopathic Institute by
            psychiatrist William Healy, the first mental health facility specifical-
            ly for children is established, marking the beginning of the child
            guidance movement.   **PSYCH**

1909   American physicist William David Coolidge develops a method of producing fine tungsten wires for use as filaments in light bulbs. **TECH**

1909   Bakelite becomes the first thermosetting plastic, one that once set does not soften under heat. Made of phenol and formaldehyde, it is invented by Belgian-American chemist Leo Hendrik Baekeland. Bakelite will be used first for electrical insulation, then later for a number of consumer products. **TECH**

1909   On July 25, Louis Blériot becomes the first to fly across the English Channel, from France to England. **TECH**

....

"As far as the propositions of mathematics refer to reality, they are not certain; and as far as they are certain, they do not refer to reality."—Albert Einstein, German-born American mathematician and physicist; early twentieth century

....

1910s   As a pioneer of small-animal experiments, American biochemist Elmer Verner McCollum (1879–1967) establishes the first white-rat colony in the U.S. for nutrition research. He will subsequently identify vitamins A and B and prove the necessity of trace elements. McCollum will also show that a calcium deficiency produces tetany (muscular spasm). **BIO**

1910s   This decade sees the foundation of the influential Norwegian, or Bergen, school of meteorology. **EARTH**

1910   American geneticist Thomas Hunt Morgan discovers the sexual differences in the inheritance of traits now known as sex-linked inheritance. **BIO**

1910   William Burton uses thermal cracking to refine petroleum oil. **CHEM**

1910   During work on celestial mechanics, Jules-Henri Poincaré develops modern tide theories. **EARTH**

June 22, 1910   The first commercial flight of a dirigible, or airship, is made, in Germany. Piloted by Count von Zeppelin and carrying twenty passengers, the dirigible travels five hundred miles, from Friedrichshafen to Düsseldorf, in nine hours. **EARTH**

1910   British mathematicians Bertrand Russell and Alfred North Whitehead begin publication of their *Principia Mathematica*, the most definitive effort yet at rooting mathematics in logic and building it systematically. **MATH**

1910   German bacteriologist and 1908 Nobel Prize–winner Paul Ehrlich produces the arsenical compound salvarsan, the first drug effective in treating syphilis. This discovery marks the beginning of modern chemotherapy. **MED**

1910   American paleontologist Barnum Brown begins to excavate Cretaceous dinosaurs at the Red Deer River in Alberta, Canada. U.S. paleontologists Charles H. Sternberg and sons will begin a separate dig at the same site in 1912. Brown's expeditions at this rich site will last through 1915, the Sternbergs' through 1917.   **PALEO**

1910   British physicist Joseph John Thomson confirms the existence of isotopes by using positive cathode rays to measure the atomic masses of two different isotopes of neon. Frederick Soddy (*see* 1913) will further develop the concept of isotopes.   **PHYS**

1910   University of Frankfurt psychologists Max Wertheimer, Kurt Koffa, and Wolfgang Köhler reject the prevailing associationism dominating German psychology and together found the school of Gestalt psychology, dealing mostly with perception processes and behavior. Gestalt therapists will seek to restore an individual's natural mental balance by heightening awareness, emphasizing present experiences rather than recollections of the past.   **PSYCH**

1910   Eric Berne, who will become known as the father of transactional analysis, is born in Canada (*d.* 1970). Berne will advocate this form of psychotherapy to help people exchange their feelings and thoughts more effectively. Among his popular books will be *Games People Play* (1964).   **PSYCH**

1910   Scottish anthropologist James George Frazer publishes *Totemism and Exogamy*, which will influence Viennese psychoanalyst Sigmund Freud in *Totem and Taboo* (1913), in which Freud will analyze the practices of "primitive" peoples to shed light on modern Western people's neuroses.   **SOC**

1910   American sociologist Robert Merton is born. A student of Talcott Parsons (*see* 1937), Merton will attempt to unite theoretical and empirical research.   **SOC**

1910   Steel begins to be used instead of wood in car bodies, for the Ford Model T.   **TECH**

1910   The Pathé Gazette, a movie newsreel, is conceived by Frenchmen Charles and Émile Pathé. These newsreels are first presented in British and American markets.   **TECH**

1910   Cartoonist John Randolph Bray patents the cel process of animation. Nearly two decades later, in 1928, American filmmaker Walt Disney will license it to create the first Mickey Mouse cartoon, "Steamboat Willie."   **TECH**

1911   Using modern archaeological methods, Amadeo Maiuri begins the excavation of Pompeii and Herculaneum, destroyed by the eruption of Mount Vesuvius in 79.   **ARCH**

1911   A meteorite kills a dog in Nakhla, Egypt, in the only recorded case of a mammal's death by a meteorite.   **ASTRO**

1911   Working independently, Danish astronomer Ejnar Hertzsprung and, in 1913, U.S. astronomer Henry Norris Russell plot the magnitudes of stars against their colors and spectral classes. The resulting Hertzsprung-Russell diagram will provide important evidence for theories of stellar evolution.   **ASTRO**

1911   American geneticist Hermann Joseph Müller begins experimental breeding of the fruit fly (*Drosophil*). He will be best known for his discoveries of gene mutations caused by X rays and dire warnings concerning the effect of nuclear radiation on human genes.   **BIO**

1911   American geneticists Thomas Hunt Morgan and Alfred Henry Sturtevant devise the first chromosome map, found by investigating the separation frequency of chromosome crossover from one gene to another.   **BIO**

Dec. 16, 1911   Roald Amundsen reaches the Antarctic Pole just ahead of Robert Falcon Scott, who will arrive on January 14, 1912.   **EARTH**

1911   The American Nurses' Association is established. Within fifty years it will be the largest professional women's organization in the world.   **MED**

1911   Polish-French chemist and physicist Marie Curie shows conclusively that radium is an element, disproving William Thomson's argument. *See* 1906.   **PHYS**

1911   British physicist Ernest Rutherford proposes a model of the atom in which the atom is mostly empty space. A massive, positively charged atomic nucleus is surrounded by outer regions of negatively charged electrons that leave the atom electrically neutral. This model makes it clear that alpha particles are helium nuclei, not helium atoms. *See also* 1913, Geiger and Marsden.   **PHYS**

1911   Scottish physicist Charles Thomson Rees Williams invents the cloud chamber, a device for studying the paths of particles of ionizing radiation.   **PHYS**

1911   American physicist Robert Andrews Millikan calculates the electric charge of a single electron.   **PHYS**

1911   Dutch physicist Heike Kamerlingh Onnes discovers superconductivity, the absence of electrical resistance in certain substances at temperatures close to absolute zero.   **PHYS**

1911–1920   Swiss psychiatrist Eugen Bleuler introduces the terms *schizophrenia* and *ambivalence* into psychiatry. Schizophrenia, or split minds, denotes what Bleuler considers a mental split from reality.   **PSYCH**

1911   German neurologist Alois Alzheimer discovers the presenile demen-
            tia, or irreversible mental and intellectual deterioration, that will
            bear his name as Alzheimer's disease.   **PSYCH**

1911   French psychologist Alfred Binet and French physician Théodore
            Simon develop the series of graded intelligence tests to measure a
            person's intelligence quotient, or IQ, that becomes known as the
            Binet-Simon scale.   **PSYCH**

1911   American ethnologist Alice Cunningham Fletcher publishes *The
            Omaha Tribe*, her most important monograph on American Indian
            culture.   **SOC**

1911   American anthropologist Franz Boas publishes his influential work
            The Mind of Primitive Man.   **SOC**

1911   C. F. Kettering, American businessman and owner of Dayton
            Engineering Laboratories (Delco), develops the electric self-starter,
            which will be widely used for automobile and truck engines.   **TECH**

1911   The Chevrolet Motor Co. is founded by American automobile pio-
            neer W. C. Durant. The company takes its name from Durant's
            partner, Swiss-American race-car driver Louis Chevrolet.   **TECH**

1911   A sulfate process using alkali rather than acids improves paper pro-
            duction, resulting in—among other products—a sturdy brown ma-
            terial called Kraft paper.   **TECH**

1912   American archaeologist Hiram Bingham discovers the Inca strong-
            holds of Machu Picchu and Vitcos near Cuzco, Peru.   **ARCH**

1912   Harvard astronomer Henrietta Leavitt discovers that the period of
            pulsation of a Cepheid variable star, one that varies in brightness in
            a regular way, increases with the star's luminosity or intrinsic
            brightness. This period-luminosity curve, as it is called, will become
            the basis for determining the distances of galaxies and distant
            stars. *See* 1914, Shapley.   **ASTRO**

1912   Austrian-American physicist Victor Franz Hess discovers evidence
            of the existence of cosmic rays.   **ASTRO**

1912   Dutch physical chemist Peter Joseph William Debye develops equa-
            tions describing the behavior of polar molecules or dipoles, mole-
            cules with pairs of separated opposite electric charges. His work
            leads to the concept of the dipole moment, the product of the posi-
            tive charge and the distance between charges.   **CHEM**

1912	German geologist Alfred L. Wegener proposes the theory of continental drift, arguing that the granite continents float on the basalt ocean floor, changing position over the ages. He claims that all the continents once formed a single landmass called Pangaea. At first rejected, his ideas bear similarities to the theory of plate tectonics (*see* 1960, Henry H. Hess), which holds that it is plates bearing continents, not the continents themselves, that move. **EARTH**
1912	For the next two years, Russian K. Silovski applies ultrasonic techniques to detect icebergs and submerged ice. **EARTH**
1912	A compendium on the hydrology of the Mediterranean Sea, including numerous temperature and salinity stations, is published by N. Nielson. **EARTH**
Apr. 15, 1912	Following the sinking of the *Titanic* on the night of April 14–15, underwater acoustics and communications becomes a rapidly growing area of study. **EARTH**
1912	British biochemist Sir Frederick G. Hopkins and Dutch physician Christian Eijkman establish the role of the accessory food factors called vitamins and are the first to pinpoint a dietary-deficiency disease. Polish-American biochemist Casimir Funk, theorizing that some diseases are caused by a lack of certain substances in the diet, coins the term *vitamin* for these missing substances. **MED**
1912	English amateur archaeologist Charles Dawson claims to have discovered the missing link between apes and humans at Piltdown in Sussex, England. This so-called Piltdown man skull will fool paleontologists until 1953, when it will be shown to be a hoax, an artful combination of an ape's jaw and a modern human skull. **PALEO**
1912	German physicist Max Theodor Felix von Laue discovers how to use crystals for X-ray diffraction, permitting measurement of the wavelength of X rays. **PHYS**
1912	British physicist Joseph Thomson studies canal rays (*see* 1886, Goldberg), which he calls positive rays, since they are streams of positively charged atomic nuclei. He discovers also that there are at least two different varieties of neon atoms. **PHYS**
1912	Émile Durkheim publishes his *Elementary Forms of Religious Life*, a major work in the development of cultural anthropology. **SOC**
c. 1912	German chemist Carl Bosch improves the Haber process for making ammonia (*see* 1908) and implements it in large industrial plants. **TECH**
1912	German chemist Friedrich Bergius develops a coal hydrogenation process in which coal and heavy oil are treated with hydrogen to produce gasoline. **TECH**

1912	American chemist Irving Langmuir finds that tungsten filaments in light bulbs filled with inert gases last longer than those in vacuum light bulbs. **TECH**
1912	The first aeroboat, or amphibious aircraft, is developed, by German-American engineer Grover Loening. **TECH**
1912	An effective high-vacuum tube, which amplifies electric current, is developed by American physicist H. D. Arnold. **TECH**
1912	The Alpha Beta Food Market and Ward's Groceteria, two self-service grocery stores, the forerunners of supermarkets, open independently in California. **TECH**
1913	Danish astronomer Ejnar Hertzsprung discovers that a Cepheid variable star of absolute magnitude −2.3 has a period of 6.6 days. **ASTRO**
1913	British chemist Frederick Soddy and, independently, Polish chemist Kasimir Fajans state the radioactive displacement law, which describes the loss of mass and electric charge incurred by radioactive atoms. Soddy coins the term *isotopes* for atoms of the same element that have a differing mass and differing radioactive properties. **CHEM**
1913	American chemist Theodore William Richards finds that the atomic weight of lead varies according to the quantity of radioactive material in the lead ores, a finding that supports the concept of isotopes. **CHEM**
1913	German chemists Leonor Michaelis and Maud Lenora Menten formulate the Michaelis-Menten equation describing the rate at which enzyme-catalyzed reactions take place. **CHEM**
1913	French physicist Charles Fabry proves the existence of an ozone layer in the upper atmosphere. **EARTH**
1913–1917	Large numbers of bottles are launched to study surface currents in the Sea of Japan. **EARTH**
1913–1919	Dutch mathematician Luitzen Egbertus Jan Brouwer develops his theory of intuitionism, in which mathematics is considered to begin with a basic intuition of natural numbers. Truth claims are then made through constructivity rather than consistency, as advocated by German mathematician David Hilbert. *See* 1900. **MATH**
1913	In a book on the Riemann surface, German mathematician Hermann Weyl develops new concepts and definitions that will be important to later research on manifolds. **MATH**
1913	German surgeon A. Saloman develops the technique of mammography, an X-ray procedure to detect breast cancer. **MED**
1913	Autopsies become legal in China. **MED**
1913	Danish physicist Niels Bohr applies quantum theory to the structure of the atom, describing electron orbits and electron excitation and de-excitation. **PHYS**

1913   German physicist Johannes Stark discovers the Stark effect, a multiplication in spectral lines caused by strong electric fields.   **PHYS**

1913   Johannes Hans Geiger and Ernst Marsden provide supporting evidence for Rutherford's model of the atom (*see* 1911) when they direct a beam of alpha particles at a piece of gold foil and note that a few of the particles are deflected.   **PHYS**

1913   Swiss psychiatrist Carl Gustav Jung breaks with his teacher, Sigmund Freud, and develops his own theories. He will classify people as introverts and extroverts and theorize that certain ideas, which he will call archetypes, are inherited from the distant past and are a part of all peoples' unconscious, referred to as the collective unconscious.   **PSYCH**

1913   American psychologist J. B. Watson explains his theory of behaviorism in an article entitled "Psychology as the Behaviorist Views It." For Watson, psychology is the "science of behavior," not the traditional "science of conscious experience." Watson's aim is to predict and control behavior rather than describe and explain it. He also wishes to eliminate the traditional behavior distinction between humans and animals.   **PSYCH**

1913   Russian engineer Igor Ivan Sikorsky builds and flies the first multi-engined aircraft.   **TECH**

1913   American physicist William David Coolidge invents the Coolidge tube, a device for manufacturing X rays.   **TECH**

1913   Diesel-electric locomotives, invented by Rudolf Diesel, are put into operation in Sweden.   **TECH**

1913   In the United States, soap-laden steel wool pads are marketed under the name Brillo pads, by the Brillo Manufacturing Corp.   **TECH**

Oct. 7,   In Detroit, the Ford Motor Co. uses the assembly line system to build
1913   cars, which reduces assembly time from 12.5 to 1.5 hours.   **TECH**

1914   American astronomer Vesto Melvin Slipher discovers that thirteen of fifteen galaxies are receding from ours at hundreds of miles per second.   **ASTRO**

1914   U.S. astronomer Walter Sydney Adams invents the technique of spectroscopic parallax for determining a star's distance by comparing its apparent magnitude with its absolute magnitude as derived from its spectral characteristics.   **ASTRO**

1914   U.S. astronomer Harlow Shapley correlates the absolute magnitude and period of Cepheid variable stars, thereby providing a yardstick for determining galactic and stellar distances. *See also* 1912, Leavitt, and 1952, Boode.   **ASTRO**

1914   British physicist Henry Gwyn Jeffreys Moseley arrives at the concept of atomic number, a number representing the positive charge of the atomic nucleus. The periodic table of elements (*see* 1869) is henceforth revised in order of atomic number, beginning with hydrogen at 1 and ending with uranium at 92.   **CHEM**

1914   British physicists William Henry Bragg and William Lawrence Bragg discover that sodium chloride and certain other compounds exist as groups of ions bound by electromagnetic interaction.   **CHEM**

1914   Chemists P. Duden and J. Hess manufacture acetic acid synthetically.   **CHEM**

1914   German geologist Beno Gutenberg demonstrates the existence of a boundary in the lower depths of the earth's surface that he calls a discontinuity, because it causes an abrupt alteration in properties. Below the Gutenberg discontinuity is the earth's liquid core, above it the earth's mantle.   **EARTH**

1914   German mathematician Felix Hausdorff publishes his *Basic Features of Set Theory*, a systematic exposition that introduces the concept of Hausdorff topological spaces and marks the development of point set topology as a distinct discipline.   **MATH**

1914   American biochemist Edward Kendall isolates thyroxin, the thyroid hormone, which will be used to treat thyroid insufficiencies. Kendall's work with hormones will lead him to isolate cortisone, an anti-inflammatory used widely in medicine. In 1950, Kendall and American physician Phillip Hench will jointly receive the Nobel Prize for their work on cortisone.   **MED**

1914   Renowned German paleontologist Friedrich von Huene endorses H. G. Seeley's 1887 classification of dinosaurs into two independent orders, *Ornithischia* and *Saurischia*. Von Huene's support promotes the general acceptance of this system.   **PALEO**

1914   British physicists William Henry Bragg and William Lawrence Bragg show how to determine the wavelengths of X rays from diffraction by crystals.   **PHYS**

1914   British physicist James Chadwick shows that beta particles, unlike alpha particles, are emitted in a continuous range of energies.   **PHYS**

1914   British physicist Ernest Rutherford gives the name *proton* to the positively charged nucleus of the hydrogen atom, which is now seen to be, in a sense, the fundamental atom, as Prout had suggested in 1815. Scientists of the time theorize that the nuclei of all other atoms are composed of a combination of protons and electrons, but this theory will be revised with the discovery of the neutron by Chadwick in 1932.   **PHYS**

1914   German physicists James Franck and Gustav Hertz perform experiments confirming Niels Bohr's model of electrons' orbits.   **PHYS**

1914   English anthropologist W. H. R. Rivers publishes his *History of Melanesian Society*, a classic work based on his research in the South Pacific.   **SOC**

1914   By the beginning of World War I, all the major European powers have submarines and continue to improve upon them, the research and development focusing only on their suitability for war purposes.   **TECH**

1914   The teletype machine is developed by German-American inventor Edward E. Kleinschmidt.   **TECH**

Aug. 31,   The Panama Canal opens to traffic, carrying ships between the
1914   Atlantic and Pacific oceans. Operating by a system of locks, the canal spans 50.7 miles.   **TECH**

1915   Scottish astronomer Robert Innes discovers Proxima Centauri, a faint companion to the double star Alpha Centauri. At 4.5 light-years away it is the closest star to earth except the sun.   **ASTRO**

1915   U.S. astronomer Walter Sydney Adams demonstrates that the star Sirius B is extremely hot, dense, and small, what is called a white dwarf.   **ASTRO**

1915   Swedish biochemist Svante Arrhenius publishes the influential *Quantitative Laws in Biochemistry*.   **BIO**

1915–1917   Canadian bacteriologists Frederick William Twort and Felix Hubert d'Herelle separately discover bacteriophages, a type of virus able to infest and kill bacteria normally present in an organism.   **BIO**

1915   American geneticists Thomas Morgan, Calvin Bridges, Alfred Sturtevant, and Hermann Müller publish *The Mechanism of Mendelian Heredity*, claiming that invisible genes within the chromosomes of the cell nucleus determine an offspring's hereditary traits.   **BIO**

1915   Japanese scientists K. Yamagiwa and K. Ichikawa identify the first of a long line of cancer-producing agents called carcinogens by exposing rabbits to coal tar for long periods of time.   **MED**

1915   American paleontologist Richard Swann Lull publishes his *Triassic Life of the Connecticut Valley* (revised 1953), a classic monograph on the ancient flora and fauna of that region. In it he revises an earlier study of fossil tracks (*see* 1848, Hitchcock), ascribing them not to birds but to dinosaurs.   **PALEO**

STELLAR NEIGHBORS

*A*bout 1752, French astronomer Nicolas-Louis de Lacaille (1713–1762) discovered Alpha Centauri, which at a distance of 4.35 light-years was believed for a time to be the star nearest the solar system. Then in 1915 a faint star called Proxima Centauri was discovered at only 4.225 light-years distance, about 25 trillion miles.

As it turns out, Proxima Centauri and Alpha Centauri are part of one triple-star system called the Centauri System. Alpha Centauri is actually two stars revolving around each other every eighty years. Proxima, separated from its two siblings by a much greater distance, revolves around them once every million years.

Could any of these stars support life? The two stars of Alpha Centauri might. One is a type G2 star, about the size and color of our yellow sun; the other, a type K0, is a somewhat cooler orange star but might still be hot enough to support life. However, Proxima Centauri, which is a red dwarf (type M5), is probably too small and cool to sustain living things.

Despite its probable bleakness, Proxima Centauri is our nearest stellar neighbor. Even so, at the fastest rates of manned space travel yet achieved, it would take about 110,000 years to reach it, long enough for the crew's descendants and their relatives waiting back home to have evolved into separate species. Unless space travel becomes faster by several orders of magnitude, don't expect to see a visit to the nearest star any time soon.

1915   German physicist Arnold Johannes Wilhelm Sommerfeld proposes that electrons travel in elliptical orbits. He combines quantum theory and relativity theory in revising the model of the atom, resulting in what is known as the Bohr-Sommerfeld atom. Sommerfeld and Bohr work out the arrangement of electrons around an atom's nucleus, defining each in terms of three quantum numbers that vary in value. *See also* 1925, Pauli.   **PHYS**

1915   American physicist William Draper Harkins calculates that four hydrogen nuclei can fuse to form a helium nucleus, releasing a great deal of energy converted from the excess mass.   **PHYS**

c. 1915   American psychophysicist Stanley Smith Stevens formulates the power law of psychophysics. His developments in auditory scaling methods determine that physical continua usually conform to a psychophysical power law rather than Gustav Fechner's logarithmic law. The power function will prove controversial in psychophysics for more than thirty years.   **PSYCH**

1915   American neurologist and physiologist Walter Cannon presents a
            critique of the James-Lange theory of emotion in his book entitled
            Bodily Changes in Pain, Hunger, Fear, and Rage. Cannon's substi-
            tute for the James-Lange theory, that a physical response pre-
            cedes the appearance of emotion, will become known as the
            Cannon-Baird theory of emotion. It states that emotion is an
            emergency reaction to help humans cope in a crisis, not a follow-
            up to physical stimuli.   **PSYCH**

1915–1918   British anthropologist Bronislaw Malinowski does field research
            with the Trobriand Islanders. He will develop the theory of func-
            tionalism with his ethnographies in the 1920s and 1930s.   **SOC**

1915   The first use of poisonous gas as a military weapon occurs when the
            Germans use chlorine gas against French troops in World War I. **TECH**

1915   Heat- and shock-resistant borosilicate glass is developed in the
            United States by the Corning Glass Works and sold as cooking im-
            plements under the trade name Pyrex.   **TECH**

1916   U.S. astronomer Edward Emerson Barnard discovers Barnard's
            Star, a star with the largest known proper motion.   **ASTRO**

1916   German-American physicist Albert Einstein's general theory of rela-
            tivity (*see* 1916, physics) accounts for a long-standing anomaly about
            the orbital motion of the planet Mercury. *See* 1846, Vulcan. **ASTRO**

1916   The Ecological Society of America is founded.   **BIO**

1916   American chemist Gilbert Newton Lewis shows how variations in
            the number of electrons in the outermost shell of an atom lead to
            the formation of chemical bonds, through electron transfer or shar-
            ing. He explains that the most stable elements are those in which
            the outer shell has either eight or two electrons, whereas elements
            with different arrangements are more or less reactive. Lewis's work
            explains the valences of elements. American chemist Irving
            Langmuir independently devises a similar model. *See* 1852,
            Frankland.   **CHEM**

1916   American feminist and nurse Margaret Sanger establishes the first
            American birth-control clinic, in Brooklyn, New York.   **MED**

1916   German-American physicist Albert Einstein proposes his general
            theory of relativity, which extends his special theory of 1905 to sys-
            tems moving at changing velocities relative to each other. The gen-
            eral theory accounts for gravitational interactions, arguing that
            mass generates a gravitational field that curves space. The predic-
            tions of Einstein's theory are close to those of Newton's, but with
            several differences that are testable, and subsequent tests support
            Einstein's theory. *See* e.g., May 29, 1919, and 1925, Adams. **PHYS**

....

"A new scientific truth does not triumph by convincing its opponents and making them see light, but rather because its opponents eventually die, and a new generation grows up that is familiar with it."—Max Planck, German Nobel-winning physicist; early twentieth century

....

1916   Swiss linguist Ferdinand de Saussure publishes his compilation of lecture notes that he calls a *Course in General Linguistics*. The founder of structural linguistics, de Saussure argues that language sounds are arbitrary signs, while language itself is a systematic structure linking the sign and that which is signified.   **SOC**

1916   American radio station developer Lee De Forest broadcasts the first radio news report.   **TECH**

1917   George Ellery Hale installs a reflecting telescope on Mount Wilson in California. Its lens of 100 inches (2.54 meters) makes it the largest until the one on Mount Palomar in 1948.   **ASTRO**

1917   German astronomer Karl Schwarzschild formulates equations based on Einstein's general theory of relativity that predict the existence of what will become known as black holes. *See* 1939, Oppenheimer, and the 1960s, Wheeler.   **ASTRO**

1917   American embryologist Frank Rattray Lillie produces a major paper on questions of the origin, nature, and action of sex hormones, giving a thorough analysis of freemartinism, in which a sterile female calf is born as a co-twin with a normal bull calf.   **BIO**

1917   German physical chemist Otto Hahn and Austrian physicist Lise Meitner discover the element protactinium.   **CHEM**

1917–1919   English mathematician G. H. Hardy collaborates at Cambridge with Indian colleague Srinivasa Ramanujan on number theory.   **MATH**

1917   Dutch-American physicist Peter Joseph William Debye develops a technique for determining crystal structure by diffracting X rays through powdered crystalline solids.   **PHYS**

1917   French physicist Paul Langevin develops sonar (SOund NAvigation and Ranging), a system of echolocation used to detect underwater objects.   **TECH**

1917   Amplitude modulation for AM radio is pioneered through the development of a superheterodyne circuit by U.S. Army Signal Corps officer Edwin Armstrong.   **TECH**

1918   British archaeologist Leonard Woolley begins the excavations that will result in the discovery of Ur in ancient Iraq. *See* 1922, Woolley.   **ARCH**

c. 1918   American astronomer Harlow Shapley makes the first fairly accurate estimate of the diameter of the Milky Way galaxy. He also calculates the position of the solar system relative to the Milky Way's galactic center.   **ASTRO**

1918   British scientists James Hopwood Jeans and Harold Jeffreys propose the tidal hypothesis as an explanation of the solar system's formation, arguing that angular momentum was imparted to the protoplanets by the gravitational pull of a star that nearly collided with our sun. *See also* 1905, Chamberlin and Moulton, and 1935, Russell.   **ASTRO**

1918   Czech chemist Jaroslav Heyrovský begins the development of polarography, an electrochemical technique for measuring the ion concentration in solutions.   **CHEM**

1918   In Germany, a laboratory test is introduced that determines the rate at which red blood cells settle in a test tube in the process called erythrocyte sedimentation. An increase or decrease in settling times indicates the presence of certain disease processes.   **MED**

1918   In Germany, synthetic quinine is introduced for use as a fever reducer, a painkiller, and an antimalarial medication.   **MED**

1918   German mathematician Amalie (Emmy) Noether shows that every symmetry in physics implies a conservation law, and every conservation law a symmetry.   **PHYS**

1918–1919   Stanford University psychologist Lewis Madison Terman adapts the Binet-Simon Intelligence Scale for use in England, leading to the publication of the first standardized individual intelligence test in the United States, the Stanford-Binet Scale.   **PSYCH**

1918   Austrian psychologist and psychiatrist Alfred Adler publishes *The Theory and Practice of Individual Psychology*. Adler believes humans to be motivated by their expectations of the future and their striving toward three life goals: physical security, sexual satisfaction, and social integration. This conviction forms the basis of individual psychology.   **PSYCH**

1918   Hungarian chemist Georg Carl de Hevesy invents the technique of radioactive tracing, using a radioactive isotope of lead called radio lead.   **TECH**

1918   A wood-cellulose bandage called Ceulcotton is developed to use with battle wounds, by German-American chemist Ernst Mahler for the U.S. company Kimberly & Clark. In 1921 it will be remarketed as a female sanitary napkin called Kotex. *See also* 1936, tampon.   **TECH**

1918   The pop-up toaster is patented by American inventor Charles Strite.   **TECH**

1919 — American physicist Robert Goddard analyzes the mathematics of rocket propulsion, noting that these principles could be used to send a rocket to the moon. **ASTRO**

1919 — British chemist Francis William Aston invents the mass spectrometer for distinguishing and studying ions with different masses. The device is used to determine relative atomic masses and the relative abundance of isotopes. With it Aston shows that most stable elements occur in two or more stable isotopes, in which the nuclei have the same positive charge but a different mass or mass number. **CHEM**

1919 — Astronomers George E. Hale and Walter S. Adams note the phenomenon of polarity inversion and realize that the true length of the solar cycle is twenty-two years rather than eleven. **EARTH**

1919 — Belgian microbiologist Jules Bordet is awarded the Nobel Prize in medicine for his work in immunology. He has discovered that components in the blood act as complements to antibodies, making it possible for the antibodies to destroy bacteria—the basis for complement fixation—and maintain the body's defense against disease. **MED**

1919 — British physicist Ernest Rutherford produces the first artificial nuclear reactions when he uses subatomic bombardment to convert the nuclei of helium and nitrogen to nuclei of hydrogen and oxygen. **PHYS**

May 29, 1919 — An expedition organized by British astronomer Arthur Stanley Eddington observes a total solar eclipse from the island of Principe off West Africa. There, observations of starlight being bent by the sun's gravity confirm Einstein's general theory of relativity. **PHYS**

1919 — American physician C. F. Menninger and his sons, Karl and William, pioneer the development of community mental health programs when they open the Menninger Clinic in Topeka, Kansas. The resulting Menninger Foundation will become a nonprofit organization devoted to mental-illness prevention and treatment. **PSYCH**

1919 — J. B. Watson, the founder of behaviorism (*see* 1913), publishes a book that will provide inspiration for experimental psychologists, *Psychology from the Standpoint of a Behaviorist*. **PSYCH**

June 15–16, 1919 — British airmen John Alcock and Arthur Whitten Brown fly the first nonstop transatlantic flight, from Newfoundland to Ireland. *See also* 1927, Lindbergh. **TECH**

Nov. 8, 1919 — In Virginia, the American Telegraph & Telephone Co. introduces dial telephones. **TECH**

1920s   Soviet biochemist Alexander Ivanovich Oparin outlines his view that life gradually developed in the ocean of the ancient earth and that the primordial atmosphere consisted largely of ammonia, hydrogen, and methane. He will publish much of this theory in his 1936 book *The Origin of Life of Earth*. Stanley Miller and Harold Urey's later experiment (*see* 1952) in creating amino acids will support Oparin's theory, though by the 1990s scientists will be raising doubts about Oparin's account of the early atmosphere.   **BIO**

1920s   The Russian school of chemistry proposes the first geochemical classification of the elements.   **EARTH**

1920s   During this decade petroleum geology will develop.   **EARTH**

1920s   The modern pastoral counseling movement, a psychologically sophisticated form of religious caring, begins as an alternative to traditional theological guidance, which is less practical, and early psychiatric treatment, which is less religious in its orientation.   **PSYCH**

1920s   The specialization of psychiatric social work comes into existence. **PSYCH**

1920s   Otto Rank emphasizes the therapeutic importance of an individual's will. This "will" therapy is the forerunner of both assertiveness training and reality therapy.   **PSYCH**

1920s   Harvard and Columbia Universities take distinct approaches to anthropology, with Harvard specializing in archaeology and physical anthropology, Columbia in ethnology and linguistics.   **SOC**

1920   American astronomer Andrew Ellicott Douglass devises dendrochronology, a technique for dating objects based on the characteristic growth rings of trees in their given region.   **ARCH**

1920   Using a stellar interferometer, German-American physicist Albert Michelson determines the diameter of Betelgeuse, the first such measurement for any star other than the sun.   **ASTRO**

Apr. 26, 1920   American astronomers Heber Doust Curtis and Harlow Shapley debate whether the Andromeda "nebula" is inside or outside the Milky Way galaxy. Curtis argues correctly (as verified by Edwin Hubble; *see* 1924) that it is outside.   **ASTRO**

1920   Czech writer Karel Capek is the first to use the word *robot* as applied to mechanical people, in his play "R.U.R." ("Rossum's Universal Robots").   **BIO**

1920   English ornithologist H. Eliot Howard publishes his *Territory in Bird Life*, a study of how male birds fight over territory more often than over female birds and why they isolate themselves and maintain a certain distance from other birds.   **BIO**

1920   Austrian-born German zoologist Karl von Frisch conditions bees to go to certain locations to gather nectar by conditioning them to certain colors. He also shows that bees can orient themselves in flight by using the direction of the sky's light polarization.   **BIO**

1920   German chemist Hermann Staudinger discovers the molecular structure of polymers, which will aid in the development of plastics.   **CHEM**

c. 1920   Norwegian meteorologists Vilhelm Bjerknes and his son Jacob show that the atmosphere is made up of air masses differing in temperature, with sharp boundaries between them called fronts.   **EARTH**

c. 1920   Dutch physicist Willem Hendrik Keesom attains a temperature of 0.5 degrees above absolute zero, a new record low.   **PHYS**

c. 1920   Swiss psychologist Jean Piaget is involved in genetic epistemology, research that shows how intelligence varies qualitatively and quantitatively with age. He identifies stages in the development of a child's mental faculties, including reasoning skills, and urges schools to provide developmentally appropriate challenges for students.   **PSYCH**

1920   American psychologist Robert Sessions Woodworth develops the Woodworth personal data sheet, a screening device for military use to detect emotional instability that will become the prototype for future personality questionnaires.   **PSYCH**

Nov. 2, 1920   Station KDKA in Pittsburgh becomes the first radio broadcasting station in the world. Developed by American engineer Frank Conrad for Westinghouse, its first broadcasts give the results of the 1920 U.S. presidential race, in which Warren G. Harding is elected.   **TECH**

1921   Chinese records on the stellar explosion in 1054 are published, confirming supernova theory.   **ASTRO**

1921   British astronomer Edward Arthur Milne studies the sun's atmosphere, determining the temperature of its layers and predicting the existence of the solar wind.   **ASTRO**

1921   British biochemist Frederick Gowland Hopkins isolates glutathione, a polypeptide important in physiological oxidations, from human tissues.   **BIO**

Nov. 1921   Canadian surgeon Sir Frederick Banting and Canadian physiologist Charles Best isolate insulin. Within a few years it will be commercially produced and used for treatment of diabetes.   **MED**

1921   Physicist Alfred Landé discovers half-integer quantum numbers. The previously known quantum numbers were assumed to be whole.   **PHYS**

1921   Swiss psychiatrist Hermann Rorschach devises what will be known as the inkblot test to assess personality and aid in the diagnosis of psychiatric disorders.   **PSYCH**

1921   American chemist Thomas Midgley, Jr. discovers that tetraethyl lead serves as an antiknock additive in gasoline. He will sell this gasoline additive as Ethyl through his company, the Ethyl Corp.   **TECH**

Dec. 1, 1921   The U.S. Navy dirigible the C-7 is the first to use helium as a lifting gas.   **TECH**

1922   British archaeologist Leonard Woolley excavates ancient Ur, discovering a great deal about the Sumerian civilization of ancient Iraq. He finds evidence of a great flood that swept Sumeria about 2800 B.C. and may have given rise to the stories of the flood in the *Epic of Gilgamesh* and the Bible.   **ARCH**

....

"Lord Carnarvon: 'Can you see anything?'
Howard Carter: 'Yes, wonderful things.'"—Conversation
upon British archaeologist Howard Carter's first entering the
tomb of Egyptian pharaoh Tutankhamen; 1922

....

Nov. 4, 1922   British archaeologists George Herbert, Earl of Carnarvon, and Howard Carter discover the entrance to the tomb of Egyptian pharaoh Tutankhamen. Inside they find an abundance of ancient Egyptian artifacts that have lain untouched for thousands of years.   **ARCH**

1922   Russian mathematician Alexander Alexandrovich Friedmann suggests that the universe has been expanding from an original dense core of matter. *See also* 1927, Lemaître.   **ASTRO**

1922   Scottish bacteriologist Alexander Fleming isolates lysozyme from tears and mucus, finding it to have bacteria-killing properties, the first example of a human enzyme to have this capability.   **BIO**

1922   Polish mathematician Stefan Banach begins to introduce the concept of normed linear spaces. Now, completely normed ones are called Banach spaces.   **MATH**

1922   American biochemist Elmer McCollum discovers a factor in fat that is essential to life—vitamin D. Like vitamin A, which McCollum had isolated in 1913, it is not soluble in water. Later, McCollum will contribute to the discovery of vitamin E.   **MED**

1922   Sickle cell anemia is named. This hereditary blood disorder, a chronic anemia common in African-Americans, was first recognized by U.S. physician James Herrick in 1910.   **MED**

1922   American paleontologist Roy Chapman Andrews begins a series of Central Asiatic Expeditions in the Gobi Desert of Mongolia. These excavations will unearth fossils of early mammals as well as Cretaceous dinosaurs.   **PALEO**

A MATHEMATICAL WOMAN

*I*n 1922, German mathematician Amalie (Emmy) Noether (1882–1935) became the first woman to join the faculty of the University of Göttingen. Her career had been an uphill struggle since her days as a student at the University of Erlangen where, because of her gender, she was at first not allowed to matriculate and had to attend as an auditor only. Once graduated with a Ph.D. summa cum laude, she found it impossible to get a university appointment. The mathematician David Hilbert championed her cause and her achievements spoke for themselves, most notably her formulation of Noether's theorem in 1918, describing the relation between mathematical symmetries and physical conservation laws. Finally, in 1922, she was hired at Göttingen as an "unofficial associate professor."

Noether stayed at Göttingen until 1933, when she was dismissed for reasons that had nothing to do with her gender. Adolf Hitler had come to power and, along with other Jewish faculty, she received a notice saying, "I hereby withdraw from you the right to teach at the University of Göttingen." Noether emigrated to America, where she spent the last two years of her life lecturing and researching at Bryn Mawr College and the Institute for Advanced Studies at Princeton University.

1922   At the Flaming Cliffs in Bain-Dzak, Mongolia, Andrews uncovers the remains of a primitive horned dinosaur, *Protoceratops*, and its fossilized egg shells. The next year many fossil eggs are found, the first dinosaur eggs ever to be discovered. **PALEO**

1922   Dow Co. chemists William Hale and Edgar Britton discover the Hale-Britton process, a cheaper, more efficient way to produce phenol. This method permits greater production of phenol-based pesticides and fungicides. **TECH**

1923   British astronomer Arthur Stanley Eddington explains the relationship between a star's mass and its luminosity, describing the tension throughout its history between gravitational contraction and outward radiation. He speculates that white dwarf stars are made of degenerate matter. **ASTRO**

1923   American physiologists Joseph Erlanger and Herbert Gasser develop a method to study the electric currents in nerves. They eventually determine the rate at which nerve fibers conduct impulses and ascertain that the velocity varies with the nerve fiber's thickness. In 1944 these scientists will share the Nobel Prize for their work. **BIO**

1923   Dutch physicist Dirk Coster and Hungarian chemist Georg C. de Hevesy discover the element hafnium.   **CHEM**

1923   Chemist G. N. Lewis formulates the Lewis theory, which establishes a relationship between acid-base reactions and oxidation-reduction reactions. A Lewis acid is a substance that can accept a pair of electrons, a Lewis base one that can donate an electron pair.   **CHEM**

1923   Dutch physical chemist Peter Debye and German chemist Erich Huckel develop their Debye-Huckel equations to explain the incomplete dissociation of certain compounds in solution.   **CHEM**

1923   Danish chemist Johannes Nicolaus Bronsted develops the concept of acid-base pairs, in which an acid transfers a hydrogen ion, or proton, to a base.   **CHEM**

1923   Swedish chemist Theodor Svedberg invents the ultracentrifuge, a high-speed centrifuge for separating out small colloidal particles and macromolecules.   **CHEM**

1923   An effective vaccine against whooping cough or pertussis is produced in Copenhagen. Years later this vaccine will finally be replaced by the triple immunization (DPT) against diphtheria, pertussis, and tetanus.   **MED**

1923   American physicist Arthur Holly Compton discovers the phenomenon now called the Compton effect: the reduction in the energy of the high-energy electromagnetic rays known as X rays and gamma rays when they are scattered by free electrons, and the corresponding gain in energy by the electrons. This effect demonstrates the particle aspects of an energetic wave. Compton coins the word *photon* for a unit of electromagnetic radiation considered as a particle.   **PHYS**

1923   French physicist Louis-Victor-Pierre-Raymond de Broglie proposes that every particle should have an associated matter wave whose wavelength is inversely related to the particle's momentum. This theory leads to the consideration of the wave aspects of particles, as Compton (*see* above) drew attention to the particle aspects of waves. *See also* 1927, Davisson.   **PHYS**

1923   Austrian psychologist Otto Rank publishes *The Trauma of Birth*, in which he claims that the act of birth, not the Oedipus complex as Freud teaches, is what gives rise to human anxiety. This clash in views will ultimately lead to a split between Rank and his mentor Freud. After 1934 Rank will live and lecture in the United States, where he will exert great influence on psychotherapy.   **PSYCH**

1923   American neurologist and physiologist Walter B. Cannon publishes his findings on the effects of traumatic shock following World War I.   **PSYCH**

1923	The sliding closure that will become known as the zipper is introduced by the B. F. Goodrich Co. Within five years, it will be used widely in men's and women's clothing. Accounts of the origin of the name vary, but the invention itself is a descendant of Whitcomb Judson's clasp locker of 1893. **TECH**

....

"Zip! It's open! Zip! It's closed!"—Gilbert Frankau, English writer, unwittingly lending a name to the recently created moving fastener he had just seen demonstrated; c. 1923

....

1924	American Edwin Powell Hubble, working with the new Mount Wilson telescope, discovers that the Andromeda "nebula" is a separate galaxy outside the Milky Way. **ASTRO**
1924	The Harvard Observatory completes the publication of the *Henry Draper* (or *Standard Draper*) *Catalogue* (1918–1924), listing 225,000 stars and their spectral types. U.S. astronomer Annie Jump Cannon is the principal author. *See also* 1949, *Henry Draper Extension.* **ASTRO**
1924	German biochemist Otto Warburg discovers cytochrome oxidase, an enzyme of importance in biological oxidations. **BIO**
1924	Russian-born British biochemist David Keilin discovers cytochrome, a pigment widely distributed in animals and plants that plays an important role in cellular respiration. **BIO**
1924	U.S. biochemist Harry Steenbock shows that inactive precursors of vitamin D exist in food and that exposure to sunlight (irradiation) produces them and "adds" vitamin D to foods. After this discovery the irradiating of food will become common. **BIO**
1924	Australian-born South African anthropologist Raymond Arthur Dart discovers a fossil skull of *Australopithecus africanus* ("southern ape from Africa"), a hominid or humanlike primate. Australopithecine fossils will later be found in East Africa as well. Living from 4 million to 1. million years ago, australopithecines were the earliest known hominids; they walked erect but had ape-sized brains. *See* 1974, Johanson. **PALEO**
1924	Indian physicist Satyendra Nath Bose and German-American physicist Albert Einstein develop the Bose-Einstein statistics, a statistical method for handling the subatomic particles called bosons, for Bose. Bosons will come to be defined as elementary particles with an integral spin. *See also* 1926, Fermi and Dirac. **PHYS**
1924	Bell Laboratories is established by American Telephone & Telegraph and General Electric to carry out physics research . **PHYS**
1924	Two U.S. Army Air Corps biplanes, flown by Lowell Smith and Erik Nelson, complete the first round-the-world flight. **TECH**

1924   The development of coal-based synthetic gasoline is studied at the I. G. Farben chemical complex in Germany.   **TECH**

1925   The Tennessee legislature passes the first state law prohibiting the teaching of Darwin's theory of evolution in any Tennessee school.   **BIO**

1925   German chemist Walter Karl Noddack, his future wife Ida Eva Tacke, and Otto C. Berg together discover the element rhenium.   **CHEM**

1925   German oceanographers, using sonar, discover the Mid-Atlantic Ridge, an underwater mountain range running down the middle of the Atlantic Ocean.   **EARTH**

1925   Russian scientist Pyotr A. Molchanov attempts the first radio-wave telemetry with balloon-borne instruments.   **EARTH**

1925   The first international symposium of the International Astronomical Union meets in Rome.   **EARTH**

1925   U.S. astronomer Walter Sydney Adams discovers a red or Einstein shift in the spectral lines of white dwarf stars that is caused by the stars' massive gravity, as predicted by Einstein's general theory of relativity.   **PHYS**

1925   Pierre Auger discovers the Auger effect, the ejection of an electron (an Auger electron) from an atom without the emission of a gamma-ray or X-ray photon, as a consequence of the de-excitation of an excited electron in the atom.   **PHYS**

1925   British chemist Francis Aston discovers the packing fraction, which is the algebraic difference between the relative atomic mass of an isotope and its mass number divided by the mass number. It refers to the energy change, also called the binding energy, produced by packing subatomic particles into a nucleus.   **PHYS**

1925   Austrian-born U.S. physicist Wolfgang Pauli states the Pauli exclusion principle, that no two electrons in an atom can have the same set of quantum numbers, or numbers characterizing how electrons are arranged around their atomic nucleus. Pauli proposes that a fourth quantum number is needed in addition to the three identified by Bohr and Sommerfeld. *See* 1915, Sommerfeld and Bohr.   **PHYS**

1925   Dutch physicists George Eugene Uhlenbeck and Samuel Abraham Goudsmit define particle spin as the fourth quantum number.   **PHYS**

1925   Dutch physical chemist Peter Debye suggests using paramagnetic substances to lower the temperature of liquid helium to get it even closer to absolute zero than has yet been achieved. American chemist William F. Giauque makes the same suggestion independently.   **PHYS**

1925   German physicist Werner Karl Heisenberg develops matrix mechanics, a mathematical technique for studying the energy levels of electrons.   **PHYS**

Advertisement for a Frigidaire refrigerator and freezer, 1925. (*Hagley Museum and Library*)

1925   Chinese psychologist Chen He-quin uses the diary, or journal, method to keep track of and study his child's physical and emotional development. This is the first official documentation of its kind in China.   **PSYCH**

1925   Psychologist Albert Bandura is born in Canada. He will be responsible for developing the theory of social learning, the view that the basic way humans learn new behavior is by watching and imitating—modeling—others.   **PSYCH**

1925   French anthropologist Marcel Mauss publishes *The Gift*, which analyzes the social bond of debt created by gift giving.   **SOC**

1925   American political scientist Charles E. Merriam publishes *New Aspects of Politics*, which argues that the discipline should make greater use of statistics in support of empirical observation. *See also* 1930, Harold Lasswell.   **SOC**

1925   The Leica, a 35-millimeter camera with an adjustable lens and shutter speed, is developed by E. Leitz G.m.b.H. of Germany. This camera permits photos that vary in their depth of field and lighting.   **TECH**

1925   A deep-freezing process (patented in 1926) for cooked foods is developed by Americans Clarence Birdseye and Charles Seabrook.   **TECH**

1926   U.S. astronomer Edwin Powell Hubble classifies galaxies by their structure, as elliptical, spiral, or irregular.   **ASTRO**

1926   While studying cytochromes, German biochemist Otto Warburg shows that they possess the same iron-containing heme—the complex molecular group that joins with protein to form hemoglobin—that hemoglobin does.   **BIO**

1926   American physiologist Walter B. Cannon coins the term *homeostasis* to describe an organism's capacity to maintain its internal equilibrium.   **BIO**

1926   U.S. biochemist James Batcheller Sumner crystallizes the first pure enzyme, jack bean urease, proving that enzymes are proteins and can act catalytically.   **BIO**

1926   Swiss-Norwegian geochemist Victor Goldschmidt codifies the isomorphism rule.   **EARTH**

1926   American researcher W. E. Brown detects slight irregularities in the motion of the earth.   **EARTH**

May 4, 1926   Two Americans, Richard E. Byrd and Floyd Bennett, are the first to fly over the North Pole, in a fifteen-hour nonstop flight. *See also* November 28–29, 1929.   **EARTH**

1926   American bacteriologist Thomas Rivera distinguishes between bacteria and viruses, thus establishing virology as a separate area of study.   **MED**

1926   German paleontologist Friedrich von Huene publishes a monograph on the late Cretaceous dinosaurs of Argentina.   **PALEO**

1926   Austrian physicist Erwin Schrödinger develops wave mechanics, a model of the atom in which the electron is regarded as a wave rather than a particle. This model accounts for hitherto unexplained aspects of electron orbits. Central to wave mechanics is the Schrödinger wave equation. **PHYS**

1926   German physicist Max Born develops the concept of the wave packet to describe the probabilistic aspect of electron waves. Born, German physicist Werner Heisenberg, and Austrian physicist Erwin Schrödinger are considered the founders of quantum mechanics, a system of mechanics developed from quantum theory (*see* 1900, Planck) to explain the properties of molecules, atoms, and subatomic particles. **PHYS**

....

"It looked almost magical as it rose, without any appreciably greater noise or flame."—Robert Goddard, American physicist, describing the flight of his first liquid-fuel rocket on his aunt's farm in Massachusetts; 1926

....

1926   Italian physicist Enrico Fermi and British physicist Paul Adrien Maurice Dirac develop the Fermi-Dirac statistics, which apply to all subatomic particles with half-integral spins, now called fermions. Such particles contrast with bosons, which have an integral spin and are treated with the Bose-Einstein statistics (*see* 1924). Protons and electrons are fermions. **PHYS**

1926   Physicist John Desmond Bernal invents the Bernal chart, which assists researchers in using X-ray diffraction photographs to discover the structure of crystals. **PHYS**

1926   Russian physiologist Ivan Pavlov publishes his *Conditioned Reflexes*, an account of dogs salivating at the sound of a bell after being conditioned to eat after a bell rang. Pavlov's experiments will lend credence to the theory that human learning and behavior result, in part, from a conditioned reflex. **PSYCH**

1926   The International Institute of African Languages is founded, to encourage linguistic and anthropological research in Africa. **SOC**

1926   American chemist Waldo Lonsbury Semon develops an early synthetic rubber called Koroseal for B. F. Goodrich. This durable rubberlike material is based on the polymer polyvinyl chloride. **TECH**

1926   In a demonstration, the first motion picture with synchronized sound is projected. The first sound feature will be *The Jazz Singer* (1927). **TECH**

1926   NBC, the National Broadcasting Company, a network initially of nine radio stations, is founded by American David Sarnoff. **TECH**

1926   On March 16, Robert H. Goddard launches the world's first liquid-fuel rocket, from a farm near Auburn, Massachusetts. **TECH**

1927   Belgian astronomer Georges Lemaître, independently of A. A. Friedmann (*see* 1922), theorizes that the universe has been expanding from an original small, dense core or "cosmic egg." This hypothesis is an early version of what will become accepted as the Big Bang theory.   **ASTRO**

1927   In Germany, the first rocket society is organized to promote rocket experimentation. Wernher von Braun (*see* 1932 and 1942) is involved, as is Rumanian Hermann Oberth, who envisions high-altitude research rockets, space travel, and space stations.   **ASTRO**

1927   Swedish astronomer Bertil Lindblad proposes that the Milky Way galaxy rotates, completing one cycle every 210 million years. **ASTRO**

1927   American scientist Thomas Morgan publishes *Experimental Embryology*.   **BIO**

1927   British biologist Charles Elton publishes *Animal Ecology*, a landmark study of ecology as scientific natural history.   **BIO**

1927   Cellulose acetate is developed.   **CHEM**

1927   Canadian anthropologist Davidson Black discovers a fossil molar of *Sinanthropus pekinensis*, or Peking man, in a cave near Peking (now Beijing) China. This extinct relative of modern humans will come to be considered an example of *Homo erectus*.   **PALEO**

1927   Danish physicist Niels Bohr develops the concept of complementarity, which suggests that different but complementary models may be needed to explain the full range of atomic and subatomic phenomena.   **PHYS**

· ·

"We are all agreed that your theory is crazy. The question that divides us is whether it is crazy enough to have a chance of being correct."—Niels Bohr, Danish physicist, speaking for a group of colleagues reviewing a particle theory proposed by Werner Heisenberg and Wolfgang Pauli; early twentieth century

· ·

1927   German physicist Werner Heisenberg states the uncertainty principle or principle of indeterminism, that it is impossible to know both the position and the momentum of a subatomic particle with complete precision. *See also* 1812, Laplace.   **PHYS**

1927   American physicist Clinton Joseph Davisson and British physicist George Paget Thomson independently discover electron diffraction, which demonstrates the wave aspect of electrons. *See also* 1923, de Broglie.   **PHYS**

1927   German-American physicist Albert A. Michelson obtains a still more accurate value for the speed of light of 199,798 kilometers per second.   **PHYS**

1927   German physicists Fritz Wolfgang London and Walter Heitler use quantum mechanics to explain the electron bond of the hydrogen molecule. Quantum mechanics will later prove a valuable aid in understanding chemistry.   **PHYS**

1927   American parapsychologist Joseph Banks Rhine begins research at Duke University to provide support for the existence of extrasensory perception (ESP), the ability to gain information unavailable to the five senses. His research will also provide evidence to support psychokinesis, clairvoyance, telepathy, and precognition.   **PSYCH**

1927   The first underwater passage from New York to New Jersey is put into use with the opening of the Holland Tunnel, named after its chief engineer, Clifton Holland.   **TECH**

1927   Transatlantic telephone service is offered between New York and London.   **TECH**

1927   Television is demonstrated for the first time in the United States by AT&T executive Walter Gifford, who broadcasts images of Secretary of Commerce Herbert Hoover from Washington, D.C., to a group of viewers in New York.   **TECH**

1927   American inventors John and Mack Rust develop the all-mechanical cotton picker, which when popularized two decades later will lead African-Americans northward in search of jobs to replace those lost on southern farms.   **TECH**

1927   The U.S. dairy company Borden begins to offer homogenized milk.   **TECH**

May 20–21, 1927   American aviator Charles Augustus Lindbergh sets off in *The Spirit of St. Louis* on the first solo nonstop transatlantic flight, from Roosevelt Field, Long Island, to Le Bourget Field outside Paris. The flight takes 33 hours, 29 minutes. *See also* June 15–16, 1919.   **TECH**

1928   German chemists Otto Paul Hermann Diels and Kurt Alder discover the Diels-Alder reaction or diene synthesis, in which two compounds react in such a way as to yield a ring compound.   **CHEM**

1928   The first ultrasound echograph is developed.   **EARTH**

Dec. 20, 1928   The first flight over Antarctica occurs.   **EARTH**

1928   Hungarian-born American mathematician John von Neumann develops the mathematical field of game theory.   **MATH**

1928   American neurosurgeons Harvey Cushing and W. T. Bowie introduce the process of surgical diathermy or blood vessel cauterization, reducing operating time and decreasing the risk of blood loss.   **MED**

1928　　Greek-American pathologist George Papanicolaou develops the test for cervical cancer that will be referred to as the Pap smear. It will prevent thousands of cancer deaths through early detection of malignant change. **MED**

1928　　During an unrelated experiment, British bacteriologist Alexander Fleming isolates the mold called *Penicillium natatum*. This discovery is ignored until 1939, however, when British biochemist Ernst Chain and British pathologist Howard Florey take up Fleming's work and produce pure penicillin. **MED**

1928　　Indian physicist Chandrasekhara Venkata Raman discovers the Raman effect, an inelastic scattering of electromagnetic radiation. This effect will be used in Raman spectroscopy to study the details of molecular structure. **PHYS**

1928　　Physicists George Gamow, R. H. Fowler, and Lothar W. Nordheim develop the concept of electron tunneling. **PHYS**

1928　　Physicist Arnold Sommerfeld discovers that in a conductor electrons behave like a degenerate gas and only a few electrons with high energy participate in conducting electricity. **PHYS**

1928　　Hungarian-American physicist Eugene Paul Wigner develops the concept of parity of atomic states. **PHYS**

1928　　In *Anthropology and Modern Life*, American ethnologist Franz Boas attacks theories of racial superiority that have been prevalent for decades. **SOC**

1928　　American anthropologist Margaret Mead publishes *Coming of Age in Samoa*, a landmark study of cultural traditions related to becoming an adult in Polynesian society. **SOC**

....

"One of the jobs of the anthropologist is to get people to see that many of the things that we think of as universal were only invented yesterday and don't fit anymore today." —Margaret Mead, American anthropologist; mid-twentieth century

....

1928　　W. Müller produces an improved Geiger counter (*see* 1908, Geiger), now known as a Geiger-Müller counter. **TECH**

1928　　American Amelia Earhart flies from Newfoundland to Wales, becoming the first woman to pilot an airplane alone across the Atlantic Ocean. **TECH**

1928　　A commercial bread-slicing machine is developed, by U.S. inventor Otto Frederick Rohwedder. Two years later the Continental Bakery will sell the first loaves of prepackaged sliced bread, under the label Wonder Bread. **TECH**

1929   Astronomer Edwin Hubble confirms that the universe is expanding and formulates Hubble's law, that the increase in the velocity at which a galaxy is receding from ours is proportionate to the distance of that galaxy.   **ASTRO**

1929   American biochemist Edward Adelbert Doisy and German chemist Adolf Butenandt independently isolate a female sex hormone, estrogen, from the estrogen group.   **BIO**

1929   American biologist Hermann Joseph Müller finds that the rate of gene mutation can be greatly increased by using X rays on genes.   **BIO**

1929   U.S. chemist William Francis Giauque discovers oxygen-16 to be the most common isotope of oxygen, with oxygen-17 and oxygen-18 less common.   **CHEM**

1929   Alexander Eugenevic Fersman formulates the concept of the geochemical migration of the elements.   **EARTH**

Nov. 28–29,   U.S. explorer Richard E. Byrd and his crew are the first to fly over
1929   the South Pole and back. *See also* May 4, 1926.   **EARTH**

1929   German psychiatrist Hans Berger reports using electrodes, placed against the head, to record the electrical impulses called brain waves. The first electroencephalograph (EEG) is introduced to help in the diagnosis of neurological disorders.   **PSYCH**

1929   American psychologist Karl Spencer Lashley publishes *Brain Mechanisms and Intelligence*. In it he proposes the law of mass action, which states that the rate and accuracy of learning is proportionate to the amount of brain tissue available, and the principle of equipotentiality, that each part of the brain is as important as any other. Lashley will be known best for his work on brain function localization and research into how brain functions are generalized.   **PSYCH**

1929   German physicist Walther Wilhelm Georg Franz Bothe invents the coincidence counter, a device for studying cosmic rays that machine-registers an event only when a particle passes through two detectors virtually simultaneously.   **TECH**

1929   British physicist John Douglas Cockcroft and Irish physicist Ernest Thomas Walton invent the voltage multiplier, the first particle accelerator, a device using electromagnetic fields to accelerate subatomic particles to high speeds.   **TECH**

1929   The 16-millimeter movie camera, projector, and film are introduced to the public by Eastman Kodak.   **TECH**

1929   On September 24, U.S. pilot James Doolittle shows that instrument-guided flying is possible when he takes off and lands relying completely on instruments in the first "blind" flight.   **TECH**

1929   German automobile maker Fritz von Opel carries out the first flight powered by a rocket engine, traveling almost two miles in seventy-five seconds. **TECH**

1930s   Russian-American physicist George Gamow popularizes the theory of the Big Bang, the explosive origin of the universe. **ASTRO**

1930s   While studying the competition of yeast and protozoa, Soviet biologist G. F. Gauze helps develop the principle that two species cannot simultaneously occupy the same ecological niche. **BIO**

1930s   Evolutionist Theodosius Dobzhansky writes *Genetics and the Origin of the Species* in which he shows that the facts of genetics are compatible with Darwinian natural selection, the chief cause of sustained changes in gene frequencies and a population's evolutionary changes. **BIO**

1930s   Chinese paleontologists M. N. Bien and Chung Chien Young excavate the so-called Lufeng series of late Triassic dinosaurs. Also discovered at this site are mammal-like reptiles related to the ancestors of modern mammals. **PALEO**

1930s   American physicist Robert Oppenheimer demonstrates that bombardment by deuterons, the atomic nuclei of hydrogen-2, or deuterium (*see* 1931, Urey), is equivalent to bombardment by neutrons. **PHYS**

1930s   Austrian researcher Manfred Sakel introduces insulin coma therapy, a somatic process to treat schizophrenia by insulin administration. Later discovered to be a potentially fatal procedure, this therapy will lose popularity in coming decades. **PSYCH**

1930s   Australian-American psychologist Elton Mayo is responsible for the Hawthorne experiments in industrial psychology that identify work as a group activity and demonstrate that a sense of belonging, of identification with a group, is more important than the physical working conditions in sustaining worker morale. Much later research in social organization will be based on these findings. **PSYCH**

1930s   Keynesian economic theory, named for U.S. economist John Maynard Keynes, calls for government intervention to boost a recessionary economy, encourages the development of econometrics, and provides a technique that combines theory with statistical and mathematical analysis in an attempt to improve the accuracy of economic forecasts. *See also* 1936, Keynes. **SOC**

1930   Archaeologists translate the Edwin Smith papyrus, which dates from 1550 B.C. and was acquired by U.S. Egyptologist Edwin Smith in 1862. This papyrus turns out to be an invaluable record of the surgical practices of ancient Egypt, based on an even older text written probably about 2500 B.C. **ARCH**

1930   Russian-German optician Bernhard V. Schmidt invents the Schmidt telescope, which is free of the aberration known as coma. **ASTRO**

1930   Swiss-American astronomer Robert J. Trumpler shows that the Milky Way galaxy is about 60 percent smaller than in previous estimates, which had failed to account for interstellar dust that dims starlight and creates the illusion of greater distance. **ASTRO**

1930   French astronomer Bernard Ferdinand Lyot invents the coronagraph, a telescope for observing the inner corona of the sun in the absence of an eclipse. **ASTRO**

Feb. 18,   American astronomer Clyde William Tombaugh discovers Pluto,
1930   the ninth planet from the sun and the last to be discovered. **ASTRO**

1930   American biochemist John Howard Northrop crystallizes pepsin and shows it to be a protein. **BIO**

1930   British naturalist Henry Ridley writes on theories of long-distance plant dispersal in *The Dispersal of Plants Throughout the World*. **BIO**

1930   Russian botanist Trofim Lysenko, in an attempt to improve Soviet agriculture, turns to the earlier discovery of vernalization, the moisturizing and near-freezing of seed. He claims that winter wheat can be changed so that it can be sown in the spring and its offspring can be changed through vernalization so as to be sown as spring wheat. This concept contradicts theories of evolution that have been claiming that acquired characteristics are not inherited. **BIO**

1930   English biologist Ronald Fisher publishes *The Genetic Theory of Natural Selection*, which reestablishes Darwin's theory of evolution by claiming that mutations occur by chance and natural selection controls the direction of evolution by weeding out harmful mutations and perpetuating useful ones. **BIO**

1930   American chemist Thomas Midgley Jr. discover difluorodichloromethane, or Freon, which will be used as a coolant in refrigerators and air conditioners. **CHEM**

1930   English biochemist William Thomas Astbury uses X-ray diffraction techniques to analyze the three-dimensional structure of proteins. **CHEM**

1930   The electrophoresis technique for studying particles in suspension is developed, for later use in the study of proteins. **CHEM**

June 11,   American naturalists Charles Beebe and Otis Barton take a dive in
1930   the first bathysphere, built to study the ocean depths. The unmaneuverable, watertight sphere of metal is capable of withstanding intense water pressures. **EARTH**

1930   British physicist Paul Dirac proposes the existence of antiparticles, particles identical to known particles in mass but with a different charge. The antiproton has a negative charge, the antielectron (or positron) a positive one. Antiparticles make up a form of matter now called antimatter. **PHYS**

1930   Superfluidity, the property of liquid helium at very low temperatures that allows it to flow without friction, is discovered. **PHYS**

1930   In his *Principles of Quantum Mechanics* Paul Dirac develops a general mathematical theory in which wave mechanics and matrix mechanics represent special cases. **PHYS**

1930   American political scientist Harold Lasswell publishes *Psychopathology and Politics*, which makes connections between politics and psychology. Lasswell and Charles E. Merriam (*see* 1925) are the leaders of the so-called Chicago school of political science, which emphasizes psychological factors and statistical analysis. It will influence the development of behaviorism in the late 1940s (*see* c. 1945). **SOC**

c. 1930   Snorkels, short pipes with one end that goes into the mouth and the other above the water's surface, come into use to aid in underwater exploration. Rubber fins come into use in 1933. **TECH**

1930   American physicist Ernest Orlando Lawrence invents the cyclotron, a particle accelerator that speeds up subatomic particles by using a magnetic field to push them in spirals. **TECH**

1930   American electrical engineer Vann Bush produces the first partially electronic computer, called a differential analyzer, capable of solving differential equations. **TECH**

1930   British engineer Frank Whittle is the first to invent and patent a practical jet engine. **TECH**

1930   The lightweight thermoplastic polymer trade-named Plexiglas is developed by Canadian research student William Chalmers. **TECH**

1930   The flash bulb for cameras is patented by German inventor Johannes Ostermeir. **TECH**

1931   The small planetoid Eros swings closer to the earth than any other celestial body except the moon, allowing astronomers to measure its parallax precisely and adjust their estimates of the scale of the solar system. **ASTRO**

1931   Karl G. Jansky of Bell Laboratories accidentally discovers radio radiation coming from the sky, thereby founding radio astronomy. *See also* 1933, Jansky. **ASTRO**

1931   German chemist Adolf Friedrich Johann Butenandt isolates the male sex hormone androsterone. **BIO**

Building the George Washington Bridge, New York City. (*Port Authority of New York*)

1931   English bacteriologist William Joseph Elford discovers that viruses range in size from those of large protein molecules to those of tiny bacteria.   **BIO**

1931   American pathologist Ernest Goodpasture devises a technique for culturing viruses in eggs.   **BIO**

July 2, 1931   British geneticist and biologist J. B. S. Haldane argues that biology should be regarded as an independent science, being different in its orientation from the physical sciences. **BIO**

1931   American chemist Harold Clayton Urey discovers deuterium (heavy hydrogen, or hydrogen-2), an isotope of hydrogen. **CHEM**

1931   American chemist Linus Carl Pauling develops the concept of resonance, which uses quantum mechanics to explain electron sharing in organic compounds. **CHEM**

1931   Swiss physicist Auguste Piccard uses a sealed gondola attached to a balloon to ascend into the thin air of the stratosphere, reaching a height of ten miles. **EARTH**

1931   Austrian mathematician Kurt Gödel develops the statement known as Gödel's proof, showing that in any system based on any set of axioms there will always be statements that cannot be proven or disproven on the basis of those axioms. *See also* 1900, Hilbert. **MATH**

1931   On Mount Carmel in Palestine and again in 1935 at Swanscombe, England, important discoveries of hominid skulls are made. The Swanscombe skull has characteristics similar to those of modern humans. **PALEO**

1931   Austrian-American physicist Wolfgang Pauli proposes the existence of an electrically neutral, virtually massless particle to account for the energy missing in beta decay. In 1932 Italian physicist Enrico Fermi will give it the name *neutrino*. **PHYS**

1931   Through his work on mental trauma, American neurologist and physiologist Walter Cannon discovers the hormone called sympathin, an adrenalinelike substance that works in the sympathic nervous system. **PSYCH**

1931   The 1,644-foot George Washington Bridge connecting New York and New Jersey opens. At the time it is the world's longest suspension bridge. Its cables were constructed by John A. Roebling's Sons, descendants of a designer of the Brooklyn Bridge. **TECH**

1931   The refrigerant gas Freon 12 is used to replace less stable gases in refrigerators. **TECH**

1932   Under scientists Walter Domberger and Wernher von Braun, the German Ordnance Corps begins researching rocket technology. **ASTRO**

1932   Using spectroscopy, astronomer T. Dunham discovers large quantities of carbon dioxide on Venus. **ASTRO**

1932   German biochemist Gerhard Domagk synthesizes prontosil, the first sulfa drug to be tested clinically for its bacteria-inhibiting properties. **BIO**

1932   British biologist R. G. Canti takes some of the first pictures of cell division, using microcinematography. **BIO**

1932	German-born British biochemist Hans Krebs discovers the urea cycle, showing that when the amino acid arginine breaks down and is reconstituted it produces a urea molecule, the chief nitrogen-containing waste in humans. **BIO**
Aug. 26, 1932	U.S. geneticist Thomas Hunt Morgan argues that genes can exert an influence outside the cells in which they are located, claiming that one of these extracellular gene activities results in hormone production. **BIO**
c. 1932	The artificial respirator called the iron lung is invented. **MED**
1932	American biochemist Charles King isolates and identifies vitamin C. *See also* 1933, Reichstein. **MED**
1932	American heart specialist A. S. Hyman develops the first clinical cardiac stimulator, calling it an artificial cardiac pacemaker. **MED**
1932	In India, Edward Lewis discovers a jaw fragment from *Ramapithecus*, which in 1981 will be shown to be an extinct primate that is probably an ancestor of the orangutan rather than the common ancestor of apes and hominids, as long believed. **PALEO**
1932	British physicist James Chadwick discovers the neutron, an electrically neutral particle that is a component of atomic nuclei. **PHYS**
1932	German physicist Werner Heisenberg develops the model of an atomic nucleus containing both protons and neutrons. He suggests that exchange forces (binding forces resulting from the interchange of particles) account for the stability of the nucleus. This model will be further developed by Hideki Yukawa. *See* 1935. **PHYS**
1932	Studying cosmic rays, American physicist Carl David Anderson discovers the antielectron predicted by Paul Dirac in 1930. Anderson calls it a positron. **PHYS**
1932	British physicist John Cockcroft and Irish physicist Ernest Walton produce the first nuclear reaction to result from the bombardment of an element by artificially accelerated particles. They produce helium by bombarding lithium with hydrogen nuclei. **PHYS**
1932	Hungarian-born physicist Leo Szilard grasps the possibility of a nuclear chain reaction, an idea that will not be realized for another decade. *See* December 2, 1942. **PHYS**
c. 1932	Hungarian psychiatrist Ladislas von Meduna invents metrazol shock therapy, one of the chemically induced forms of convulsive therapy used on schizophrenics. **PSYCH**
1932	British physiologist Charles Scott Sherrington is awarded the Nobel Prize for his research on how neurons function. Since irregularities in neurotransmitter levels are linked to depression and schizophrenic disorders, Sherrington's work helps establish greater understanding of these mental illnesses and their treatment. **PSYCH**

1932   Austrian psychoanalyst Melanie Klein publishes *The Psychoanalysis of Children*, illustrating how anxieties affect a child's developing ego, superego, and sexuality and cause emotional disturbances. She also develops play therapy, in which children show and release their anxieties through playing with toys.   **PSYCH**

1932   British psychologist Sir Frederic C. Bartlett publishes *Remembering*, in which he argues that all new learning builds on existing knowledge.   **PSYCH**

1932   American child development scientist Beth Wellman is the first to demonstrate that children's intelligence can diminish in deprived environments and increase in enriched ones.   **PSYCH**

1932   German electrical engineer Ernst August Friedrich Ruska invents the electron microscope.   **TECH**

1932   The first synthetic light-polarizing film, Polaroid film, is developed by U.S. inventor Edwin Herbert Land.   **TECH**

1933   In the first discovery of radio astronomy, Karl G. Jansky detects powerful radio-wave radiation coming from the center of the Milky Way. *See also* 1931, Jansky, and 1937, radio telescope.   **ASTRO**

1933   German-American astronomer Walter Baade and others develop the theory of neutron stars, arguing that a star larger than 1.4 solar masses would collapse into small, dense objects composed of neutrons.   **ASTRO**

1933   Polish-born Swiss chemist Tadeus Reichstein successfully synthesizes vitamin C.   **BIO**

1933   American geneticist Thomas Morgan receives the Nobel Prize for proving that chromosomes carry hereditary traits.   **BIO**

1933   American chemist Gilbert N. Lewis discovers deuterium oxide, or heavy water.   **CHEM**

1933   Hubert James and Albert Sprague Coolidge apply quantum mechanics to deduce the strength of the covalent bond. Their highly accurate results lend support to quantum theory.   **CHEM**

1933   A prototype defibrillator, to electrically restore an irregular heartbeat to normal, is introduced.   **MED**

1933   German-American physicist Otto Stern demonstrates the wave aspects and magnetic characteristics of molecular beams: streams of molecules, atoms, or ions traveling at low pressure in the same direction.   **PHYS**

1933   American chemist William F. Giauque uses the magnetic techniques he and Paul Dirac had earlier developed (*see* 1925, Debye) to reach a new record low temperature of 0.25° K.   **PHYS**

1933	Walther Meissner discovers the Meissner effect, that there is a falling off of magnetic flux in the interior of a superconducting material when it is cooled below a critical temperature. **PHYS**
1933	Wiley Post becomes the first pilot to circle the globe solo. **TECH**
1933	American Edwin H. Armstrong refines the process of frequency modulation (FM), a method of transmitting radio waves without static. **TECH**
1933	The walkie-talkie, a portable pair of short-distance radios, is invented by the U.S. Army Corps of Engineers and Motorola employee Paul Galvin. **TECH**
1933	The first milk fortified with vitamin D is sold commercially by the Borden Co. **TECH**
1934	German-American astronomer Walter Baade and Swiss astronomer Fritz Zwicky identify the differences between novae and supernovae, and suggest that neutron stars are the product of supernova eruptions. *See* 1968, Crab Nebula. **ASTRO**
1934	Dutch botanist F. W. Went demonstrates the existence of plant hormones. **BIO**
1934	German chemist Adolf Butenandt isolates progesterone, a female hormone vital to successful gestation. **BIO**
1934	The pH meter for electronically measuring acidity and alkalinity is invented by Arnold O. Beckman. **CHEM**
1934	Russian mathematician Aleksander O. Gelfond publishes Gelfond's theorem, which solves Hilbert's seventh problem. *See* 1900. **MATH**
1934	Sodium pentothal is introduced for use as an intravenous anesthetic. **MED**
1934	French physicists Irène and Frédéric Joliot-Curie are the first to achieve artificial radioactivity when they create the radioactive isotope phosphorus-30 by bombarding the nucleus of an aluminum atom with alpha particles. **PHYS**
1934	Italian physicist Enrico Fermi studies the effects of bombarding of uranium atoms with neutrons. **PHYS**
1934	Enrico Fermi develops the concept of the weak interaction, the fundamental event that accounts for the beta decay of particles and atomic nuclei. **PHYS**
1934	Soviet physicist Pavel Alekseyevich Cherenkov discovers Cherenkov radiation, the wake of light produced by particles moving faster than light in a medium other than a vacuum, a phemomenom explained by Russian physicists Igor Y. Tamm and Ilya M. Frank. This form of radiation proves useful in calculating the speed of very fast particles. **PHYS**

Ruth Benedict in 1939 with two Blackfoot Native Americans. (*Vassar College Library*)

1934	British physicist James Chadwick and Austrian-American physicist Maurice Goldhaber determine the mass of the neutron. **PHYS**
c. 1934–1943	American psychiatrist Harry Stack Sullivan serves as director of the William Alanson White Foundation, during which time he contributes his theory of interpersonal relations, that personality development and adjustment are determined by the results of interactions with significant others in a person's life (family, friends, peers, spouse), not solely by biological and sexual factors. **PSYCH**
1934	German-born psychologist Erich Fromm emigrates to the United States, where his prolific work will highlight the importance of social influences—especially alienation—on individual personalities. His publications will include *Escape from Freedom* (1941). **PSYCH**
1934	American anthropologist Ruth Benedict publishes *Patterns of Culture*, an account of her work with the Zuni and Hopi Native American peoples. This book contributes to the development of the field of cultural psychology. **SOC**

1935   U.S. astronomer Henry Norris Russell shows that the catastrophic theories of solar system formation advanced by Chamberlin and Moulton in 1905 and Jeans and Jeffreys in 1918 violate the laws of conservation. Future studies by astronomers (including those of American Lyman Spitzer in 1939) will further disprove the idea that the solar system could have resulted from a near collision of stars. *See* 1944, Weizsäcker, for the currently accepted theory of the solar system's origin. **ASTRO**

1935   German astronomer Rupert Wildt discovers methane and ammonia on the large planets such as Jupiter and Saturn that are now known as gas giants. **ASTRO**

1935   American biochemist Wendall Stanley isolates a virus in crystals, proving it is protein in nature, much the same way John Howard Northrop crystallized pepsin. *See* 1930, Northrop. **BIO**

1935   German biologist Hans Spemann is awarded the Nobel Prize for his discovery of the organizer effect in embryo development. **BIO**

1935   The Richter scale for measuring the severity of earthquakes is developed by U.S. seismologist Charles Richter. **EARTH**

1935   German pathologist and chemotherapist Gerhard Domagk discovers the first sulfonamide (sulfa drug) for combating bacterial diseases. His resulting 1939 Nobel Prize for medicine will go unclaimed, as the Nazis will forbid him to accept it. **MED**

1935   Swedish biochemist Ulf von Euler discovers prostaglandins, a group of fatty acids made naturally in the body that act much like hormones. Von Euler finds them in semen, but they will also be discovered in many different bodily tissues and found to vary in their chemical structure. **MED**

1935   Canadian-American physicist Arthur Jeffrey Dempster discovers uranium-235, an isotope of uranium that will be used in producing the first sustained nuclear chain reaction. *See* 1942, Fermi. **PHYS**

1935   Japanese physicist Hideki Yukawa develops the theory of the strong interaction, the fundamental interaction that binds particles in the atomic nucleus. He proposes the existence of an exchange particle binding the nuclear particles or nucleons. Later called a *mesotron* or *meson*, such a particle is predicted to be intermediate in mass between electrons and protons. **PHYS**

1935   American chemist William F. Giauque cools helium to a new record low temperature of 0.1° K. **PHYS**

1935   In Akron, Ohio, stockbroker Bill W. and surgeon Dr. Bob S. found Alcoholics Anonymous (AA), the first self-help fellowship. Toward the end of the century, AA will inspire numerous other programs centered on mutual support to recover from addiction. **PSYCH**

1935   Psychologists Henry A. Murray and Conway Lloyd Morgan intro-
            duce a projective test to study personality. Their Thematic
            Apperception Test consists of thirty pictures and one blank, to and
            around which the patients assign stories. Information about the pa-
            tient's personality and motivation is then obtained from the stories
            and later used for diagnostic purposes.   **PSYCH**

1935   Portuguese neurologist Antonio Egas Moniz develops the lobotomy,
            a form of brain surgery, to relieve some forms of mental distur-
            bance. The procedure involves cutting fibers in the brain that
            connect the frontal lobes with the anterior ones. In time, the
            lobotomy's benefits will prove inconclusive and its side effects dan-
            gerous, so that it will be discontinued after the mid-1950s.   **PSYCH**

1935   U.S. anthropologist Margaret Mead publishes *Sex and Temperament*,
            which examines gender-based social expectations in three cultures. **SOC**

1935   American pollster George Gallup founds the American Institute of
            Public Opinion in Princeton, New Jersey. The following year his
            correct prediction of the outcome of the 1936 presidential election
            confirms the validity of sampling as a method for determining pub-
            lic opinion. Scientific polling will become an important tool of so-
            cial scientists, politicians, and market researchers.   **SOC**

1935   Robert H. Goddard becomes the first to fire a liquid-fuel rocket
            faster than the speed of sound.   **TECH**

1935   Scottish physicist Robert Alexander Watson-Watt invents radar
            (Radio Detection And Ranging), which uses microwaves (short-
            wavelength radio waves) to locate and track objects. German scien-
            tists who were working independently to develop radar had already
            tested it successfully in 1934.   **TECH**

1935   The Rural Electrification Administration (REA) is established by U.S.
            President Franklin D. Roosevelt to subsidize, through loans and un-
            derwriting, the development of electrical service for rural areas of
            the country.   **TECH**

1935   The U.S. Army demonstrates the B-17 bomber, an all-metal, four-
            engine monoplane that will be used extensively in World War II. **TECH**

1935   Polyethylene, a plastic made of polymerized ethylene that will
            eventually have many uses, is invented in Britain by Imperial
            Chemical Industries.   **TECH**

1935   Kodachrome color film, using a three-color process, is introduced for
            16-millimeter movie cameras by Eastman Kodak. In Hollywood, the
            first three-color Technicolor feature, *Becky Sharp*, is released.   **TECH**

1936   The quartz clock becomes a standard part of astronomic instru-
            mentation.   **ASTRO**

1936   André Leallemard, of the Strasbourg and Paris observatories, invents the first electronic telescope accessory—the image-intensifying tube—which becomes important in the study of faint objects.   **ASTRO**

1936   British geologist Arthur Holmes begins to use the uranium-lead absolute dating method on Precambrian minerals.   **EARTH**

1936   French-American surgeon Alexis Carrel collaborates with American navigator Charles Lindbergh to invent the first artificial heart or cardiac pump.   **MED**

1936   Hungarian-born American physicist Eugene Paul Wigner introduces the concept of the nuclear cross section in developing the mathematics of neutron absorption by atomic nuclei.   **PHYS**

1936   British economist John Maynard Keynes publishes *The General Theory of Employment, Interest, and Money*, in which he argues for government intervention in the market and deficit spending as a remedy for recession. Keynes becomes one of the chief architects of modern macroeconomic theory.   **SOC**

1936   The Houdry catalytic cracking process of producing gasoline from oil is employed by Socony-Vacuum and Sun Oil. This process, developed by French-American engineer Eugène Houdry, works at a lower pressure and temperature than previous refining processes.   **TECH**

1936   Southwestern U.S. states are provided with inexpensive electric power after the completion of the 726-foot-high Boulder Dam, known after 1947 as Hoover Dam.   **TECH**

1936   Douglas Aircraft debuts the DC-3, an early example of the commercial passenger plane. This two-engine vehicle transports up to twenty-one passengers.   **TECH**

1936   An electronic television system is set up by the British Broadcasting Company.   **TECH**

1936   The tampon, developed by American physician Earl Haas, is produced commercially for the first time by Tampax, Inc. *See also* 1918, Kotex.   **TECH**

1937   The first radio telescope, with a 9.4-meter (31-foot) dish, is installed by U.S. astronomer Grote Reber in Illinois.   **ASTRO**

1937   British plant pathologist Frederick Charles Bawden shows that the tobacco mosaic virus is not all protein but also contains small amounts of ribonucleic acid (RNA). It will eventually be discovered that viruses contain either RNA or DNA (deoxyribonucleic acid).   **BIO**

1937   German-born British biochemist Hans Adolf Krebs discovers the citric acid cycle, later called the Krebs cycle. This series of chemical body reactions is the main pathway of terminal oxidation in the process of utilizing carbohydrates, fats, and proteins.   **BIO**

1937   American biochemist Conrad Arnold Elvehjem discovers that nicotinic acid (niacin) and nicotinamide (niacinamide) are vitamins that prevent and cure pellagra.   **BIO**

1937   Swedish chemist Arne Tiselius introduces electrophoresis, the movement of charged colloidal particles through a medium in which they are dispersed as a result of changes in electrical potential. The process will quickly become important in biochemistry, microbiology, immunology, and chemistry.   **BIO**

1937   Italian physicists Emilio Gino Segré and Carlo Perrier discover the element technetium. With no stable isotope, it is the first of many elements to be manufactured rather than discovered in nature. **CHEM**

1937   German scientists develop polyurethane.   **CHEM**

1937   British mathematician Alan Mathison Turing describes a "Turing machine," a hypothetical device that can solve any computable problem. Turing's work will contribute to the development of digital computers in the 1940s.   **MATH**

1937   American physician D. W. Gordon Murray introduces heparin, a complex organic acid that prevents blood clotting, into general medical practice.   **MED**

1937   Physicists H. A. Jahn and Edward Teller predict the Jahn-Teller effect, a distortion of the structure of nonlinear molecules or ions that would be likely to have degenerate orbitals.   **PHYS**

1937   American physicist Carl David Anderson discovers a particle that is at first believed to be a meson (*see* 1935, Yukawa) and is thus called a mu-meson. But when it is shown that this particle does not behave like a meson, it is renamed a muon and placed in a class of particles called leptons, which interact by the electromagnetic and weak interactions.   **PHYS**

1937   Physicist H. A. Kramers develops the concept of charge conjugation, a property that determines the difference between a particle and its antiparticle.   **PHYS**

1937   Italian physicians Ugo Cerletti and Lucio Bini pioneer electric shock treatment for the symptomatic relief of schizophrenia. Such electroconvulsive treatment (ECT), although controversial, will become standard for forms of depression until the introduction of antipsychotic drugs in the 1950s.   **PSYCH**

1937   German-American psychiatrist and psychoanalyst Karen Horney publishes *The Neurotic Personality of Our Time*, in which she explores the concept of basic anxiety.   **PSYCH**

1937   American psychologist Gordon Willard Allport publishes *Personality: A Psychological Interpretation*, with which he begins to make his mark as a specialist in personal dispositions, functional autonomy, and the mature personality. Both this book and his 1961 *Pattern and Growth in Personality* will be professionally well received.   **PSYCH**

1937   Yale University begins recording its Human Relation Area Files (HRAF), a compilation of ethnographic data for the statistical comparison of cultures.   **SOC**

1937   American sociologist Talcott Parsons publishes *The Structure of Social Action*, which bridges the gap between American and European schools of sociology. Parsons will become known for his structural-functional theory, a grand unifying theory of nearly every aspect of society.   **SOC**

1937   Russian-American sociologist Pitirim A. Sorokin publishes *Social and Cultural Dynamics*, in which he expounds influential theories of social process and the typology of cultures.   **SOC**

1937   Canadian physicist James Hillier invents the first electron microscope, which improves vastly on optical microscopes. His device reaches a magnification of seven thousand times, in contrast to the two thousandfold magnification of the best optical microscope. **TECH**

1937   German-born American physicist Erwin Wilhelm Mueller invents the field-emission microscope, which allows direct observation of atoms.   **TECH**

1937   While working for Du Pont, American chemist Wallace Hume Carothers patents nylon, the first fully synthetic fiber. Nylon will be used in many products previously made with silk and wool.   **TECH**

1937   The explosion of the German dirigible *Hindenburg* at Lakehurst, New Jersey, killing thirty-six people, marks the end of the use of hydrogen-borne dirigibles for air travel.   **TECH**

1937   Great Britain and other European countries, as well as parts of South America and Asia, adopt the phone number 999 as a universal distress signal for police and firefighters. In 1968 New York will become the first U.S. state to adopt a universal emergency phone number, in this case 911.   **TECH**

1937   Using principles of electrostatics and photoconductivity, American student Chester Carlson develops a dry-copy process he calls Xerography, which revolutionizes office technology.   **TECH**

1937   U.S. grocery store owner Sylvan Goodman develops the first large-sized grocery shopping cart, from folding chairs and hand-held shopping baskets.   **TECH**

July 4, 1937   German pilot Hanna Reitsch is the first to fly a helicopter successfully. Her FW-61 helicopter was built by Heinrich Focke.   **TECH**

1938   German physicists Hans Bethe and Carl von Weizsäcker independently develop the theory that stars are powered by thermonuclear fusion.   **ASTRO**

1938   British physicist Paul Dirac links the Hubble constant, which concerns the rate at which galaxies recede from each other, to constants describing subatomic particles.   **ASTRO**

1938   American physicist J. Robert Oppenheimer and George Volkoff predict the existence of neutron stars rotating at a rapid rate. *See* 1967, Bell.   **ASTRO**

1938   A coelacanth, a species of fish believed extinct for 70 million years, is discovered alive in the waters off South Africa.   **BIO**

1938   In South Africa, Scottish–South African paleontologist Robert Broom discovers hominid fossils he classifies as a new genus and species, *Paranthropus robustus*. The species is of a heavier, more robust build than *Australopithecus africanus* (*see* 1924, Dart). Some later paleontologists will classify Broom's find as *Australopithecus robustus*. The remains date from 2 to 1.5 million years ago.   **PALEO**

1938   Austrian-born American physicist Isidor Isaac Rabi develops the technique of magnetic resonance, which allows measurement of the energies absorbed and emitted by the particles of a molecular beam.   **PHYS**

1938   The law of baryon conservation is proposed. Baryons include protons and neutrons.   **PHYS**

Dec. 18, 1938   German physical chemist Otto Hahn achieves nuclear fission, the splitting of an atomic nucleus into two parts, when he bombards uranium-235 with neutrons. The results will not be published until the following year (*see* 1939).   **PHYS**

1938   American behaviorist B. F. Skinner publishes the results of his first experiments with the Skinner box, a simple piece of laboratory equipment that makes possible a series of systematic experiments in operant conditioning on rats and pigeons. His work will be considered different from, but equal in value to, Ivan Pavlov's earlier conditioned response experiments with dogs.   **PSYCH**

1938   Dutch physicist Frits Zernike invents the phase-contrast microscope, which uses light diffraction to improve resolution.   **TECH**

1938   The rear-engined Volkswagen ("people's car"), also known as the Beetle, is first produced in Germany, designed by Austrian engineer Ferdinand Porsche.   **TECH**

1938   Fiberglass is developed by Owens-Illinois and Corning. Able to
             be woven or spun, this material will prove useful in many appli-
             cations.   **TECH**

1938   American chemist Roy Plunkett invents the material trade-named
             Teflon (polytetrafluoroethylene) while working for Du Pont. It is
             originally sold in Britain, under the trade name Fluon.   **TECH**

1938   Hungarian brothers Ladislao and George Biro patent the first ball-
             point pen.   **TECH**

1939   U.S. physicist J. Robert Oppenheimer theorizes that a star greater
             than 3.2 solar masses will collapse from its own weight into a sin-
             gle point, an object that will become known as a black hole. **ASTRO**

1939   Indian astronomer Subrahmanyan Chandrasekhar determines the
             Chandrasekhar limit, the maximum possible mass for a star pre-
             vented from collapsing by degeneracy pressure. For a white dwarf
             star the limit is 1.4 times the mass of the sun; heavier stars may
             become neutron stars. *See also* 1934, Baade-Zwicky.   **ASTRO**

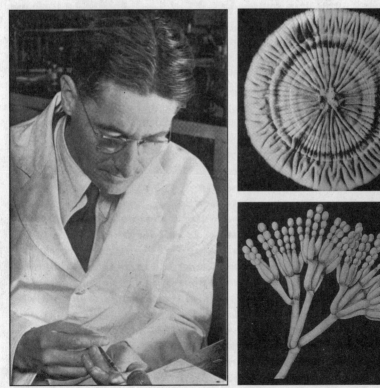

Florey and the invention of penicillin. (*Reportagebild, Stockholm*)

| 1939 | Russian-born British biochemist David Keilin further demonstrates the existence and importance of essential minerals (essential trace elements) with his discovery that zinc is necessary to life. **BIO** |

1939   Russian-born British biochemist David Keilin further demonstrates the existence and importance of essential minerals (essential trace elements) with his discovery that zinc is necessary to life. **BIO**

1939   DDT, a hydrocarbon pesticide, is developed by Swiss chemist Paul H. Müller for the Geigy Co. It is first used in Switzerland, then, due to its efficacy and low cost, becomes widely popular. **BIO**

1939   French physicist Marguerite Perey discovers the element francium. **CHEM**

1939   The French survey of mathematics called *Éléments de mathématique* begins publication under the name of Nicolas Bourbaki, a pseudonym for a group of mathematicians. The work emphasizes logical structure and an axiomatic approach. **MATH**

1939   French-born American microbiologist René Jules Dubos isolates the antibiotic substance tyrothricin. Though not very effective, it is for a time one of the few tools physicians have against infection. **MED**

1939   British pathologist Howard Florey and British biochemist Ernst Chain produce pure penicillin, the first powerful antibiotic. *See* 1928, Alexander Fleming. **MED**

Sept. 1, 1939   World War II begins when German dictator Adolf Hitler invades Poland, prompting Great Britain and France to declare war on September 3. The war will spur the development of numerous technologies, including the atomic bomb. **MISC**

1939   Hungarian-born American physicist Leo Szilard hears of Otto Hahn's discovery of nuclear fission and observes that it can be used to produce a nuclear chain reaction (*see* 1932, Szilard), which can be put to destructive use in a bomb. **PHYS**

....

"Some recent work by E. Fermi and L. Szilard which has been communicated to me in manuscript leads me to expect that the element uranium may be turned into a new and important source of energy in the near future. Certain aspects of the situation which has arisen seem to call for watchfulness and, if necessary, quick action on the part of the Administration.... In the course of the last four months it has been made almost certain...that it may become possible to set up a nuclear chain reaction in a large mass of uranium, by which vast amounts of power and large quantities of radium-like elements would be generated....This new phenomenon would lead also to the construction of bombs."
—Albert Einstein, German-American physicist, in letter to President Franklin D. Roosevelt; 1939

....

1939   Swiss-born American physicist Felix Bloch calculates the magnetic moment (a measure of magnetic strength) of the neutron. This discovery indicates that the electrically neutral particle is made up of smaller charged particles. Independently, American physicist Edward Mills Purcell makes the same discovery.   **PHYS**

1939   Under pressure from Hungarian-born physicists Leo Szilard, Edward Teller, and Eugene Paul Wigner, German-born American physicist Albert Einstein sends a letter to President Franklin D. Roosevelt urging him to develop an atomic bomb before the Germans do.   **PHYS**

1939   W. C. Herring discovers a way of calculating the properties of substances from quantum principles, a technique he applies in explaining the properties of beryllium.   **PHYS**

1939   German physical chemist Otto Hahn's achievement of nuclear fission (*see* December 18, 1938) is announced in a paper dated January 26 and published by his colleague Austrian physicist Lise Meitner and her nephew Otto Robert Frisch.   **PHYS**

1939   American psychologist Myrtle B. McGraw demonstrates the swimming reflex in infants. She will later pioneer in studying twins.   **PSYCH**

1939   U.S. psychologist David Wechsler introduces the Wechsler-Bellevue Adult Intelligence Scale, which measures verbal, numerical, social, and perceptuomotor abilities.   **PSYCH**

1939   Fluorescent lighting is developed by General Electric.   **TECH**

1939   Pan American Airways introduces commercial passenger airline service with a four-engine Boeing craft traveling from Port Washington, New York, to Marseilles, France.   **TECH**

1939   FM radios are sold commercially for the first time.   **TECH**

1939   The Germans fly the first turbojet, a Heinkel He-178 plane powered by a Heinkel S3B turbojet engine.   **TECH**

1940s   Ecological studies show that unproductive land can often be reclaimed and made productive again by correcting its nutritional deficiencies and not overfertilizing it.   **BIO**

1940s   American geneticists George Wells Beadle and Edward Laurie Tatum provide one of the first important clues as to how chromosomes and their genes copy exactly from cell to cell when they find that genes direct enzyme formation through the units called polypeptides that make them up.   **BIO**

1940s   Norwegian-American meteorologist Jacob Bjerknes identifies the jet stream, a narrow, eastward wind current above the lower troposphere.   **EARTH**

A CIGAR IS NOT ALWAYS JUST A CIGAR

*L*egend has it that Austrian psychiatrist Sigmund Freud (1856–1939), asked whether there was some deeper significance to the cigar he always carried, said, "Sometimes a cigar is just a cigar." Whether this story is true or not, Freud was an incessant cigar smoker who claimed that smoking helped him work harder and maintain self-control. Once when his seventeen-year-old nephew Harry refused a cigarette, Freud told him, "My boy, smoking is one of the greatest and cheapest enjoyments in life, and if you decide in advance not to smoke, I can only feel sorry for you."

In fact, however, Freud knew there were deeper reasons for his inability to give up his habit, even when it became a matter of life and death. In an 1897 letter to a colleague, Wilhelm Fliess, Freud said that all addictions, including smoking, are substitutes for the "single great habit, the 'primal addiction'"—masturbation. The founder of psychoanalysis saw the problem but could not treat it: he was unable to quit smoking, even in 1923 when a cancerous growth was found on his jaw and palate. In 1930, after years of operations, oral prostheses, and declining health, Freud finally gave up smoking, saying, "I am better than before, but not happier." It was too late. On September 23, 1939, the cancer caused by Freud's cigars finally killed him.

1940s   I. Efremov and other Soviet paleontologists in Mongolia discover fossils of *Syrmosaurus*, an armored dinosaur that links the plated dinosaurs of the Jurassic period with the armored dinosaurs of the Cretaceous. **PALEO**

1940s   Psychologists at the University of Minnesota develop the Minnesota Multiphasic Personality Inventory (MMPI) test to measure more than one personality dimension at a time. It will be used more than any other personality test and be considered reliable in indicating psychological pathology. *See also* 1989. **PSYCH**

1940s   Canadian researcher Han Selye, studying the results of injecting rats with hormones, discovers the general adaptation syndrome, in which intense physiological changes in body organs occur in response to stress. The body changes consist of the alarm reaction, resistance, and exhaustion. Selye will continue to study the effects of stress, publishing major works in 1950 and 1976. **PSYCH**

1940s   American child psychologist and pediatrician Arnold Gesell researches childhood stages of mental and emotional growth. The Gesell developmental scale comes into wide use during this decade. He is the first psychologist to observe patients/clients through one-way mirrors. **PSYCH**

1940s   At McGill University, neurosurgeon William Penfield and his col-
           league Herbert Jasper give one of the first demonstrations in neuro-
           science of the human brain's information storage and retrieval ca-
           pabilities. With electrodes, they stimulate exposed temporal brain
           lobes on neurological patients under a local anesthetic, a process
           that evokes vivid memories of isolated and insignificant past
           events.   **PSYCH**

1940   Italian physicist Emilio Segré, Dale Corson, and K. R. Mackenzie
           discover the element astatine.   **CHEM**

1940   American physicists Edwin H. McMillan and Philip H. Abelson discov-
           er neptunium, the first known transuranium element, or element with
           an atomic number greater than 92, the number of uranium.   **CHEM**

1940   American physicist Glenn Theodore Seaborg and his colleagues
           discover the element plutonium.   **CHEM**

1940   Canadian-American biochemist Martin David Kamen discovers car-
           bon-14, an isotope of carbon with a half-life of about 5,700 years.
           See 1947, Libby.   **CHEM**

1940   The British Association Seismological Committee begins to publish
           the seismic wave travel timetables known as the Jeffreys and
           Bullen tables. They will be superseded in 1991 by timetables based
           on tomography (CT scanning).   **EARTH**

1940   Nine-year-old Milton Sirotta is the first to use the googol, the number
           10 raised to the hundredth power, or 1 followed by 100 zeroes. **MATH**

Sept. 1940 Paintings dating from the Cro-Magnon era some 17,000 years ago
           are discovered on the walls of a cave in Lascaux, France. **PALEO**

1940   U.S. physicist Philip Hauge Abelson proposes a process for enrich-
           ing uranium, by accumulating the rare isotope uranium-235 in
           quantities sufficient for use in an atomic bomb. The process in-
           volves the evaporation and gaseous diffusion of the liquid uranium
           hexafluoride.   **PHYS**

1940   U.S. physicist Donald William Kerst invents the betatron, an accel-
           erator that pushes electrons to speeds close to that of light, now
           making electron bombardment practical.   **PHYS**

1940   British anthropologist Edward Evan Evans-Pritchard publishes *The
           Nuer*, the first work in an influential trilogy that will include *Kinship
           and Marriage Among the Nuer* (1951) and *Nuer Religion* (1956). **SOC**

1940   U.S. coal executive Carson Smith and engineer Harold Silver invent
           a deep-cutting, continuous-digging machine able to carve a nearly
           twenty-foot-wide tunnel. Upon the rights to the machine being pur-
           chased by manufacturer Joseph Joy, the implement becomes
           known as the Joy machine.   **TECH**

1940   The Russian MIG-1 fighter plane is introduced.   **TECH**

NYLON DAY

A lthough it was 1937 when American chemist Wallace Hume Carothers patented the strong polymeric fiber built of diamines and dicarboxylic acids that would rival silk, the substance now known as nylon did not reach the market until 1938, in the form of toothbrush bristles and later, more dramatically, women's hosiery.

The first toothbrush with nylon bristles, the Dr. West's Miracle Tuft Toothbrush, was first sold in 1938, but because of the toughness of the nylon it met with only limited success. To introduce its nylon hosiery the manufacturer and patent holder Du Pont orchestrated a more wide-ranging plan: a nationwide launch called Nylon Day. On May 15, 1940, when the first nylon hosiery was sold, women lined the streets in front of stores in anticipation, stormed notions counters, and made the new product the most sought-after item to date.

By the close of 1940, 3 million dozen pairs of nylon stockings had been sold across the United States. For the next four years, until the end of World War II, nylon would be used primarily for parachutes and other military purposes. But starting on Nylon Day, nylon came to dominate people's lives more intimately. Despite wartime shortages, the synthetic fiber virtually replaced silk as the standard for sheer in stockings, even providing the basis for their new name, nylons.

1940	The four-cylinder general purpose field vehicle called the jeep is developed by U.S. engineer Karl Pabst for the Bantam Car Co. More than 600,000 jeeps will be produced for use in World War II. **TECH**
1940	The first U.S. superhighway with tunnels, the 160-mile Pennsylvania Turnpike, opens. **TECH**
1940	Nylon stockings are sold for the first time in the United States. **TECH**
1941	Previously unexplained lines in the spectrum of the solar corona, known as coronium lines, are found to be produced by iron, calcium, and nickel ionized by the corona's intense heat of about 1 million° C. **ASTRO**
1941	Czechoslovakian physical chemist Jaroslav Heyrovský develops the technique of polarimetry, for analyzing solutions of an unknown composition. **CHEM**
1941	Arnold O. Beckman invents the spectrophotometer, a device for measuring a material's chemical composition based on reflected wavelengths of light. **CHEM**

SEGREGATED BLOOD

*A*ll human blood looks the same, but medical attempts at blood transfusion before the twentieth century showed, sometimes fatally, that there were differences. Some patients were helped by receiving blood from outside donors, but others died more quickly as a result. Not until 1900 did Austrian physician Karl Landsteiner show that human blood occurs in four classes—O, A, B, and AB—and that a simple set of rules governed which class was compatible with which (O could be given to any receiver, AB only to AB receivers, A to A and AB, and B to B and AB). Mixing incompatible blood types could result in clumping of red blood cells, blocked vessels, and death.

The difficulty was in finding donor blood of the type needed when and where it was needed, often under the most pressing emergency conditions. Conscious of this problem, an African-American physician named Charles Drew, a medical professor at Howard University, became interested in the idea of storing blood in "blood banks" for use in transfusions. However, blood storage had many problems, because refrigeration extended blood's therapeutic benefits for only a few hours and freezing destroyed red blood cells. But the imminence of war in Europe at the end of the 1930s made it important to find a solution. While working with blood chemist John Scudder at Columbia University in 1938–1940, Drew discovered that blood plasma (the yellowish fluid part of blood in which cells are suspended) could be stored for long periods and was effective in treating blood loss and burn victims.

Drew therefore proposed that plasma banks be set up for massive wartime programs. He directed the Plasma for France and Plasma for Britain projects and, in 1941, was named medical director of the American Red Cross's National Blood Bank program. He directed the preparation of liquid plasma and researched ways to prepare frozen and dried plasma.

Then Drew found out that the U.S. military would accept blood only from Caucasians. If African-American blood was accidentally accepted, it had to be isolated and transfused only to African-Americans. Unlike the segregation of blood types that had made transfusions possible, this segregation was a result purely of racial prejudice and had no medical basis. Drew protested but was told that the whites-only policy was required to ensure the general population's cooperation with blood drives.

Drew resigned and returned to Howard University to continue teaching. In 1949 he took a position as surgical consultant to the U.S. Armed Forces, at a point when the military no longer insisted on segregated blood.

1941   American physician Dickinson Woodruff Richards, German physician Werner Forssmann, and French-American physician André Cournand develop a procedure in which a tiny plastic tube or catheter is passed into the heart through a blood vessel to withdraw blood samples, to test cardiac output and blood pressure. This technique of cardiac catheterization will advance the diagnosis of heart disease and heart defects. **MED**

Dec. 6, 1941   One day before the Japanese attack on Pearl Harbor will bring the United States into World War II, President Franklin D. Roosevelt signs a secret directive ordering the development of a nuclear fission bomb in an operation known as the Manhattan Project. **PHYS**

1941   Terylene, a polyester fiber composed of terephthalic acid and ethylene glycol, is developed by British chemist John Rey Whinfield. It will become known in the United States as Dacron and be sold by Du Pont. **TECH**

1942   Radio waves from the sun are detected in England. **ASTRO**

1942   U.S. astronomer Grote Reber makes the first radio maps of the universe. Among his discoveries is the first known radio galaxy, Cygnus A, some 700 million light-years away. **ASTRO**

1942   American biochemist Vincent du Vigneaud isolates vitamin H (biotin). **BIO**

1942   Italian-born American microbiologist Salvador Edward Luria is able to photograph bacteriophages with the magnifying aid of the electron microscope, the first time a virus has been recorded as something greater than a speck. **BIO**

1942   Curare, a substance used for centuries by South American Indians as a poison, is introduced as a muscle relaxant for patients in surgery. **MED**

1942   On December 2, on a converted squash court at the University of Chicago, Italian-born American physicist Enrico Fermi achieves the first sustained nuclear chain reaction. This uranium-235–based fission reaction, produced in a structure called an atomic pile, will lead to the development of nuclear weapons and nuclear power. **PHYS**

1942   American psychologist William Herbert Sheldon (1899–1977) publishes his constitutional theory of personality, claiming that body structure alone determines personality. In his system, body type is classified in terms of three components: ectomorphy, endomorphy, and mesomorphy. **PSYCH**

The Birth of the Atomic Age, a painting of Fermi and his colleagues overseeing the first chain-reacting pile at the University of Chicago. (*Chicago Historical Society*)

1942	American theoretical physicist John V. Atanasoff and his assistant Clifford Berry build the first computer that successfully uses vacuum tubes to perform calculations. The machine is called the Atanasoff Berry Computer, or ABC. **TECH**
Oct. 1, 1942	In the first U.S. jet plane flight, Robert Stanley flies the Bell XP-59 *Airacomet* at Muroc Army Base, California. **TECH**
Oct. 3, 1942	Wernher von Braun and other scientists in Peenemünde, Germany, successfully launch the world's first ballistic missile, the twelve-ton AS-4 rocket that is the predecessor of the V-2 rockets that will wreak havoc on London in 1944 and 1945. **TECH**
1943	Chinese-born American biochemist Choh Hao Li isolates a hormone that stimulates the adrenal cortex to produce and release cortical hormones. It is called adrenocorticotropic hormone (ACTH). **BIO**
1943	Swiss chemist Albert Hoffman synthesizes lysergic acid diethylamide, or LSD, which will become widely used as a hallucinogen in the 1960s. **CHEM**
1943	Swiss chemists produce xylocaine (lidocaine) for use as a local anesthetic. It is faster acting and longer lasting than procaine, making it a popular choice of physicians. **MED**
1943	Austrian-born psychiatrist Leo Kanner is the first to describe infantile autism, a brain disease of childhood characterized by withdrawal, language disturbance, mutism, fear of change, emotional detachment, and repetitive rhythmic movements. **PSYCH**

1943   Neurophysiologist Warren McCulloch and mathematician Walter Pitts show that the human brain's fundamental mechanisms can be described in terms of symbolic (Boolean) logic. They find that electrical impulses pass along the axon and trigger chemical processes that cause adjoining neurons either to fire or not fire. The discovery suggests that human thought mechanisms may be reproducible on complex computer systems.   **PSYCH**

1943   Construction on the Pentagon, the largest office building in the world at 6.5 million square feet, is complete. It cost $83 million.   **TECH**

1944   German astronomer Carl F. von Weizsäcker reexamines Pierre Simon de Laplace's nebula hypothesis of the origin of the solar system (*see* 1796, Laplace). His elaborations on it, as well as later revisions by Swedish astrophysicist Hannes Alfven and British astronomer Fred Hoyle, establish the theory that the planets formed from the coalescing of smaller particles called planetesimals, which in turn arose from eddies in an original planetary nebula. *See also* 1905, Chamberlin.   **ASTRO**

1944   German-American astronomer Walter Baade distinguishes two populations of stars: population I (younger stars found in the spiral arms of galaxies) and population II (older stars found in galactic cores).   **ASTRO**

1944   Dutch astronomer Hendrik van de Hulst predicts that interstellar hydrogen emits radiation with a 21-cm wavelength, a prediction later verified by Ewen and Purcell. *See* 1951, Ewen and Purcell.   **ASTRO**

1944   U.S. astronomer Gerard P. Kuiper discovers that there is an atmosphere on the Saturnian moon Titan.   **ASTRO**

1944   Astronomer Carl Seyfert discovers several spiral galaxies with compact nuclei radiating enormous quantities of energy at all wavelengths, which will become known as Seyfert galaxies. *See* 1957, Ryle.   **ASTRO**

1944   American geneticist T. M. Sonneborn explains that genes cannot operate except in the presence of other substances he calls primers, which as yet remain unidentified.   **BIO**

1944   Canadian bacteriologist Oswald Theodore Avery proves that deoxyribonucleic acid (DNA) is the fundamental substance that determines heredity.   **BIO**

1944   American paleontologist George Gaylord Simpson becomes a leading figure in evolutionary thought with such as works as his *Tempo and Mode in Evolution*.   **BIO**

1944   American physicist Glenn T. Seaborg and his colleagues discover the elements americium and curium.   **CHEM**

MUSICAL MUMMY

*I*n 1944 the oldest complete mummy was found in Saqqâra, Egypt. The preserved body was that of a court musician named Wati from about 2400 B.C.

Egyptian mummification is believed to have begun about 2600 B.C., during the fourth dynasty. The oldest-known mummy fragment is the skull of a woman from about that time, found near the Great Pyramid of Cheops at Giza in 1989.

1944   British biochemists Archer Martin and Richard Synge invent paper chromatography, a technique for analyzing mixtures using absorbent paper.   **CHEM**

1944   U.S. chemists Robert Burns Woodward and William von Eggers Doering artificially synthesize quinine.   **CHEM**

1944   American mathematicians John von Neumann and Oskar Morgenstern publish *The Theory of Games and Economic Behavior*, a major work in the development of game theory.   **MATH**

1944   Dutch physician Willem Kolff produces the first kidney machine, to cleanse the blood of people whose own kidneys have failed.   **MED**

1944   Austrian-born psychoanalyst Helene Deutsch publishes *The Psychology of Women*, which corroborates many Freudian ideas. She was the first female psychoanalyst to be analyzed by Freud.   **PSYCH**

1944   German-American psychologist Kurt Lewin becomes the director of the Research Center for Group Dynamics at the Massachusetts Institute of Technology. His work will focus on motivation problems in groups and individuals, child development, and personality characteristics. He will establish what will become known as field theory, a method for analyzing causal relations and building scientific constructs.   **PSYCH**

1944   The first nuclear reactors, built to convert uranium into plutonium for atomic bombs, begin operation in Washington State.   **TECH**

1944   At the California Institute of Technology (Caltech), research begins on U.S. high-altitude rockets.   **TECH**

1944   At Harvard University, the Harvard-IBM Automatic Sequence Controlled Calculator is developed under the direction of Howard Hathaway Aiken. It contains more than 750,000 parts and takes a few seconds to complete simple arithmetic calculations.   **TECH**

1944   The U.S. National System of Interstate Highways is set up by a congressional federal highways act designating the construction of forty thousand miles of highway across the country.   **TECH**

1944   Kodacolor negative film is developed for color snapshots by Eastman Kodak.   **TECH**

June 1944   The German Messerschmitt Me-163B Komet becomes the first rocket-engined fighter plane to go into production.   **TECH**

Sept. 7, 1944   The first V-2 rockets, developed by German rocket engineer Wernher von Braun, are fired by the Germans at London.   **TECH**

....

"Basic research is what I am doing when I don't know what I am doing."—Wernher von Braun, German-American rocket engineer; mid-twentieth century

....

1945   British science-fiction writer Arthur C. Clarke arrives at the concept of communication satellites in geosynchronous orbits (a stationary orbit above a particular longitude on earth) to provide worldwide communication. *See* 1962, *Telstar I.*   **ASTRO**

1945   American microbiologists Salvador Luria and Alfred Day Hershey show that bacteriophages mutate, which will explain why flu and the common cold are difficult to develop an immunity against.   **BIO**

1945   Cambridge University geneticists J. F. Danielli and D. G. Catchside report being the first to have witnessed the process whereby genes influence cellular activity.   **BIO**

1945   American physicist Edwin McMillan and, independently, Soviet physicist Vladimir I. Veksler invent the synchrocyclotron, an accelerator that produces particle energies in excess of 20 million electron volts.   **PHYS**

1945   American anthropologist Ralph Linton publishes *Cultural Background of Personality*, which develops an interdisciplinary approach to the study of culture and personality.   **SOC**

c. 1945   Inspired by the Chicago school (*see* 1930, Harold Lasswell), behaviorism becomes dominant in political science from the late 1940s to the 1960s. Behaviorists attempt to explain and predict political behavior across cultures and throughout historical periods, using empirical methodologies previously employed by other social sciences. See *1960s.*   **SOC**

1945   A pilot is killed in Germany in the first attempt at manned rocket flight.   **TECH**

1945   At the end of World War II, more than 120 German scientists, including rocket designers Wernher von Braun and Walter Domberger, surrender to the United States and begin working for their former enemies. The Soviets recruit their own German scientists, and both the Soviets and Americans capture rocket equipment. **TECH**

....

"The physicists have known sin; and this is a knowledge which they cannot lose."—J. Robert Oppenheimer, American physicist, on the project he led to develop the atomic bomb; first detonated 1945

....

1945   The White Sands Proving Ground in New Mexico is established for rocket research, launching its first captured V-2 rocket in 1946. **TECH**

1945   The fluoridation of water supplies to retard tooth decay begins, in Grand Rapids, Michigan. **TECH**

1945   Frozen orange juice, a concentrate of fresh juice, is developed in the United States. **TECH**

ALAMOGORDO, JULY 16, 1945

*A*t 5:30 A.M. on July 16, 1945, the first man-made atomic bomb was exploded in a test site at Alamogordo Air Base, New Mexico. The U.S. War Department issued a release about the test, saying in part:

Mounted on a steel tower, a revolutionary weapon destined to change war as we know it, or which may even be the instrumentality to end all wars, was set off with an impact which signaled man's entrance into a new physical world....At the appointed time there was a blinding flash lighting up the whole area brighter than the brightest daylight. A mountain range three miles from the observation point stood out in bold relief. Then came a tremendous sustained roar and a heavy pressure wave which knocked out two men outside the control center. Immediately thereafter, a huge multicolored surging cloud boiled to an altitude of over 40,000 feet. Clouds in its path disappeared. Soon the shifting substratosphere winds dispersed the now gray mass....The test was over, the project a success....

1945 — Five thousand U.S. homes now have television sets—three years from now the number will be 1 million. By 1968, Americans will own 78 million television sets. **TECH**

July 16, 1945 — The first atomic bomb is detonated just before dawn in a secret test at Alamogordo, New Mexico. Its force is equivalent to about twenty thousand tons of conventional high explosives. **TECH**

Aug. 6, 1945 — Hiroshima, Japan, is devastated by an American atomic bomb based on uranium-235 in the first public display and wartime use of nuclear weapons. **TECH**

Aug. 9, 1945 — Nagasaki, Japan, is destroyed by a plutonium-based atomic bomb. The surrender of Japan to the Allies will follow five days later (August 14), ending World War II. **TECH**

1946 — The radio source Cygnus A is discovered. In 1951, astronomers at Mount Palomar will identify it with a distant cluster of galaxies in the constellation Cygnus, making Cygnus A the first radio galaxy. **ASTRO**

1946 — German-born microbiologist Max Delbrück and American microbiologist Alfred Day Hershey show that the genetic material of different virus strains can be combined to form a new strain. **BIO**

1946 — American chemist Vincent Schaefer creates the first artificially induced precipitation when he seeds clouds with dry ice, resulting in a snowstorm. Later, seeding clouds with other chemicals, he will succeed in producing rain. **EARTH**

1946 — In *Foundations of Algebraic Geometry*, French mathematician André Weil develops a theory of polynomial equations in any number of indeterminates and with coefficients in an arbitrary field. Weil makes a number of conjectures concerning algebraic topology that are eventually proven true. *See* 1974, Pierre Deligne. **MATH**

1946 — The Atomic Energy Commission releases radioisotopes (radionuclides) for medical use. Nuclear medicine will explore their diagnostic, therapeutic, and investigative uses. **MED**

1946 — Swiss-born American physicist Felix Bloch and American physicist Edward Mills Purcell independently develop the technique of nuclear magnetic resonance (NMR), for determining nuclear moments and measuring magnetic fields. This process will be the basis for the medical technique of magnetic resonance imaging (MRI), a noninvasive way of producing images of the body's interior. **PHYS**

1946 — Physicist Willis Eugene Lamb discovers the Lamb shift, a small energy difference between two levels in the hydrogen spectrum. This discovery will contribute to the development of quantum electrodynamics (QED). *See* 1948, Feynman. **PHYS**

1946   Abraham Pais and C. Moller coin the term *lepton* to describe particles such as electrons and muons that are not affected by the strong force.   **PHYS**

c. 1946   The field of artificial intelligence (AI) begins as the first computers are developed. AI—often defined as a multidisciplinary field encompassing computer science, neuroscience, philosophy, psychology, robotics, and linguistics—will attempt to reproduce with machines the methods and results of human reasoning and brain activity.   **PSYCH**

....

"I propose to consider the question, 'Can Machines Think?'"
—Alan Mathison Turing, British computer scientist; 1936

"No, I'm not interested in developing a powerful brain.
All I'm after is just a mediocre brain, something like the
president of the American Telephone and Telegraph
Company."—Remarks attributed to Turing at a
meeting with Bell Corp. executives

....

1946   American pediatrician Benjamin Spock writes *The Common Sense Book of Baby and Child Care*, encouraging parents to show more affection toward their infants and be less structured in their feeding habits. Later retitled *Baby and Child Care*, Spock's book will become an all-time bestseller on the subject of child rearing.   **PSYCH**

1946   In psychoanalysis the idea of brief therapy begins to evolve. Any form of this therapy is goal specific and has relatively limited and delineated objectives. Brief therapy may be completed in ten to sixty-five sessions, whereas traditional psychoanalysis can take up to five hundred sessions. Further, brief therapy strives to focus on the present problem and work on modifying current variables. **PSYCH**

1946   American anthropologist Ruth Benedict publishes *The Chrysanthemum and the Sword*, a classic study of Japanese culture and society.   **SOC**

1946   U.S. postwar testing of nuclear weapons begins in the Pacific Ocean.   **TECH**

1946   At the California Institute of Technology (Caltech), it is found that a liquid polysulfide polymer is an effective propellant for space vehicles. **TECH**

ENIAC computer. (*Hagley Museum and Library*)

1946   The first automatic electronic digital computer, the ENIAC, is constructed at Harvard University by electrical engineers John Presper Eckert and John William Manchly in consultation with John Atanasoff. This electronic numerical integrator and computer contains radio tubes and runs by electrical power to perform hundreds of computations per second.   **TECH**

1946   The word *automation* is used for the first time, by Ford Motor Co. engineer Delmar Harder to describe the fourteen-minute process by which Ford engines are produced.   **TECH**

1947   American chemist Willard Frank Libby invents the technique of carbon dating, in which the radioactive isotope carbon-14 discovered by Martin Kamen in 1940 is used to determine the age of archaeological objects dating as far back as 45,000 years.   **ARCH**

1947   The Dead Sea Scrolls are discovered in earthen jars in a cave near Khirbet Qumran in what is now Israel. These scrolls contain religious texts offering insights into ancient Judaism and early Christianity. More than ten more caves with other such scrolls are discovered in the 1950s and 1960s.   **ARCH**

1947	From a group of molds, American microbiologists isolate chloramphenicol, the first broad-spectrum antibiotic. **BIO**
1947	American chemists J. A. Marinsky, L. E. Glendenin, and C. D. Coryell discover promethium, the last element from the periodic table to be identified. **CHEM**
c. 1947	Researchers abandon the idea that the oceans' floors are flat and produce arguments in favor of the continental drift hypothesis. **EARTH**
1947	Nikolai Vasilevich Belov develops his theory concerning maximum ionic density. **EARTH**
1947	American geobiologist Maurice Ewing conducts systematic studies of the North Atlantic, using depth probes, and determines the existence there of a huge abyssal plain. **EARTH**
1947	British physicist Cecil Frank Powell discovers the subatomic particle called a pi-meson or pion, the first true meson to be discovered. *See* 1935, Yukawa and 1937, Anderson. **PHYS**
1947	Hungarian-British physicist Dennis Gabor develops the theory of holography, though full implementation of it will await the invention of the laser in 1960. **PHYS**
1947	Austrian-born psychoanalyst Anna Freud, daughter of Sigmund Freud, founds the London Hampstead Child-Therapy Clinic. In 1936 she had introduced the theory of ego defense mechanisms such as repression. She becomes well known for her work in the psychoanalysis of children. **PSYCH**
1947	The Institute of Sex Research is founded as an affiliate of Indiana University by Alfred C. Kinsey. In the next five years, Kinsey and three colleagues will publish the results of research on male and female sexuality known as the *Kinsey Reports*. These findings will be used to correct prevalent misconceptions about female sexual arousal, childhood sexuality, and homosexuality. **PSYCH**
1947	The first self-sealing tubeless automobile tires are sold, by B. F. Goodrich. **TECH**
1947	The eight-engine *Spruce Goose*, then the largest aircraft in the world, is introduced by its designer Howard Hughes in a one-mile flight in Long Beach Harbor, California. **TECH**
1947	The first Levittown suburban housing development is erected, on Long Island, by American construction designer Abraham Levitt and his sons. Over the next decade, thousands of these moderately priced homes will be mass-produced on Long Island, in Pennsylvania, and in New Jersey. **TECH**
1947	The Radarange, the first microwave oven for commercial use, is built and demonstrated by the Raytheon Co., but it is not an immediate success. **TECH**

THE EDSEL OF THE KITCHEN

*I**n 1947, when the U.S. manufacturer Raytheon introduced the first microwave oven, the company predicted it would revolutionize cooking. They had reason to be confident. After all, it had been five years since Raytheon scientist Percy Spencer had discovered that the magnetron, or electronic tube, he was testing would manipulate food molecules into a heated, cooked state, and the company had used the war years to develop a working prototype.*

But the public test of the Radarange was a failure. Since the oven lacked modern-day browning devices, the tested foods, unlike those in the publicity photos, were pale and rubbery. Worse, at the size of a standard oven and a cost of $3,000, the first microwave was hardly an affordable convenience. Not until Amana Refrigeration introduced a $495 table-top microwave oven in 1967, built with a smaller electron tube developed by Japanese engineer Keishi Ogura, did the product sell. Until then the microwave oven was as popular as the 1957 giant meant to revolutionize its own industry, the Ford Edsel.

c. 1947   Diesel-electric trains are replacing steam locomotives on U.S. railroad lines.   **TECH**

Oct. 14,   In the first piloted supersonic airplane flight, Capt. Charles E.
1947   Yeager flies the Bell X-1 rocket-powered plane *Glamorous Glennis*, named for his wife, faster than the speed of sound at Muroc Air Force Base in California.   **TECH**

1948   Austrian-born astronomers Hermann Bondi and Thomas Gold theorize that the universe is expanding but has no beginning or end. New matter, they say, is constantly being created from nothing. This model of what becomes called the steady-state universe is later popularized by Fred Hoyle.   **ASTRO**

1948   U.S. researchers at White Sands, New Mexico, launch a monkey named Albert in a V-2 rocket's nose cone.   **ASTRO**

1948   The Hale telescope at Mount Palomar, California, named for U.S. astronomer George Ellery Hale, becomes the largest reflecting telescope in the world, as it is to the present day. Its lens is 5.08 meters (200 inches) in diameter. *See also* 1897, Hale.   **ASTRO**

1948   U.S. astronomer Gerard P. Kuiper discovers Miranda, the fifth known moon of Uranus.   **ASTRO**

1948   American microbiologist John Franklin Enders, along with U.S. virologist Thomas H. Weller and U.S. physician Frederick Chapman Robbins, develops a technique to study viruses within living cells. Using chicken eggs, Enders grows viruses in the developing embryos, then adds penicillin to prevent bacteria growth without destroying the viruses. This method becomes useful in finding ways to battle viral diseases.   **BIO**

1948   After years of study on mice, American geneticist George Small locates the specific gene sites (histocompatibility genes) concerned with the acceptance or rejection of tissue transferred from one organism to another. He will be awarded the 1980 Nobel Prize in medicine and physiology for this work.   **BIO**

THE WAR ON FUNGI

*A*s long as there have been people there have been fungi to torment them. Neither plants nor animals, fungi such as mold, yeast, and mushrooms are a distinct kingdom of living things that absorb nutrients directly from the environment, either from dead organic matter or parasitically from living hosts. Some varieties have long been useful—yeast in baking and brewing, mushrooms as food—but others are more inclined to use people as food. Fungi spoil granaries, rot books, and cause maddening itches in warm, moist body crevices such as the vagina and the spaces between toes. However, it was not until 1948 that two American women discovered the first safe fungicide for human use.

Nystatin, named in honor of New York State, which funded the scientists' work, was the discovery of microbiologist Elizabeth Hazen and chemist Rachel Brown. Hazen and Brown were convinced, based on previous research, that an antifungal organism existed in certain soils. While vacationing in Virginia, Hazen collected a soil sample from a friend's cow pasture and sent it to Brown in New York for analysis. Brown then isolated an antitoxin agent in the soil. The two used it to develop nystatin, the first broadly effective antifungal antibiotic.

Since then, nystatin has appeared in the form of oral and vaginal tablets, ointments, powder, and liquid medication. Horticulturists also use nystatin to combat Dutch elm disease. Its mold-destroying ability prevents spoilage in everything from bananas to zebra feed. In 1966, when the Arno River overflowed in Italy, nystatin was used to stop mold from ruining priceless paintings and books damaged by flood waters. And, perhaps most important to anyone with toes, the fungicide works against athlete's foot.

1948   Soviet geneticist and biologist I. V. Michurin's alternative theory of genetics wins out over neo-Mendelism in the Soviet Union, where Michurin becomes heralded as a great and original thinker. His fundamental theory is that heredity can be altered by changing the environment.   **BIO**

1948   American biochemists Stanford Moore and William Howard Stein invent starch chromatography.   **CHEM**

1948   O. F. Tuttle and N. C. Bowen develop the first petrogenetic grid and apply it to metamorphosis and serpentinization.   **EARTH**

....

"If, in some cataclysm, all of scientific information were to be destroyed, and only one sentence passed on to the next generation of creatures, what statement would contain the most information with the fewest words?...All things are made of atoms—little particles that move around in perpetual motion, attracting each other when they are a little distance apart, but repelling upon being squeezed into each other. In that one sentence...there is an enormous amount of information about the world, if just a little imagination and thinking are applied."—Richard Feynman, American physicist; twentieth century

....

1948   Swiss physicist Auguste Piccard builds the first bathyscaphe, an improvement upon the bathysphere for deep-sea dives. Piccard tests, rebuilds, and continues to improve upon the craft.   **EARTH**

1948   U.S. mathematician Norbert Weiner publishes *Cybernetics*, a landmark investigation of the mathematics of computer-controlled systems.   **MATH**

1948   American botanist Benjamin Duggar isolates and introduces Aureomycin, a tetracycline, which proves second only to penicillin in combating infection.   **MED**

1948   The United Nations establishes the World Health Organization, stating that "the health of all peoples is fundamental to the attainment of peace and security."   **MED**

1948   German-born American physicist Maria Goeppert Mayer and, independently, German physicist Johannes Hans Daniel Jensen advance the shell model of the atomic nucleus, introducing the concept of magic numbers for the numbers of protons or neutrons that produce the most stable structures.   **PHYS**

SOMETHING TO DIGEST

*S*ince the Nobel Prize was instituted in 1901, more than three hundred people have received awards for science. Only nine of them have been women. The first American woman to do so was biochemist Gerty Theresa Radnitz Cori (1896–1957), who shared the prize for physiology or medicine with her husband Carl Ferdinand Cori in 1947.

The couple won the award for discovering the series of steps by which the human body converts glycogen into glucose and back again to glycogen, the process now known as the Cori cycle. Glycogen, a starchlike substance, is the main form in which carbohydrates are stored in animals, especially in liver and muscle tissue. Glucose is the simple sugar that is the body's major source of energy. By showing how glycogen and glucose are converted into one another, Gerty and Carl Cori contributed to our understanding of how cells obtain energy from food.

The other eight women awarded Nobel Prizes in science are:

- French physicist and radiochemist Marie Curie (1903, physics; 1911, chemistry).
- French chemist Irène Joliot-Curie (1935, chemistry).
- American physicist Maria Goeppert Mayer (1963, physics).
- American chemist Dorothy Crowfoot Hodgkin (1964, chemistry).
- American Rosalyn Sussman Yalow (1977, physiology or medicine).
- American geneticist Barbara McClintock (1983, physiology or medicine).
- Italian neuroembryologist Rita Levi-Montalcini (1986, physiology or medicine).
- American biochemist Gertrude Elion (1988, physiology or medicine).

1948   American physicist Richard Phillips Feynman develops the theory of quantum electrodynamics or QED, the study of the properties of electromagnetic radiation and its interaction with charged matter in terms of quantum mechanics. Julian S. Schwinger and Shin'ichiro Tomonaga independently develop the theory. **PHYS**

c. 1948   At Cornell University, the first major attempt is made to put together a pseudobrain out of electrical circuits. **PSYCH**

1948   In *Male and Female: A Study of the Sexes in a Changing World*, American anthropologist Margaret Mead argues that many aspects of gender identity are determined by cultural practices. **SOC**

1948   American economist Paul Samuelson publishes *Economics*, which will long remain a standard textbook. A Keynesian, Samuelson will win a Nobel Prize in 1970 for his role in developing the mathematical basis of economics.   **SOC**

1948   The transistor, which will greatly reduce the size of electronic devices, is developed for Bell Laboratories by U.S. physicists William Shockley, John Bardeen, and Walter Brattain.   **TECH**

1948   The long-playing vinyl phonograph record is developed and demonstrated by CBS engineer Peter Goldmark. The twelve-inch record runs at a speed of 33⅓ r.p.m. and plays for about forty-five minutes.   **TECH**

1948   Hexachlorophene, a bacteria-killing compound, is an active ingredient in Dial, the first deodorant soap.   **TECH**

1949   Physicist George Gamow predicts that if there was a Big Bang at the creation of the universe, there should be a homogeneous background of radio radiation indicating an average temperature of the universe of about 5° K. *See* 1964, Penzias.   **ASTRO**

1949   German-American astronomer Walter Baade discovers the asteroid Icarus.   **ASTRO**

1949   Astronomer Ralph Belknap Baldwin theorizes that meteoritic impacts account for lunar features.   **ASTRO**

1949   U.S. astronomer Fred L. Whipple theorizes that comets are "dirty snowballs" composed of ice and dust.   **ASTRO**

1949   Astronomer Gerard P. Kuiper discovers Nereid, one of Neptune's two satellites.   **ASTRO**

1949   Publication of the *Henry Draper Extension* begun in 1925 is completed. With the *Henry Draper Catalogue* of 1918–1924 (*see* 1924), both based primarily on the work of U.S. astronomer Annie Jump Cannon, the works together catalog some 350,000 stars.   **ASTRO**

1949   British anatomist Peter Brian Medawar develops a technique leading to the reduction of problems associated with tissue transplants. Working with mice embyros, Medawar discovers they have not yet developed an immunological system to reject foreign proteins, so that when these embyros begin independent life and form antibodies they do not treat injected foreign cells as invaders.   **BIO**

1949   The first photograph of genes, the units that transmit physical characteristics from one generation to the next, is taken by Daniel Chapin Pease and Richard Baker at the University of Southern California.   **BIO**

1949   American physicist Glenn T. Seaborg and his colleagues discover the element berkelium.   **CHEM**

SNAKE PIT CURES

*T*he horrific images of Olivia de Havilland being "treated" for mental illness in the 1948 movie The Snake Pit were restrained compared to some techniques that have been employed in real asylums. Along with the shock therapy and straitjackets shown in the movie, here are some of the more arcane, barbaric, and bizarre treatments of mental illness offered throughout history:

Apples. Those suffering from madness were once allowed to eat nothing but apples for thirty days.

Bad news. In this sixteenth-century therapeutic technique, manic patients were given frequent unpleasant and depressing news.

Bleeding. Blood was let out of the patient's body, based on the belief that too much hot blood caused insanity.

Branking. Starting in sixteenth-century Scotland, the insane were put in iron or leather headpieces (branks), complete with a mouth gag.

Carbon dioxide therapy. As recently as the 1940s, neurotics were prescribed carbon dioxide inhalation to the point of coma.

Diamonds. As early as 1582, diamonds were worn to cure depression and prevent nightmares.

Fish. Citerrochen fish, which are naturally charged with electricity, were placed on patients' foreheads as a shocking apparatus.

Human skin belts. Skin belts made from human corpses were worn by those suffering from hysteria.

Malaria. In early twentieth-century America, intentional infection with malaria was used as a form of therapy for the general paralysis of the insane.

Peas. Head wounds were inflicted on patients, then stuffed with dried peas. The peas were supposed to produce a counterirritation to combat the mental irritation in the brain.

Withholding afternoon tea. In early nineteenth-century England, hot drinks were believed to cause suicide.

This list by no means exhausts the questionable practices undertaken in the name of restoring mental health. Since antiquity water has been a favorite therapy, usually cold and dropped from heights onto patients' heads, or used to immerse them to the point of drowning. Whipping was once a form of shock therapy, and sneezing powder was popular. Perhaps the most radical treatment was one recommended by an American neurologist in 1877: rest, seclusion, good food, and a massage.

1949   British chemist Derek H. R. Barton begins to study complex organic molecules. He will eventually demonstrate the high dependence that chemical properties have on molecular shape.   **CHEM**

1949   British biochemist Dorothy Crowfoot Hodgkin is the first to enlist the aid of an electronic computer in discovering the structure of an organic compound, in this case penicillin.   **CHEM**

1949   V-2 rockets are used by the United States to explore the upper atmosphere.   **EARTH**

1949   Psychopharmacologist J. F. J. Cade publishes the first report on lithium's antimanic effects. Although lithium was discovered in 1817 by Swedish chemist Johan Arfwedson as a naturally occurring salt, it will not be approved in the United States for the treatment of affective disorders until 1970.   **PSYCH**

1949   Writer George Orwell coins the term *brainwashing* in his novel *Nineteen Eighty-Four*.   **PSYCH**

1949   The Wechsler Intelligence Scale for Children (WISC) is published as an intelligence test for children five to fifteen years old.   **PSYCH**

1949   French anthropologist Claude Lévi-Strauss publishes his first major work, *Elementary Structures of Kinship*. In this and later titles, including *Structural Anthropology* (1958) and *The Savage Mind* (1962), he expounds his theory of structuralism, which will become important not only to anthropology but to literary studies.   **SOC**

1949   A rocket-testing site is founded at Cape Canaveral, Florida, the future site of U.S. space launches.   **TECH**

1949   U.S. engineers build and launch the first multistage rocket, made up of a smaller rocket on top of a V-2.   **TECH**

Sept. 22, 1949   The Soviet Union explodes its first fission bomb.   **TECH**

1950s   Metal-shadowcasting and freeze-drying techniques are developed in the microscopic study of viruses.   **BIO**

1950s   American biochemists Edmond H. Fischer and Edwin G. Krebs discover a cellular regulatory mechanism used to control a variety of metabolic processes important to life.   **BIO**

1950s   Researchers find that they can increase plant root systems by inoculating them with soil fungi or mycorrhizae. The fungi colonize and extend down to the root system, providing more root-surface area for water and nutrient absorption.   **BIO**

1950s   Some insect pests are successfully controlled biophysically, by sterilizing males with radiation.   **BIO**

1950s   Prompted by studies of paleomagnetism in the late 1940s, geologists begin to accept the concept of continents moving relative to magnetic poles and to one another. This change represents the beginning of significant studies of continental drift, sea-floor spreading, and plate tectonics. *See also* 1912, Alfred Wegener, and 1960, Henry H. Hess.   **EARTH**

1950s   Several nations, such as Iceland and New Zealand, begin to access geothermal energy from water that is naturally heated in volcanic and earthquake areas, where molten rock is close to the surface and hot springs and geysers plentiful.   **EARTH**

1950s   During this decade, scientific researchers in every discipline learn to make use of computers. Computers will be used in calculating planetary orbits, weather patterns, molecular structures, population trends, and more.   **MISC**

1950s   Two main classes of elementary particles, fundamental units smaller than the atom, are identified. Hadrons, including nucleons (protons and neutrons), mesons, and hyperons interact by the force known as the strong interaction and are found to have a complex internal structure. Leptons, including electrons, neutrinos, and muons, interact either by the weak or electromagnetic interactions (or forces) and have no apparent internal structure.   **PHYS**

1950s   Psychiatrist Nathan Kline introduces reserpine as the first major tranquilizer.   **PSYCH**

1950s   German psychoanalyst Ludwig Binswanger formulates a mode of therapy from the ideas of existentialism. He claims that neurosis must be explained by its meaning to the patient, not in terms of its origin or etiology. Existential therapy in all its forms becomes not a "school" of psychology but rather an understanding and therapy based on personal values, concrete experience, and respect for each patient.   **PSYCH**

1950s   German-American psychologist Stanley Milgram experiments with human obedience, finding that people will go to the extent of torturing others in order to obey authority figures. Milgram suggests that this tendency helps to explain people's compliance with Nazi brutality during World War II.   **PSYCH**

1950s   Research psychologists Neal Miller and John Dollard introduce the frustration-aggression hypothesis, that frustration always causes a certain amount of aggression. This hypothesis will play a part in evaluating and diagnosing mental health problems like depression.   **PSYCH**

1950s   Between now and the 1960s, the monoamine (MAO) inhibitors and tricyclic antidepressants are discovered and developed.   **PSYCH**

1950   Dutch astronomer Jan Hendrik Oort suggests that comets originate
            in a vast cloud of material revolving around the sun far beyond
            Pluto, a region that becomes known as the Oort Cloud. Astronomer
            Gerard Kuiper will posit the existence of a disk-shaped belt of
            comets just beyond Pluto.   **ASTRO**

1950   American biochemist William Cumming Rose conclusively estab-
            lishes the protein-building role of the essential amino acids:
            isoleucine, leucine, lysine, methionine, phenylalanine, threonine,
            tryptophan, valine, and histidine.   **BIO**

1950   Using the electron microscope, Belgian cytologist Albert Claude dis-
            covers the structural network of membranous vesicles in cells' cy-
            toplasm called the endoplasmic reticulum.   **BIO**

1950   German-born American biochemist Konrad Emil Bloch, using stable
            carbon-13 and radioactive carbon-14 as tracers, shows detailed
            changes occurring with the buildup of the cholesterol molecule in
            the body.   **BIO**

1950   American physicist Glenn T. Seaborg and his colleagues discover
            the element californium.   **CHEM**

1950   In Paris, an international meeting agrees to adopt a new astronomi-
            cal unit, the ephemeridical unit, to measure time. It is based on the
            earth's movement around the sun.   **EARTH**

1950   A French team led by Maurice Herzog climbs Annapurna, the
            first 8,000-meter peak (26,000 feet) ever scaled, in north-central
            Nepal.   **EARTH**

Mar. 23,   An international technical organ of the United Nations, the World Me-
1950   teorological Organization, is founded, replacing the International
            Meteorological Organization begun in 1873.   **EARTH**

1950   German-French physicist Alfred Kastler develops an optical pump-
            ing system, which uses electromagnetic waves to excite atoms and
            is a precursor to the laser.   **PHYS**

c. 1950   American psychiatrist Jacob L. Moreno develops psychodrama
            (therapy involving role playing to bring about emotional catharsis)
            and a social psychology methodology called sociometry, a tech-
            nique for measuring attraction and repulsion among people.   **PSYCH**

1950   German-born psychoanalyst Erik H. Erikson writes his first work on
            the developmental stages in humans. The stages he elaborates are
            trust vs. mistrust, autonomy vs. doubt, industry vs. inferiority,
            identity vs. diffusion, intimacy vs. isolation, generativity vs. stagna-
            tion, and integrity vs. despair.   **PSYCH**

1950	American social psychologist Stanley Schachter begins developing a psychological cognitive theory of emotion, claiming that humans cannot discriminate emotions unless they have some cognitive indication of what their feelings relate. **PSYCH**
1950	American psychology professor James J. Gibson writes *The Perception of the Visual World*, a book on human perception that explores the role human senses take in selecting information from stimuli. His theory comes to be called psychophysical correspondence. **PSYCH**
1950	British mathematician Alan Mathison Turing proposes the "Turing Test" for determining whether a machine thinks: If a person communicating with a computer cannot tell whether its responses come from a human or a machine, the computer can be considered intelligent. **TECH**
1950	Orlon, a polymerized acrylonitrile fiber that will be widely employed in clothing, is introduced by Du Pont, as developed in consultation with William Hale Church. **TECH**
1950	The first Xerox machine is built by the Haloid Co. of New York. **TECH**
1951	Dutch-American astronomer Dirk Brouwer is the first to use a computer to calculate planetary orbits. **ASTRO**
1951	Using spectroscopic analysis, U.S. astronomer William Wilson Morgan shows that the Milky Way galaxy has a spiral structure like that of its neighbor the Andromeda galaxy (M31). **ASTRO**
1951	U.S. astronomers Harold Irving Ewen and Edward Mills Purcell discover radio emissions from hydrogen clouds in interstellar space (*see* 1944, van de Hulst). Their 21-centimeter-wavelength radiations will allow astronomers to map the structure of the galaxy and confirm that the galaxy rotates once every 200 million years. **ASTRO**
1951	Henrietta Lacks, a thirty-one-year-old cervical cancer patient, dies in Baltimore. Cells from her cervical tumor are preserved and, when multiplied, become the first continuously cultured strain of cancer cells, called HeLa cells. **BIO**
1951	German biochemist Feodor Felix Konrad Lynen is the first to isolate acetyl coenzyme A, a compound important in biochemical functions and as an intermediate in the Krebs cycle, the cycle of intracellular chemical reactions by which organisms convert food chemicals to energy. **BIO**
1951	Insect sterilization by irradiation is determined to be an effective method for lowering insect levels, according to findings by U.S. Department of Agriculture entomologist Edward Knipling. **BIO**
1951	Drawing on quantum theory, American physicist John Bardeen develops an explanation of superconductivity. **PHYS**

1951   The Chrysler Corporation introduces power steering in their high-end automobiles. Eventually, power steering will be installed in other Chrysler models, as well as those made by other automobile companies.   **TECH**

1951   The Univac computer is introduced for business use by Remington Rand.   **TECH**

1951   Color television programming is transmitted for the first time, by CBS, though color TV sets will not be marketed commercially until 1954.   **TECH**

Dec. 1951   An experimental reactor in Idaho generates the first electricity from nuclear power.   **TECH**

1952   Archaeologists discover signs of human settlement at a site near Clovis, New Mexico, dating from 11,500 years ago. The remains of these "Clovis people" are the earliest undisputed evidence of human settlement in the Americas.   **ARCH**

1952   Michael Ventris deciphers the ancient Cretan language known as Linear B.   **ARCH**

1952   U.S. astronomer Walter Baade discovers an error in the Cepheid luminosity scale (*see* 1912, Leavitt, and 1914, Shapley), based on differences between Cepheids in population I and population II stars. As a result, he determines that other galaxies are about twice as far away as previously thought.   **ASTRO**

1952   Astronomers Adrian Blaauw and Georg Herbig discover evidence of ongoing star formation in the Milky Way galaxy, while Martin Schwarzschild investigates signs of stellar evolution in globular clusters.   **ASTRO**

1952   British biochemist Frederick Sanger uses paper chromatography to show that the protein hormone insulin consists of fifty amino acids along two interconnected chains. He also shows their exact order on each chain.   **BIO**

1952   U.S. biologists Robert Briggs and Thomas J. King successfully transplant living nuclei from blast cells to enucleated frog's eggs.   **BIO**

1952   After working with implanted tumors in chick embryos, Italian embryologist Rita Levi-Montalcini shows the nerve growth factor to be a soluble substance that the tumor releases, which hastens nerve growth.   **BIO**

1952   American biophysicist Rosalyn Sussman Yalow develops the radioimmune assay, a method for detecting and following antibodies and other minute biologically active proteins and hormones present in the body.   **BIO**

1952   American physicist Albert Ghiorso and his colleagues discover the element einsteinium.   **CHEM**

1952   U.S. chemists Stanley Lloyd Miller and Harold Clayton Urey demon-
             strate that simple chemical compounds such as water, hydrogen,
             ammonia and methane—like those believed to have composed the
             earth's early atmosphere and ocean—can interact with electrical
             discharges to produce more complex organic compounds and even
             amino acids. This experiment supports the theory that life originat-
             ed on earth from simpler, nonliving substances.   **CHEM**

1952   British biochemist Arthur J. P. Martin develops gas chromatogra-
             phy.   **CHEM**

1952   American chemist William Gardner Plann develops zone refining, a
             technique for reducing the impurities in metals, alloys, semicon-
             ductors,. and other substances.   **CHEM**

1952   German physician and philosopher Albert Schweitzer receives the
             Nobel Peace Prize for his work with the sick in Africa.   **MED**

1952   U.S. biochemists discover an antibacterial called isoniazid, which
             will be used in the long-term treatment of tuberculosis.   **MED**

1952   In the United States erythromycin, an antibiotic used to treat skin,
             chest, throat, and ear infections is isolated.   **MED**

1952   Fossil remains of a giant extinct ape, called *Gigantopithecus*, are
             discovered in Asia.   **PALEO**

1952   Polish physicists Marian Danysz and Jerzy Pniewski discover the
             K meson or kaon, about 0.5 the mass of a proton, and the lambda
             particle, approximately 1.2 times the mass of a proton. Particles more
             massive than protons will eventually be grouped as hyperons.   **PHYS**

1952   The American Psychiatric Association publishes its first *Diagnostic
             and Statistical Manual of Mental Disorders* (DSM-1), which will serve
             as a mental disorders classification system and be the diagnostic
             standard of the APA. *See also* 1979, World Health Organization. **PSYCH**

1952   Martinique-born psychiatrist Frantz Omar Fanon examines the sig-
             nificance of racism and cultural prejudice in his book *Black Skin,
             White Masks*. After suffering under French colonial rule, Fanon says
             that racial oppression can cause debilitating mental illness. In
             1953, while practicing psychiatry in Algeria, Fanon will join with
             the Algerian Liberation Movement and attempt to overthrow
             French rule. He will eventually call for violent revolution to end
             colonial tyranny.   **PSYCH**

1952   British anthropologist Alfred Reginald Radcliffe-Brown publishes
             Structure and Function in Primitive Society, on his theory of structur-
             al functionalism.   **SOC**

1952   Japanese-made hand-held transistor radios are first marketed in the
             United States by Sony.   **TECH**

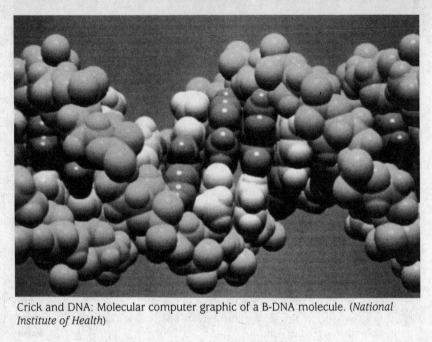

Crick and DNA: Molecular computer graphic of a B-DNA molecule. (*National Institute of Health*)

1952   Japan's first 35 mm single-lens reflex camera, the Asahiflex, is manufactured by Asahi Optical Co. of Japan.   **TECH**

May 2, 1952 Using a De Havilland Comet, BOAC institutes the first jetliner service between London and Johannesburg, South Africa.   **TECH**

Nov. 1,   The U.S. detonates the first hydrogen bomb, destroying the Pacific
1952   island of Elugelab in the process. This fusion bomb releases energy equivalent to 10.4 million tons of high explosive, about 700 times the force of the Hiroshima fission bomb.   **TECH**

1953   Superclusters of galaxies—clusters of clusters—are discovered. **ASTRO**

1953   American biologist Robert William Briggs and Thomas J. King succeed in growing tadpoles from eggs whose nucleus has been replaced with one from a partly differentiated cell of a developing embryo.   **BIO**

1953   British biophysicists Francis Crick and Maurice Wilkins, with American biochemist James Watson, discover the double-helix structure of the deoxyribonucleic acid (DNA) molecule.   **BIO**

1953   American physicist Albert Ghiorso and his colleagues discover the element fermium.   **CHEM**

1953	German chemist Karl W. Ziegler and Italian chemist Giulio Natta develop isotactic polymers, nonbranching, uniformly ordered polymer chains useful in industry. These chains employ catalysts that combine monomers into polymers in a regular way. **CHEM**
1953	American geologists Maurice Ewing and Bruce Charles Heezen discover an underwater canyon running the length of the Mid-Atlantic Ridge (*see* 1925). In 1956, they will propose the existence of a world-girdling formation of mountains called the Mid-Oceanic Ridge, accompanied by a formation of canyons called the Great Global Rift. The discovery that the rift separates the earth's crust into plates contributes to the developing theory of plate tectonics (*see* 1960, Henry H. Hess). **EARTH**
1953–1979	It is official U.S. Weather Service policy to use women's names for tropical cyclones, hurricanes, and typhoons. Afterward, names of both genders will be used for storm names. **EARTH**
May 29, 1953	New Zealander Edmund P. Hillary and his Nepalese guide Tenzing Norkay reach the top of Mount Everest. At 8,848 meters (29,028 feet) high, this mountain on the Tibet–Nepal border is the world's tallest. Tibetans call Everest *Chomolungma,* "Goddess Mother of the World." **EARTH**
1953	The world's first successful open-heart surgery, using U.S. surgeon John Gibbon Jr.'s newly developed heart-lung machine, is performed. **MED**
1953	American physician and epidemiologist Jonas Edward Salk begins preliminary testing of a poliomyelitis vaccine he developed in 1952. By 1955 this polio vaccine will be used worldwide to dramatically reduce the incidence of this disease. Virologist Albert Bruce Sabin will develop an oral polio vaccine in 1957. **MED**
1953	U.S. physicist Donald Arthur Glaser invents the bubble chamber, a device for detecting ionizing radiation. **PHYS**
1953	American physicist Murray Gell-Mann investigates the property of the elementary particles called kaons and hyperons that is known as strangeness, the tendency to decay slowly by way of the weak interaction even though the particles are subject to the strong interaction. To these particles Gell-Mann assigns a quantum number s (for strangeness number) that has an integral value and does not equal zero. **PHYS**
1953	A regularly recurring sleep stage characterized by rapid eye movement (REM) is discovered. This REM stage, which appears spontaneously about every ninety minutes during sleep, is considered to indicate the presence of dreams in humans. **PSYCH**

1953   African-American psychologist Mamie Phipps Clark assists in the preparation of a social science brief addressing self-awareness and self-esteem in black children. This brief will form the basis of the 1954 U.S. Supreme Court decision on public school desegregation.   **PSYCH**

1953   American political scientist David Easton publishes *The Political System*, which develops the approach known as systems analysis. Drawing metaphors from physics and biology, Easton treats the political system as one part of an overall social system. His strategy provides a framework for many topics of study, including the interaction of elites, interest groups, and political parties.   **SOC**

1953   American physicist Charles Hard Townes and, independently, Soviet physicists A. M. Prokhorov and N. G. Basov, invent the maser (Microwave Amplification by Stimulated Emission of Radiation), a device for producing a coherent beam of microwave radiation.   **TECH**

1953   IBM introduces the IBM 701, its first computer for scientific and business use.   **TECH**

1953   The plastic valve for aerosol cans that now bears his name is developed by U.S. inventor Robert Abplanalp.   **TECH**

1953   The Ziegler process, a catalytic technique used in making low-cost polyethylene plastics, is developed by German chemist Karl W. Ziegler.   **TECH**

1953   Cinemascope, a film process that widens the view projected on the screen, is used for the first time in the film *The Robe*.   **TECH**

1953   *Bwana Devil*, the first three-dimensional, or 3-D, film is shown in theaters. The technique requires special viewing devices to appreciate the 3-D effects.   **TECH**

1954   In Egypt, Kamal el-Malakh and his colleagues discover two chambers near the base of the Great Pyramid of Khufu. In one they find a 142-foot boat probably meant to transport the deceased pharaoh to the next world.   **ARCH**

1954   American biochemist Vincent du Vigneaud synthesizes the hormone oxytocin, the first naturally occurring protein to be synthesized with the exact makeup it has naturally in the body.   **BIO**

1954   Polish-American biochemist Daniel Israel Arnon obtains intact chloroplasts from spinach-leaf cells that have been disrupted and shown their ability to photosynthesize extracellularly.   **BIO**

1954   Russian-born American physicist George Gamow proposes the existence of a multinucleotide genetic code.   **BIO**

1954   The microprobe is invented for use in experimental mineralogy.   **EARTH**

1954	The National Geographic Society and the Mount Palomar Observatory together publish the *National Geographic–Palomar Sky Atlas*. **EARTH**
Feb. 15, 1954	Off the coast of West Africa, two French naval officers descend to a depth of 4,050 meters (13,300 feet) in Auguste Piccard's bathyscaphe. **EARTH**
1954	Scientists at the University of California build the bevatron, a particle accelerator capable of accelerating protons to energies of 5 or 6 billion electron volts. **PHYS**
1954	CERN, the European organization for Nuclear Research, is founded in Geneva, Switzerland. **PHYS**
1954	Chinese-American physicist Chen Ning Yang and American physicist Robert Mills develop the mathematics of Yang-Mills gauge-invariant fields, concerning symmetry at the level of fundamental interactions. **PHYS**
1954	Abraham Pais coins the term *baryon* to describe particles such as protons and neutrons that are affected by the strong force. This definition will be applied later to hadrons (*see* 1962, Okun). Baryons will be understood to be a subclass of hadrons, those with a half-integral spin. Nucleons (protons and neutrons) will be considered a subclass of baryons. **PHYS**
Mar. 1954	Chlorpromazine is approved for use as an antipsychotic in the United States, under the trade name Thorazine. **PSYCH**
June 1954	In the United States the Durham Rule, named for defendant Monte Durham, becomes law. It states that a criminal is not guilty if his unlawful behavior is the result of "mental defect or disease." **PSYCH**
1954	Silicon transistors are introduced by Texas Instruments. **TECH**
1954	The oxygen steel-manufacturing furnace, already popular in Europe, is introduced to the United States in a steel mill in Detroit. **TECH**
1954	BHA, butylated hydroxyanisole, is approved by the U.S. Food and Drug Administration for use as a preservative in foods. **TECH**
1954	U.S. salesman Raymond Kroc purchases the franchise rights to the California-based McDonald brothers' hamburger chain and begins to develop it into the largest fast-food restaurant chain in the world. **TECH**
1954	The U.S.S. *Nautilus*, the first submarine powered by an onboard nuclear reactor, is launched. It will remain in service until 1980. **TECH**
c. 1955	The Schwarzschild radius, named for the German astronomer Karl Schwarzschild, is identified. It is the radius that must be exceeded for light to escape an object of a given mass, and marks the event horizon of a black hole. *See* 1960s, Wheeler. **ASTRO**

1955   The United States and the U.S.S.R. initiate separate satellite programs, with the U.S.S.R. being the first to launch a satellite, two years later.   **ASTRO**

1955   British astronomer Martin Ryle invents the radio interferometer, a device that improves the resolution of radio telescopes.   **ASTRO**

1955   U.S. astronomers detect radio emissions from Jupiter.   **ASTRO**

1955   Measuring the polarization of light, Dutch astronomer Jan Hendrik Oort confirms a 1953 hypothesis by I. S. Shklovskii that radio emission from the Crab nebula is the result of synchrotron radiation.   **ASTRO**

1955   Belgian cytologist Christian René de Duve discovers and names lysosomes.   **BIO**

1955   American physicist Albert Ghiorso and his colleagues discover the element mendelevium.   **CHEM**

1955   Using high temperatures and pressures and with chromium as a catalyst, scientists produce the first synthetic diamonds out of graphite.   **CHEM**

1955   Mathematicians Henri Cartan and Samuel Eilenberg develop homological algebra, an innovation that unites abstract algebra and algebraic topology.   **MATH**

1955   At the urging of social activist Margaret Sanger, U.S. biologist and endocrinologist Gregory Pincus develops the first successful birth-control pill, based on his discovery that the hormone norethindrone is effective in preventing conception.   **MED**

1955   Italian physicist Emilio Segré and American physicist Owen Chamberlain discover the first known antiprotons, negatively charged particles that have the mass of protons.   **PHYS**

1955   Two types of K mesons with differing modes of decay are detected, the tau and the theta.   **PHYS**

1955   American clinical psychologist Albert Ellis develops Rational-Emotive Therapy (RET), which emphasizes how the holding of unrealistic expectations and irrational thinking and beliefs can cause and perpetuate human misery. RET works to overcome problems created by false beliefs and to correct the human tendency toward irrational thought.   **PSYCH**

1955   American clinical psychologist George Kelly publishes his two-volume work *The Psychology of Personal Constructs*. Kelly's personal construct theory is based on the idea that the most important determinant of human behavior is the individual's own conception of the world and the people he or she meets. Kelly will be the first to found a psychological clinic for training in a theory.   **PSYCH**

This is your future   3D Color TV Wall Panel   Slide-back Roof   Personal Helicopter and Roof Landing Area   Moving Stairway   House-control Panel

Glass Walls   Dust-free Floors   Menu Selector and Microwave Stove   Garden-less Fruit   Ultrasonic Laundry   Electrical Heat Unit   Photovacuum Broom

Ad for the ideal kitchen of the 1950s with formica, plastic, nylon, and other features.

1955	U.S. anthropologist Julian Steward publishes his *Theory of Culture Change: The Methodology of Multilinear Evolution*, a study of cultural evolution. **SOC**
1955	American physicist Erwin Wilhelm Mueller invents the field ion microscope, which is capable of magnifications of more that a million times. It is the first device that can yield images of individual atoms. **TECH**
1955	The IBM 752, the company's first computer designed exclusively for business use, is produced. **TECH**
1956	Microwave radiation detected on Venus indicates that its surface temperature is as high as 600° F. **ASTRO**
1956	U.S. biologists T. T. Puck, S. J. Cieciura, and P. I. Marcus grow clones of human cells successfully in vitro. **BIO**
1956	Using the electron microscope, Romanian-born American physiologist George Emil Palade discovers that microsomes (small bodies in cell cytoplasm) contain RNA, and renames them ribosomes. They are later found to be the protein-manufacturing site in the cell. **BIO**
1956	Chinese-born American biochemist Choh Hao Li isolates the human growth hormone from the pituitary gland. He also studies the structure of ACTH and the melanocyte-stimulating hormone (MSH). **BIO**
1956	American biochemist Earl Sutherland Jr. isolates cyclic adenosine monophosphate (AMP). **BIO**
1956	In the United States the Federal Water Pollution Control Act passes, one of the early modern attempts at marine protection. **BIO**

1956   American biochemist Mahlon Bush Hoagland discovers small RNA molecules in cytoplasm and shows that each variety has the capacity to combine with a particular amino acid.   **BIO**

1956   Halothane, a colorless liquid inhaled as a vapor to induce and maintain general anesthesia, is introduced.   **MED**

1956   U.S. physicists Frederick Reines and Clyde Lorrain Cowan discover antineutrinos.   **PHYS**

1956   Chinese physicists Chen Ning Yang and Tsung-dao Lee show that the property called parity, the quality of being odd or even, is conserved in the strong and electromagnetic interactions but not in the weak interaction.   **PHYS**

1956   The existence of antineutrons, differing from neutrons in the orientation of their magnetic field, is predicted.   **PHYS**

1956   American anthropologist Gregory Bateson formulates the double-bind theory of communication patterns, which argues that schizophrenia develops in children whose parents give contradictory messages, often sent subliminally.   **PSYCH**

1956   The Dartmouth Summer Research Project on Artificial Intelligence is held to explore the idea that intelligence can be described so precisely that a machine can be made to simulate it. Among those attending the conference are neurologist and mathematician Marvin Minsky, Herbert Simon, and Allen Newell. Minsky and conference host John McCarthy will found the AI lab at MIT, Simon and Newell the one at Carnegie Mellon in Pittsburgh.   **PSYCH**

1956   Americans William C. Boyd and his wife Lyle Boyd identify thirteen "races" of *Homo sapiens*, based on blood groups.   **SOC**

1956   American sociologist C. Wright Mills publishes *The Power Elite*, an analysis of American class structure, in which he critiques the highly theoretical sociology of Talcott Parsons and others, believing they neglect such issues as group conflict and social change.   **SOC**

1956   The first nuclear-powered jet engine is tested in Idaho. It is meant to power a bomber that can fly for months without refueling, but the project will be canceled in 1961 after intercontinental ballistic missiles make it obsolete.   **TECH**

1956   Dutch-born American physicist Nicolaas Bloembergen invents the continuous maser.   **TECH**

1956   A videotape-recording machine is shown publicly by the U.S.-based Ampex Corporation.   **TECH**

1957   British astronomer Martin Ryle argues that energy fluctuations in Seyfert galaxies (*see* 1944) result from the ejection of matter at near-light speed.   **ASTRO**

Oct. 4, 1957	The Soviet Union launches *Sputnik I*, the world's first artificial satellite, into orbit. The United States reacts by beginning a space race with the Soviet Union. **ASTRO**
Nov. 3, 1957	The U.S.S.R. launches the satellite *Sputnik II*, which carries a dog named Laika. **ASTRO**
1957	British biochemist John Kendrew solves for the first time the three-dimensional structure of a protein. **BIO**
1957	American biochemist Melvin Calvin discovers and isolates all the details of plant photosynthesis. **BIO**

THE RIGHT STUFF

*A*fter the Soviet Union launched the satellite Sputnik in 1957, the United States was determined to put a man in space before the Russians did. They didn't succeed—Russian cosmonaut Yuri Gagarin became the first person to orbit the earth, in 1961—but the United States's Project Mercury became a focus for national attention and pride just the same.

Project Mercury was publicly announced on October 7, 1958. The original seven Mercury astronauts, famed for the cool, professional courage Tom Wolfe called the right stuff in his 1979 book of the same name, were:

> M. Scott Carpenter
> L. Gordon Cooper Jr.
> John H. Glenn Jr.
> Virgil I. Grissom
> Walter M. Schirra Jr.
> Alan B. Shepard Jr.
> Donald K. Slayton

Shepard became the first American in space in a suborbital flight, on May 5, 1961. John Glenn became the first American to orbit the earth, on February 20, 1962. And L. Gordon Cooper Jr., became the first American to spend more than a day in space, on May 15–16, 1963.

After Project Mercury ended, Grissom established another record of a grimmer kind. On January 27, 1967, he and fellow astronauts Edward H. White II and Roger Chaffee were in the Apollo I space capsule during a training exercise at Cape Kennedy, Florida. A flash fire cost them their lives, making them the first American astronauts to die in the line of duty.

1957   Gibberelins—plant hormones used to increase plant size, especially in wine and table grapes—are isolated from a fungus of the genus *Gibberella*.   **BIO**

1957   G. Evelyn Hutchinson defines the concept of the ecological niche as the place or function of a given organism within its ecosystem, which is a collection of living things and the environment in which they live.   **BIO**

. . . .

"There is a story, perhaps apocryphal, of the distinguished British biologist J. B. S. Haldane, who found himself in the company of a group of theologians. On being asked what one could conclude as to the nature of the Creator from a study of his creation, Haldane is said to have answered, 'An inordinate fondness for beetles.'"—G. Evelyn Hutchinson, British biologist, on colleague J. B. S. Haldane, 1959. Of the formally named animals and plants, 57 percent are insects, and nearly half of those are beetles.

. . . .

1957   The lightweight plastic called polypropylene is invented.   **CHEM**

1957   American seismologist Charles Richter establishes a new relationship between the magnitude and the energy produced by an earthquake.   **EARTH**

1957   Researchers in seventy countries engage in the systematic, coordinated study of the earth and its atmosphere during the International Geophysical Year. One study, for instance, focuses on measuring the flattening of the earth at its poles.   **EARTH**

1957   British bacteriologist Alick Isaacs discovers interferon, an antiviral protein produced by the body in response to viral infections. It will be used against a wide variety of drug-resistant viral diseases and in cancer research.   **MED**

1957   Amniocentesis, the study of amniotic fluid extracted from the amniotic sac with a needle and syringe, is developed to test for genetic disorders.   **MED**

1957   American physicists John Bardeen, Leon N. Cooper, and John R. Schrieffer advance the so-called BCS theory to explain the phenomenon of superconductivity.   **PHYS**

c. 1957   U.S. researchers Allen Newell, Herbert Simon, and J. C. Shaw develop their Logic Theorist program, one of the first artificial intelligence programs.   **PSYCH**

1957	American social psychologist Leon Festinger presents his cognitive dissonance theory, having to do with the relationship among cognitive elements such as self-knowledge, behavior, and environment. Festinger's research concentrates on the discrepancies between attitude and behavior and on the consequences of decisions. **PSYCH**
1957	In his work *Syntactic Structures*, American linguist Noam Chomsky proposes the revolutionary theory of transformational-generative grammar, in which he argues that innate structures in the mind are the basis for human languages. This theory seeks to uncover the underlying structure and rules that govern the production of sentences. **SOC**
1957	The Wankel rotary engine, an improved internal combustion engine, is developed by German engineer Franz Wankel for use in automobiles and other types of machinery. **TECH**
1957	Soy protein foodstuffs are more easily created with the development of an improved spinning process to mix soy flour and alkaline liquids. **TECH**
1958	U.S. physicist Eugene N. Parker discovers the solar wind, a flow of charged, subatomic particles emanating from the sun. **ASTRO**
1958	U.S. astrophysicist Herbert Friedman discovers X rays emanating from the sun that are probably produced in its corona. **ASTRO**
Jan. 31, 1958	The United States launches its first satellite, *Explorer I*. In addition, American scientists discover the earth's Van Allen radiation belt and launch four more satellites and three lunar probes. **ASTRO**
Oct. 7, 1958	The United States announces its Project Mercury, the first American manned space program. **ASTRO**
1958	English biochemist Francis Crick writes on a principle he calls the central dogma of molecular biology: "Once 'information' has passed into protein it cannot get out again.... The transfer of information from nucleic acid to nucleic acid may be possible, but transfer from protein to protein, or from protein to nucleic acid, is impossible." **BIO**
1958	Russian scientist Ilya Darevsky discovers the first known example of an all-female vertebrate species, a lizard species in Soviet Armenia that reproduces without male fertilization. **BIO**
1958	U.S. geneticist Joshua Lederberg is awarded a Nobel Prize for his work on genetic mechanisms. U.S. geneticists George Beadle and Edward Tatum also win Nobel prizes, for discovering how genes transmit hereditary characteristics. **BIO**
1958	American physicist Albert Ghiorso and his colleagues discover the element nobelium. **CHEM**

| 1958 | Scottish physician Ian McDonald pioneers the use of high-frequency sound waves (ultrasound) as a diagnostic and therapeutic tool. Ultrasound is used to destroy diseased tissue and restore damaged tissue.   **MED** |

1958   German physicist Rudolf Ludwig Mössbauer discovers the Mössbauer effect, a sharp narrowing of the energy spread (range of wavelengths) of gamma-ray emission from atoms in certain solids possessing a lattice configuration. Atoms of the same crystal will absorb only gamma rays of the same energy spread. *See also* 1960, Mössbauer.   **PHYS**

1958   The Council of Mental Health of the American Medical Association validates the therapeutic use of hypnosis.   **PSYCH**

1958   American psychologist Arnold Lazarus is the first to use the term *behavior therapy* in describing certain mental illness treatment strategies.   **PSYCH**

1958   U.S. experimental and comparative psychologists Harry F. Harlow and John Bowlby experiment with baby monkeys, mannequin mothers, and the idea of maternal deprivation. They prove that behavioral disturbances and detachment occur when adequate interaction, holding, and bonding do not take place between mother and child.   **PSYCH**

1958   Social psychologist Fritz Heider publishes what will become a classic treatise on social psychology, *The Psychology of Interpersonal Relations*. In it Heider presents his balance theory and explains why individuals strive for cognitive consistency—how an individual organizes beliefs and perceptions in a consistent, organized way.   **PSYCH**

1958   The Boeing 707, the first U.S. jet for passenger service, is put into operation by Boeing Aircraft.   **TECH**

1958   A saccharin-based artificial sweetener is introduced to the American market.   **TECH**

1959   The United States experimentally launches two monkeys and a chimpanzee into space.   **ASTRO**

1959   The Soviet unmanned spacecraft *Luna 1* makes the first flyby of the moon.   **ASTRO**

Sept. 12,   The Soviet unmanned spacecraft *Luna 2*, launched today, is the
1959   first vehicle to reach the moon, where it crashes on Sept. 14.   **ASTRO**

Oct. 7,   The Soviet unmanned craft *Luna 3* takes the first pictures of the
1959   moon's far side.   **ASTRO**

1959   American scientist Christian Boehmer Anfinsen publishes *The Molecular Basis of Evolution*, based on his work with enzymes.   **BIO**

1959   Severo Ochoa and Arthur Kronberg are awarded the Nobel Prize
          for discoveries related to compounds within chromosomes that
          play a role in heredity.   **BIO**

1959   The U.S. satellite *Vanguard II* becomes the first to transmit weather
          information to earth.   **EARTH**

1959   The U.S. satellite *Explorer 6* takes the first television pictures of the
          earth's cloud cover as seen from space.   **EARTH**

1959   British anthropologists Louis and Mary Leakey discover fossils of
          Zinjanthropus boisei in the Olduvai Gorge of what is now Tanzania,
          Africa. Believed to have lived 2.5 to 1 million years ago, this thick-
          boned hominid with large back teeth is now classified either as
          Australopithecus robustus or *Australopithecus boisei*.   **PALEO**

1959   Japanese physicists Saburo Fukui and Shotaro Miyamoto invent the
          spark chamber, a device to selectively detect ionizing particles. **PHYS**

1959   German-born psychiatrist Viktor Frankl publishes *Man's Search for
          Meaning*, a popular mental-health book emphasizing the impor-
          tance of free will.   **PSYCH**

1959   The drug haloperidol, or Haldol, is first synthesized, for use with
          psychotic disorders.   **PSYCH**

Louis Leakey at Olduvai Gorge, the site where the *Australopithecus* skull was
found in 1959. (*The Bettman Archive*)

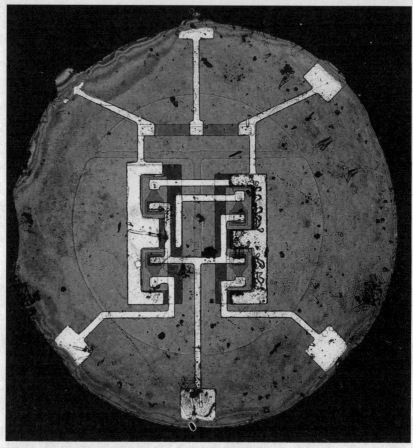

Robert Norton Noyce's integrated circuit. (*AT&T*)

1959   The first ground-based nuclear rocket engine is tested, with the goal of designing nuclear rockets to fly into space. After many experiments the program will be scrapped in 1973 as the space effort is scaled back.   **TECH**

1959   The microchip, an integrated circuit made of a single silicon wafer, is invented by American engineers Jack Kilby of Texas Instruments and Robert Noyce of Fairchild Semiconductors.   **TECH**

1959   Sony introduces the first transistorized television set.   **TECH**

1959   The first pantyhose are developed, by Glen Raven Mills in North Carolina.   **TECH**

1960s   U.S. physicist John Archibald Wheeler coins the term *black hole* for a collapsed star whose surface gravity is so great that nothing, not even light, can escape it.   **ASTRO**

1960s   In the United States a creationist movement begins to gain strength advocating the belief that God literally created all life forms as described in the biblical book of Genesis and demanding that this doctrine be taught in the public schools. Creationists have never accepted the theory of evolution as expressed by Darwin in 1859.   **BIO**

1960s   Ecology becomes identified for the first time with environmental concerns like pesticides, pollutants, and preservation. Prior to this time, ecology was linked mostly to agriculture and related economic issues.   **BIO**

1960s   U.S. biologist Daniel Mazia uncouples centrosomal and nuclear replication in the fertilized eggs of sand dollars and sea urchins. With his assistants he proves that centrosome replication can occur in the absence of nuclear replication.   **BIO**

1960s   By mid-decade some scientists observe what they consider evidence of global warming due to the greenhouse effect. *See* 1863, Tyndall.   **EARTH**

1960s   Biofeedback becomes popular as a short-term therapy to help people learn healthy responses to stress. In it, a machine tells the patient when he is controlling his response (slowing the heart rate and breathing, and relaxing the muscles). Eventually, the patient learns to control his responses without the machine. Biofeedback will come to be used to treat migraine headaches, anxiety and panic attacks, and hypertension.   **PSYCH**

1960s   Encounter groups, meant to help emotionally well people achieve high-level mental health, begin to reach their peak in American society. By discussing the meaning of life on a profound level, these groups try to cultivate self-actualization.   **PSYCH**

1960s   Family therapy, the treatment of entire families, develops as a result of theories claiming that many mental illnesses are caused by abnormal family communication patterns.   **PSYCH**

1960s   Stanford psychiatrist and scientist Kenneth Colby develops a computer program simulating a neurotic individual. Colby's artificial neurotic will be followed by a more sophisticated artificial paranoid Colby will name Perry. Both programs are attempts to use computers to study the structure of mental illness and create a dynamic model that trainee analysts can practice on.   **PSYCH**

1960s American neurophysiologist David Hunter Hubel and Swedish neurobiologist Torsten Nils Wiesel find in experiments that a patch placed over one eye of a kitten during its critical period of neural growth leads to permanent blindness in that eye. The blindness is not reversible, however, because, while the one eye is patched, inputs arriving from the unpatched eye take over the visual cortex's allotment for the patched eye. **PSYCH**

1960s Many political scientists react against behaviorism (*see* c. 1945), which they view as having placed an excessive emphasis on methodology and the preservation of the status quo. They call instead for more emphasis on contemporary problems and human values. **SOC**

1960s The emerging field of cognitive anthropology seeks to understand the structure of cultures as systems of knowledge. **SOC**

1960s By the early part of this decade, radar is in use for such civilian purposes as air traffic control, weather forecasting, and police procedures. **TECH**

1960s Late in the decade, Nils Nilsson, Bertram Raphael, and their colleagues at the Stanford Research Institute develop a robot they name Shakey that is able to distinguish boxes from pyramids and follow simple instructions. **TECH**

1960 At L'Anse aux Meadows in north Newfoundland, Helge Ingstad and George Decker rediscover a Viking settlement dating to the eleventh century, indicating that Vikings settled in North America several centuries before Columbus. **ARCH**

1960 American astronomer Frank Drake organizes Project Ozma, a four-hundred-hour radio search for extraterrestrial life that yields negative results. **ASTRO**

1960 U.S. astronomer Allen Sandage identifies several starlike objects emitting radio waves, the first being 3C48. Maarten Schmidt will show in 1963 that these objects are quasars. **ASTRO**

1960 American zoologists Kenneth Norris and John Prescott determine that marine mammals (in this case dolphins) use echolocation to find the range and direction of objects in the water. **BIO**

May 16, 1960 University of California–Berkeley biochemists A. Tsugita and Heinz Fraenkel-Conrat describe their discovery of the first definite link between a mutation, or change in inheritance code, and an alteration in the molecule manufactured according to that code. **BIO**

1960 *Tiros I,* launched by the United States, is the first weather satellite. It is equipped to take thousands of photographs of the earth and its cloud cover and transmit them back. **EARTH**

1960   U.S. geologist Henry H. Hess proposes the concept of sea-floor spreading, a key idea in plate tectonics. Hess suggests that new crust forms at rifts, especially in the sea floor, where lithospheric plates move apart. *See also* 1912, Alfred Wegener.   **EARTH**

c. 1960   The "new math," an educational system that constructs mathematical relationships from set theory, is introduced in American public schools.   **MATH**

1960   The General Conference of Weights and Measures sets a new standard for the meter: 1,650,763.73 wavelengths of the spectral line of a certain isotope of krypton.   **MISC**

c. 1960   Fossil bones of primitive Triassic saurischians found in the Ischigualasto beds of Argentina appear to be from of the oldest dinosaurs then known.   **PALEO**

1960   An international team of geologists discovers dinosaur footprints on the Arctic island of West Spitzbergen (Svalbard). The tracks will be identified in 1961 as those of the early Cretaceous dinosaur the *Iguanodon*.   **PALEO**

1960   Scientists use the Mössbauer effect (*see* 1958) to test the general theory of relativity. Monochromatic gamma rays fired from the top of a building at a crystal at its base prove to increase in wavelength, owing to the stronger gravitational field at the bottom, an effect predicted by the theory of general relativity.   **PHYS**

1960   American physicist Luis Walter Alvarez discovers resonance particles, which exist for so short a time (10^{-24} second) that they can be regarded as the excited state of more stable particles.   **PHYS**

1960   Polish-American chemist Leo Sternback discovers a drug marketed as Librium, a benzodiazepine for the treatment of anxiety and tension.   **PSYCH**

1960   American physicist Theodore Harold Maiman invents the laser (Light Amplification by Stimulated Emission of Radiation), a device that produces an intense beam of coherent light. The laser will have many applications in physics research, industry, electronics, and surgery.   **TECH**

1960   The first electronic wristwatch, the Accutron, is developed by Bulova. It operates with a tuning fork that vibrates 360 times per second.   **TECH**

1960   Aluminum cans come into use in the United States as containers for soft drinks and food products.   **TECH**

....

"I invite you to sit down in front of your television set when your station goes on the air, and stay there. You will see a vast wasteland—a procession of game shows, violence, audience participation shows, formula comedies about totally unbelievable families...blood and thunder...mayhem, violence, sadism, murder...private eyes, more violence, and cartoons...and, endlessly, commercials—many screaming, cajoling, and offending."—Newton Minow, chairman of the U.S. Federal Communications Commission, in speech to National Association of Broadcasters; 1961

....

Apr. 12, 1961	Riding aboard the *Vostok 1*, Soviet cosmonaut Yuri A. Gagarin becomes the first human to reach outer space and the first to orbit the earth. **ASTRO**
May 5, 1961	U.S. astronaut Alan B. Shepard Jr. is the first American in space. His *Freedom 7* space capsule makes a fifteen-minute suborbital flight. **ASTRO**
May 21, 1961	U.S. president John F. Kennedy promises to send a man to the moon and back by the end of the decade. *See* July 20, 1969. **ASTRO**
July 21, 1961	Virgil I. Grissom becomes the second American in space, during a suborbital flight aboard the *Liberty Bell 7*. **ASTRO**
Aug. 7, 1961	Soviet cosmonaut Gherman S. Titov, aboard the *Vostok 2*, becomes the second Soviet in space and the first human to spend more than a day in space, completing seventeen earth orbits during his 25½-hour flight. **ASTRO**
1961	Biochemists at the Oak Ridge National Laboratory in Tennessee observe in a test tube for the first time the genetic process by which proteins are synthesized. **BIO**
1961	American physicist Albert Ghiorso and his colleagues discover the element lawrencium. **CHEM**
1961	American scientist Edward Lorenz begins to develop the mathematics that will become chaos theory. **MATH**
1961	The rubella (German measles) virus is identified and isolated. A live vaccine for long-lasting immunity from it will become available within the next decade. **MED**
1961	American physicist Murray Gell-Mann develops a classification system for the elementary particles called hadrons (*see* 1962, Okun), categorizing them in families according to properties that vary regularly in value. He calls his system the Eightfold Way. Israeli physicist Yuval Ne'emen independently develops a similar system around the same time. **PHYS**

1961   British physicist Jeffrey Goldstone formulates what is known as Goldstone's theorem, which predicts the existence of a spin-zero massless particle called a Goldstone boson in certain situations of symmetry.   **PHYS**

1961   Soviet military scientists set a record, still unbroken, for the largest nuclear explosion, testing a fifty-eight-megaton weapon.   **TECH**

1962   The unmanned U.S. spacecraft *Mariner 2* completes the first flyby of Venus, transmitting pictures back to earth.   **ASTRO**

Feb. 20,   Circling the earth three times aboard the *Friendship 7*, John Glenn
1962   becomes the first American to orbit the earth.   **ASTRO**

1962   American author and scientist Rachel Carson publishes *Silent Spring*, an alarming and revealing glimpse into how chemicals in the environment damage ecosystems.   **BIO**

1962   American chemist Linus Pauling and Austrian-born French biochemist Émile Zuckerkandl suggest that changes in genetic material can be used as a kind of biological clock to date the time one species separated from another.   **BIO**

CHAOS, OR WHY YOU CAN'T PREDICT THE WEATHER

*I*n 1961, MIT meteorologist Edward N. Lorenz was forced to pause while running a lengthy computer calculation of weather patterns. He didn't want to start over from scratch, so he saved some of his intermediate results and, when he came back, had the computer begin from that new starting point. He then discovered that the final results were quite different from those he had gotten earlier by running the same calculation uninterrupted.

Searching for the source of the discrepancy, Lorenz found that the computer had rounded off the figures slightly differently when saving them than when using them continuously. Although this discrepancy affected only the eighth decimal place in the original numbers, it was enough to cause enormous differences in the final results. Lorenz had found that weather systems are highly sensitive to initial conditions. They are, in short, chaotic systems. The weather in New York on the third Sunday of next December cannot be predicted, because it depends on the initial conditions around the globe today—and those conditions cannot be known with complete accuracy.

Since Lorenz's discovery, chaos theory—the study of chaotic systems, using nonlinear equations that involve several variables—has been applied not only to weather but to turbulent flow, planetary dynamics, electrical oscillations, and many other areas.

1962   British-born Canadian chemist Neil Bartlett combines the noble gas xenon with platinum fluoride to produce xenon fluoroplatinate in the first known case of a noble gas bonding with another element to form a compound.   **CHEM**

1962   Japanese physicians introduce the first flexible fiber-optic endoscope, a device consisting of a tube and an optical system for seeing inside a hollow organ or body cavity.   **MED**

1962   In Britain the first beta-adrenergic blocking agent (a drug used mostly to treat heart disorders) is developed.   **MED**

1962   In South Africa, paleontologists A. W. Crompton and Alan J. Charig report the discovery of the oldest known ornithischian dinosaurs, dating from the late Triassic.   **PALEO**

1962   British physicist B. D. Josephson predicts the Josephson effects, a group of electrical results that occur at low temperatures when two superconducting materials are separated by a thin layer of insulation.   **PHYS**

1962   German-born British physicist Heinz London develops a technique for inducing very low temperatures with a mixture of helium-3 and helium-4. With this and other methods, temperatures of a millionth of a degree above absolute zero will eventually be obtained.   **PHYS**

1962   American physicists discover two varieties of neutrinos, one associated with the muon, one with the electron. Scientists will later infer the existence of another variety, associated with the tauon. *See* 1974, Perl.   **PHYS**

1962   L. B. Okun coins the term *hadron* to describe the class of particles including protons and neutrons that are affected by the strong force. *See also* 1954, Pais, baryons.   **PHYS**

1962   German psychiatrist Karl Leonard uses for the first time the term *bipolar disorder* to describe manic-depressive psychosis.   **PSYCH**

1962   American behaviorist Abraham Maslow publishes *Toward a Psychology of Being*. In this work and his 1954 *Motivation and Personality*, Maslow describes two basic types of human motivation: deficiency motivation (the need for shelter, food, and water) and growth motivation (the striving for knowledge and self-actualization).   **PSYCH**

1962   British anthropologist Victor Turner publishes his *Forest of Symbols*, a seminal work on African ritual and symbolism.   **SOC**

1962   The United States launches *Telstar I*, the first commercial communications satellite, which provides television and voice communications between the United States and Europe. *See also* 1945, Clarke.   **TECH**

1962   Diet-Rite Cola becomes the first low-calorie soda with a sugar substitute to be sold nationally. This beverage is sweetened with cyclamate.   **TECH**

1962   The Aluminum Corp. of America helps to develop a can with dis-
            cardable pull tabs, an innovation test marketed in Virginia with
            Iron City Beer.   **TECH**

1963   The radio telescope at Arecibo, Puerto Rico, is completed, with a
            dish 305 meters (1,000 feet) in diameter.   **ASTRO**

1963   Dutch-American astronomer Maarten Schmidt discovers the first
            quasar when he identifies the large red shift of object 3C273, a
            very distant extragalactic radio source receding at great speed.
            Hong-Yee Chiu will coin the term *quasar* to describe it the following
            year.   **ASTRO**

1963   The *Syncom 2* is the first satellite to be launched into a geosynchro-
            nous orbit, stationary above a given longitude on earth. **ASTRO**

1963   Scientists detect hydroxyl groups (combinations of one hydrogen
            and one oxygen atom) in space, providing the first evidence that
            interstellar space contains matter in forms other than individual
            atoms.   **ASTRO**

May 15–16, L. Gordon Cooper becomes the first American to spend more than
1963   a day in space, orbiting the earth twenty-two times in the last flight
            of the Project Mercury.   **ASTRO**

June 16,   Riding aboard the *Vostok 6*, Soviet cosmonaut Valentina V.
1963   Tereshkova becomes the first woman in space. She completes
            forty-eight earth orbits during a seventy-one-hour flight. **ASTRO**

Sept. 1963 Columbia University geneticist Ruth Sager reports finding the
            genetic system called nonchromosomal inheritance. This system
            involves genes but follows different rules from the chromosomal
            system, including the fact that nonchromosomal genes do not
            seem to mutate as chromosomal ones do, that they appear to be
            transmitted to the offspring by the female only, that the two sys-
            tems have different sorting times, and that the systems produce
            different numbers of possible kinds of progeny.   **BIO**

1963   Geologists discover the phenomenon of periodic magnetic reversal
            in the earth's crust, evident from the pattern of alternating magnet-
            ic polarity in the ocean floor near mid-ocean rifts. The discovery
            lends support to the theory of sea-floor spreading and plate tecton-
            ics (*see* 1960, Henry H. Hess).   **EARTH**

1963   American mathematician Paul J. Cohen shows that German mathe-
            matician Georg Cantor's continuum hypothesis concerning transfi-
            nite numbers (*see* c.1895) is neither consistent nor inconsistent
            with the axioms of set theory.   **MATH**

1963   Valium (diazepam), marketed now by Roche Laboratory, will quick-
            ly become the most widely used tranquilizer in the world. **PSYCH**

1963   The word *psychedelic* is first used. It originally means mind mani-
            festing but will soon become associated with drug intoxication and
            visual hallucinations.   **PSYCH**

1963   Researchers A. Carlson and M. Lindquist are the first to propose
            the dopamine hypothesis, that the neurotransmitter dopamine is
            linked to schizophrenia. It will become one of the most
            researched biochemical theories of schizophrenia since the illness
            was identified.   **PSYCH**

1963   After studying child development with Jean Piaget in Geneva, artifi-
            cial intelligence specialist Seymour Papert comes to MIT to begin
            working with Marvin Minsky. Papert will develop the AI program
            LOGO as a language for helping children develop their problem-
            solving skills. He will also hypothesize that many steps in mental
            growth are based less on the acquisition of new skills than on gain-
            ing new ways to administer already established abilities, a concept
            that becomes known as Papert's principle.   **PSYCH**

1963   MIT computer scientist Joseph Weizenbaum writes the AI program
            Eliza, to parody a Rogerian psychoanalyst's noncommittal ques-
            tioning style. Weizenbaum then is appalled at how attached some
            of Eliza's "psych patients" become to their mentor. In his 1976
            book *Computer Power and Human Reason*, he denounces artificial
            intelligence and questions why people become willing to accept
            machines as all-knowing and all-powerful.   **PSYCH**

1963   The father of artificial intelligence, John McCarthy, leaves MIT,
            where he had developed Lisp, the most popular AI language in the
            United States, to establish another major AI laboratory at Stanford
            University.   **PSYCH**

1963   The first commercial nuclear reactor, Jersey Central Power's Oyster
            Creek facility, is opened.   **TECH**

1963   The electronic transistorized telephone service called Touch-Tone is
            marketed in Pennsylvania by AT&T.   **TECH**

··
*"There are three great things in the world: there is
religion, there is science, and there is gossip."*
—Robert Frost, American poet; 1963
··

1964   The U.S. *Ranger 7* spacecraft transmits more than four thousand
            photographs of the moon's surface before crashing.   **ASTRO**

1964   The U.S. unmanned spacecraft *Mariner 4* completes the first flyby
            of Mars.   **ASTRO**

May 1964   German-American physicist Arno Allan Penzias and American as-
            tronomer Robert Woodrow Wilson detect radio-wave background ra-
            diation indicating an average temperature of the universe of 3° K.
            The cosmic background radiation corroborates the Big Bang theory.
            See 1949, Gamow.   **ASTRO**

1964   Three Soviets aboard the *Voskhod 1* are the first humans to ride as
            a team aboard a single capsule.   **ASTRO**

1964   Egyptian-born British biologist and geneticist William Donald
            Hamilton writes on the genetic evolution of social behavior, claim-
            ing that the traits of social species like ants and bees can be ex-
            plained as a mechanism designed to transmit genes. This concept
            will later develop into the field of sociobiology.   **BIO**

1964   U.S. microbiologists Keith Porter and Thomas F. Roth discover, em-
            bedded in the cell membrane of an egg cell, the first cell receptors. **BIO**

June 14,   Australian geneticist Pamela Abel, working with German geneticist
1964   T. A. Trautner at the University of Cologne, reports that evidence
            has been found showing the genetic code of life to be universally
            the same in all living things. Drs. Abel and Trautner report taking
            genes from one organism and making them work in the environ-
            ment of another, completely alien, organism.   **BIO**

c. 1964   American chemist Bruce Merrifield invents a simplified technique
            for synthesizing proteins and peptides. Later automated, this
            method will become useful in gene synthesis in the 1980s.   **CHEM**

1964   An international research program is developed to take advantage
            of a period of minimal solar activity known as "the year of the qui-
            et Sun."   **EARTH**

c. 1964   U.S. physician Stanley Dudrick introduces total parenteral nutrition
            (TPN), an intravenous feeding system that meets the total caloric
            needs of a patient unable to eat or drink normally.   **MED**

1964   British anthropologist Louis Leakey and his colleagues announce
            the discovery of fossils of *Homo habilis* in the Olduvai Gorge of
            what is now Tanzania. The earliest known member of the genus
            Homo, this first hominid species to make stone tools is now be-
            lieved to have lived as early as 2.5 million years ago.   **PALEO**

1964   American physicist Murray Gell-Mann further develops his Eightfold
            Way of classifying hadrons (*see* 1961) by reference to more funda-
            mental particles he calls quarks, an allusion to James Joyce's novel
            Finnegans Wake. A few kinds of quarks and their oppositely
            charged counterparts, antiquarks, interact to form all the many va-
            rieties of hadrons, a class of particles that includes protons and
            neutrons. Quarks have fractional rather than whole electric
            charges.   **PHYS**

1964   A particle with a strangeness number of −2 is discovered. Its proper-
        ties correspond precisely to those that Gell-Mann had predicted for
        an empty spot in his classification system called the Eightfold Way.
        This discovery lends credibility to Gell-Mann's quark theory.   **PHYS**

1964   American physicists Val Logsden Fitch and James Watson Cronin
        disprove the accepted belief that CP (charge conjugation and parity,
        two properties of particles) is always conserved when they discover
        that neutral kaons occasionally violate CP conservation. The CPT
        theorem, still accepted, adds a third characteristic, time (T), to the
        symmetry. No violation of CPT symmetry has yet been detected,
        though the characteristics of C, P, and T or any two of them may
        each be violated.   **PHYS**

1964   Physicists Sheldon Lee Glashow and James D. Bjorken propose the
        existence of quarks possessing a property they call charm. The hy-
        pothesis will be confirmed by Samuel Ting and Burton Richter in
        1974.   **PHYS**

1964   Physicist Peter Higgs predicts the existence of a spin-zero particle
        with a nonzero mass, now called the Higgs boson.   **PHYS**

1965   Astronomers Herbert Friedman, Edward Byram, and Talbot Chubb
        discover an intense X-ray source in the constellation Cygnus, which
        becomes known as Cygnus X-1. *See* 1970, satellite observatory.   **ASTRO**

1965   Cosmic masers are discovered. These are interstellar gas clouds
        whose intense radio emission lines indicate that their molecules are
        being pumped to more highly excited levels by the radiation of
        nearby stars.   **ASTRO**

1965   Astronomers at the Arecibo Observatory in Puerto Rico discover
        the retrograde rotation of Venus and the rotation of Mercury.   **ASTRO**

Mar. 18,   Soviet cosmonaut Alexei A. Leonov is the first human to "walk" in
1965   space, leaving his spacecraft the *Voskhod 2* while in orbit.   **ASTRO**

June 3–7,   The first American two-person crew in space, Virgil I. Grissom and
1965   John W. Young, carries out the first in-orbit maneuvers of a
             manned spacecraft, the *Gemini 3*.   **ASTRO**

June 3–7,   Edward H. White II becomes the first American to walk in space
1965   and the first human to use a personal propulsion pack during a
             space walk. His thirty-six-minute EVA (extravehicular activity) takes
             place outside his *Gemini 4* spacecraft.   **ASTRO**

Dec. 15,   Coming within one foot of each other, the *Gemini 6A* and the *Gemini
1965*   7* are the first manned spacecraft to rendezvous in space.   **ASTRO**

1965   Pheromones, artificial sex attractants, are developed for insect
        control.   **BIO**

1965   It is discovered that algae chloroplasts have their own DNA.   **BIO**

1965   French biochemist Jacques-Lucien Monod wins the Nobel Prize in physiology and medicine for his work with François Jacob and André-Michael Lwoff on the regulatory activities of genes. Monod is considered the discoverer of the operon system that controls bacteria gene action.   **BIO**

1965   Scientists now suspect the existence of "hotspots," junctures at tectonic plates through which heat leaks up into the ocean, and hotspots are in fact detected in the early 1970s.   **EARTH**

1965   Using computer power, Hugh C. Williams and his colleagues discover the first complete solution to the "cattle of the sun" problem posed by Archimedes about 300 B.C. The solution has in excess of 200,000 digits.   **MATH**

1965   American paleontologist Elso Sterrenberg Barghoorn discovers the first microfossils, the fossilized remains of ancient single-celled organisms dating as far back as 3.5 billion years.   **PALEO**

1965   Physicists Moo-Young Han and Yoichiro Nambu develop the concept of color charge, a property of quarks.   **PHYS**

1965   Psychologists Robert Melzack and Patrick Ward develop the gate control theory of pain, which holds that selective brain processes increase or decrease sensitivity to pain.   **PSYCH**

1965   Austrian-born psychoanalyst Anna Freud, the daughter of Sigmund Freud, publishes *Normality and Pathology in Childhood*, a cumulation of her theories on child psychotherapy and the prevention of mental illness.   **PSYCH**

1965   American pediatrician and psychoanalyst Donald Winnicott emphasizes that infancy is a critical time in human development that is relevant to later psychopathology.   **PSYCH**

....

"For more than half a century, the automobile has brought death, injury and the most inestimable sorrow and deprivation to millions of people."—Ralph Nader, American consumer advocate; 1965

....

1965   American consumer advocate Ralph Nader exposes the safety defects of American automobiles, particularly the Chevrolet Corvair, in his book *Unsafe at Any Speed*.   **TECH**

1965   In April, The United States launches SNAP-10A (Systems for Nuclear Auxiliary Power), the first and only American nuclear reactor to be placed in orbit. In contrast, the Soviet Union will launch thirty-three reactors into space from 1968 to 1988, most of them to power spy satellites. *See* 1978, Cosmos-954.   **TECH**

1965	On November 9, one of the biggest electrical blackouts in history occurs when a faulty relay in a Canadian power plant leads to a loss of electricity in New York City and much of the northeastern United States and southern Canada. **TECH**
1966	The U.S. *ESSA I* satellite becomes the first weather satellite capable of viewing the whole earth. **ASTRO**
Feb. 3, 1966	The Soviet unmanned spacecraft *Luna 9* makes the first soft landing on the moon. *See* July 20, 1969, *Apollo 11*, for the first manned lunar landing. **ASTRO**
1966	The Soviet unmanned spacecraft *Luna 10* completes the first orbit of the moon. *See* December 21–27, 1968, *Apollo 8*, for the first manned orbit. **ASTRO**
Mar. 16–17, 1966	The *Gemini 8* docks with an unmanned target vehicle in the first space docking. **ASTRO**
June 2, 1966	The unmanned spacecraft *Surveyor 1* becomes the first U.S. vehicle to land on the moon. It transmits photographs of the lunar surface for six weeks. **ASTRO**
1966	Austrian scientist Konrad Lorenz publishes his controversial book *On Aggression*. Lorenz, who pioneered the study of animal behavior (ethology), argues that animals—including humans—inherit many of their behavioral patterns such as aggression and maternal bonding. In this book he argues that the impersonal weapons of war have allowed humans to develop an unnatural level of aggression. **BIO**
1966	Robert Ardrey publishes *The Territorial Imperative*, which argues that humans, like other animals, are driven by territoriality. **BIO**
1966	In the United States, the first antiviral drug to block influenza infections, amantadine hydrochloride, is licensed. **MED**
1966	British psychiatrist Gordon Allen German sets up the first east-central African academic psychiatry unit, in Uganda. He will show that mental disorders are as prevalent in developing nations as in industrialized ones. **PSYCH**
1966	British-American chemist and psychologist Raymond Cattell publishes his *Handbook of Multivariate Experimental Psychology*. This research is the practical application of the Cattell 16PF personality inventory, one of the major personality tests used in North America. **PSYCH**
1966	U.S. gynecologist William Howell Masters and American psychologist Virginia Johnson publish the first of their reports on the psychology, physiology, and anatomy of human sexual activity, *Human Sexual Response*. They will devise methods of sex therapy after investigating human sexuality via the electroencephalograph (EEG), the electrocardiogram (ECG), and motion picture cameras in a laboratory setting. **PSYCH**

Oct. 6, 1966	A partial meltdown occurs at the Fermi nuclear reactor near Detroit, when a metal plate comes loose and blocks the cooling water. **TECH**

| 1967 | British astronomer Jocelyn Bell discovers the first pulsar, in the constellation Vulpecula. This object emitting intense, regular radio-wave pulses will turn out to be a rapidly rotating neutron star. **ASTRO** |

| 1967 | The unmanned Soviet *Venera 4* spacecraft is the first to enter the atmosphere of Venus. **ASTRO** |

| 1967 | The *Venera 4* parachutes a probe into the atmosphere of Venus, which is discovered to be composed mostly of carbon dioxide. The U.S. spacecraft the *Mariner 5* flies by Venus on the following day. **ASTRO** |

| Jan. 27, 1967 | The first deaths of U.S. astronauts in the line of duty take place when a flash fire in the *Apollo 1* space capsule during a test at Cape Kennedy, Florida, kills Virgil I. Grissom, Edward H. White II, and Roger Chaffee. **ASTRO** |

| Apr. 24, 1967 | The first human death during a space mission occurs when the Soviet *Soyuz 1* spacecraft crashes during reentry, killing cosmonaut Vladimir M. Komarov. **ASTRO** |

| 1967 | Sociobiologist Edward O. Wilson and R. H. MacArthur publish *The Theory of Island Biogeography*, marking the beginning of a school of ecology that focuses on biogeographical equilibrium, or balanced and stable ecosystems. **BIO** |

| 1967 | Austrian-born British molecular biologist Max F. Perutz and his colleague Hilary Muirhead build the first high-resolution model of the atomic structure of oxyhemoglobin. **BIO** |

| 1967 | British biologist John B. Gurden is the first to successfully clone a vertebrate, in this instance a South African clawed frog, using the technique of nuclear transplantation. **BIO** |

| 1967 | American geneticist Sewall Wright receives the National Medal of Science for his work in genetic studies and evolution research. He originated the mathematical theory of evolution which argues that mathematical chance, as well as mutation and natural selection, affect evolutionary change. **BIO** |

| 1967 | U.S. biochemists at the Roswell Park Memorial Institute in Buffalo, New York, discover the complex structure of a protein enzyme called ribonuclease that breaks down RNA. Since ribonuclease exerts control over cell growth, the discovery of its structure is thought to help explain why cancer cells spread. **BIO** |

1967	Harvard biophysicist Walter Gilbert, German-born biochemist Benno Müller-Hill, and molecular biologist Mark Ptashne isolate and identify for the first time two of the cell substances believed to control the process of making genes either operational or dormant. **BIO**
1967	On March 18, the U.S. oil tanker *Torrey Canyon* is grounded off the coast of Cornwall, England, creating an oil spill that damages 120 miles of British and French coastline. **EARTH**
1967	American cardiovascular surgeon René Favaloro develops the coronary artery bypass operation to graft on additional blood vessels in the heart to get around narrowed or obstructed arteries. It will come into general use as a treatment for coronary artery disease. **MED**
1967	American biochemist Maurice Hilleman develops a live-virus vaccine against mumps. **MED**
1967	By now (*see* 1945) fluoridation—the addition of fluoride to the water supply with the aim of combating tooth decay—has been widely adopted throughout the United States. **MED**
Dec. 3, 1967	South African cardiovascular surgeon Christiaan Barnard performs the first human heart transplant, in Cape Town. His patient, Louis Washkansky, lives for eighteen days before succumbing to postoperative pneumonia. **MED**
1967	Elwyn Simons discovers the skull of the primate *Aegyptopithecus*, which at 30 million years of age is the oldest known ancestor in the line leading to humans. **PALEO**
1967	American psychologist Aaron T. Beck designs the Beck Depression Inventory (BDI), a test to measure the depth of a person's depression. **PSYCH**
1967	Neuropsychologist Roger Sperry, at the California Institute of Technology (Caltech), reports on his research concerning the split brain. This type of radical surgery on patients with severe seizures involves severing the corpus callosum, a network of fibers that connects the brain's two hemispheres. As a result, each hemisphere operates in isolation. This research will lead to further studies of how each hemisphere specializes in processing information. **PSYCH**
1967	The Amana Refrigeration Co. introduces the first small microwave oven in the United States for home use. **TECH**
1968	The Soviet unmanned spacecraft *Zond 5* becomes the first to return to earth after orbiting the moon. **ASTRO**
1968	Astronomers at Green Bank, West Virginia, discover a pulsar or neutron star in the Crab Nebula, thus corroborating the Baade-Zwicky theory (*see* 1934) that neutron stars form in the aftermath of supernovae (*see also* 1054, supernova). **ASTRO**

....

"A scientist can discover a new star but he cannot make one.
He would have to ask an engineer to do it for him."
—**Gordon L. Glegg, American engineer; 1969**

....

1968	Using the U.S. Third Orbiting Solar Observatory, astronomers discover gamma radiation emanating from the center of the Milky Way. **ASTRO**
1968	Scientists detect water and ammonia molecules in interstellar clouds, thereby showing that complex compounds can form in space. **ASTRO**
Nov. 8, 1968	The U.S. spacecraft *Pioneer 9*, launched today, will achieve an orbit around the sun and return solar-radiation data to the earth. **ASTRO**
Dec. 21–27, 1968	During the *Apollo 8* mission, U.S. astronauts Frank Borman, James A. Lovell Jr., and William A. Anders are the first humans to orbit the moon and the first to see its dark side, the one never visible from the earth. **ASTRO**
1968	The U.S. House of Representatives declares Lake Erie a "dead" lake, due to its pollution levels. **BIO**
1968	In August, University of Illinois chemical geneticist Sol Speigelman announces at the Twelfth International Congress of Genetics that he has developed the first method of observing evolution in a test tube. It will allow scientists not only to observe but to manipulate molecular events associated with evolutionary change under controlled laboratory conditions. **BIO**
1968	The U.S. government declares Bikini Island, the former site of nuclear bomb tests, to be "safe" and its displaced inhabitants return. Ten years later, however, the medical hazards of nuclear fallout are reassessed and the inhabitants again removed. **MED**
1968	American cardiovascular surgeons Charles Dotter and Melvin Judkins introduce angioplasty, the widening or unblocking of a blood vessel or heart valve by using a balloon catheter. **MED**
1968	American paleontologist Robert Bakker proposes that dinosaurs were warm-blooded and highly active, not cold-blooded and sluggish, as had been previously believed. Bakker's ideas will gradually gain adherents as well as detractors. **PALEO**
1968	U.S. physicists trap neutrinos emanating from the sun in an underground tank in South Dakota, but the quantities collected are only one-third that predicted by solar theory. **PHYS**

337

1968   American physicists Steven Weinberg and Sheldon Lee Glashow, with Pakistani physicist Abdus Salam, propose the electroweak theory, which gives a unified description of the electromagnetic and weak interactions.   **PHYS**

1968   American behaviorist B. F. Skinner writes about his technique of programmed instruction in *The Technology of Teaching*, which presents ordered information to students, each bit of which must be understood before the student can proceed. Many teaching machines will then be designed to incorporate Skinner's ideas.   **PSYCH**

1968   The three-digit emergency telephone number 911 is first used, in New York. Over the next two decades it will become widely instituted across the country. *See also* 1937, 999 distress signal.   **TECH**

1968   The Jacuzzi whirling bath is demonstrated in California by Jacuzzi Bros., a farm pump manufacturer.   **TECH**

1969   Astronomers Thomas Gold and Franco Pacini develop their theory that pulsars are neutron stars rotating at a rapid rate.   **ASTRO**

1969   Japanese geologists discover meteorites on the Antarctic ice cap.   **ASTRO**

Jan. 14–15, 1969   The Soviet *Soyuz 4* and *Soyuz 5* spacecraft are the first manned vehicles to dock in space.   **ASTRO**

May 18–26, 1969   In a dress rehearsal for the moon landing, the *Apollo 10* lunar lander descends to within fifty thousand feet of the moon's surface.   **ASTRO**

July 20, 1969   At 10:56 P.M. E.D.T. in the course of the July 16–24 *Apollo 11* mission, Neil A. Armstrong becomes the first human to set foot on the moon. Edwin E. "Buzz" Aldrin Jr. follows him onto the surface while Michael Collins orbits in the command module.   **ASTRO**

Oct. 11–13, 1969   The Soviet spacecraft *Soyuz 6, 7,* and *8* orbit simultaneously, in the first triple launch of manned spacecraft.   **ASTRO**

Nov.14–24, 1969   The U.S. spacecraft *Apollo 12* completes the second manned lunar landing, as Charles Conrad Jr. and Alan L. Bean become the third and fourth men on the moon.   **ASTRO**

1969   The modern five-kingdom classification of living things is by now firmly established. Organisms are grouped into the kingdoms of Monera or Prokaryotae (bacteria), Protista or Protoctista (algae, protozoans, slime molds), Fungi, Plantae, and Animalia.   **BIO**

1969   Exploratory researchers at Merck Laboratories in Rahway, New Jersey, and Rockefeller University in New York City announce independently that they have synthesized the enzyme ribonuclease for the first time.   **BIO**

1969   Harvard University research scientists report isolating of a gene from an organism.   **BIO**

Neil Armstrong, the first man on the moon. (*NASA*)

1969   American physicist Albert Ghiorso and his colleagues discover element 104, rutherfordium.   **CHEM**

1969   The American underwater laboratory Tektite I houses scientists studying the physiological and psychological reactions of humans to a hostile, isolated environment.   **EARTH**

1969   The U.S. oil tanker *Manhattan* becomes the first commercial ship to navigate the Northwest Passage.   **EARTH**

1969–1970   In a two-year voyage, Norwegian explorer Thor Heyerdahl sails across the Atlantic in the *Ra II*, a reed boat made in the ancient Egyptian fashion to demonstrate that such a voyage was possible in antiquity.   **EARTH**

1969   American experimental psychologist John Bowlby extends his earlier studies of childhood attachment and loss to the hospital setting. He identifies the separation stages of protest, despair, and detachment that occur when a child is hospitalized. His findings will lead to related research on the human grief process in death and dying.   **PSYCH**

1969   Chemical and biological warfare materials are banned from production in the United States by President Richard Nixon.   **TECH**

1970s   A series of Soviet *Venera* spacecraft—*Venera 8* (1972), *9* and *10* (1975), and *11* and *12* (1978)—study the surface and atmosphere of the planet Venus.   **ASTRO**

1970s   U.S. astronomer John A. Eddy, following up on the work of British astronomer Edward W. Maunder (*see* 1893), discovers that there have been several periods of very low sunspot activity throughout history, called Maunder minima. One such period occurred in 1645–1715, another in 1400–1510; both were also periods of extreme cold.   **ASTRO**

1970s   The cloning of plants from protoplasts becomes an active area of research.   **BIO**

1970s   Superovulation (hormone-induced excess) and embryo transfer become routine in the U.S. cattle industry. These steps increase cattle production by thousands of calves per year.   **BIO**

1970s   At General Electric, biochemist Ananda Chakrabarty develops oil-eating bacteria. This new strain will be the subject of a 1980 U.S. Supreme Court ruling stating that "a live, human-made microorganism is patentable subject matter."   **BIO**

1970s   American scientists at the Brookhaven National Laboratory on Long Island build a cell that contains both plant and animal cells.   **BIO**

1970s   Between now and the 1980s, biochemical systematics advance to reveal that a range of common animals once thought to be a single species is in fact complexes of several different species, based on DNA or protein differences.   **BIO**

1970s   Late in this decade, U.S. biochemists Sidney Altman and Thomas R. Cech discover independently that RNA is not just a passive carrier of genetic information but can process such information, actively promote chemical reactions, and even reproduce itself.   **BIO**

1970s   American researchers succeed in teaching sign language to two primates, Washoe the chimpanzee and Koko the gorilla. Scientists disagree whether the results prove that such animals are capable of authentic language or have merely undergone conditioning.   **BIO**

1970s   American cardiologists Meyer Friedman and Ray Rosenman are the first to identify a behavior pattern known as Type A, characterized by impatience, a rapid pace, and trying to do too many things at one time. It is suspected at the time that Type A behavior leads to cardiac risk and mental stress.   **PSYCH**

1970s   Assertiveness training in group settings is used to enhance individual social skills and self-concept. Its basis is the belief that when people react passively to others it can make them feel mistreated and used.   **PSYCH**

1970s–1990s Psychological self-help groups become widespread. The common therapeutic factors of these groups are helping others, a shared experience, support networks, information sharing, gaining feedback, and learning special methods of coping.   **PSYCH**

1970s   The basic action of the neurotransmitter called GABA (gamma-aminobutyric acid) is worked out. Unlike most other transmitters, GABA works as an inhibitor and, along with serotonin (the transmitter involved in sleep and sensory perception), helps keep the mind from running amok.   **PSYCH**

1970s   British psychologist Lawrence Weiskrantz studies blindsight, a visual phenomenon occurring in people who develop visual-field gaps following brain injuries. Blindsight allows people to identify objects in their blind areas without their being aware of it, because they have vision they do not know they have. Weiskrantz's experiments suggest that different aspects of vision are separately processed and vision itself is processed separately from awareness.   **PSYCH**

1970   American archaeologist J. M. Adovasio claims to have discovered human remains at Meadowcroft, Pennsylvania, dating from 19,000 years ago, some 7,500 years earlier than previously known sites (*see* 1952, Clovis). Claims of similar antiquity will be made for other sites in the Americas but their dates will be disputed, leading in the 1990s to an unresolved controversy about the date of the first human migration to the Americas. Some will place it at about 12,000 years ago, others 35,000 years ago or even earlier.   **ARCH**

1970   A satellite observatory is launched to locate and study celestial X-ray sources. Information from the satellite provides evidence that Cygnus X-1, discovered in 1965, is the first known black hole.   **ASTRO**

1970   The Soviet *Venera 7* spacecraft becomes the first to land on the surface of Venus.   **ASTRO**

1970   British physicist Stephen William Hawking suggests that black holes may evaporate over long periods as they gradually release subatomic particles.   **ASTRO**

1970   Large reflecting telescopes are completed at Kitt Peak, Arizona, and Mauna Kea, Hawaii. A 100-meter (328-foot) radio telescope is completed at Bonn, Germany.   **ASTRO**

1970   The Chinese and Japanese launch their first artificial satellites. **ASTRO**

| 1970 | Sri Lanka–born American biochemist Cyril Ponnamperuma discovers several kinds of amino acids in a meteorite, showing that amino acids have been formed beyond the earth. **ASTRO** |

| Apr. 11–17, 1970 | The U.S. *Apollo 13* lunar mission is aborted when an oxygen tank malfunctions. After several tense days, the astronauts return safely to earth. **ASTRO** |

| 1970 | The so-called telomere hypothesis is proposed as an explanation for certain characteristics of cellular aging. This argument states that a small amount of DNA from telomeres (chromosomal ends) is lost each time DNA replicates itself, and these accumulated deletions eventually result in cellular senescence. **BIO** |

| 1970 | Molecular biologists at the University of California–Berkeley report fusing together two separate genes inside bacteria to form a single enzyme-producing gene that performs the functions of both genes. They claim this is an important clue as to how evolution occurred at the most basic level of molecular activity. **BIO** |

| 1970 | The human growth hormone is synthesized. **CHEM** |

| 1970 | American physicist Albert Ghiorso and his colleagues discover element 105, hahnium. **CHEM** |

| Apr. 21, 1970 | The first Earth Day is celebrated. In the 1970s an international "green movement" develops, expressing concern about environmental damage. **EARTH** |

| Nov. 13, 1970 | Cyclones originating in the Bay of Bengal hit the low-lying islands and coasts of Bangladesh, killing an estimated 200,000 to 500,000 people. **EARTH** |

| 1970 | French anthropologist Louis Dumont publishes *Homo Hierarchicus*, an influential study of the caste system in India. **SOC** |

| c. 1970 | Researchers develop techniques to use fine glass fibers to conduct light, which can be modulated to carry pulses of information. This technology, called fiber optics, will revolutionize communication in coming decades, replacing copper wires with cheaper, less bulky glass fibers. **TECH** |

| 1970 | British-born U.S. physicist Albert Victor Crewe invents the scanning electron microscope. **TECH** |

| 1970 | The Concorde supersonic jet airplane reaches speeds of two times the speed of sound. **TECH** |

| 1970 | U.S. scientist Ted Hoff, working for Intel, invents the microprocessor, a silicon chip containing the central processor of a computer. The versatile chip will lead to the proliferation of small, inexpensive computers for home and business use. Intel microprocessors will be marketed commercially for the first time in 1971. **TECH** |

1971   Italian astronomer Paolo Maffei discovers Maffei One and Maffei Two, member galaxies of the Local Group.   **ASTRO**

1971   Orbiting Mars, the U.S. unmanned *Mariner 9* spacecraft becomes the first such vehicle to orbit another planet.   **ASTRO**

1971   American physicist Irwin Ira Shapiro discovers what are now known as superliminal sources—components of quasars that appear to be moving away from each other faster than the speed of light.   **ASTRO**

1971   British physicist Stephen Hawking proposes the existence of mini black holes formed when the universe was created. He suggests that these might be detected by a final explosive evaporation that would take place only now, after 15 billion years of slow evaporation.   **ASTRO**

Jan. 31,   *Apollo 14*, launched today and returning to earth on February 9,
1971   completes the third successful manned lunar landing, the first after the near-disaster of *Apollo 13*.   **ASTRO**

Apr. 18,   The Soviet Union launches the *Salyut 1*, the first earth-orbiting
1971   space station. Cosmonauts occupy the station for twenty-three days (June 7–29) but are killed during reentry into the earth's atmosphere.   **ASTRO**

June 2–19,   Soviet cosmonauts aboard the *Soyuz 9* set a new space endurance
1971   record of more than seventeen and a half days.   **ASTRO**

July 26,   *Apollo 15*, launched today and returning to earth on August 7, com-
1971   pletes the fourth successful manned lunar landing. Its Lunar Rover becomes the first wheeled vehicle to ride on the moon's surface.   **ASTRO**

1971   Sociobiologist Edward O. Wilson publishes his fundamental work on insect societies.   **BIO**

1971   British ethologist Jane Goodall publishes *In the Shadow of Man*, an account of her years observing the chimpanzees of Gombe Stream National Park, Tanzania.   **BIO**

1971   The use of the insecticide DDT (dichloro-diphenyltrichloroethane) is banned in the United States for all but essential uses because of its being linked with severe bird and animal birth anomalies.   **BIO**

1971   Thousands of gallons of dioxin waste from an herbicide factory spill on the roads of Times Beach, Missouri, causing a major toxic chemical disaster. By 1983 the town's entire population will be evacuated.   **EARTH**

1971   British paleontologist Harry Whittington begins a major reexamination of Charles Walcott's interpretation of the Cambrian fossils of the Burgess Shale (*see* 1909). Over the next two decades, Whittington and colleagues Simon Conway Morris and Derek Briggs will propose that the Burgess Shale fauna include many phyla (basic body plans) that are now extinct, in contradiction to Walcott's view that these fauna were early examples of present-day phyla. *See also* 1989, Gould.   **PALEO**

1971   B. F. Skinner publishes *Beyond Freedom and Dignity*, repeating his belief that behavioral free will is an illusion. In it he argues that when humans are behaving freely they are free only from negative reinforcement; their behavior is still dependent on positive reinforcement from their past and is always shaped by the expected consequences.   **PSYCH**

1971   The National Railroad Passenger Corp., also known as Amtrak, is appointed by Congress to assume all U.S. passenger train business to stem the decline of private passenger rail service as railroads face increased competition from planes, buses, and cars.   **TECH**

1971   Chicago's Union Stockyards close, ending the city's century-old role in meat production.   **TECH**

Apr. 16–27,   *Apollo 16* completes the fifth manned lunar landing.   **ASTRO**
1972

Dec. 7–19,   U.S. spacecraft *Apollo 17* completes the sixth and last manned lunar landing.   **ASTRO**
1972

1972   The Marine Protection, Research, and Sanctuaries Act, or more familiarly the Ocean Dumping Act, gives the U.S. Environmental Protection Agency and the National Oceanic and Atmospheric Administration important control over waste dumping. It is an early effort to protect delicate oceanic ecosystems.   **BIO**

1972   The first of a series of U.S. *Landsat* satellites is launched to study the earth, including its mineral and agricultural resources.   **EARTH**

Dec. 23,   An earthquake in Managua, Nicaragua, destroys much of the center
1972   of the capital, killing at least five thousand people. The Somoza government fails to distribute internationally provided relief supplies.   **EARTH**

1972   The lumpectomy procedure is introduced for the treatment of breast cancer. Instead of removing the entire breast, this operation removes only the cancerous tissue and leaves the remaining part of the breast intact.   **MED**

B. F. Skinner in his lab. (*B. F. Skinner Foundation, Harvard University*)

1972   American paleontologists Niles Eldredge and Stephen Jay Gould
            publish their theory of punctuated equilibrium, which holds that
            evolution proceeds through relatively short bursts of rapid change
            followed by long periods of stasis.   **PALEO**

1972   American physicist Murray Gell-Mann establishes quantum chromo-
            dynamics (QCD), a theory describing how quarks combine to form
            hadrons in terms of a characteristic called color charge.   **PHYS**

1972   In October, using laser beams, American physicist Kenneth M.
            Evenson and his colleagues obtain a new level of precision in mea-
            suring the speed of light: 186,282.3959 miles per second.   **PHYS**

1972	The first computerized axial tomography (CAT) scanner goes into operation to study the brain. This combined use of a computer and X rays provides physicians with clearer, more detailed information about tissue than X rays alone can. The CAT scanner's inventors are British engineer Godfrey Hounsfield and American physicist Allan Cormack. **PSYCH**
1972	In his doctoral work at MIT, artificial intelligence researcher Terry Winograd develops one of the best-known computer language programs, which he calls SHRDLU. With it he tries to simplify words and make them less likely to be misinterpreted. **PSYCH**
1973–1974	Astronauts aboard the U.S. space station *Skylab* set a new space endurance record of 84 days. **ASTRO**
1973	The unmanned U.S. spacecraft *Mariner 10* becomes the first to visit the two planets Venus and Mercury, transmitting the first television pictures of Venus and completing the first flyby of Mercury. **ASTRO**
1973	The Soviet unmanned spacecraft *Mars 2* and *3* are the first to enter the atmosphere of Mars. The capsules land but stop transmitting shortly after that. *See* 1976, *Viking 1* and *2*. **ASTRO**
1973	American physicist Edward P. Tryon proposes his theory that the universe originated as a random quantum fluctuation in a vacuum, given the prediction of quantum mechanics that particles can appear and disappear in a vacuum. **ASTRO**
May 14,* 1973	The U.S. launches *Skylab*, its first orbiting space station. **ASTRO**
Dec. 3, 1973	After passing through the asteroid belt, the U.S. unmanned spacecraft *Pioneer 10* (launched March 3, 1972) becomes the first probe to fly past Jupiter. In 1986, it will also become the first man-made craft to leave the solar system. **ASTRO**
1973	For the first time, a calf is created from a frozen embryo. **BIO**
1973	Genetic engineering begins when American biochemists Stanley Cohen and Herbert Boyer show that if DNA is broken into fragments and combined with new genes, these genes can be inserted into bacterial cells, where they will reproduce whenever the cells divide in two. **BIO**
Oct. 1973	Many industrialized countries receive a rude awakening about energy dependence when an oil embargo from now to March 1974 by the Organization of Petroleum Exporting Countries (OPEC) touches off energy shortages. **EARTH**

1973   Pakistani physicist Abdus Salam suggests that a Grand Unified Theory (GUT) attempting to combine the strong, weak, and electro-magnetic interactions would imply that protons are slightly unstable and will occasionally decay to positrons and neutrons. The first GUT is presented in 1974 (*see* Glasbow and Georgi).   **PHYS**

1973   Physicists predict the existence of solitons, which are stable, particle-like, solitary wave states.   **PHYS**

1973   Physicist Paul Musset and his colleagues discover neutral currents in neutrino reactions, a discovery that tends to confirm the electroweak theory.   **PHYS**

1973   Physicist David Politzer theorizes that quarks exhibit asymptotic freedom in that the forces between them become weaker as the distance between them grows shorter, then vanishes entirely when the distance reaches zero.   **PHYS**

1973   Scottish scientists at Aberdeen University isolate endorphins, which, with a structure and action similar to morphine, act as the brain's own opiate. Endorphins will come to be considered natural painkillers.   **PSYCH**

1973–1976   The first examples of neurotransmitters are isolated. The discovery of these molecular substances, which serve as information processors in the brain, will provide neuroscientists with the material to describe and evaluate fundamental aspects of cognition.   **PSYCH**

1973   Anthropologist Clifford Geertz publishes his *The Interpretation of Culture*, which outlines an influential approach to the study of cultural symbols.   **SOC**

1973   American physicists build a continuous-wave laser that can be tuned or modulated.   **TECH**

1973   The Universal Product Code (UPC) system is promoted by U.S. supermarket owners and food producers to speed the process of checking by electronically scanning the price of products.   **TECH**

1974   The U.S. unmanned spacecraft *Pioneer 11* transmits the first close-up color photographs of Jupiter, then travels on to Saturn (*see* 1979).   **ASTRO**

1974   U.S. astronomer Charles Kowal discovers Leda, the thirteenth known satellite of Jupiter. In 1975, he finds a fourteenth satellite.   **ASTRO**

1974   The skeleton structure of a cell, its cytoskeleton, is revealed for the first time by using monoclonal antibodies and fluorescence.   **BIO**

1974   Scientists in the United States and the Soviet Union discover element 106.   **CHEM**

1974   American scientists F. Sherwood Rowland and Mario Molina show that chlorofluorocarbons, or CFCs, such as Freon (*see* 1930, Midgley) released from spray cans and refrigeration units can erode the ozone layer in the upper atmosphere, permitting more ultraviolet (UV) radiation to reach the earth's surface. Such an increase in UV rays could raise the incidence of skin cancer and eye cataracts and also disrupt ecosystems by destroying ocean plankton and soil bacteria. Concerned about protecting the ozone layer, the United States bans the use of CFCs in spray cans.   **EARTH**

1974   Belgian mathematician Pierre Deligne proves the last of French mathematician André Weil's conjectures concerning algebraic topology (*see* 1946). Weil's conjecture is a generalized version of the Riemann hypothesis (*see* 1857), which remains unconfirmed.   **MATH**

1974   In East Africa, American paleontologist Donald Johanson discovers the partial skeleton of Lucy, an Australopithecine dating back more than 3 million years. Lucy would have been three and a half feet tall and walked erect. Her kind is given the species name *Australopithecus afarensis*. This skeleton is the most complete ever found for a hominid of this period.   **PALEO**

1974   U.S. physicists Samuel Ting and Burton Richter independently discover a new subatomic unit called the J-Psi particle that provides evidence for the existence of "charmed" quarks. *See* 1964, Glashow and Bjorken.   **PHYS**

1974   American physicist Martin L. Perl discovers the tau particle or tauon, a type of lepton.   **PHYS**

1974   Working independently, American physicists Burton Richter and Samuel Chao Chung produce particles that are shown to contain c-quarks (charmed quarks), counterparts of s-quarks (strange quarks), a discovery that lends support to quark theory.   **PHYS**

1974   Physicists Sheldon Lee Glashow and Howard Georgi set forth the first grand unified theory (GUT), unifying the strong, weak, and electromagnetic forces.   **PHYS**

1974   A silicon photovoltaic cell for harnessing solar power is developed by engineer Joseph Lindmayer, the head of Solarex, Inc.   **TECH**

1974   A text-editing computer with a cathode-ray tube video screen and its own printer is put on the American market by Vydek.   **TECH**

1975   Farmers in Shensi Province, China, discover the tomb of Chinese emperor Ch'in Shih Huang Ti (*d.* 210 B.C.), which proves notable for 7,500 life-sized terra-cotta human statues placed there as guards for the deceased emperor.   **ARCH**

1975   Astronomer Alan E. E. Rogers rediscovers the concept of very long baseline interferometry for improving the resolution of radio telescopes, an idea originally proposed, but not implemented, by Roger Jennison in 1953.   **ASTRO**

July 17, 1975   The first docking in space between U.S. and Soviet spacecraft occurs, as the *Soyuz 19* performs a rendezvous with an *Apollo* spacecraft. **ASTRO**

1975   U.S. gene researchers David Baltimore, Howard Temin, and Renato Dulbecco win a Nobel Prize for their work on interactions between tumor viruses and the genetic material of cells.   **BIO**

B.Y.O.C., OR BUILD YOUR OWN COMPUTER

*T*he first personal computer on the market had no keyboard, no monitor, and no software. It was simply a set of parts that the user assembled and programmed by flicking the little switches on its front panel. However inauspicious, the Altair computer, first marketed in 1975, marked the beginning of the personal computer industry.

The Altair was developed by Ed Roberts, owner of MITS, a struggling calculator company in Albuquerque, New Mexico. He knew that in 1971 scientists at Intel, a young company in northern California's Silicon Valley, had introduced something called a microprocessor, a silicon chip that contained the central processor of a computer. Because of its small size and versatility, it could potentially lead to a new generation of small, inexpensive computers, but the leading computer manufacturers saw no market for such things.

In the midst of a calculator price war, Roberts was desperate for a new product, so he built a small computer based on Intel's 8080 microprocessor. Called the Altair and sold at the ridiculously low price of five hundred dollars, the computer first appeared on the cover of Popular Electronics magazine in January 1975. Within weeks, Roberts's company could barely keep up with demand. Altair enthusiasts formed clubs to discuss the product, write programs, and design add-on devices. As one member of Silicon Valley's Homebrew Club said, "You read about technological revolutions, the Industrial Revolution, and here was one of those sort of things happening and I was a part of it."

That member was Stephen Wozniak, who, with Steve Jobs, invented a computer inspired by the Altair. In 1977 the second version of that machine, the Apple II, became the first computer on the market to be accessible not just to hobbyists but to the general public. From then on, computers increasingly became a visible part of everyday life.

1975 | Argentinean-born British geneticist César Milstein announces the use of genetic cloning to create monoclonal antibodies (MABs). This cloning process allows antibodies to be custom-made to neutralize one specific antigen. **BIO**

1975 | U.S. mathematician Benoit Mandelbrot coins the term *fractals* to describe irregular mathematical patterns and structures generated by a process that involves successive subdivision. **MATH**

1975 | Mitchell J. Feigenbaum discovers Feigenbaum's number (approximately 4.6692), the ratio that the consecutive differences of iterated functions tend to approach. **MATH**

1975 | The Betamax, a home video recorder, is introduced to the market by the Sony Corp. of Japan. **TECH**

1975 | The first personal computer, the Altair, is put on the market by American inventor Ed Roberts. **TECH**

1975 | Americans William Henry Gates III and Paul Gardner Allen found Microsoft, which will become the world's most successful manufacturer of computer software. **TECH**

1976 | The 6-meter (236-inch) reflecting telescope on Mount Semirodriki in the U.S.S.R. becomes the world's largest but remains inoperative, due to technical problems. **ASTRO**

1976 | The U.S. unmanned spacecraft *Viking 1* and *2* are the first to complete successful landings on Mars (see 1973, *Mars 2* and *3*), transmitting back pictures of the planet's surface. The *Viking 1* lands on July 20, *Viking 2* on Sept. 3. Both craft continue to operate for several years, going silent by 1982. **ASTRO**

1976 | U.S. astronomers discover rings around the planet Uranus. **ASTRO**

1976 | Astronomers discover a covering of frozen methane on Pluto. **ASTRO**

1976 | Astronomer Tom Kibble predicts the existence of cosmic strings—very thin, massive objects millions of light-years in length formed by ripples in the universe following the Big Bang. These strings would account for the observed large-scale structure of the universe, including cosmic voids (regions of apparently empty space) and galactic superclusters. **ASTRO**

1976 | The assertion that four colors are needed to color any map is verified computationally. **MATH**

1976 | Cimetidine (Tagamet) becomes available for the treatment of peptic ulcers. It is the first of many drugs made to block the action of histamine and inhibit gastric secretions. By 1990 it will be the most prescribed drug in the United States. **MED**

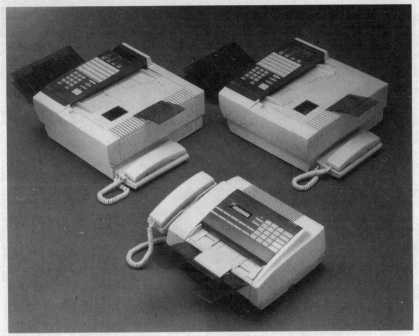

Fax machines. (*Okidata*)

1976   U.S. health authorities investigate a severe form of pneumonia after an outbreak of the disease kills twenty-nine American Legion convention attendees in Philadelphia. This so-called Legionnaires' disease is found to be caused by the *Legionella pneumophilia* bacteria, which thrives in a variety of moist conditions.   **MED**

1976   American scientist Baruch Blumberg is awarded the Nobel Prize in medicine for his discovery of the hepatitis B virus.   **MED**

1976   Chinese gynecologists develop the technique of chorionic villus sampling to aid in the early diagnosis of congenital birth defects. This test, involving a tissue sample from the placenta, provides results earlier than an amniocentesis.   **MED**

1976   American psychologist Herbert Benson publishes *The Relaxation Response*, concerning the physiological effect at work during therapeutic techniques used to control panic and general anxiety symptoms.   **PSYCH**

1976   Austrian psychologist Bruno Bettelheim publishes *The Uses of Enchantment*, in which he argues that the "evil" in fairy tales is valuable to children in that it can help them recognize and assimilate "good" and "bad" parts of their own psychological makeup.   **PSYCH**

The first Apple I computer. (*Apple Computer, Inc.*)

1976	American economist Milton Friedman wins the Nobel Prize. As a leader of the monetarist school, a branch of neoclassical economics that opposes Keynesian government intervention, he supports laissez-faire policies and argues that monetary policy (control of the money supply) is the most important factor in stabilizing the economy. **SOC**
1976	Americans Stephen Wozniak and Steven Jobs design a prototype for a computer that will be the first product of Apple Computer. **TECH**
1976	Facsimile or fax machines, which transmit type or images via telephone lines, gain in popularity for office use. **TECH**
Jan. 21, 1976	Air France and British Airways begin the first regularly scheduled commercial flights of supersonic transports (SSTs). Air France flies from Paris to Rio de Janeiro, British Airways from London to Bahrain. **TECH**
1977	American physicist Alan Guth postulates an inflationary universe, one that underwent exponential expansion after the Big Bang. **ASTRO**
1977	Beginning on December 10, Soviet cosmonauts set a new space endurance record of ninety-six days aboard the space station *Salyut 6*. **ASTRO**
1977	Scientists aboard the submersible *Alvin* discover deep ocean vents near the Galapagos Islands, where hot, mineral-laden water spews into the sea. The vents sustain an ecology of sulfur-eating bacteria and other life forms, including large clams and tube worms. **EARTH**

1977	Amendments to the Clean Water Act give the U.S. Environmental Protection Agency more authority to regulate waste discharges into rivers, lakes, and coastal waters as awareness about pollution continues to grow. **EARTH**
1977	Physicist Leon Max Lederman discovers the upsilon particle, which supports the quark theory of baryons. **PHYS**
Feb. 4–6, 1977	At a Yale University conference on behavioral medicine a new branch of medicine formally comes into existence. As an extension of psychomatic medicine, behavioral medicine investigates the psychosocial factors in illness and health. A well-known type of behavioral medicine is biofeedback. **PSYCH**
1977	The Apple II computer is marketed by American inventors Stephen Wozniak and Steve Jobs, the first personal computer to be accessible not just to hobbyists but to the public at large. *See also* 1975, the Altair, and 1976, Apple. **TECH**
Aug. 23, 1977	The first successful man-powered aircraft, the *Gossamer Condor*, invented by American Paul MacCready, is flown three miles by Bryan Allen. **TECH**
1978	The Soviet satellite *Cosmos-954*, containing a nuclear reactor, falls to earth, showering Canada with radioactive debris. **ASTRO**
1978	Vladimir Remek of Czechoslovakia, aboard the Soviet *Soyuz 28*, becomes the first person in space who is not from the United States or the Soviet Union. **ASTRO**
1978	U.S. astronomer James Christy discovers Charon, Pluto's only satellite. **ASTRO**
1978	The first known satellite of an asteroid is discovered orbiting the asteroid Herculina. **ASTRO**
May 20, 1978	The U.S. robot spacecraft *Pioneer 12* is launched on a one-year mission to study Venus. Over the next fourteen years, it will send more than 100 gigabits of data, including radar pictures of most of the planet's surface, back to earth. *See* October 8, 1992. **ASTRO**
Dec. 9, 1978	The *Pioneer 13* U.S. robotic spacecraft, launched in August, now carries four probes into the atmosphere of Venus while its companion, *Pioneer 12*, relays data back to earth. **ASTRO**
1978	American molecular geneticists Daniel Nathans and Hamilton C. Smith along with Swiss geneticist Werner Arber win the Nobel Prize for their discovery of restriction enzymes and the enzymes' application to problems in molecular genetics. **BIO**
1978	The genome of the virus SV40 is determined, the first step in working out the human genome, which is a complete single set of chromosomes with its associated genes. **BIO**

1978   In England, the world's first successful human pregnancy by in vit-
            ro (test tube) fertilization comes to term as Louise Brown is deliv-
            ered by doctors Patrick Steptoe and Robert Edwards on July 25. **BIO**

1978   The United States launches the satellite *Sensat I* to study the earth's
            oceans.   **EARTH**

1978   British scientists introduce the Laparoscope, a type of endoscope
            used to examine the fallopian tubes, appendix, gallbladder, and liv-
            er for disease and obstruction.   **MED**

1978   In Montana, U.S. paleontologists John R. Horner and Bob Makela
            discover the first known nest of baby dinosaurs, indicating that di-
            nosaur babies were cared for by adults. The new species is called
            the *Maiasaura* ("Good mother lizard"). *See also* 1979, Horner. **PALEO**

1978   Using deuterium as fuel, the Princeton Large Torus nuclear fusion
            reactor attains a temperature of 60 million degrees F, for one-twen-
            tieth of a second. In so doing it reaches nearer to the temperature
            of the sun (100 million° F) than any other reactor, though it is still
            not a practical source of energy.   **TECH**

1979   Aboard the *Salyut 6*, Soviet cosmonauts begin a new space en-
            durance record of 175 days.   **ASTRO**

1979   The U.S. unmanned spacecraft *Voyager 1* and *Voyager 2*, launched
            in 1977, reach the planet Jupiter, transmitting back to earth spec-
            tacular images and abundant information. Among the discoveries
            are a ring around the planet, two new moons, and details of the
            surfaces of Io, Ganymede, Europa, and Callisto, the four moons
            first observed by Galileo in 1610. Both spacecraft will go on to
            Saturn and Uranus, in 1980–1981 and 1986. Then *Voyager 2* will
            go on to Neptune in 1989.   **ASTRO**

1979   The U.S. unmanned spacecraft *Pioneer 11* becomes the first probe
            to reach Saturn, where it discovers several new moons and the
            planet's magnetic field.   **ASTRO**

1979   British physician Dick Rees, using the nine-banded armadillo as a
            source of the vaccine organism, discovers the first leprosy vaccine. **MED**

1979   From excess traces of iridium in late Cretaceous rocks, American
            scientist Luis Walter Alvarez theorizes that a large comet or aster-
            oid struck the earth 65 million years ago, raising clouds of dust that
            reduced the amount of solar radiation penetrating the atmosphere
            and triggering the mass extinctions of that period. Among the vic-
            tims of this hypothetical meteorite were the dinosaurs. *See also*
            1991, Sigardsson.   **PALEO**

1979   From now into the 1980s, American paleontologist John Horner, digging in Montana, will discover evidence of maiasaur (*see* 1978, Horner) colonial nesting grounds and herding behavior. This herd is believed to have comprised ten thousand dinosaurs. Horner will also discover egg clutches laid by hypsilophodontid dinosaurs. His findings will provide new insight into the social behavior of dinosaurs.   **PALEO**

1979   Scientists discover evidence of gluons, the exchange particles that bind quarks together.   **PHYS**

1979   The World Health Organization publishes its *International Classification of Diseases* (ICD-9-CM), which covers mental diseases and will prove compatible with the U.S. classification system DSM-III. *See* 1952, American Psychiatric Association.   **PSYCH**

1979   The American Psychological Association gives its Distinguished Scientific Award to South Africa–born psychiatrist Joseph Wolpe, for his work in the systematic desensitization of military patients traumatized by combat.   **PSYCH**

Mar. 28, 1979   A partial meltdown occurs in Unit 2 of the Three Mile Island nuclear reactor near Harrisburg, Pennsylvania, as a result of design flaws, operator mistakes, and mechanical failure. Some radioactive material is released and nearly 150,000 people are evacuated from the surrounding area.   **TECH**

1980s   Unmanned flights to Venus in this decade include the Soviet spacecraft *Venera 15* and *16* (1983). In 1986 the American spacecraft *Vega 1* and *2* drop probes on Venus while en route to Halley's Comet. *See* March 1986.   **ASTRO**

1980s   U.S. animal researchers begin using computer monitoring in animal studies to evaluate physiological and behavioral reactions to different experiences.   **BIO**

1980s   Late this decade, researchers at the Cetus Corp. of California develop the polymerase chain reaction (PRC), a genetic engineering technique that uses the enzyme DNA polymerase to make thousands of copies of small samples of genetic material.   **BIO**

1980s   The problem of acid rain begins to gain international attention. Acid rain, atmospheric water contaminated with industrial pollutants, causes long-term devastation to the environment.   **EARTH**

1980s   In terms of global averages, the 1980s go on record as the warmest decade since recording began in the nineteenth century.   **EARTH**

1980s   New discoveries are made about four-dimensional spaces, by such mathematicians as Mike Freedman, Simon Donaldson, and Clifford Taubes. Freedman finds a way of classifying some of these spaces, Donaldson shows that some are not smooth, and Taubes demonstrates that the infinity of nonsmooth four-dimensional spaces is uncountable.   **MATH**

1980s   Some employers provide access to mental health programs for their employees on a low-cost or even no-cost basis. These Employee Assistance Programs (EAPs) provide confidential counseling on a short-term basis. After sufficient time has elapsed, it will be shown that EAPs reduce absenteeism and resignations, thus providing a more stable work force.   **PSYCH**

1980s   U.S. neurophysiologist Michael M. Merzenich and American psychophysiologist Jon Kaas develop the idea that a "hard-wired" brain circuit—one with fixed neural connections—does not adequately explain phantom pain, the perception of pain from a missing limb. Experiments on a monkey with an amputated finger indicate that a remapping of the cortex takes place in such situations. *See also* 1991, Poris.   **PSYCH**

1980   The Very Large Array (VLA) radio telescope in Socorro, New Mexico, opens for business. Its resolution is equivalent to that of a single seventeen-mile dish.   **ASTRO**

1980   The quasar 3C273 is observed emitting gamma rays. Scientists then discover a nebulous region around it, suggesting that it may be in the center of a galaxy.   **ASTRO**

1980   Uwe Fink and others discover a thin atmosphere on Pluto.   **ASTRO**

1980   Aboard the *Salyut 6*, Soviet cosmonauts begin a new space endurance record of 184 days.   **ASTRO**

1980   The U.S. spacecraft *Voyager 1* flies by Saturn. With *Voyager 2*, which arrives there on August 27, 1981, this probe sends back copious information to the earth, discovering two new Saturnian moons in addition to the twelve known ones.   **ASTRO**

1980   Lymphocyte adhesion molecules are identified, leading to a burst of information on adhesion molecules' structure, expression, and function. This knowledge will prove vital to understanding intercellular interactions as they affect the human immune system and disease processes like AIDS.   **BIO**

1980   American molecular biologist Frederick Sanger wins the Nobel Prize in chemistry for his recent discovery of introns, made possible by new methods of determining the exact sequence of DNA and RNA nucleotides and molecules.   **BIO**

1980   The U.S. *Magsat* satellite maps the earth's magnetic field.   **EARTH**

May 18, 1980	The volcano Mount St. Helens in Washington State erupts, killing dozens of people. **EARTH**
1980	American mathematicians Robert Griess Jr. and his colleagues finish a comprehensive classification of finite simple groups, the building blocks of modern algebra. **MATH**
1980	Mathematicians Leonard Adleman and Robert Rumely develop a new test for prime numbers. **MATH**
c. 1980	Apheresis, a new technique of giving blood, is introduced. It allows only a single component like plasma, platelets, or white cells to be taken from circulation, reducing the chances of hepatitis transmission and rejection reactions. **MED**
1980	Physicians in Europe and the United States start removing bone marrow in patients getting large doses of radiation during therapy. This marrow is frozen and saved for later reimplantation. **MED**
1980	American and Soviet scientists suggest that neutrinos, previously believed to be massless, do have mass, possibly $\frac{1}{13,000}$ that of electrons. **PHYS**
1980	At Stanford University, the undulator, a device to increase the power of synchrotron radiation, is invented. **PHYS**
1980	Klaus von Klitzing discovers the quantum Hall effect, an observable example of quantum behavior. This effect involves discrete, not continuous, changes in resistance in a plate in a magnetic field at very low temperatures. **PHYS**
1980	British research psychiatrist T. J. Crow publishes his hypothesis that schizophrenia is a "two syndrome" disease process, and names two schizophrenia subtypes as Type I and Type II. The first condition has a sudden onset and responds well to antipsychotic medication; the second develops slowly and responds poorly to such drugs. **PSYCH**
1980	Scientists develop the scanning tunneling microscope, which can produce images of individual atoms on the surface of a material. **TECH**
1980	American businessman Ted Turner establishes the Cable News Network (CNN). Over the next few years, cable television stations of all kinds will proliferate. **TECH**
1980	Rollerblades, bootlike skates that each have a row of four wheels, are patented by Canadian hockey player Scott Olsen. **TECH**
1980	The first IBM personal computer, employing the Microsoft operating system MS-DOS, is marketed, with great success. **TECH**
Dec. 3, 1980	In the first long-distance solar-powered flight, American Janice Brown flies six miles in the aircraft *Solar Challenger*. **TECH**

1981	Stephen Boughn discovers variations of 0.3 percent in directions 90° apart in the cosmic background radiation. **ASTRO**
1981	Joseph P. Cassinelli discovers R136a, the most massive star yet known, 2,500 times more massive than the sun. **ASTRO**
1981	William B. Hubbard theorizes that there is a partial ring around Neptune. *See* confirmation: 1984, European Southern Observatory. **ASTRO**
1981	Hyron Spinrad and John Stauffer discover the most distant galaxies yet known, about 10 billion light-years away. **ASTRO**
1981	John Stocke discovers narrow-line quasars, which have spectra consisting of narrow emission lines. **ASTRO**
1981	A. D. Linde and, independently, Andreas Albrecht and Paul Steinhardt develop the theory of the new inflationary universe, building on the ideas of Alan Guth. *See* 1977. **ASTRO**
Apr. 12–14, 1981	The U.S. space shuttle *Columbia*, the first spacecraft designed for regular reuse, is launched on its first voyage around the earth, with Robert L. Crippen and John W. Young as crew. This shuttle is also known as the Space Transportation System (STS). **ASTRO**
1981	The U.S. spacecraft *Voyager 2* flies by Saturn. *See* 1980, *Voyager 1*. **ASTRO**
1981	Geneticists in China are the first to successfully clone a fish, the golden carp. **BIO**
1981	The entire sequence of nucleotides in the DNA of a mitochondrion, the cell's energy producer, is determined. **BIO**
1981	Soviet scientists discover element 107. **CHEM**
1981	Scientists develop a technique for producing "glassy," extraordinarily light and strong metal alloys from rapidly cooled molten metal. **CHEM**
1981	The first experimental work in Ocean Acoustic Tomography (CT scanning) is conducted by Robert C. Spindel and Peter F. Worcester studying such below-the-surface features of oceans as temperatures and currents. **EARTH**
1981	British scientists introduce the nuclear magnetic resonator, a diagnostic tool used extensively to study the brain and spinal cord, heart, major blood vessels, joints, eyes, and ears. This technique makes use of magnetic resonance imaging (MRI) to provide images of the body's organs and structures without surgery or radiation. **MED**
1981	A vaccine against serum hepatitis is approved in the United States. It will be in heavy demand well into the next decade. **MED**

SUPER VISION

*T*he world's most powerful microscope is the scanning tunneling microscope (STM) invented at the IBM Zürich laboratory in Switzerland in 1981. With a magnification factor of 100 million, it can resolve to one-hundredth the diameter of a single atom. This device works by holding a fine conducting probe to the surface of a sample. The probe's tip tapers down to a single atom. As electrons tunnel between the sample and the probe, the probe's movement yields a contour map of the surface.

In 1990, IBM scientists in California used an STM to reposition individual xenon atoms on a nickel surface. In the process they succeeded in producing the world's smallest graffiti—the initials IBM spelled out in atoms.

June 1981	The Centers for Disease Control in Atlanta, Georgia, report unusual cases of pneumocystis pneumonia among homosexual men. The cases will lead to the diagnosis of the new and deadly ailment called AIDS for Acquired Immune Deficiency Syndrome. *See* August 1982. **MED**
1981	Archaeologists in northern Spain discover the remains of a Neanderthal religious sanctuary. Its limestone altar and remnants of burnt offerings indicate that Neanderthals practiced religious rituals. **PALEO**
1981	In the Awash River Valley of Ethiopia hominid fossil bones are discovered dating from 4 million years ago. **PALEO**
1981	American psychologist Eleanor Rosch expands her Theory of Prototypes and Basic Level Categories, challenging Aristotle's classical theory of categorization and establishing categorization as a subfield of cognitive psychology. **PSYCH**
1981	U.S. economist James Tobin wins a Nobel Prize for his studies concerning the impact of financial markets on spending and investment. **SOC**
1981	Adam Heller, Barry Miller, and Ferdinand Thiel develop a liquid junction cell that converts up to 11.5 percent of solar energy to electric power. **TECH**
1982	The *Mary Rose*, the flagship of King Henry VIII, is raised from the bottom of England's Portsmouth Harbor, where French warships sank it on July 19, 1545. Artifacts found inside include musical instruments, board games, boots, and jerkins. **ARCH**

| 1982 | The unmanned U.S.S.R. spacecraft *Venera 13* and *14* complete the first successful soft landings on Venus.   **ASTRO** |

| Apr. 19, 1982 | The Soviet space station *Salyut 7* is launched, in which cosmonauts set a new space endurance record of 211 days.   **ASTRO** |

| 1982 | On the fifth flight of the U.S. space shuttle *Columbia*, its first operational mission, the crew successfully deploys a satellite.   **ASTRO** |

| 1982 | Genetically identical twin calves Chris and Becky are born. Their embryo was split by Colorado State University researcher Tim Williams when it was about a week old, then the two halves were implanted in the uteri of separate cows.   **BIO** |

| 1982 | West German scientists discover element 109.   **CHEM** |

| 1982 | Ronald Bracewell introduces a quicker version of the Hartley technique to replace the Fourier transform. It becomes known as the Hartley-Bracewell algorithm or the Hartley transform.   **MATH** |

| 1982 | British physician Michael Epstein identifies a herpeslike virus found in a type of lymphoma and associated with infectious mononucleosis, the Epstein–Barr virus.   **MED** |

| 1982 | The U.S. pharmaceutical company Eli Lilly markets the first genetically engineered human insulin.   **MED** |

| Aug. 1982 | A fatal immune system disorder transmitted sexually or through contaminated blood is termed AIDS (Acquired Immune Deficiency Syndrome). At the time of discovery, the highest-risk groups are homosexual men and intravenous drug users, but it will spread to other groups. Eroding the body's ability to fight disease, AIDS manifests itself through such ailments as pneumonia and a form of cancer known as Kaposi's sarcoma. Over the next few years it will become a worldwide epidemic.   **MED** |

THE HEAVIEST ELEMENT

*T*he element with the highest atomic number and heaviest atomic mass is provisionally known as unnilennium (Une). Produced by West German scientists on August 29, 1982, its atomic number is 109 (i.e., it has 109 protons in its nucleus) and its atomic mass 266.

Unnilennium is not, however, the most recent element to be discovered. Element 108, provisionally called unniloctium (Uno), was identified in West Germany in 1984 from observations of three atoms. Soviet scientists made a less well substantiated claim to have discovered this element later that year.

Dec. 2,   The first artificial heart is implanted, in the chest of a sixty-two-
1982   year-old Utah man suffering from heart disease. The operation is a
             success and the patient's discharge is planned, but ninety-two
             days after the surgery the patient develops a flulike illness and
             soon dies.   **MED**

1982   Physicist Blas Cabrera reports the discovery of a magnetic mono-
             pole, a particle with a single magnetic pole, as predicted by the
             Grand Unified Theory. However, this discovery is not confirmed by
             further experiments.   **PHYS**

1982   Roger Schank of Yale University publishes *Dynamic Memory: A
             Theory of Reminding and Learning in Computers and People*, in which
             he describes his attempts to develop and write an AI program capa-
             ble of understanding what it reads and of drawing upon its memo-
             ry to come to conclusions and answers as humans do.   **PSYCH**

1983   Scientists develop a chemical method of dating objects based on
             changes observable in obsidian.   **ARCH**

1983   The satellite known as IRAS is launched on a ten-month mission to
             search for the infrared radiation that would indicate planet forma-
             tion around stars beyond the sun. IRAS does discover such evi-
             dence, around the star Beta Pictoris, fifty-six light-years from the
             earth. Astronomers now believe that a disk of gas and dust sur-
             rounds this star. *See also* 1991, Hubble, and 1985, Houck. **ASTRO**

June 18,   Sally Ride becomes the first American woman in space, during the
1983   second flight of the second space shuttle *Challenger*. On this mis-
             sion a satellite is deployed and retrieved.   **ASTRO**

Aug. 30,   On its third mission, the space shuttle *Challenger* carries the first
1983   African-American in space, Guion Bluford Jr.   **ASTRO**

1983   U.S. geneticist Barbara McClintock is awarded the Nobel Prize for
             her discovery of mobile genes in the chromosomes of plants. **BIO**

1983   The world's first artificially made chromosome is created at
             Harvard University.   **BIO**

1983   The process of group transfer polymerization (GTP) is introduced. **CHEM**

1983   American scientist Carl Sagan and others theorize that a nuclear
             war could trigger a nuclear winter, in which fusion explosions raise
             clouds of dust that reduce sunlight enough to cause mass starvation
             and extinctions. This theory is inspired by Luis Alvarez's hypothesis
             (*see* 1979) that a meteorite collision indirectly exterminated the di-
             nosaurs.   **EARTH**

1983   American physician John E. Buster reports on an artificial insemination procedure in which a female donor receives the sperm of the prospective father, the sperm fertilizes the donor's ovum, and then the egg is gently washed out of the donor's uterus and implanted in the uterus of the infertile patient. Buster claims a 40 percent success rate for this technique.   **MED**

1983   In Kenya, paleontologists find a jawbone of *Sivapithecus*, a primate 16 to 18 million years old.   **PALEO**

1983   Italian physicist Carlo Rubbia and Dutch physicist Simon van der Meer discover three exchange particles with the mass predicted by the electroweak theory: the two W bosons, one positive (W^+) and one negative (W^-), and the neutral Z boson (Z^0).   **PHYS**

1983   The Center for the Study of Language and Information is established at Stanford University, combining resources from such language-related fields as psychology, philosophy, linguistics, and computer science.   **PSYCH**

1983   French neurologist A. Roch-Lecours discovers that humans are born with two language areas in the brain. The right hemisphere has a certain potential that is lost in adult life as the left begins to dominate early in life, probably within the first year.   **PSYCH**

1983   Cellular telephones, made by Motorola, are first test-marketed in Chicago. These phones use computers and multiple transmitters to receive and transfer calls.   **TECH**

1983   Aspartame-based Nutrasweet is used for the first time to sweeten beverages. In the next decade it will be used in a variety of foods, including salad dressings and desserts.   **TECH**

1984   Archaeologists discover Altit-Yam, an underwater site off the coast of Israel that preserves the remains of an 8,000-year-old settlement.   **ARCH**

1984   Lindow man is discovered in a peat bog in Germany. This 2,200-year-old preserved body is believed to be that of a Druid victim of human sacrifice.   **ARCH**

1984   Scientists at the European Southern Observatory, near Santiago, Chile, confirm the existence of a partial ring around Neptune, as suggested by William Hubbard in 1981.   **ASTRO**

1984   J. C. Bhattacharyya in India discovers two more rings of Saturn.   **ASTRO**

Feb. 3–7, 1984   On the fourth *Challenger* mission, two astronauts use jet-propelled backpacks in the first untethered space walks.   **ASTRO**

Feb. 8, 1984   Soviet cosmonauts Leonid Kizim, Vladimir Solovyov, and Oleg Atkov begin setting a new space endurance record, spending 237 days (until October 2, 1985) aboard the *Salyut 7*.   **ASTRO**

| Apr. 7, 1984 | Astronauts on the fifth *Challenger* mission, launched today, deploy the Long Duration Exposure Facility, an orbiting platform designed for long-range space experiments. On the same mission a disabled satellite is captured, repaired, and redeployed for the first time. **ASTRO** |

| Aug. 30, 1984 | The *Discovery*, the third space shuttle, makes its first voyage. **ASTRO** |

| 1984 | Large-scale biological research begins in private industry with the establishment of the Monsanto Life Sciences Research Center in Missouri built to create new drugs, crop plants, and microbial pesticides. **BIO** |

| 1984 | American scientist Allan Wilson at the University of California–Berkeley clones a pair of gene fragments from a preserved pelt of an animal that has been extinct for hundreds of years, the South African quagga, related to the zebra. **BIO** |

| 1984 | Sheep are successfully cloned. **BIO** |

| 1984 | U.S. geneticists analyzing DNA find that chimpanzees are more closely related to humans than either are to gorillas or other apes; the genetic difference is 1 percent. From this evidence it is deduced that humans and chimpanzees diverged from a common ancestor some 5 to 6 million years ago. **BIO** |

....

"Society increasingly has neglected the substructure of biology, to its own peril."—Edward O. Wilson, American entomologist and sociobiologist; 1984

....

| 1984–1985 | Severe droughts lead to famine in Ethiopia–Eritrea. The famine is accompanied by epidemic disease and complicated by the refusal of warring factions to allow free passage of aid shipments. More than one million people die. **BIO** |

| 1984 | West German scientists discover element 108. **CHEM** |

| 1984 | An electrically conductive polymer called MEEP is introduced, which will be applied to the manufacture of lightweight batteries. **CHEM** |

| Dec. 3, 1984 | In Bhopal, India, a leak of lethal methyl isocyanate gas from a Union Carbide plant creates a toxic cloud over the city, killing more than 3,500 people and injuring at least 200,000 more. **EARTH** |

| 1984 | In April, French scientist Luc Montagnier of the Pasteur Institute in Paris and Robert Gallo, a physician with the U.S. National Cancer Institute, announce their discovery of a virus believed to cause AIDS. They call it HTLV-III or HIV, for human immunodeficiency virus. A dispute will arise over who initially discovered the virus, with the French scientist being officially credited in 1987. **MED** |

1984   Near Lake Turkana, Kenya, British paleontologist Richard Leakey discovers the nearly complete skeleton of Turkana boy, who lived some 1.6 million years ago. He is seen as one of the earliest confirmed specimens of *Homo erectus*, though some classify him as *Homo ergaster*, a closely related species. **PALEO**

1984   A fossilized jawbone found by Andrew Hill in Kenya is believed to come from a 5-million-year-old specimen of *Australopithecus afarensis*, the earliest known hominid. **PALEO**

1984   U.S. scientist D. Schechtman and others discover the first quasicrystal, a crystal-like substance that violates the rules for crystal patterns. **PHYS**

1984   The first one-megabit random access memory (RAM) chip is developed in the United States by Bell Laboratories. It stores four times as much data as any chip produced to date. **TECH**

1985   The luxury ocean liner *Titanic* is located on the ocean bottom in the North Atlantic. Using a remote-controlled camera, French and American oceanographers study this ship that sank in 1912 after hitting an iceberg. **ARCH**

1985   Construction begins on the Keck telescope, the world's largest, on Mauna Kea in Hawaii. **ASTRO**

1985   James R. Houck discovers eight infrared galaxies, located by the IRAS satellite. *See* 1983. **ASTRO**

1985   Mark Morris discovers string-shaped radio sources, possibly low-energy cosmic strings (*see* 1976, Kibble) at the center of the Milky Way. **ASTRO**

1985   Observing an eclipse of Pluto by its satellite Charon, Edward F. Tedesco determines that Pluto's diameter is less than nineteen hundred miles. **ASTRO**

1985   Neil Turok theorizes that cosmic strings are responsible for the formation of the groups of galaxies called Abell clusters. **ASTRO**

1985   The *Atlantis*, the fourth space shuttle, makes its first flight. **ASTRO**

c. 1985 The U.S. Department of Agriculture announces the success of the first bioinsecticide. **BIO**

1985   Indian-born American botanist Subhash Minocha succeeds in producing clones of a Venus flytrap. **BIO**

1985   American zoologist Dian Fossey is murdered, probably by enemies made during her years of protecting the mountain gorillas of Rwanda's Virunga Mountains from poachers. Her years observing the gorillas, beginning in 1967, were described in *Gorillas in the Mist* (1983). **BIO**

Nova, the world's most powerful laser, in 1985. (*Lawrence Livermore National Laboratory, University of California*)

ELEPHANT TALK

*I*n 1985, while studying a herd of elephants, Cornell University animal researcher Katherine Payne detected a spasmodic throbbing in the air that seemed to correspond with movements of the elephants' foreheads. Further study with ultrasonic recording equipment showed that the sound and the movements were not coincidental. Elephants in fact communicate by using low-frequency sounds. They can locate each other with this technique even when initially separated by great distances, and male elephants use it to find ready-to-mate females that are miles out of smelling range.

1985   American chemist Richard Smalley and British chemist Harry Kroto discover buckminsterfullerene, a third form of pure carbon (in addition to graphite and diamond) composed of hollow, geodesic, spherical molecules of sixty atoms each. Chemists foresee a wide range of applications in industry and medicine for these "buckyballs" and for related forms of pure carbon, collectively known as fullerenes. The molecules are named in honor of American architect R. Buckminster Fuller, inventor of the geodesic dome.   **CHEM**

1985   U.S. researchers report the discovery of lanxides, substances with characteristics of both metal and ceramics.   **CHEM**

1985   The British Antarctic Expedition detects a "hole" that forms annually in the ozone layer above Antarctica. The opening represents a substantial reduction below the naturally occurring concentration of ozone.   **EARTH**

1985   Positron Emission Tomography (PET) scans are developed to reveal the metabolic activity levels of the brain and heart. These scans show the rate at which abnormal and healthy tissues consume glucose and other biochemicals.   **MED**

Aug. 1985   The National Institutes of Health suggests that other viruses, in addition to HTLV-III (HIV), may cause AIDS. *See* April 1984.   **MED**

Dec. 1985   Researchers at the University of California–San Francisco announce that passage of the AIDS virus is blocked by using condoms.   **MED**

1985   In an underground test, a nuclear X-ray laser produces X rays 1 million times brighter than previously obtained.   **PHYS**

1985   Psychiatrist Leopold Bellak proposes that many supposed cases of schizophrenia are misdiagnoses, claiming that as many as 10 percent of the schizophrenia cases diagnosed are really examples of what is now called attention-deficit disorder (ADD).   **PSYCH**

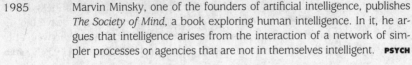

1985	Marvin Minsky, one of the founders of artificial intelligence, publishes *The Society of Mind*, a book exploring human intelligence. In it, he argues that intelligence arises from the interaction of a network of simpler processes or agencies that are not in themselves intelligent. **PSYCH**
1986	Archaeologists in Mexico discover a stone stele from about A.D. 1, inscribed with writing in an undecipherable language. **ARCH**
1986	Harold L. Dibble develops a computerized surveying system, based on an electronic theodolite (a surveying device for measuring horizontal and vertical angles), for use in archaeological digs. **ARCH**
1986	At Tell Leilan, in northern Mesopotamia, archaeologist Harvey Weiss discovers the largest cache of cuneiform tablets since the 1930s. These 1,100 tablets are inscribed in the exinct Semitic language Akkadian and date from the eighteenth century B.C. **ARCH**
1986	Astronomers discover that the Milky Way and its neighboring galaxies in the local supercluster are moving toward a hypothetical Great Attractor, a point in the direction of the Southern Cross. *See* 1990. **ASTRO**
1986	The U.S. spacecraft *Voyager 2* flies by Uranus, sending pictures and information back to earth. Ten new moons of Uranus are discovered. **ASTRO**

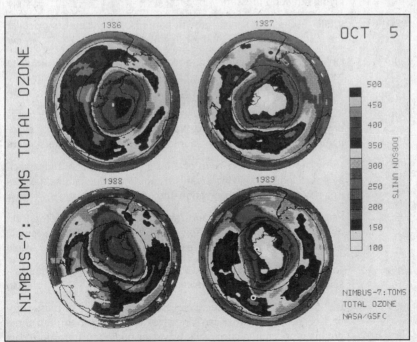

The ozone layer at different times. (*NASA*)

1986
: The U.S. unmanned spacecraft *Pioneer 10*, launched fourteen years ago in 1972, becomes the first human-made object to leave the region of the solar system where the planets orbit. Along the way it became the first craft to fly past Jupiter, in 1973. *See also* 1993.   **ASTRO**

Jan. 28, 1986
: In the worst space flight disaster in history, the space shuttle *Challenger* explodes seventy-three seconds after takeoff, killing its crew of seven, including teacher Christa McAuliffe.   **ASTRO**

Feb. 20, 1986
: The Soviet Union launches the *Mir* space station, in which cosmonauts will set new records for continuous habitation in space. **ASTRO**

Mar. 1986
: Several spacecraft make close approaches to Halley's Comet, including the Japanese *Suisei* on March 8 and *Sakigake* (March 10) probes and the European Space Agency *Giotto* probe (March 13).   **ASTRO**

1986
: The U.S. Department of Agriculture grants the first license to market a living organism produced by genetic engineering. It is a virus to vaccinate against a herpes disease in swine, registered to the Biologics Corp. of Omaha.   **BIO**

1986
: Brooklyn-born U.S. physicist Arthur Ashkin discovers a new method for observing and manipulating biological particles by applying radiation pressure with a laser.   **BIO**

1986
: While researching cancer growth patterns, U.S. scientists discover the first gene known to inhibit cell growth.   **BIO**

1986
: On August 21, in Cameroon, a cloud of toxic gas rises from Lake Nios, which has a volcanic crater. The cloud kills approximately 1,700 people and injures more than 500 more.   **EARTH**

1986
: Mathematicians Ramachandran Balasubramanian and colleagues prove a conjecture by Edward Waring dating from 1770, that every natural number is the sum of, at most, nineteen fourth powers. **MATH**

1986
: Using the radiation pressure of a laser, Arthur Ashkin and associates trap individual living organisms and individual atoms, permitting new methods of observation and handling.   **MISC**

1986
: Paleontologists Tim White and Donald Johanson discover fossil remains, including the first known limb bones, of OH62, a female *Homo habilis* dating back 1.8 million years.   **PALEO**

1986
: A complete frog, dating back 35 to 40 million years, is found fossilized in amber in the Dominican Republic.   **PALEO**

1986
: U.S. linguist Joseph H. Greenberg uses the technique of mass comparison of Native American languages to classify them into three groups representing successive waves of migration from northeast Asia.   **PALEO**

1986	Swiss physicist Karl Alexander Müller and German physicist Johannes Georg Bednorz discover superconductivity in certain ceramics at temperatures of 30° K, which is very cold, but warmer than any results obtained so far. This discovery leads to further experiments yielding superconductivity at still higher temperatures, making practical applications possible. **PHYS**
1986	Working independently, U.S. and German researchers observe individual quantum jumps in single atoms for the first time. **PHYS**
1986	Ephraim Fishbach claims to have discovered a fifth fundamental force referred to as the hypercharge, detectable in certain subatomic interactions. **PHYS**
1986	American biophysicist Michael Phelps and pediatric neurologist Harry Chugani use positron emission tomography (PET scans) to discover that the primary brain metabolic activity in infants five weeks or younger occurs in areas of the brain that control the primitive sensory and motor activities. The results suggest that newborns have a limited capacity for high-order functioning, including thought, a capacity that increases slowly as they grow. **PSYCH**
1986	Nintendo video games are introduced in the United States by the Japanese game-manufacturing company of the same name, founded in 1898. By the start of the next decade, U.S. sales of the games will top $3 billion. **TECH**
Apr. 28, 1986	In the worst nuclear accident in history, the Chernobyl 4 reactor in the Soviet republic of Ukraine undergoes a meltdown. Thirty-one firemen and plant workers are killed and radioactive fallout covers a wide region. **TECH**
Dec.14–23, 1986	Americans Dick Rutan and Jeana Yeager complete the first nonstop around-the-world flight without refueling. Their airplane, *Voyager*, departs from and returns to Edwards Air Force Base in California. **TECH**
1987	Further remains of Clovis people named for the New Mexico town near where they were first found are identified in Washington State. These prehistoric ancestors of Native Americans lived about 11,500 years ago. **ARCH**
1987	R. Brent Tully reports the discovery of the Pisces-Cetus Supercluster complex, the largest known structure in the universe. **ASTRO**
1987	Benjamin Zuckerman and Eric E. Becklin report the discovery of a brown dwarf star in orbit around the white dwarf star Giclas 29-38. **ASTRO**
Feb. 24, 1987	Canadian astronomer Ian Shelter discovers a supernova in the Large Magellanic Cloud, a galaxy near the Milky Way. This Supernova 1987A is the closest supernova since the one observed by Kepler in 1604. **ASTRO**

1987   Soviet cosmonaut Yuri V. Romanenko sets a new record for a single endurance flight aboard the space station *Mir*, after 326.5 days beginning February 8 and ending December 29.   **ASTRO**

1987   The U.S. Supreme Court strikes down a Louisiana law requiring the teaching of "creation science" in public schools whenever evolution is taught. This ruling follows a string of lawsuits pitting evolution against creationism in public schools.   **BIO**

Apr. 24, 1987   Plant pathologists Steve Lindow of the United States and Nickolas Panopoulos of Greece develop a mutant of a common parasite, *Pseudomonas syringae*. This genetically altered bacterium is designed to retard frost formation on plants, giving them the ability to withstand some subzero temperatures. On this day, when the mutant bacteria is applied on a field, it is the first time scientists are allowed to release man-made microbes into the environment.   **BIO**

1987   Chemists H. Naarmann and N. Theophilou develop a polyacetylene-iodine compound that serves as an efficient conductor of electricity.   **CHEM**

Sept. 1987   In Montreal, an international agreement is signed restricting the release of ozone-destroying halocarbons into the atmosphere.   **EARTH**

Nov. 1987   The periodic late fall appearance of the Antarctic ozone hole (*see* 1985) is larger in magnitude and duration than in previous years. The layer of ozone over Antarctica is less than 50 percent of its 1979 value.   **EARTH**

1987   Tretinoin (Retin-A), a prescription product used to treat acne for more than a decade, is shown to improve the skin's quality and diminish wrinkles. However, the side effects of its use such as skin irritation will deter some from using this "youth potion."   **MED**

1987   Mexican surgeon Ignacio Navarro develops a surgical procedure to treat severe cases of Parkinson's disease. The procedure involves implanting the patient's adrenal tissue into the brain, causing the brain to produce dopamine, the substance deficient in Parkinson's disease.   **MED**

1987   The anti-AIDS drug AZT (azidothymidine, or zidovudine) receives FDA approval.   **MED**

1987   Near the Milk River, in Alberta, Canada, Kevin Aulenback discovers dinosaur eggs containing fossilized unhatched dinosaurs, in only the second such find.   **PALEO**

1987   Scientists at IBM produce a standing wave called a dark pulse soliton, which propagates through an optical fiber without spreading.   **PHYS**

1987   Physicists Michael K. Moe and others determine that selenium-82 has the longest half-life ever recorded for a radioactive substance.   **PHYS**

1987   Researchers in Mexico, Europe, and the United States perform the first fetal brain tissue transplant into patients suffering from Parkinson's disease.   **PSYCH**

1987   The U.S. drug company Eli Lilly introduces the antidepressant Prozac (fluoxetine), which initially appears to have few side effects and will become the most widely prescribed antidepressant in the country. Later, however, it will become the center of a controversy over charges that taking it leads to suicide, murder, and self-mutilation. Despite these charges, the FDA will not require warning labels on it and Prozac will continue to be prescribed worldwide.   **PSYCH**

1988   The Shroud of Turin, a linen cloth marked with an image of a bearded man and believed by many to be the burial shroud of Jesus, is dated with carbon-14 at about 1300, some thirteen hundred years too late to have covered Jesus. The evidence now shows that the cloth was woven soon before it was first displayed in France in the 1350s.   **ARCH**

1988   On Rome's Palatine Hill a wall dating from the seventh century B.C. is discovered, which supports the legendary date of 735 B.C. for the founding of Rome.   **ARCH**

1988   Archaeologists Tom Dillehay and Michael Collins claim that charcoal dating of a site at Monte Verde, Chile, indicates that the ancestors of Native Americans arrived in the New World at least 33,000 years ago, nearly three times earlier than the accepted date of 12,000 years.   **ARCH**

1988   Simon J. Lilly identifies a galaxy that is 12 billion light-years away, indicating that it formed 12 billion years ago, early in the universe's history.   **ASTRO**

July 1988   The U.S.S.R. launches *Phobos 1* and *2*, unmanned spacecraft designed to study the Martian moon Phobos, but loses contact with both spacecraft before their missions can be completed.   **ASTRO**

Sept. 29, 1988   The space shuttle *Discovery* is launched in the first U.S. manned space mission since the *Challenger* disaster of January 28, 1986.   **ASTRO**

1988   The development of a method to identify a person from the DNA in a single hair is announced.   **BIO**

1988   American biochemist Sidney Fox makes proteinlike substances called proteinoids that self-organize in water to form cell-like units known as microspheres that closely resemble ancient protocells.   **BIO**

1988   Scottish researchers report that some cancers involve the loss of a specific piece of genetic material, bolstering the theory that cancer development is caused by activation of cancer-causing genes and the loss of cancer-controlling genes in the body.   **BIO**

1988	It is estimated that some 10 million chemical compounds are known to science, with the number growing by approximately 400,000 every year. **CHEM**

1988   Government scientist James E. Hansen testifies before the U.S. Senate that he is "99 percent sure that accumulation of greenhouse gases is responsible for global warming trends." His remarks contribute to a growing public sense of urgency on this issue. **EARTH**

1988   Scientists will determine that 1988 was the warmest year on record for average temperatures worldwide as thousands of heat-related deaths occur internationally. Links to the greenhouse effect are suspected but cannot be confirmed. **EARTH**

1988   A Joint Symposium on Ozone Depletion, Greenhouse Gases, and Climate Change is held at the U.S. National Academy of Sciences. **EARTH**

1988   Mathematician Silvio Micali and colleagues report the development of a method for generating purely random numbers, based on the problem of factoring large numbers that are the products of two large primes. **MATH**

1988   In Israel, fossils of early humans are found that bear many characteristics of modern *Homo sapiens sapiens*. Dating back 90,000 to 100,000 years, they are more than twice as old as the previously known specimens of modern humans. **PALEO**

1988   Scientists at the University of Arkansas discover a warm-temperature superconductor based on thallium that attains superconductivity at a record high temperature of 125° K. Later this year, scientists develop a motor that employs these warm-temperature superconductors. **PHYS**

c. 1988   American psychologist David Sack and colleagues at the National Institutes of Mental Health find that partial sleep deprivation can reverse some of the effects of severe depression. **PSYCH**

1988   Canadian psychiatrist Colin Ross conducts a major study which discovers that out of 236 persons diagnosed as having multiple personality disorder, 41 percent had previously been diagnosed as schizophrenics. This result represents a trend toward more careful examination of persons presenting symptoms of probable mental illness and it also illustrates growth in the recognition of multiple personality disorder. **PSYCH**

1988   University of California–Irvine psychiatrist Richard Haier reports that high intelligence may be the result of an efficiently organized brain. His experiments with PET scans of people taking a series of visual tests show that those who performed best used less energy in the cortical areas of the brain, where abstract reasoning takes place, than those who performed poorly. Haier claims that his experiments show that the high scorers used their brains more efficiently. **PSYCH**

1988	The positron transmission microscope is invented. **TECH**
1989	American archaeologists excavate the Babylonian city of Mashkan-shapir. Built about 1840 B.C., it is one of the oldest known cities. **ARCH**
1989	Astronomers report evidence that a pulsar—an extremely dense, rapidly spinning star—has formed in the debris left over from Supernova 1987A. **ASTRO**
1989	Astronomers theorize that the Andromeda and M32 galaxies have black holes at their centers. **ASTRO**
1989	A whirlpool of rotating gas expelled from the core of the Milky Way, possibly caused by a black hole at the galaxy's center, is discovered. **ASTRO**
1989	While mapping the location of galaxies, astrophysicists discover the largest structure yet known in the universe, a sheet of galaxies that comes to be called the Great Wall. **ASTRO**
1989	Studies of the Saturnian moon Titan indicate that it is not covered by a global ocean, so that in all the solar system the earth remains the only known body with liquid on its surface. **ASTRO**
May 4, 1989	The U.S. unmanned spacecraft *Magellan* is launched from the shuttle *Discovery* in the first instance of a space probe being launched from a shuttle. *See also* August 10, 1990. **ASTRO**
Aug. 1989	The U.S. spacecraft *Voyager 2* becomes the first probe to fly past Neptune. It discovers three new moons, detects volcanic activity on the Neptunian moon Triton, and confirms the existence of partial rings around the planet. **ASTRO**
Oct. 18, 1989	The United States launches the *Galileo* spacecraft, scheduled to reach Jupiter by 1995 to study the planet's atmosphere and satellite system. *See also* February 1990. **ASTRO**
Dec. 21, 1989	Col. Vladimir Titov and Musa Manarov set a team endurance flight record aboard the Soviet space station *Mir* after 366 days beginning December 21, 1988. **ASTRO**
1989	In his book *Wonderful Life*, Harvard biologist Stephen Jay Gould argues that the "explosion" of life forms (570 million years ago) produced many more basic body plans than exist today. This controversial theory, based on recent reinterpretations of Canada's Burgess Shale fossils (*see* 1971, Whittington), suggests that only a fraction of the phyla then living survived the mass extinction at the end of the Cambrian period. **BIO**
1989	The Texas State Board of Education formally votes, for the first time, to require the teaching of evolution in all biology textbooks. **BIO**
1989	U.S. geneticists Steven Rosenberg, R. Michael Blaese, and W. French Anderson discover human gene transfer. **BIO**

OLD BLOOM

*T**he earliest flower thus far discovered is a flowering angiosperm called the Koonwarra plant, thought to be 120 million years old. The fossil of the flower was discovered in 1989 not far from Melbourne, Australia, by Drs. Leo Hickey and David Taylor of Yale University. With its two leaves and one bloom the Koonwarra is similar in appearance to the black pepper plant.*

1989	The first robot honeybee able to use the waggle dance to communicate with other bees is developed by a team of engineers and entomologists. **BIO**
1989	Scientists determine that dogs have some color vision. **BIO**
1989	In May, for the first time, U.S. geneticists at the National Institutes of Health inject genetically engineered nonhuman cells into a human patient. These cells will be used to mark and trace other cells in an experimental therapy for skin cancer. **BIO**
1989	Under millions of atmospheres of pressure, hydrogen is converted into a metal-like phase that may be superconducting. **CHEM**
1989	Scientists from the United States and India find evidence that tectonic plates clashed some 2.5 billion years ago in what is now India's Kolar schist belt, indicating that tectonic processes were under way early in earth's history. **EARTH**
1989	Using a computer model, William F. Ruddman and John E. Ketzbach demonstrate that a tectonic uplifting of the Tibetan plateau and the Rocky Mountains caused global cooling and weather patterns that may have set off the recent ice ages. **EARTH**
1989	U.S. scientists complete an ocean-mapping project which reveals that the mid-Atlantic Ridge is comprised of a string of sixteen spreading centers. **EARTH**
1989	The oldest known rock is discovered, dated at 3.96 billion years, soon after the earth's formation 4.6 billion years ago. **EARTH**
1989	More than eighty nations, including the United States and the twelve nations of the European Community, agree to plans to phase out ozone-destroying chlorofluorocarbons (CFCs) by the year 2000. **EARTH**
1989	On March 24, the *Exxon Valdez* oil tanker is the source of a massive oil spill of about 250,000 barrels in Prince William Sound off the Alaskan coast. The spill causes a series of related ecological disasters, including 350,000 to 2.4 million seabirds killed by the spilled oil, according to an estimate in a 1991 study. **EARTH**

1989   Using a new algorithm to compute pi, mathematicians extend the calculation of pi to 1 billion digits.   **MATH**

1989   Researchers Francis Collins of the United States and La-Chee Tsui of Canada discover the gene that causes cystic fibrosis, the most common deadly genetic disease in North America.   **MED**

1989   U.S. scientists David Goeddel, William Korh, Diane Pennica, and Gordon Behar are named inventors of the year for their invention of t-PA, a drug used to dissolve blood clots in heart attack patients. **MED**

1989   Research determines that azidothymidine (AZT) can curb the progression of AIDS in HIV-infected patients who present no symptoms of the disease. However, studies also show that some patients develop viruses resistant to AZT. *See* 1987.   **MED**

1989   Researchers announce that they have pinpointed a set of genes that seem to make some families more susceptible than others to the debilitating nerve disease multiple sclerosis (MS).   **MED**

1989   In Culpeper, Virginia, quarry workers uncover the largest set of dinosaur tracks in North America: about one thousand well-preserved footprints dating from 210 million years ago.   **PALEO**

1989   Based on evidence from fossil skulls, scientists argue that Neanderthals and anatomically modern humans evolved near each other, possibly interbreeding, in the Near East as long ago as 145,000 years.   **PALEO**

1989   Evidence is discovered that anatomically modern humans inhabited southwestern Europe forty thousand years ago, earlier than previously believed.   **PALEO**

1989   Researchers at the University of Utah claim to have discovered cold fusion of atomic nuclei, with a resulting release of energy, at room temperature. The experiment is never successfully reproduced and the claim is generally discredited.   **PHYS**

1989   Japanese physicists report the first experimental confirmation that the sun generates neutrinos.   **PHYS**

1989   Funding for the construction of the Superconducting Super Collider is approved by the U.S. Congress, which will vote to terminate the unfinished project in 1993.   **PHYS**

1989   U.S. researchers James W. Tetrud and J. William Langstrom report that they have developed Deprenyl, the first drug shown to delay symptoms of neurological disease. It prevents brain cell death and slows the progress of Parkinson's disease.   **PSYCH**

1989   The University of Minnesota Press releases a new version of the world's most widely used psychological profile test, the MMPI (*see* 1940s). Criticized for an alleged sexist bias, the test was reviewed and redeveloped to be gender neutral. It also includes more recent psychological disorders such as drug abuse, eating disorders, and Type A personality.   **PSYCH**

1989   University of Texas researchers present the first evidence that stuttering and spasmodic dysphonia (difficulty in speaking) are caused not by emotional disturbance but by biochemical abnormalities in the brain.   **PSYCH**

1990s   The United Nations estimates that the population of the lesser-developed and developing countries will rise by almost 3 billion by the year 2020.   **BIO**

1990   Microscopic study of horses' teeth removed from a site in Ukraine shows that horses were ridden about six thousand years ago, considerably earlier than according to previous estimates.   **ARCH**

1990   Scientists confirm the existence of a concentration of mass called the Great Attractor, which changes the rate at which the Milky Way and nearby galaxies spread apart as the universe expands. *See also* 1986, Milky Way.   **ASTRO**

1990   By launching a satellite into lunar orbit, Japan becomes the third country in history, after the United States and the U.S.S.R., to send a spacecraft to the moon.   **ASTRO**

Feb. 1990   The U.S. unmanned spacecraft *Galileo*, launched October 18, 1989, flies by Venus, gaining a gravity assist on its way to Jupiter. *See also* October 29, 1991.   **ASTRO**

Apr. 25, 1990   The Hubble Space Telescope, the first telescope intended for permanent earth orbit, is launched aboard the space shuttle *Discovery*. A joint project of the United States and the European Space Agency, this telescope proves to have obscured vision resulting from technical flaws that another shuttle crew will attempt to repair in December 1993.   **ASTRO**

Aug. 10, 1990   The U.S. unmanned spacecraft *Magellan*, launched May 4, 1989, reaches Venus. In the next two years it will use radar to penetrate the thick Venusian cloud cover and transmit back detailed maps of most of the planet's surface.   **ASTRO**

Oct. 6, 1990   The United States launches the unmanned spacecraft *Ulysses* to study the poles of the sun and the interstellar space above and below those poles. The craft is scheduled to approach the sun first in 1994, then again in 1995. *See also* February 8, 1992.   **ASTRO**

1990   Tigers conceived through in vitro fertilization are born, in Omaha, Nebraska.   **BIO**

1990	Researchers expand the genetic alphabet of four nucleotides by adding two artificial nucleic acids that can be recognized and built into new DNA and RNA molecules by cellular biochemical machinery. **BIO**
1990	New evidence indicates that humans are destroying tropical rain forests at a rate faster than previously believed. **BIO**
1990	American physicist Donald Huffman and German colleague Wolfgang Krätschmer patent a method for producing buckminster-fullerene molecules (buckyballs) in larger quantities than previously possible (*see* 1985, Richard Smalley). **CHEM**
1990	Inexpensive synthetic diamonds are developed that conduct heat 50 percent better than natural ones and withstand ten times as much laser power. The synthetic diamonds are made from isotopically purified carbon. **CHEM**
1990	Scientists make aerogels, very low density solid materials, out of silica and other substances. **CHEM**
1990	Scientists from the United States and the U.S.S.R. discover the first known fresh-water geothermal vents, in the floor of Lake Baikal, Russia. These vents confirm that the lake is a spreading area, a place where new crust is forming. Should this spreading continue, over the course of several hundred million years Asia could split apart and the lake become an ocean between two tectonic plates. **EARTH**
1990	Undersea core samples drilled in the Ontong–Java Plateau provide evidence for a superplume, a giant mass of hot material that bursts through to the earth's crust in a relatively short time, in the Cretaceous period. According to current theory, superplumes affect the shape of the crust, tectonic movement, geomagnetism, climate, and the course of evolution. **EARTH**
1990	Hundreds of climate experts sign a statement predicting global warming unless the nations of the world act to stop the increase of greenhouse gases in the atmosphere. However, the United States refuses to set specific targets for limiting carbon dioxide emissions. **EARTH**
1990	Meteorologists develop new techniques to determine the probability that atmospheric chaos will disrupt any given long-term forecast. **EARTH**
Oct. 17, 1990	In the San Francisco Bay area, an earthquake measuring 7.1 on the Richter scale kills sixty-seven people and injures more than three thousand. **EARTH**
1990	A 155-digit Fermat number is factored by two computer scientists, breaking existing records. **MATH**
1990	The *Journal of the American Medical Association* publishes the results of a study linking dopamine receptor genes to alcoholism. **MED**

1990   The first fetus-to-fetus tissue graft in the United States is performed. **MED**

1990   *The New England Journal of Medicine* publishes a study supporting the idea that genetic factors influence weight gain.   **MED**

1990   Daniell Rudman of the Medical College of Wisconsin (Milwaukee) and colleagues report that treatment with the human growth hormone can reverse the physical effects of aging. Mass production of this hormone has been made possible by the advent of genetic engineering.   **MED**

1990   British physicians Norman Winston and Alan Handyside are the first to implant a woman with embryos screened in a test tube for genetic defects. Handyside says that refining the technique will allow physicians to screen for any genetic disorder. Previously, genetic screening was not possible until the tenth week of pregnancy, when an amniocentesis could be performed.   **MED**

1990   American rheumatologist Lawrence E. Shellman discovers the gene that causes osteoarthritis, the most common form of arthritis.   **MED**

1990   Several researchers present evidence of a link between very low frequency electromagnetic fields and human cancer.   **MED**

1990   Researchers discover that the number of years a person smokes cigarettes is the most important risk factor in carotid artery disease.   **MED**

1990   Researchers find that a high-fiber diet can help protect against colon cancer.   **MED**

1990   Secondhand tobacco smoke—smoke inhaled by nonsmokers—is called a "known human carcinogen" in a draft EPA report.   **MED**

1990   On September 14, the first United States government-approved infusion of genetically engineered cells into a human for therapeutic purposes is successfully performed when a four-year-old girl with an inherited immune disorder (adenosine deaminase deficiency) begins receiving monthly injections of genetically engineered white-blood cells.   **MED**

Dec. 1990 The U.S. government approves the first significantly new contraceptive in twenty-five years, Norplant. This hormone-releasing system to be implanted under a woman's skin for long-term protection is introduced as the most effective contraceptive on the market.   **MED**

1990   Scientists present evidence that humans settled Australia as early as fifty thousand years ago.   **PALEO**

1990   Scientists analyze DNA from a magnolia leaf that is 20 million years old, the oldest genetic material ever tested. It provides insight into the evolution of plants.   **PALEO**

1990   In Egypt, paleontologists discover the fossil remains of a 40-million-year-old whale with feet, providing a clue to the evolution of cetaceans.   **PALEO**

1990	Scientists report discovering the fossil of *Sinornis*, a 135-million-year-old bird from China. More recent and less primitive in appearance than *Archaeopteryx* (*see* 1861), it is the oldest bird with modern flight features. **PALEO**
1990	Using a scanning tunneling microscope, researchers at IBM are able to move individual atoms on a surface for the first time. **PHYS**
1990	Physicists use new data on Z particles to develop strict limits concerning the number of particle families and refine their estimates of the top quark mass. **PHYS**
1990	American neuroscientist Solomon Snyder grows a human brain cell in a lab at the Johns Hopkins University School of Medicine. This cell, a neuron from the most highly evolved portion of the brain, will allow for more detailed studies of the brain. **PSYCH**
1990	Psychologists discover that faces usually found to be attractive have features that approximate the mathematical average of all faces in the area's population. **PSYCH**
1990	Two separate studies of twins, one on men and another on women, suggest that genes may have an important influence on the development of one's sexual orientation. **PSYCH**
1990	"Smart" materials and structures are developed that sense such conditions as pressure and temperature, then respond with changes in their properties, such as their conductivity or shape. **TECH**
1991	The 5,000-year-old body of a man preserved in ice is discovered in the Alps between Austria and Italy. Dubbed the "iceman," he carries tools that provide clues to life in Europe about 3000 B.C. **ARCH**
1991	American astronomers discover a quasar 12 billion light-years away, the most distant object ever identified. **ASTRO**
1991	The *Magellan* space probe completes its first radar survey of the planet Venus, mapping more than 90 percent of its surface, revealing thousands of cracks and craters, enormous lava flows, and features indicating quakes and volcanic activity. **ASTRO**
1991	British astronomers report indirect evidence for a planet orbiting a distant pulsar or neutron star. **ASTRO**
1991	Using the Hubble Space Telescope's spectrograph, astronomers analyze the disk of gas and dust orbiting the star Beta Pictoris (*see* 1983, IRAS). By late 1992 the Hubble telescope will uncover evidence of similar protoplanetary disks around fifteen new stars in the Orion nebula. **ASTRO**
Apr. 7, 1991	The U.S. Gamma Ray Observatory is launched into earth orbit to study celestial gamma-ray sources, particularly supernovae, quasars, neutron stars, and black holes. **ASTRO**

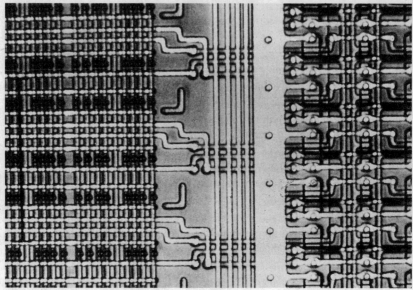

An electronic neural network chip. The chip represents the possible architecture of brain cells. (*AT&T*)

Oct. 29,
1991

The U.S. unmanned spacecraft *Galileo* takes the first close-up photograph of an asteroid in space, of 951 *Gaspra*, from a distance of ten thousand miles.   **ASTRO**

1991

The World Resources Institute estimates that the world's forests are being destroyed by deforestation at a rate of eighty acres per minute, or some 40 to 50 million acres a year.   **BIO**

1991

At a meeting of the International Union of Biological Sciences in Amsterdam, British mycologist David Hawksworth estimates that the total of fungi types worldwide could be as high as 1.6 million. At the same conference on biodiversity, some biologists claim that humans may share the world with 100 million other species but are rapidly causing hundreds of extinctions via global warming, habitat destruction, and the introduction of species foreign to a region. **BIO**

1991–1992

Under a scanning electron microscope, U.S. geologist John Watterson studies gold grains (placer gold) from Lillian Creek, Alaska, and discovers that the grains are attached to bacteria. Among the possible explanations are that the gold is a chemical residue left after bacterial breakdown in the humic acids of Alaskan soil, or that the gold comes from extracellular enzyme activity. Watterson estimates that a 0.1 millimeter gold grain takes at least a year to grow.   **BIO**

1991   The British journal *Nature* publishes a study by British scientists claiming to have discovered the gene on the Y chromosome that determines maleness in mice. When the researchers inject the gene into female mouse embryos, some of the embryos became male.   **BIO**

1991   Contrary to the theories of Gregor Mendel (*see* 1866), geneticists find that genes may behave differently, depending on which parent they were inherited from.   **BIO**

1991   In the United States, on September 26, the privately financed *Biosphere 2* project begins. Eight men and women are locked in a sealed structure containing five sample earth environments. Over the next two years they will study the feasibility of sustaining a closed ecology. The project draws much media attention, though its scientific standards are criticized in many quarters.   **BIO**

1991   American organic chemist Joel Hawkins uses X-ray diffraction to generate the first image of a buckyball molecule (*see* 1985, Richard Smalley), corroborating the existence of this form of pure carbon, also called buckminsterfullerene. American physicist Arthur Hebard demonstrates that buckyballs doped with potassium or rubidium are superconductive.   **CHEM**

1991   The newly revised U.S. Clean Air Act identifies 189 chemicals commonly found in the air as toxic. Environmental Defense Fund senior scientist Michael Oppenheimer says that more than 150 million Americans live in areas where air pollution levels still violate federal health standards.   **EARTH**

1991   The Environmental Protection Agency estimates that more than 1 million of America's 5 million underground storage tanks, most of which hold petroleum products, are currently leaking. The EPA asserts that the damage done to groundwater supplies and ecosystems is only beginning to be evaluated.   **EARTH**

1991   Tomography (CT scanning) is applied to studies of the earth's interior. On that basis, the International Association of Seismology and Physics of the Earth's Interior develops new seismic-wave travel timetables that supersede the 1940 Jeffreys and Bullen tables.   **EARTH**

1991   U.S. scientists R. C. Capo and D. J. DePaolo report that the ratio of two isotopes of strontium can be used to determine past climates.   **EARTH**

1991   The eruption of Mount Pinatubo on Luzon Island in the Philippines is the largest in the twentieth century. Within ten days its cloud spreads seven thousand miles to reach from Indonesia to Central Africa. The quantities of sulfur dioxide, ash, and aerosol material issued by it lead to lower global temperatures and accelerate the erosion of the ozone layer.   **EARTH**

1991   American geologists Eldridge M. Moore and Ian W. D. Dalziel propose that Antarctica and the western coast of North America were originally linked 500 million years ago.   **EARTH**

1991   American geologists led by Haraldur Sigardsson analyze glass fragments from Haiti that confirm the theory (*see* 1979, Alvarez) that a large object from outer space rammed into the earth 65 million years ago.   **EARTH**

1991   The U.N. Intergovernmental Negotiating Committee on Climate Change meets in Chantilly, Virginia. Its delegates, from 130 countries, structure a treaty to "curb the threat of global warming."   **EARTH**

1991   Retreating Iraqi troops set hundreds of Kuwaiti oil wells on fire during the Persian Gulf War through February and March. Smoke from the burning wells blankets the area, and soot is detected well north of Turkey, as far west as Egypt, the Sudan, and Ethiopia, and as far east as India and China. The smoke also contributes to a cyclone in Bangladesh that takes more than 100,000 lives.   **EARTH**

1991   Twenty-four countries with interests in Antarctica sign a treaty banning oil exploration there for the next fifty years.   **EARTH**

1991   As of this year there have been thirteen epidemiological studies linking secondhand cigarette smoke and diseases in nonsmoking people exposed to smoke.   **MED**

1991   British geneticists claim to have located a gene that, when mutated, causes a hereditary type of Alzheimer's disease.   **MED**

1991   A characteristic gene mutation is found in people prone to developing colon cancer.   **MED**

1991   *The New England Journal of Medicine* reports on the longest and largest estrogen-after-menopause investigation, which concludes that the benefits of estrogen replacement, evaluated on an individual basis, outweigh the risk of cancer.   **MED**

1991   Researchers at Israel's Weizmann Institute of Science say that it may be possible to vaccinate against the insulin-dependent form of diabetes after manipulating T-cells, which has allowed researchers to keep mice from developing diabetes.   **MED**

1991   The first woman named to the National Inventors Hall of Fame in Akron, Ohio, is seventy-three-year-old Gertrude Belle Elion, who helped develop drugs to fight leukemia, septic shock, and tissue rejection in patients having kidney transplants.   **MED**

1991   The American Heart Association recommends limiting meat in the diet, claiming it is not a necessary food.   **MED**

1991   By now, more than 366,000 cases of AIDS have been reported in 162 countries and 10 million adults are believed to be infected with the HIV virus that causes AIDS. The World Health Organization estimates that by the year 2000 some 40 million people will be infected. **MED**

1991   French diver Henri Cosquer discovers paintings and engravings in an undersea cave in the Calanque region of France. The artwork, which includes paintings of marine birds called auks, dates from at least two different periods—one 27,000 years ago, the other 19,000 years ago. **PALEO**

1991   Physicists in England achieve controlled nuclear fusion with a mixture of tritium and deuterium (two forms of hydrogen) producing almost 2 megawatts of power, a new record for experimental fusion reactors. Though this fuel is more efficient than the pure deutrium previously used, fusion has still not become a commercially viable energy source. **PHYS**

1991   The journal *Cell* reports that geneticists have located the gene that causes the most common form of inherited mental retardation, the "Fragile X" syndrome. **PSYCH**

1991   U.S. neurobiologist Simon LeVay announces that the brains of homosexual men are structurally different from those of heterosexual men. The affected brain area, a segment of the hypothalamus, is believed to influence male sexual behavior. **PSYCH**

1991   American cognitive scientist Daniel C. Dennett publishes *Consciousness Explained*, in which he argues that there is no central, conscious "audience" in the brain, nor a single, unified stream of consciousness. Rather, consciousness consists of multiple drafts composed by neural processes of "content fixation" playing semi-independent roles and generating the illusion of a single, conscious self. **PSYCH**

1991   U.S. neuroscientist Timothy Pons announces the results of experiments on monkeys that support and extend Michael Merzenich's cortical remapping theory. *See* 1980s, Merzenich and Kaas. **PSYCH**

1991   American psychologist Jan Belsky argues that girls who grow up in dangerous environments have a tendency to experience the onset of puberty earlier than other girls. Her controversial explanation is that children in such conditions are encouraged by evolution to have offspring early and often, to increase the chances that some will survive. **SOC**

1992   A 5,000-year-old city, possibly the legendary trade city Ubar, is discovered in the Arabian Desert. **ARCH**

1992   European and American astronomers announce the discovery of two black holes, V404 Cygni and Nova Muscae, each orbited rapidly by a star. **ASTRO**

1992	European astronomer Mart de Groot demonstrates that the blue supergiant star P Cygni has brightened steadily over the past 300 years, thus providing evidence of stellar evolution. **ASTRO**
1992	The Hubble Space Telescope detects the hottest star yet known, the white dwarf NGC 2440. Its surface temperature is 360,000° C, more than thirty times hotter than the sun's. **ASTRO**
1992	A cometlike object titled QB1 is found at a distance of 39 to 45 astronomical units (the distance between the earth and the sun), at least as far out as Pluto. It may be the first known comet in the hypothetical Kuiper belt. *See* 1950. **ASTRO**
1992	Studies indicate that the Milky Way galaxy, as well as thousands of others, is moving across the sky at 375 kilometers per second. **ASTRO**
Feb. 8, 1992	The unmanned U.S. spacecraft *Ulysses* (*see* October 6, 1990) flies by Jupiter, using the planet's gravity to speed it on its way toward the sun. The spacecraft studies Jupiter's magnetic field in the process. **ASTRO**
Apr. 23, 1992	The Cosmic Background Explorer (COBE) science team reports that the U.S. *COBE* satellite, launched in 1989, has discovered small temperature variations or "ripples" in the universe's microwave background radiation. These variations support the Big Bang theory by indicating that there were fluctuations in the density of gas in the early universe soon after the Big Bang. Then, as the universe expanded, density variations like these led to the formation of galaxies, galaxy clusters, and other large-scale structures. **ASTRO**
May 7, 1992	The fifth, and possibly last, U.S. space shuttle, *Endeavour*, is launched on its first mission, during which astronauts retrieve a satellite stranded in a useless orbit and launch it into the correct one. The earlier shuttles were the *Columbia*, *Discovery*, and *Atlantis*. The second space shuttle, the *Challenger*, exploded in flight. *See* January 28, 1986. **ASTRO**
Sept. 12, 1992	The U.S. space shuttle *Endeavour*, launched today, carries the first African-American woman astronaut, Mae C. Jemison, and the first married couple in space, Mark C. Lee and N. Jan Davis. **ASTRO**
Sept. 25, 1992	NASA launches the *Mars Observer* spacecraft, the first U.S. probe sent to Mars since the *Viking* in 1975. The rendezvous with Mars, planned for August 1993, will fail to take place due to loss of radio contact with the probe. **ASTRO**
Oct. 12, 1992	On the five hundredth anniversary of Columbus's discovery of America, U.S. astronomers begin a planned ten-year search of the sky for radio signals indicating extraterrestrial intelligence. **ASTRO**

Oct. 8, 1992

NASA scientists lose radio contact with the *Pioneer 12*, which is presumed to have broken up as it plunged through the upper atmosphere of Venus. This robotic spacecraft has remained operational for fourteen years, far exceeding initial expectations. *See* May 20, 1978. **ASTRO**

1992

Teams of scientists working in the United States, France, and elsewhere, complete the first comprehensive maps of two human chromosomes, the Y chromosome and chromosome 21. These maps are an important step forward for the Human Genome Project, a multiyear effort to determine the entire human genome. **BIO**

1992

U.S. biologists Joseph Manson and Richard Wrangham report that their recent studies show that all primate aggression, including that of humans, is more complex than just a stress reaction or an atavistic animal instinct. They claim that private aggression is an ancient evolutionary strategy linked more to coalition building and maintaining harmony than to wanton murder and violence. **BIO**

1992

Scientists report locating what they think to be the oldest and largest living organism on earth, a giant mold called *Armillaria bulbosa*, found growing beneath a Crystal Falls, Michigan, forest. **BIO**

1992

An eleven-day United Nations Conference on Environment and Development, known as the Earth Summit, is held in Rio de Janeiro, Brazil. Some of the issues discussed are a funding agreement to provide environmental aid to developing countries, a so-called World Statement of Principles for the sustainable management and conservation of forests, and various other conventions on climate change and biodiversity. **BIO**

1992

Researchers from Yale University and New York City's American Museum of Natural History report extracting DNA fragments from an extinct termite embedded in amber for 30 million years, proving that genetic molecules can survive far longer than had been thought possible. **BIO**

1992

The National Institutes of Health (NIH) withdraws funds from an academic conference searching for a genetic basis for criminal behavior, objecting to the notion that violence and crime might have genetic causes. **BIO**

1992

Scientists isolate a cluster of proteins that imitates the process by which baker's yeast copies its genes. This experiment proves to be a major step toward understanding how higher organisms copy their genes. **BIO**

1992

A panel of experts finds that DNA fingerprinting is useful in identifying criminals, but insists that standards for its use must be developed. **BIO**

1992   While studying specimens of the rock called shungite, Russian-American mineralogist Semeon Tsipursky discovers naturally-occurring buckyballs, or buckminsterfullerene molecules, which had previously been found only in the laboratory (*see* 1985, Richard Smalley).   **CHEM**

1992   American scientists succeed in forming the first buckyball polymers and in making diamonds from buckyballs at lower temperatures and pressures than are needed to transform graphite into diamonds. Like diamonds and graphite, buckyballs are a form of pure carbon.   **CHEM**

1992   Scientists for the NEC Corp. in Japan synthesize buckytubes, hollow cylinders of carbon atoms that may be useful for their great strength and electric conductivity.   **CHEM**

1992   The ozone hole over Antarctica grows to its largest size ever.   **EARTH**

1992   Scientists studying the climate of the last ice age by analyzing samples of ancient ice from Greenland determine that the climate changed significantly in that period over spans as short as one or two years.   **EARTH**

1992   Scientists find new laboratory evidence that the atmospheres of Mars, Venus, and the earth were formed partly from noble gases trapped in the icy nuclei of comets.   **EARTH**

1992   On June 28, the largest earthquake in California in forty years strikes near the town of Landers.   **EARTH**

1992   Using a Cray supercomputer, British scientist David Slowinski discovers the largest prime number to date, called the thirty-second Mersenne prime, which is 227,832 digits long.   **MATH**

1992   Harvard University Medical School's *Harvard Health Letter* lists what it considers the seven best screening tests in preventive medicine, based on health professionals' guidelines: blood-pressure screening for hypertension, serum cholesterol for coronary artery disease, a stool smear for occult blood, the sigmoidoscopy for colon and rectal cancer, a clinical exam for breast cancer, mammography for breast cancer, and the Pap smear for cervical cancer.   **MED**

1992   Researchers find evidence that Alzheimer's disease may develop as the result of an imbalance in two biochemical pathways that break down a precursor of beta amyloid, an ingredient of the plaques that attack the brain in this disease.   **MED**

1992   Researchers are divided on the benefits of the drug azidothymidine (AZT) in prolonging the lives of AIDS patients.   **MED**

1992   Three studies find that the symptoms of Parkinson's disease can be improved through transplanting fetal brain tissue.   **MED**

1992   American paleontologist Paul Sereno identifies the 230-million-year-old *Herrerasaurus* as the earliest carnivore in the dinosaur family. This 400-pound, 15-foot-long reptile was probably an ancestor of *Tyrannosaurus rex*.   **PALEO**

1992   The "Eve" hypothesis is undermined when flaws are revealed in molecular research that had led scientists in the 1980s to trace the human lineage back to a common female ancestor in Africa some 200,000 years ago.   **PALEO**

1992   Li Tianyuan of China and Dennis Etler of the United States announce the discovery of two extremely old Chinese skulls. If their date of 350,000 years ago is correct, the fossils are the oldest complete human skulls yet found in eastern Asia. Li and Etler claim that these specimens are intermediate between *Homo erectus* and modern humans.   **PALEO**

1992   In the Yucatán Peninsula of Mexico, geologists find evidence of a crater from the crash of a meteorite or comet 65 million years ago, an event hypothesized by Luis Alvarez in 1979. Paleontologists disagree on whether this collision was responsible for the extinction of the dinosaurs.   **PALEO**

1992   The federal government, the Cheyenne River Sioux tribe, and the private Black Hills Institute of Geological Research become embroiled in a dispute over ownership of a *Tyrannosaurus rex* skeleton referred to as Sue.   **PALEO**

1992   In February, American paleoanthropologists Andrew Hill and Steven Ward announce their discovery of the oldest *Homo* specimen yet known. This skull fragment, from Kenya's Lake Baringo Basin, is 2.4 million years old, half a million years older than previously known specimens. Its discovery corroborates the theory that stone-tool-making hominids first emerged about 2.5 million years ago.   **PALEO**

1992   Researchers observe the unusual behavior of electrons confined to spaces small enough for quantum effects to become significant.   **PHYS**

1992   Researchers make the best measurement to date of the neutrino's mass.   **PHYS**

1993   U.S. archaeologists John S. Justeson and Terrence Kaufman report their decipherment of an epi-Olmec stone stela or monument from Mexico dating from 159.   **ARCH**

1993   Archaeologists discover evidence of a human campsite in northern Alaska dating from 11,700 years ago, the first solid evidence of human activity in the northern part of the migration route from Asia to the Americas believed to have been traveled by ancestors of the Native Americans. *See* 10,000 B.C.   **ARCH**

1993	U.S. astronomer Douglas Lin presents evidence that the Milky Way is much larger than formerly believed and is surrounded by a halo of "dark matter" invisible to telescopes. These findings support the view that most of the universe is composed of such dark matter. **ASTRO**
1993	American scientists report that *Voyagers 1* and *2*, now far beyond Pluto, have detected intense, low-frequency radio emissions from the heliopause, the outer boundary of the solar system. This point, marking the juncture where interstellar gases interact with the solar wind, is believed to be 8 to 12 billion miles from the sun. *Voyager 1* is expected to reach it in about fifteen years. **ASTRO**
1993	Evidence from the COBE satellite (*see* April 23, 1992) indicates that 99.97 percent of the radiant energy of the universe was released within a year of the Big Bang. This discovery adds support to the Big Bang theory. **ASTRO**
Mar. 27, 1993	Supernova SN1993J appears in Galaxy M-81, about 12 million light-years from the earth. This supernova's X-ray emissions are the first to be analyzed by an X-ray camera orbiting the earth. **ASTRO**
Aug. 1993	NASA loses radio contact with the U.S. *Mars Observer* spacecraft (*see* September 25, 1992), bringing the mission to an end before the planned rendezvous with Mars. **ASTRO**
Dec. 1993	Space shuttle astronauts succeed in repairing the optical problems of the Hubble Space Telescope. *See* April 25, 1990. **ASTRO**
1993	The British journal *Nature* reports that British geneticists have identified the gene whose mutation leads to amyotrophic lateral sclerosis (ALS, or Lou Gehrig's disease), an incurable muscle-wasting neural disease. **BIO**

THE GREAT PUMPKIN

*N*ot all produce is grown to uniform supermarket size. Every year, local, national, and international contests are held to display potentially record-breaking gargantuan fruits and vegetables. From the 1993 Guinness Book of World Records, here is a sampling of the largest varieties of a few common fruits and vegetables:

Apple. 3.1 lbs. (V. Loveridge, Ross-on-Wye, Great Britain, 1965).
Cabbage. 124 lbs. (B. Lavery, Llanharry, Great Britain, 1989).
Pumpkin. 816 lbs., 8 oz. (E. and R. Gancarz, Wrightstown, N.J., 1990).
Tomato. 7 lbs., 12 oz. (G. Graham, Edmond, Okla., 1986).
Watermelon. 262 lbs. (B. Carson, Arrington, Tenn., 1990).

1993   U.S. researchers at the National Cancer Institute claim to have linked a genetic marker on the X chromosome to homosexual orientation.   **BIO**

1993   Researchers clone human embryos for the first time.   **BIO**

1993   American chemists synthesize the largest molecule yet created in a laboratory from carbon and hydrogen alone. This lumpy, ball-shaped molecule consists of 1,134 carbon atoms and 1,146 hydrogen atoms.   **CHEM**

1993   A devastating flood, perhaps the worst in U.S. history, hits the Midwest. The Mississippi and Missouri Rivers and their tributaries overflow their banks, submerging towns and farmland in several states and wreaking havoc in such cities as Des Moines, Iowa; Kansas City, Kansas; and St. Louis, Missouri.   **EARTH**

Sept. 1993   A 6.1 magnitude earthquake near Latur, India, destroys more than 20 villages, killing about 10,000 people.   **EARTH**

1993   British mathematician Andrew Wiles reportedly proves Fermat's Last Theorem (*see* 1637), perhaps the most famous unsolved mathematical problem.   **MATH**

1993   U.S. health officials investigate a mysterious, deadly disease afflicting Navajos in New Mexico and Arizona. The disease is determined to be linked to a virus found in rodent droppings.   **MED**

1993   American molecular biologist Raúl J. Cano extracts DNA from a weevil fossilized in amber for 120 to 135 million years.   **PALEO**

1993   U.S. paleontologist John R. Horner reports the discovery of red blood cells in the fossilized leg bone of a 65-million-year-old *Tyrannosaurus rex* found in Montana. Horner hopes that DNA can be extracted from the dinosaur's cells.   **PALEO**

1993   U.S. and Mongolian paleontologists announce the discovery of a 75-million-year-old fossil animal they believe to be a flightless bird transitional between dinosaurs and modern birds. Other scientists disagree, saying that the creature, *Mononychus*, was a dinosaur not ancestral to modern birds.   **PALEO**

1993   Spanish paleontologists find evidence that hominids in Spain were beginning to evolve Neanderthal features as early as 300,000 years ago, much earlier than previously thought.   **PALEO**

1993   American physicists run a supercomputer calculation that appears to confirm the theory of quantum chromodynamics. *See* 1972, Gell-Mann.   **PHYS**

1993   The U.S. Congress votes to terminate funding for the unfinished Superconducting Super Collider. *See* 1989.   **PHYS**

1993   Princeton University researchers set a new record for energy
            production from controlled nuclear fusion, generating more than 3
            megawatts, and later 5 megawatts, of power.   **PHYS**

1993   Researchers develop nanowires, virtual strings of atoms of a few
            nanometers in thickness that may be useful in magnetic recording
            technology.   **TECH**

1994   American archaeologists report evidence of local production of tin
            in Turkey as early as 3,000 B.C. Previously, it was believed that tin
            in the Bronze Age Middle East was imported from such distant
            areas as Afghanistan.   **ARCH**

1994   American scientists report the discovery of genetic traces of
            tuberculosis infection in a thousand-year-old pre-Columbian
            mummy from Peru, proving that Europeans did not introduce the
            disease to the Americas.   **ARCH**

1994   British astronomers report the discovery of the closest known
            galaxy, a dwarf galaxy in the constellation Sagittarius 50,000
            light-years from the Milky Way's center.   **ASTRO**

1994   The U.S. spacecraft *Galileo* transmits the first complete image of a
            moon orbiting an asteroid, 243 Ida.   **ASTRO**

1994   American volcanologists Tobias Fischer and Stanley Williams
            discover a pattern of geological signs that can help predict when a
            volcano is about to erupt. The research results from a 1993
            eruption in Colombia that severely injured Williams and killed nine
            others.   **EARTH**

Jan. 17   Los Angeles suffers a magnitude 6.7 earthquake centered in
1994   Northridge that kills 61 people and costs an estimated $15 billion
            in damages.   **EARTH**

1994   An American medical team reports the first account of successful
            gene therapy to be published in a scientific journal. The team used
            a receptor gene that lowers cholesterol to treat a patient suffering
            from an inherited high-cholesterol disorder.   **MED**

Apr. 1994   American researchers report the discovery of a gene mutation that
            may lead to many forms of cancer.   **MED**

1994   In Pakistan, paleontologist J. G. M. Thewissen and his colleagues
            discover the most solid fossil evidence to date of an ancestral
            whale intermediate between land and sea. The 50-million-year-old
            whale, *Ambulocetus natans,* had large hind legs that were functional
            on land and in water.   **PALEO**

1994   American anthropologist Donald Johanson and his colleagues piece
            together the first nearly complete skull of the human ancestor
            Australopithecus afarensis from fragments found in 1992 at Hadar,
            Ethiopia. *See also* 1974, Lucy.   **PALEO**

1994   American scientists report the discovery of the earliest known land life, tubular microorganisms from Arizona dating from 1.2 billion years ago.   **PALEO**

1994   New Zealand physicist Daniel F. Walls and his colleagues show theoretically that the relationship between the complementarity and uncertainty principles must always hold in quantum experiments employing closely spaced double slits.   **PHYS**

1994   An international team of physicists at Fermilab in Illinois discovers evidence for the top quark, a fundamental particle sought for nearly two decades.   **PHYS**

1994   A comprehensive survey in the *Archives of General Psychiatry* indicates that nearly half of all American adults experience a mental disorder at some point in their lives.   **PSYCH**

APPENDIX:
BIRTH AND DEATH DATES

Abbe, Cleveland	1838–1916	Balard, Antoine-Jérôme	1802–1876
Abel, Niels Henrik	1802–1829	Balboa, Vasco Núñez	c. 1475–1519
Abelson, Philip Hauge	1913–	Balmer, Johann Jakob	1825–1898
Acheson, Edward Goodrich	1856–1931	Banting, Sir Frederick Grant	1891–1941
Adler, Alfred	1870–1937	Bardeen, John	1908–1991
Agassiz, Louis	1807–1873	Barnard, Christiaan	1922–
Aiken, Howard H.	1900–1973	Barnard, Edward Emerson	1857–1923
al-Khwārizmī, Muhammad	780–850	Barth, Heinrich	1821–1865
Albertus Magnus	1193–1280	Bateson, William	1861–1926
Aldrin, Edwin E. (Buzz)	1930–	Baudot, Jean-Maurice-Émile	1845–1903
Alhazen (al-Hasan)	965–1039	Bauer, Sebastian Wilhelm	1822–1875
Alpini, Prospero	1553–1616	Beau de Rochas, Alphonse	1815–1893
Alvarez, Luis Walter	1911–1988	Becquerel,	
Ampère, André-Marie	1775–1836	Alexandre-Edmond	1820–1891
Amundsen, Roald	1872–1928	Becquerel, Antoine–Henri	1852–1908
Anaximander	610–547 B.C.	Beg, Ulugh	1394–1449
Anders, William A.	1933–	Behring, Emil Adolf von	1854–1917
Ångström, Anders Jonas	1814–1874	Bell, Alexander Graham	1847–1922
Anning, Mary	1799–1847	Bell, Sir Charles	1774–1842
Archimedes	c. 287–212 B.C.	Benedict, Ruth	1887–1948
Arfwedson, Johan A.	1792–1841	Bennett, Floyd	1890–1928
Aristotle	384–322 B.C.	Benz, Carl Friedrich	1844–1929
Arkwright, Sir Richard	1732–1792	Bering, Vitus J.	1681–1741
Armstrong, Neil	1930–	Bernard, Claude	1813–1878
Arrhenius, Svante	1859–1927	Bernoulli, Daniel	1700–1782
Arzachel	fl. c. 1075	Bernoulli, Jakob	1654–1705
Avogadro, Amedeo	1776–1856	Berthelot,	
Baade, Walter	1893–1960	Pierre-Eugéne-Marcelin	1866–1934
Babbage, Charles	1792–1871	Berzelius, Jöns Jakob	1779–1848
Bacon, Francis	1561–1626	Bessel, Friedrich Wilhelm	1784–1846
Bacon, Roger	c. 1220–1292	Bessemer, Sir Henry	1813–1898
Baekeland, Leo Hendrik	1863–1944	Best, Charles	1899–1978
Baer, Karl Ernst von	1792–1876	Bettelheim, Bruno	1903–1990
Bain, Alexander	1818–1903	Binet, Alfred	1857–1911
Baird, J. L.	1888–1946	Bingham, Hiram	1875–1956

Coriolis,			Doolittle, James	1896–1993
Gaspard-Gustave de	1792–1843		Doppler, Christian Johann	1803–1853
Corliss, George Henry	1817–1888		Dorn, Friedrich E.	1848–1916
Coronado, Francisco de	c. 1510–1554		Doughty, Charles Montagu	1843–1926
Cort, Henry	1740–1800		Dove, Heinrich	1803–1879
Cortés, Hernando	1485–1547		Drake, Sir Francis	1540–1596
Coster, Dirk	1889–1950		Drebbel, Cornelis van	1572–1633
Coulomb,			Dubois, Marie Eugène	1858–1940
Charles-Augustin de	1736–1806		Dujardin, Félix	1801–1860
Courtois, Bernard	1777–1838		Dunlop, John	1840–1921
Cousteau, Jacques-Yves	1910–		Durkheim, Émile	1858–1971
Crick, Francis	1916–		Duryea, Charles	1861–1938
Crile, George Washington	1864–1943		Duryea, James Frank	1869–1967
Crippen, Robert L.	1937–		Dutrochet, René	1776–1847
Crompton, Samuel	1753–1827		Dutton, Clarence Edward	1841–1912
Cronstedt, Baron Axel F.	1722–1765		Eddington, Sir Arthur Stanley	1882–1944
Crookes, Sir William	1832–1919		Edison, Thomas A.	1847–1931
Cross, Charles Frederick	1855–1935		Ehrlich, Paul	1854–1915
Cugnot, Nicolas-Joseph	1725–1804		Eijkman, Christiaan	1858–1930
Curie, Marie Sklodowska	1867–1934		Einstein, Albert	1879–1955
Curie, Pierre	1859–1906		Ekeberg, Anders G.	1767–1813
Cuvier, Baron	1769–1832		Elhuyar, Fausto d'	1755–1833
da Vinci, Leonardo	1452–1519		Elhuyar, Juan	1754–1804
da Gama, Vasco	c. 1460–1524		Enders, John Franklin	1897–1985
Daguerre,			Eratosthenes	c. 276–c. 194 B.C.
Louis-Jacques-Mandé	1789–1851		Ericsson, John	1803–1889
Daimler, Gottlieb	1834–1900		Esmarch, Friedrich A. von	1823–1908
Dalton, John	1766–1844		Espy, James	1785–1860
Dart, Raymond	1893–1988		Euclid	fl. c. 300 B.C.
Darwin, Charles	1809–1882		Eudoxus of Cnidus	c. 408–355 B.C.
Davenport, Thomas	1802–1851		Euler, Leonhard	1707–1783
Davy, Sir Humphry	1778–1829		Eustachio, Bartolommeo	c. 1520–1574
Debierne, André-Louis	1874–1949		Evans, Oliver	1755–1819
Deere, John	1804–1886		Evans-Pritchard,	
De Forest, Lee	1873–1961		Edward Evan	1902–1973
Delbrück, Max	1906–1981		Eyre, Edward John	1815–1901
Demarçay, Eùgene-Anatole	1852–1903		Fahrenheit, Daniel Gabriel	1686–1736
Democritus	c. 460–370 B.C.		Fallopius, Gabriele	1523–1562
Descartes, René	1596–1650		Faraday, Michael	1791–1867
de Vries, Hugo	1848–1935		Fauchard, Pierre	1678–1761
Dias, Bartolomeu	c. 1450–1500		Fenton, Roger	1819–1869
Diesel, Rudolf	1858–1913		Fermat, Pierre de	1601–1665
Dirac, Paul Adrien Maurice	1902–1984		Fermi, Enrico	1901–1954
Domagk, Gerhard	1895–1964		Ferraris, Galileo	1847–1897
Dooley, Thomas	1927–1961		Feynman, Richard Phillips	1918–1988

Fibonacci, Leonardo	1170–1230	Goethals,	
Fischer, Emil	1852–1919	George Washington	1858–1928
Fitch, John	1743–1798	Golgi, Camillo	1844–1926
FitzGerald, George Francis	1851–1901	Gomberg, Moses	1866–1947
Flagg, Josiah	1763–1816	Goodwin, Hannibal W.	1822–1900
Flammarion, Camille	1842–1925	Goodyear, Charles	1800–1860
Fleming, Sir Alexander	1881–1955	Gorgas, William C.	1854–1920
Fleming, Sir John	1849–1945	Graaff, Robert J. van de	1901–1966
Ford, Henry	1863–1947	Gramme, Zénobe Théophile	1826–1901
Fourier, Jean-Baptiste-Joseph	1768–1830	Gregor, William	1761–1817
Fournier, Pierre-Simon	1712–1768	Grew, Nehemiah	1641–1712
Franck, James	1882–1964	Grissom, Virgil I.	1926–1967
Franklin, Benjamin	1706–1790	Grotefend, Georg Friedrich	1775–1853
Fraunhofer, Joseph von	1787–1826	Guericke, Otto von	1602–1686
Frazer, Sir James George	1854–1941	Gutenberg, Johannes	c. 1398–c. 1468
Frege, Gottlob	1848–1925	Haeckel, Ernst	1834–1919
Frémont, John Charles	1813–1890	Hahn, Otto	1879–1968
Frere, John	1740–1807	Haldane, J. B. S.	1892–1964
Fresnel, Augustin	1788–1827	Hale, George Ellery	1868–1938
Freud, Anna	1895–1982	Hall, Asaph	1829–1907
Freud, Sigmund	1856–1939	Hall, Sir James	1761–1832
Frobisher, Sir Martin	c. 1535–1594	Hall, Marshall	1790–1857
Fulton, Robert	1765–1815	Haller, Albrecht von	1708–1777
Funk, Casimir	1884–1967	Halley, Edmund	1656–1742
Gadolin, Johan	1760–1852	Hardy, G. H.	1877–1947
Gagarin, Yuri A.	1934–1968	Hargreaves, James	c. 1720–1778
Galen, Claudius	c. 130–c. 199	Harrison, John	1693–1776
Galilei, Galileo	1564–1642	Hartley, David	1705–1757
Gall, Franz Joseph	1758–1828	Harvey, William	1578–1657
Galle, Johann Gottfried	1812–1910	Hatchett, Charles	1765–1847
Galois, Evariste	1811–1832	Hawking, Stephen William	1942–
Galton, Sir Francis	1822–1911	Heaviside, Oliver	1850–1925
Galvani, Luigi	1737–1798	Heisenberg, Werner Karl	1901–1976
Gatling, Richard Jordan	1818–1903	Helmholtz, Hermann	
Gauss, Carl Friedrich	1777–1855	Ludwig Ferdinand von	1821–1894
Gay-Lussac, Joseph-Louis	1778–1850	Henry the Navigator,	
Geiger, Johannes Hans	1882–1945	Prince of Portugal	1394–1460
Gell-Mann, Murray	1929–	Henry, Joseph	1797–1878
Gesner, Conrad von	1516–1565	Hero of Alexandria	fl. A.D. 62
Ghiorso, Albert	1915–	Herodotus	c. 485–428 B.C.
Gibbs, Josiah Willard	1839–1903	Herschel, John	1792–1871
Gilbert, William	1544–1603	Herschel, Sir William	1738–1822
Glenn, John	1921–	Hertz, Heinrich Rudolph	1857–1894
Goddard, Robert H.	1882–1945	Hertzsprung, Ejnar	1873–1967
Gödel, Kurt	1906–1978	Hess, Harry	1906–1969

Hess, Victor Franz	1883–1964	Kekule von Stradonitz,	
Hevesy, Georg C. de	1885–1966	Friedrich A.	1829–1896
Hewitt, Peter C.	1861–1921	Kelvin,	
Hilbert, David	1862–1943	William Thomson, Lord	1824–1907
Hippocrates	c. 460–c. 370 B.C.	Kennelly, Arthur Edwin	1861–1939
Hisinger, Wilhelm	1766–1852	Kenny, Sister Elizabeth	1880–1952
Holland, John P.	1840–1914	Kepler, Johannes	1571–1630
Hollerith, Hermann	1860–1929	Kingsley, Norman W.	1829–1913
Hooke, Robert	1635–1703	Kircher, Athanasius	1601–1680
Hopkins,		Kirchhoff, Gottlieb Sigismund	1704–1833
Sir Frederick Gowland	1861–1947	Kirchhoff, Gustav Robert	1824–1887
Hoppe-Seyler, Ernst Felix	1825–1895	Kirkwood, Daniel	1814–1895
Howe, Elias	1819–1867	Klaproth, Martin H.	1743–1817
Hubble, Edwin P.	1889–1953	Klaus, Karl K.	1796–1864
Hudson, Henry	fl. 1607–1611	Klietsch, Karl	1841–1926
Hughes, David E.	1831–1900	Koch, Robert	1843–1910
Hughes, Howard	1905–1976	Koldewey, Robert	1855–1925
Humboldt, Alexander von	1769–1859	Kölliker, Albrecht von	1817–1905
Hunter, John	1728–1793	Krebs, Sir Hans Adolf	1900–1981
Huntsman, Benjamin	1704–1776	Kroeber, Alfred Lewis	1876–1960
Hutton, James	1726–1797	La Salle,	
Huxley, Julian	1887–1975	René-Robert Cavelier de	1643–1687
Huxley, Thomas Henry	1825–1895	Laënnec, René T. H.	1781–1826
Huygens, Christiaan	1629–1695	Lagrange, Joseph-Louis	1736–1813
Hyatt, John W.	1837–1920	Lamarck, Jean-Baptiste de	1744–1829
Imhotep	c. 2980–2950 B.C.	Land, Edwin Herbert	1909–1991
Ivanovsky, Dmitry	1864–1920	Landsteiner, Karl	1868–1943
Ives, Frederic Eugene	1856–1937	Langley, Samuel Pierpont	1834–1906
James, William	1842–1910	Langmuir, Irving	1881–1957
Jansky, Karl G.	1905–1950	Laplace, Pierre Simon de	1749–1827
Janssen,		Lassell, William	1799–1880
Pierre-Jules-César	1824–1907	Lavoisier, Antoine-Laurent	1743–1794
Jenner, Edward	1749–1823	Lawrence, Ernest O.	1901–1958
Jenner, Sir William	1815–1898	Layard, Sir Austen Henry	1817–1894
Joliet, Louis	1645–1700	Leakey, Louis	1903–1972
Joliot-Curie, Frédéric	1900–1958	Leakey, Mary	1913–
Joliot-Curie, Irène	1897–1956	Leakey, Richard	1944–
Jones, Sir William	1746–1794	Leavitt, Henrietta Swan	1868–1921
Jouffroy d'Abbans,		Leblanc, Maurice	1857–1923
Marquis de	1751–1832	Lee, Tsung-dao	1926–
Joule, James P.	1818–1889	Leeuwenhoek, Anton van	1632–1723
Jung, Carl Gustav	1875–1961	Leibniz,	
Kamerlingh Onnes, Heike	1853–1926	Gottfried Wilhelm	1646–1716
Kant, Immanuel	1724–1804	Lemaître, Georges-Henri	1894–1966
Kay, John	1704–1764	Lenoir, Jean-Joseph Étienne	1822–1900

Leonov, Alexei A.	1934–	Marx, Karl	1818–1883
Levene, Aaron	1869–1940	Maspero,	
Leverrier, Urbain-Jean-Joseph	1811–1877	Gaston-Camille-Charles	1846–1916
Lévi-Strauss, Claude	1908–	Maury, Matthew Fontaine	1806–1873
Lewis, Meriwether	1774–1809	Maxwell, James Clerk	1831–1879
Libby, Willard Frank	1908–1980	Mayer, Maria Goeppert	1906–1972
Liebig, Justus von	1803–1873	Mayow, John	1641–1679
Lilienthan, Otto	1848–1896	Mead, Margaret	1901–1978
Lindbergh, Charles A.	1902–1974	Meitner, Lise	1878–1968
Linde,		Mendel, Gregor J.	1822–1884
Carl Paul Gottfried von	1842–1934	Mendeleyev,	
Linnaeus, Carolus	1707–1778	Dmitry Ivanovich	1834–1907
Linton, Ralph	1893–1953	Mercator, Gerardus (Kremer)	1512–1594
Lister, Joseph	1827–1912	Mergenthaler, Ottmar	1854–1899
Lister, Joseph Jackson	1786–1869	Merrifield, Bruce	1921–
Livingstone, David	1813–1873	Mesmer, Franz Anton	1734–1815
Lobachevsky,		Meyer, Adolf	1866–1950
Nikolai Ivanovich	1792–1856	Michelson, Albert Abraham	1852–1931
Lockyer, Sir Joseph N.	1836–1920	Mill, James	1773–1836
Long, Crawford W.	1815–1878	Miller, Stanley Lloyd	1930–
Lorenz, Edward	1917–	Miller, Willoughby D.	1853–1907
Lorenz, Konrad	1903–1989	Millikan, Robert Andrews	1868–1953
Lovell Jr., James A.	1928–	Milne, John	1850–1913
Lowe, Thaddeus		Mohl, Hugh von	1805–1872
Sobieski Coulincourt	1832–1913	Mohorovičić, Andrija	1857–1936
Lowell, Percival	1855–1916	Moissan, Henri	1852–1907
Lower, Richard	1631–1691	Monier, Joseph	1823–1906
Lumière, Auguste	1862–1954	Morgan, Louis Henry	1818–1881
Lumière, Louis	1864–1948	Morgan, Thomas Hunt	1866–1945
McAdam, John	1756–1836	Morgenstern, Oskar	1902–1977
McClintock, Barbara	1902–1992	Morley, Edward Williams	1838–1923
McCormick, Cyrus Hall	1809–1884	Morse, Samuel F. B.	1791–1872
Mackenzie, Sir Alexander	1764–1820	Mosander, Carl Gustaf	1797–1858
McMillan, Edwin M.	1907–	Müller, Franz J.	1740–1825
Magellan, Ferdinand	c. 1480–1521	Müller, Johannes Peter	1801–1858
Maiman, Theodore	1927–	Müller, Paul H.	1899–1965
Malinowski, Bronislaw	1884–1942	Murchison, Sir Roderick I.	1792–1871
Malpighi, Marcello	1628–1694	Murdock, William	1754–1839
Malthus, Thomas Robert	1766–1834	Nansen, Fridtjof	1861–1930
Manly, Charles M.	1876–1927	Napier, John	1550–1617
Marconi, Guglielmo	1874–1937	Natta, Giulio	1903–1979
Marggraf, Andreas S.	1709–1782	Nernst, Walther Herrmann	1864–1941
Marignac, Jean-Charles de	1817–1894	Neumann, John von	1903–1957
Marquette, Jacques	1637–1675	Newcomen, Thomas	1663–1729
Marsh, Othniel Charles	1831–1899	Newton, Sir Isaac	1642–1727

Nicolet, Jean	1598–1642
Niepce, Joseph-Nicéphore	1765–1833
Nightingale, Florence	1820–1910
Nilson, Lars Fredrik	1840–1899
Nipkow, Paul Gottlieb	1860–1940
Nobel, Alfred Bernhard	1833–1896
Noddack, Ida Tacke	1896–
Noddack, Walter	1893–1960
Noether, Amalie (Emmy)	1882–1935
Nordenskjöld, Nils Adolf	1832–1901
Noyce, Robert N.	1927–1989
Obërth, Hermann	1894–1989
Ochoa, Severo	1905–1993
Oersted, Hans Christian	1777–1851
Ohm, Georg Simon	1789–1854
Olbers, Heinrich Wilhelm	1758–1840
Olds, Ransom Eli	1864–1950
Oppenheimer, Julius Robert	1904–1967
Ostwald, Friedrich Wilhelm	1853–1932
Otis, Elisha Graves	1811–1861
Otto, Nikolaus August	1832–1891
Oughtred, William	1574–1660
Owen, Sir Richard	1804–1892
Papin, Denis	1647–c. 1712
Paracelsus (Bombast von Hohenheim)	c. 1493–1541
Paré, Ambroise	1510–1590
Park, Mungo	1771–1806
Parker, Eugene N.	1927–
Parsons, Sir Charles Algernon	1854–1931
Parsons, William	1800–1867
Pascal, Blaise	1623–1662
Pasteur, Louis	1822–1895
Pauli, Wolfgang	1900–1958
Pauling, Linus Carl	1901–
Pavlov, Ivan	1849–1936
Pearson, Karl	1857–1936
Peary, Robert E.	1856–1920
Penn, William	1644–1718
Perey, Marguerite	1909–1975
Piaget, Jean	1896–1980
Piazzi, Giuseppe	1746–1826
Pickering, William Henry	1858–1938
Pinel, Philippe	1745–1826

Pizarro, Francisco	c. 1475–1541
Planck, Max	1858–1947
Plato	427–347 B.C.
Poincaré, Jules-Henri	1854–1912
Polo, Marco	c. 1254–c. 1324
Ponce de León, Juan	c. 1460–1521
Porta, Giambattista della	1535?–1615
Prévost, Pierre	1751–1839
Priestley, Joseph	1733–1804
Proust, Joseph-Louis	1754–1826
Przhevalsky, Nikolay	1839–1888
Ptolemalus, Claudius (Ptolemy)	c. 85–165
Pullman, George M.	1831–1897
Purkinje, Jan Evangelista	1787–1869
Pythagoras	c. 582–c. 507 B.C.
Rabi, Isidor Isaac	1898–1988
Radcliffe-Brown, Alfred Reginald	1881–1955
Ramsay, Sir William	1852–1916
Rassam, Hormuzd	1826–1910
Rawlinson, Sir Henry Creswicke	1810–1895
Rayleigh, 3rd Baron (John W. Strutt)	1842–1919
Reber, Grote	1911–
Redi, Francesco	1626–1697
Reed, Walter S.	1851–1902
Reich, Ferdinand	1799–1882
Renault, Louis	1877–1944
Richter, Charles Francis	1900–1985
Ride, Sally K.	1951–
Riemann, Georg Friedrich Bernhard	1826–1866
Rogers, Moses	1779–1821
Römer, Ole or Olaus	1644–1710
Röntgen, Wilhelm	1845–1923
Rorschach, Hermann	1884–1922
Ross, Sir James Clark	1800–1862
Rous, Francis	1879–1970
Rudolf, Christoff	c. 1500–1545
Russell, Bertrand Arthur William	1872–1970
Russell, Henry Norris	1877–1957
Rutherford, Daniel	1749–1819

Rutherford, Ernest	1871–1937	Speke, John Hanning	1827–1864
Sabin, Albert	1906–1993	Sperry, Elmer Ambrose	1860–1930
Sagan, Carl	1935–	Stahl, George	1660–1734
Salk, Jonas Edward	1914–	Stanley, Sir Henry M.	1841–1904
Sanctorius (Santorio Santorio)	1561–1636	Starling, Ernest	1866–1927
Sarnoff, David	1891–1971	Staudinger, Hermann	1881–1965
Saussure,		Steinmetz, Charles Proteus	1865–1923
Horace Bénédict de	1740–1799	Steno, Nicolaus	1638–1686
Savery, Thomas	c. 1650–1715	Stephenson, George	1781–1848
Scheele, Carl Wilhelm	1742–1786	Stevens, John C.	1749–1839
Schiaparelli, Giovanni	1835–1910	Stevens, Robert Livingston	1787–1856
Schleiden, Matthias Jakob	1804–1881	Stevinus, Simon	1548–1620
Schliemann, Heinrich	1822–1890	Steward, Julian H.	1902–1972
Schmidt, Bernhard	1879–1935	Stewart, Balfour	1828–1887
Schröder, Johann	1600–1664	Stieglitz, Alfred	1864–1946
Schrödinger, Erwin	1887–1961	Stoney, George Johnston	1926–1911
Schwann, Theodor	1810–1882	Strabo	c. 63 B.C.–A.D. 21
Schwarzschild, Karl	1873–1916	Strasburger,	
Schweitzer, Albert	1875–1965	Eduard Adolf	1844–1912
Scott, Robert Falcon	1868–1912	Strohmeyer, Friedrich	1776–1835
Seaborg, Glenn T.	1912–	Strutt, Jedidiah	1726–1797
Secchi, Pietro Angelo	1818–1878	Strutt, John William,	
Sedgwick, Adam	1785–1873	Lord Rayleigh	1842–1919
Seebeck, Thomas Johann	1770–1831	Stuart, John McDouall	1815–1866
Sefström, Nils G.	1787–1854	Sully, James	1842–1923
Segré, Emilio Gino	1905–1989	Sutton, Walter	1877–1916
Semmelweis, Ignaz P.	1818–1865	Sydenham, Thomas	1624–1689
Senefelder, Aloys	1771–1834	Szilard, Leo	1898–1964
Sertüner, Friedrich	1783–1841	Talbot, William H. F.	1800–1877
Seyfert, Carl K.	1911–1960	Tasman, Abel Janszoon	c. 1603–1659?
Shanks, William	1821–1882	Teller, Edward	1908–
Shapley, Harlow	1885–1972	Tennant, Smithson	1761–1815
Shepard Jr., Alan B.	1923–	Tesla, Nikola	1856–1943
Shockley, William	1910–	Thales of Miletus	c. 636–546 B.C.
Siebold,		Thénard, Louis-Jacques	1777–1857
Karl Theodor Ernst von	1804–1885	Theodoric of Freiburg	c. 1250–c. 1310
Siemens, Ernst Werner von	1816–1892	Theophrastus	c. 372–287 B.C.
Sikorsky, Igor	1889–1972	Thomas, Joseph	1856–1940
Simpson, Sir James Young	1811–1870	Thompson, Benjamin	1753–1814
Skinner, B. F	1904–1990	Thomson, Sir Joseph John	1856–1940
Smith, Adam	1723–1790	Thomson,	
Smith, William	1769–1839	William, Lord Kelvin	1824–1907
Solvay, Ernest	1838–1922	Thorndike, Edward Lee	1874–1949
Soret, Jacques L.	1827–1890	Tombaugh, Clyde William	1906–
Soto, Hernando de	c. 1500–1542	Torricelli, Evangelista	1608–1647

Travers, Morris William	1872–1961	Wells, Horace	1815–1848
Trevithick, Richard	1771–1833	Welsbach, Carl Auer von	1858–1929
Tsiolkovsky, Konstantin	1857–1935	Wertheimer, Max	1880–1943
Tull, Jethro	1674–1741	Westinghouse, George	1846–1914
Turing, Alan Mathison	1912–1954	Wheatstone, Sir Charles	1802–1875
Turner, Victor	1920–	Whipple, Fred L.	1906–
Tylor, Sir Edward B.	1832–1917	White II, Edward H.	1930–1967
Ulloa, Antonio de	1716–1795	Whitehead, Robert	1823–1905
Urey, Harold Clayton	1893–1981	Whitney, Eli	1765–1825
van't Hoff,		Whittle, Frank	1907–
Jacobus Hendricus	1852–1911	Wiener, Norbert	1894–1964
Vauquelin, Louis-Nicolas	1763–1829	Wilkes, Charles	1798–1877
Verrazano, Giovanni da	c. 1480–1528	Williams, Daniel	1858–1931
Vesalius, Andreas	1514–1564	Wills, William John	1833–1861
Vespucci, Amerigo	1454–1512	Winkler,	
Viète, François	1540–1603	Clemens Alexander	1838–1904
Virchow, Rudolf	1821–1902	Withering, William	1741–1799
Vogel, Hermann Wilhelm	1834–1889	Wöhler, Friedrich	1800–1882
Volta, Alessandro	1745–1827	Wollaston, William H.	1766–1828
Wakswan, Selman	1888–1973	Woolley, Leonard	1880–1960
Wallace, Alfred Russel	1823–1913	Wright, Sewall	1889–1988
Wasserman, August von	1866–1925	Wright, Orville	1871–1948
Watson, John Broadus	1878–1958	Wright, Wilbur	1867–1912
Watson, James	1928–	Wundt, Wilhelm	1832–1920
Watson-Watt, Robert A.	1892–1973	Yang, Chen Ning	1922–
Watt, James E.	1736–1819	Young, John W.	1930–
Weber, Max	1864–1920	Young, Thomas	1773–1829
Weber, Wilhelm Eduard	1804–1891	Zeppelin, Ferdinand von	1838–1917
Wedgwood, Thomas	1771–1831	Zhang Heng	78–139
Wegener, Alfred L.	1880–1930	Ziegler, Karl W.	1898–1973
Weismann, August	1834–1914		

BIBLIOGRAPHY

Abell, George O. *Exploration of the Universe*, 3rd ed. New York: Holt, Rinehart & Winston, 1975.

Alberto, Bruce, et al. *Molecular Biology of the Cell*. New York: Garland, 1989.

Asimov, Isaac, *Asimov's Biographical Encyclopedia of Science and Technology*, 2nd rev. ed. Garden City, NY: Doubleday, 1982.

———. *Asimov's Chronology of Science and Discovery*. New York: Harper & Row, 1989.

———. *Asimov's New Guide to Science*. New York: Basic Books, 1984.

———. *Experiencing the Earth and the Cosmos: The Growth and Future of Human Knowledge*. New York: Crown, 1982.

Asimov, Isaac, and Jason A. Shulman, ed. *Isaac Asimov's Book of Science and Nature Quotations*. New York: Weidenfeld & Nicolson, 1988.

Barnhart, Robert K. *Hammond Barnhart Dictionary of Science*. Maplewood, NJ: Barnhart Books, 1986.

Bettman, Otto. *A Pictorial History of Medicine*. Springfield, IL: Charles C. Thomas, 1956.

Borell, Merriley, and I. Bernard Cohen, ed. *Album of Science: The Biological Sciences in the 20th Century*. New York: Charles Scribner's Sons, 1989.

Boyer, Carl B. and Uta C. Merzbach. *A History of Mathematics*, 2nd ed. New York: John Wiley & Sons, 1991.

Bruno, Leonard C. *The Landmarks of Science*. New York: Facts on File, 1989.

Bynum, W. F., et al., eds. *Dictionary of the History of Science*. Princeton: Princeton University Press, 1981.

Castiglioni, Arturo. *A History of Medicine*. New York: Alfred A. Knopf, 1941.

Chandler, Caroline. *Famous Modern Men of Medicine*. New York: Dodd, Mead & Co., 1965.

Clayman, Charles, ed. *The American Medical Association Encyclopedia of Medicine*. New York: Random House, 1989.

Coe, Michael D. *Breaking the Maya Code*. New York: Thames & Hudson, 1992.

Colbert, Edwin H. *The Great Dinosaur Hunters and Their Discoveries*. New York: Dover, 1984.

Corsini, Raymond J., ed. *Concise Encylopedia of Psychology*. New York: John Wiley & Sons, 1987.

DeBono, Edward, ed. *Eureka! An Illustrated History of Inventions from the Wheel to the Computer*. London: Thames & Hudson, 1974.

Degler, Carl N. *In Search of Human Nature: The Decline and Revival of Darwinism in American Social Thought*. New York: Oxford University Press, 1991.

Dennett, Daniel C. *Consciousness Explained*. Boston: Little, Brown & Co., 1991.

Diamond, Jared. *The Third Chimpanzee: The Evolution and Future of the Human Animal*. New York: Harper Perennial, 1993.

Discover. New York.

Dolan, Josephine. *History of Nursing*. Philadelphia: W. B. Saunders, 1968.

Fancher, Raymond. *Pioneers of Psychology*. New York: W. W. Norton & Co., 1979.

Faul, Henry, and Carol Faul. *It Began with a Stone*. New York: John Wiley & Sons, 1983.

Fox, Ruth. *Milestones of Medicine*. New York: Random House, 1950.

Funk and Wagnalls New Encyclopedia. New York: Funk and Wagnalls.

Gascoigne, Robert Mortimer. *A Chronology of the History of Science, 1450–1900*. New York: Garland, 1987.

Gillispie, Charles C., ed. *Dictionary of Scientific Biography*. New York: Charles Scribner's Sons, 1981.

Gjertsen, Derek. *The Classics of Science*. New York: Lilian Barber Press, 1984.

Golob, Richard, and Eric Brus. *The Almanac of Science and Technology*. New York: Harcourt Brace Jovanovich, 1990.

Gould, Stephen Jay. *Wonderful Life: The Burgess Shale and the Nature of History*. New York: W. W. Norton & Co., 1989.

Gregory, Bruce. *Inventing Reality: Physics as Language*. New York: John Wiley & Sons, 1988.

Grolier's Academic American Encyclopedia, Online Edition.

Grun, Bernard. *The Timetables of History*. New York: Touchstone, 1982.

Harper, Patrick, ed. *The Timetable of Technology. A Record of the 20th Century's Amazing Achievements*. London: Marshall's Editions, 1982.

Harvard Health Letter. Boston: Harvard Medical School Health Publications Group.

Hellemans, Alexander, and Bryan Bunch. *The Timetables of Science*. New York: Simon & Schuster, 1988.

Hunt, Elgin F., and David C. Colander. *Social Science: An Introduction to the Study of Society*, 6th ed. New York: Macmillan, 1987.

The Information Please Almanac 1993. Boston: Houghton Mifflin, 1992.

Inglis, Brian. *A History of Medicine*. Cleveland: World Publishing Co., 1965.

Isaacs, Alan, et al. *Concise Science Dictionary*, 2nd ed. Oxford: Oxford University Press, 1991.

Johnson, George. *Machinery of the Mind: Inside the New Science of Artificial Intelligence*. New York: Times Books, 1986.

Kane, Joseph Nathan. *Famous First Facts*. New York: H. W. Wilson Co., 1981.

Karier, Clarence J. *Scientists of the Mind*. Urbana: University of Illinois Press, 1986.

Levy, Judith S., and Agnes Greenhall, ed. *The Concise Columbia Encyclopedia*. New York: Avon, 1983.

Macorini, Edgardo, ed. *The History of Science and Technology: A Narrative Chronology*, vol. 2, 1900–1970. New York: Facts on File, 1988.

Matthews, Peter, ed. *The Guinness Book of Records 1993*. New York: Bantam, 1993.

McGraw-Hill Yearbook of Science and Technology 1993. New York: McGraw-Hill, 1992.

McGrew, Rodrick. *Encyclopedia of Medical History*. New York: McGraw-Hill, 1985.

Morris, Richard B., and Graham W. Irwin, ed. *Harper Encyclopedia of the Modern World*. New York: Harper & Row, 1970.

Mount, Ellis, and Barbara List. *Milestones in Science and Technology*. New York: Oryx Press, 1987.

Natural History. New York.

The New York Times. New York.

Nuland, Sherwin. *Doctors: A Biography of Medicine*. New York: Alfred A. Knopf, 1988.

Ochoa, George, and Jeffrey Osier. *The Writer's Guide to Creating a Science Fiction Universe*. Cincinnati: Writer's Digest Books, 1993.

Ogilvie, Marilyn Bailey. *Women in Science: Antiquity through the Nineteenth Century*. Cambridge, MA: MIT Press, 1986.

Olby, R. C., et al., eds. *Companion to the History of Modern Science*. London: Routledge, 1990.

The Oxford Dictionary of Quotations, 3rd ed. Oxford: Oxford University Press, 1980.

Pacey, Arnold. *Technology in World Civilization*. Cambridge, MA: MIT Press, 1990.

Palfreman, Jon, and Doron Swade. *The Dream Machine: Exploring the Computer Age*. London: BBC Books, 1991.

Panati, Charles. *The Browser's Book of Beginnings*. Boston: Houghton Mifflin, 1984.

———. *Extraordinary Origins of Everyday Things*. New York: Harper & Row, 1987.

Parker, Steve. *The Dawn of Man*. New York: Crescent Books, 1992.

Parkinson, Claire. *Breakthroughs: A Chronology of Great Achievements in Science and Mathematics*. Boston: G. K. Hall & Co., 1985.

Patent, Dorothy. *The Quest for Artificial Intelligence*. New York: Harcourt Brace Jovanovich, 1986.

Ronan, Colin A. *Science: Its History and Development Among the World's Cultures*. New York: Facts on File, 1982.

Salzberg, Hugh W. *From Caveman to Chemist*. Washington, DC: American Chemical Society, 1991.

Science News. Washington, DC.

Scientific American. New York.

Sigerist, Henry. *Primitive and Archaic Medicine*. New York: Oxford University Press, 1967.

Struik, Dirk J. *A Concise History of Mathematics*, 4th ed. New York: Dover, 1987.

Talbott, John. *A Biographical History of Medicine*. New York: Grune and Stratton, 1970.

Torpie, Stephen, et al., ed. *American Men and Women of Science*, 18th ed. New Providence, NJ: R. R. Bowker/Reed, 1992.

Trager, James. *The People's Chronology*. New York: Henry Holt, 1992.

Trefil, James. *1,001 Things Everyone Should Know about Science*. New York: Doubleday, 1992.

Unschuld, Paul. *Medicine in China: A History of Ideas*. Berkeley: University of California Press, 1985.

Van Doren, Charles. *A History of Knowledge*. New York: Ballantine, 1991.

Walton, John, and Paul Beeson, eds. *The Oxford Companion to Medicine*. Oxford: Oxford University Press, 1986.

Webster's Medical Desk Dictionary. Springfield, MA: Merriam Webster, 1986.

Wetterau, Bruce. *The New York Public Library Book of Chronologies*. New York: Prentice Hall Press, 1990.

Wolman, Benjamin, ed. *Dictionary of Behavioral Science*, 2nd ed. New York: Academic Press, 1989.

————, ed. *International Encyclopedia of Psychiatry, Psychology, Psychoanalysis and Neurology*. New York: Aesculapius Publishers, 1977.

The World Almanac and Book of Facts 1992. New York: Pharos, 1991.

Zusne, Leonard. *Names in the History of Psychology: A Biographical Sourcebook*. Washington, DC: Hemisphere Publishing, 1975.

INDEX

INDEX

Antimatter, 268
Antineutrinos, 316
Antiprotons, 314
Apollonius of Perga, 17, 19
Appert, Nicolas, 121
Appian Way, 16–17
Appius Claudius Caecus, 16–17
Aqueducts, 10, 22, 155
Arago, François, 131–32
Arber, Werner, 353
Archer, Scott, 161
Archimedean screw, 17
Archimedes, 17–18
Archimedes' principle, 18
Architectural acoustics, 218
Architecture: arch, 9; Gothic, 34; pyramids, 6,
312; skyscraper, 204; suburban housing, 297
Arderne, John of, 38
Ardrey, Robert, 334
Arfwedson, Johan August, 128, 304
Aristaeus, 17
Aristarchus of Samos, 19, 69
Aristotle, 14–15
Armillary ring, 20, 23
Armstrong, Edwin H., 249, 273
Armstrong, Neil A., 338
Armstrong, William, 154
Arnold, H. D., 243
Arnon, Daniel Israel, 312
Arrhenius, Svante, 202, 208, 246
Arsenic, 35
Artificial intelligence (AI), 295, 318, 330
Artificial sweeteners, 320, 362
Asclepiades, 20
Ashkin, Arthur, 368
Aspdin, Joseph, 134
Astbury, William Thomas, 267
Asteroids, 117, 119, 302, 353, 380
Aston, Francis William, 251, 258
Astrolabe, 19, 29
Astronautics, 221, 228
Astronauts, American: Aldrin, Edwin E. "Buzz",
Jr., 338; Anders, William A., 337; Bean,
Alan L., 338; Bluford, Guion, Jr., 361; Borman,
Frank, 337; Chaffee, Roger, 317, 335; Collins,
Michael, 338, 371; Conrad, Charles, Jr., 338;
Cooper, L. Gordon, Jr., 317, 329; Crippen,
Robert L., 358; Davis, N. Jan, 384; Glenn,
John H., Jr., 317, 327; Grissom, Virgil I., 317,
326, 332, 335; Jemison, Mae C., 384; Lee,
Mark C., 384; Lovell, James A., Jr., 337;
McAuliffe, Christa, 368; Ride, Sally, 361;
Schirra, Walter M., Jr., 317; Shepard, Alan B.,
Jr., 317, 326; Slayton, Donald K., 317; White,
Edward H., II, 318, 332, 335; Young, Arthur, 95
Astronauts, Soviet: Atkov, Oleg, 362; Gagarin, Yuri
A., 317, 326; Kizim, Leonid, 362; Komarov,
Vladimir M., 335; Leonov, Alexei A., 332;
Manarov, Musa, 373; Romanenko, Yuri V., 370;
Solovyov, Vladimir, 362; Tereshkova, Valentina
V., 329; Titov, Col. Vladimir, 373; Titov,
Gherman S., 326

Atanasoff, John V., 289, 296
Atom, 120, 123; model of, 230, 240, 243–44,
261; model of nucleus, 271, 300; parity of
atomic states, 264; quantum jumps, 369;
radioactive disintegration of, 232; size of, 235
Atomic number, concept of, 245
Attention, study on, 160
Attention-deficit disorder (ADD), 366
Atwood, George, 106
Audubon, John James, 137
Auer, Carl, 203
Auger, Pierre, 258
Auger effect (PHYS), 258
Aulenback, Kevin, 370
Automat (food), 227
Automobiles, 219, 228; models, 206, 214, 219,
236, 280, 286; powered by gasoline, 204;
power steering, 308; safety defects, 333;
steel, 239; tires, 216, 297
Autoradiograph, 234
Avery, Oswald Theodore, 290
Avogadro, Amedeo, 125, 173
Avogadro's hypothesis (PHYS), 125, 173
Avogadro's number (constant), 132, 177
Ayrton, Hertha Marks, 203, 230
Aztecs, 47, 132

B

Baade, Walter, 272–73, 290, 302, 308
Baade-Zwicky theory (ASTRO), 336
Babbage, Charles, 119, 127, 131, 141, 144–45,
157, 161
Babbitt metals, 148
Babcock, George, 182
Babo, Lambert, 157
Bacon, Francis, 51, 58, 63–65
Bacon, Roger, 35–36
Bacteria, 50; anthrax bacillus, 191; genetically
altered, 370; mycobacterius tuberculosis, 200;
oil-eating, 340; pneumococcus, 198; virus
distinguished, 260
Bacteriology, 186
Baekeland, Leo Hendrick, 238
Bagehot, Walter, 187
Baillarger, Jules, 164
Baily, Francis, 146
Baily's beads (ASTRO), 146
Bain, Alexander, 191
Bakelite, 238
Baker, Henry, 86
Baker, Richard, 302
Bakker, Robert, 337
Balard, Antoine-Jérôme, 136
Balasubramanian, Ramachandran, 368
Baldwin, Ralph Belknap, 302
Ballistic missile, 289
Balloons, 105–6; military use, 112;
scientific use, 106, 120
Ball-point pen, 281
Balmer, Johann Jakob, 203
Baltimore, David, 349
Banach, Stefan, 254

INDEX

INDEX

C

Cabrera, Blas, 361
Cade, J. F. J., 304
Calculating machines, 68, 75, 206
Calculus, 66, 72, 75, 77, 131; differential, 68, 95; functional, 232; limit concept, 95
Calendar: Chinese, 9, 27; Coptic, 25; Gregorian, 54; Julian, 20
Calvin, Melvin, 317
Camera lucida, 126
Camera obscura, 51
Cameras, 207, 224, 260
Campbell, John, 95
Campbell, William Wallace, 222
Camper, Pieter, 95
Canal rays, 242
Cancer: and genes, 371, 382, 390; and high-fiber diet, 378; and very low frequency electromagnetic fields, 378
Cannizzaro, Stanislao, 162, 173
Cannizzaro reaction (CHEM), 162
Cannon, Annie Jump, 225, 257, 302
Cannon, Walter B., 248, 256, 260, 270
Cano, Raúl J., 389
Can opener, mechanical, 185
Canti, R. G., 270
Cantor, Georg Ferdinand, 184, 186, 188, 217, 329
Capek, Karl, 252
Capillary forces, theory of (PHYS), 122
Capo, R. C., 381
Carbolic acid, 179
Carbon-14, 285
Carbonated water, 98
Carcinogens, 246
Cardano, Geronimo, 48, 50
Carlson, A., 330
Carlson, Chester, 279
Carnot, Lazare, 120
Carnot, Nicolas-Léonard-Sadi, 134
Carothers, Wallace Hume, 279, 286
Carpenter, M. Scott, 317
Carrel, Alexis, 277
Carson, Rachel, 327
Cartan, Henri, 314
Carter, Howard, 254
Case, Jerome Increase, 152
Cassinelli, Joseph P., 358
Cassini, Giovanni, 72, 75–76
Catastrophism, 126
Catchside, D. G., 292
Cathode rays, 191, 198, 217
Cattell, Raymond, 334
Cauchy, Augustin Louis, Baron, 128, 131, 135, 189
Cauchy-Kovalevskaya theorem (MATH), 189
Cauchy-Riemann equations (MATH), 161
Cauchy's integral theorem (MATH), 135
Cavendish, Henry, 86, 97, 106, 114
Caventou, Joseph-Bienaimé, 128, 130
Caxton, William, 42
Cayley, Arthur, 152, 163, 168

Cayley, Sir George, 152, 163
Cech, Thomas R., 340
Celeripede, 128
Cell: cytoskeleton, 347; genetically engineered, 378; mitosis, 187; protoplasm, theory of, 174; receptors, 331; theory, 156
Celluloid, 166
Cellulose, 145
Cellulose acetate, 262
Celsius, Anders, 90
Cerletti, Ugo, 278
Cesalpino, Andrea, 54, 92
Chadwick, James, 245, 271, 274
Chain, Ernst, 264, 282
Chain reactions (CHEM), 208
Chakrabarty, Ananda, 340
Chalmers, William, 268
Chamberlain, Owen, 314
Chamberlin, Thomas Chrowder, 230, 275
Champlain, Samuel de, 62
Champollion, Jean-François, 132
Chandrasekhar, Subrahmanyan, 281
Chandrasekhar limit (ASTRO), 281
Chaos theory (MATH), 326–27
Chaos theory (PHYS), 228
Charig, Alan J., 328
Charles, Jacques-Alexandre-César, 81, 107
Charles's law (PHYS), 119
Chasles, Michel, 162
Chemical thermodynamics, laws of, 191
Chemistry: chemical notation, 168; chemical symbols, 126; nomenclature, 107; periodic table of elements, 183
Chen He-quin, 259
Cherenkov, Pavel Alekseyevich, 273
Cherenkov radiation, 273
Chlorofluorocarbons (CFCs), 348
Chloroform (compound), 142
Chlorophyll, 128, 230, 232
Chocolate, 46, 139, 190, 216
Choh Hao Li, 289, 315
Cholera, 164; bacillus, 200; epidemics, 143, 181; pandemic, 137
Cholesterol, 306
Chomsky, Noam, 319
Christy, James, 353
Chromatography, 232, 291, 300, 309
Chromosomes, 283; artificially made, 361; maps, 240, 385
Chronometer, 87
Chubb, Talbot, 332
Chugani, Harry, 369
Chung, Samuel Chao, 348
Chung Chien Young, 266
Church, William, 133
Church, William Hale, 307
Cieciura, S. J., 315
Cigarettes, 114
Cinemascope, 312
Cinématographe, 217
Circle, squaring the, 13, 15, 200
Citric acid, 106

INDEX

INDEX

Electrometer, 97
Electron, 240, 305; charge, 222; diffraction, 262; mass, 220; orbit model, 246; radio tube, 230
Electron tunneling, concept of, 264
Electrophoresis technique, 267, 278
Electroplating, 117
Electroweak theory (PHYS), 338, 362
Elements, geochemical classification, 252
Elements discovered: actinium, 222; aluminum, 134; americium, 290; antimony, 57; argon, 214; astatine, 285; barium, 101, 123; berkelium, 302; beryllium, 114; bismuth, 57, 93; boron, 123; cadmium, 128; calcium, 123; californium, 306; certium, 120; cesium, 172; chlorine, 101, 124; chromium, 113; cobalt, 87; curium, 290; dysprosium, 204; einsteinium, 308; element "106," 347; element "107," 358; element "108," 360, 363; element "109," 360; erbium, 152; europium, 225; fermium, 310; fluorine, 204; francium, 282; gadolinium, 204; gallium, 189; germanium, 204; hafnium, 256; hahnium, 342; helium, 183, 216; holmium, 194; hydrogen, 97; indium, 176; iodine, 124; iridium, 120; krypton, 221; lanthanum, 148; lawrencium, 326; lithium, 128; lutetium, 232; magnesium, 123; manganese, 101; mendelevium, 314; molybdenum, 103; neodymium, 203; neon, 221; neptunium, 285; nickel, 92; niobium, 118; nitrogen, 99; nobelium, 319; osmium, 120; oxygen, 101; palladium, 120; phosphorus, 74; platinum, 87; plutonium, 285; polonium, 221; potassium, 122; praseodymium, 203; promethium, 297; protactinium, 249; radium, 221, 240; radon, 223; rhenium, 258; rhodium, 120; rubidium, 172; ruthenium, 153; rutherfordium, 339; samarium, 194; scandium, 195; selenium, 128; silicon, 134; sodium, 122; strontium, 123; tantalum, 119; technetium, 278; tellurium, 106; terbium, 152; thallium, 174; thorium, 139; thulium, 195; titanium, 110; tungsten, 105; uranium, 109; vanadium, 140; xenon, 221; ytterbium, 233; yttrium, 112, 152; zirconium, 109
Elements (Euclid), 17, 34
Elevator, 162, 168
Elford, William Joseph, 269
Elion, Gertrude Belle, 301, 382
Elliptic functions, theory of (MATH), 137
Ellis, Albert, 314
Ellis, Havelock, 222
el-Malakh, Kamal, 312
Elton, Charles, 262
Elvehjem, Conrad Arnold, 278
Embolism, 170
Embryology, 75, 136, 275
Emotion, theories of, 197, 248, 307
Empedocles of Acragas (Agrigentum), 12, 93
Encke, Johann, 128
Enders, John Franklin, 299
Endorphins, 347
Energy, physical concept of, 123

Engels, Friedrich, 182
Engines: diesel, 216; four-cycle, 191; internal-combustion, 174, 191; jet, 268, 316; Wankel rotary, 319. *See also* Steam engine
Enzymes, 260, 353
Eötvös, Roland, 211
Epic of Gilgamesh, 7, 149, 185
Epidemiology, 160
Epsom salts, 80
Epstein, Michael, 360
Equinoxes, 19, 30
Eratosthenes of Cyrene, 19, 77
Erb, Wilhelm, 194
Erie Canal, 131, 134
Erikson, Erik H., 306
Erlanger, Joseph, 255
Ethics, medical, 8, 23, 179
Ethnocentrism, 234
Ethyl alcohol, 113
Etler, Dennis, 387
Euclid, 17
Eudoxus of Cnidus, 13, 15
Euler, Leonhard, 83, 85, 87, 90–91, 95, 112
Evans, Arthur John, 223
Evans, Oliver, 104, 108
Evans-Pritchard, Edward Evan, 285
Evenson, Kenneth M., 345
Evolution, theories of, 96, 99; biological, 153; education, 258, 373; Lamarckism, 123; natural selection, 124, 170–71, 177, 184, 258, 267; punctuated equilibrium, 345
Ewen, Harold Irving, 290, 307
Ewing, Maurice, 297, 311
Explorers: Africa, 112, 137, 150, 168, 191, 208; Antartic, 131, 240; Baffin Island, 53; Canary Islands, 38; Central America, 46; Greenland, 31, 53; Lewis and Clark expedition, 120, 122; North America, 46, 49, 62; North Pole, 236; Northwest passage, 228; Rocky Mountains, 89; Siberia, 54; South America, 49; South Pole, 228; Timbuktu, 137; Vikings, 34
Explosive nitroglycerine, 156
Extrasensory perception (ESP), 263
Eyde, Samuel, 227
Eyes: astigmatism, 118; cataracts, cure for, 93; contact lenses, 193; glasses, 35, 41, 106, 173; Snellen eye chart, 176

F

Fabrici, Girolamo, 63
Fabricius, David, 55, 67
Fabricius, Johann Christian, 102
Fabricius, Johannes, 60
Fabry, Charles, 243
Fahlberg, Constantine, 195
Fahrenheit, Daniel Gabriel, 84–85
Fairbanks, Thaddeus, 141
Fajans, Kasimir, 243
Fallopian tubes, 51
Fallopius, Gabriel, 51
False Geber, 37
Fankland, Edward, 161

INDEX

INDEX

Interferon (antiviral protein), 318
Introns, 356
Intuitionism, theory of (MATH), 243
Ionic dissociation, theory of (CHEM), 202
Iron, 9; for anemia, 64; production, 69, 83, 105, 139, 143, 146
Isaacs, Alick, 318
Isomers, 134
Isomorphism rule (EARTH), 260
Isotactic polymers, 311
Isotopes, 239
Ives, Frederick Eugene, 205

J

Jackson, John, 214
Jacob, François, 333
Jacobi, Carl Gustav, 137
Jacquard, Joseph-Marie, 119
Jacuzzi whirling bath, 338
Jahn, H. A., 278
Jahn-Teller effect (PHYS), 278
James, Hubert, 272
James, William, 151, 197, 202, 209, 222
Janet, Pierre Marie Felix, 225
Jansky, Karl G., 268, 272
Janssen, Pierre-Jules-César, 183
Jasper, Herbert, 285
Jeans, James Hopwood, 224, 250, 275
Jeffreys, Harold, 250, 275
Jenney, William LeBaron, 204
Jennison, Roger, 349
Jensen, Johannes Hans Daniel, 300
Jet stream, 283
Jex-Blake, Sophia Louisa, 188
Jobs, Steve, 349, 352–53
Johannsen, Wilhelm L., 236
Johanson, Donald, 348, 368, 390
Johnson, Virginia, 334
Joliot-Curie, Frédéric, 273
Joliot-Curie, Irène, 273, 301
Jones, Sir William, 99
José, Juan, 105
Josephson, B. D., 328
Josephson effects (PHYS), 328
Jost's law, 160
Joule, James P., 118, 150, 152, 157, 162
Joule's laws (PHYS), 150
Joule-Thomson effect, 162
J-Psi particle, 348
Judkins, Melvin, 337
Judson, Whitcomb L., 214, 257
Jung, Carl Gustav, 189, 244
Junine, C. G., 93
Jupiter, 59–60, 72, 105, 212, 228, 275, 347; radio emissions from, 314; space exploration, 346–47, 354, 368, 373, 384
Justeson, John S., 387

K

Kaas, Jon, 356
Kalokairinos, M., 197
Kamen, Martin David, 285, 296

Kanner, Leo, 289
Kant, Immanuel, 93, 104
Kaons, 309, 311
Kaposi, Moritz K., 187
Kapteyn, Jacobus Cornelis, 231
Kastler, Alfred, 306
Kaufman, Terrence, 387
Keesom, Willem Hendrik, 253
Keilin, David, 257, 282
Kekule von Stradonitz, Friedrich August, 168, 173–74, 177
Keller, Gottlob, 154
Kelly, George, 314
Kelvin, Lord. See Thomson, William
Kelvin scale, 159
Kendall, Edward, 245
Kendrew, John, 317
Kennelly, Arthur Edwin, 227
Kepler, Johannes, 57–58, 60, 63, 65, 369; heliocentric theory and Roman Catholic church, 63, 132, 145
Kerr, John, 189
Kerr effect (PHYS), 189
Kerst, Donald William, 285
Kesselring, Ulrich, 232
Kettering, C. F., 241
Ketzbach, John E., 374
Keynes, John Maynard, 266, 277
Kibble, Tom, 350
Kilby, Jack, 322
Kinesthesis, 113
Kinetograph camera, 212
Kinetoscope viewer, 212, 217
King, Charles, 271
King, Clarence, 186, 195
King, Samuel Archer, 174
King, Thomas J., 308, 310
Kinsey, Alfred C., 297
Kipping, Frederick Stanley, 229
Kirchhoff, Gottlieb Sigismund Constantin, 125
Kirchhoff, Gustav Robert, 170, 172, 174
Kirkwood, Daniel, 179
Kirkwood gaps (ASTRO), 179
Klaproth, Martin Heinrich, 109, 120
Klaus, Karl K., 153
Klein, Melanie, 200, 272
Kleinschmidt, Edward E., 246
Kline, Nathan, 305
K-meson, 309, 311
Knipling, Edward, 307
Knitting machines, 55
Koch, Robert, 191, 200
Koch's postulates or laws (MED), 200
Koffa, Kurt, 239
Köhler, Wolfgang, 239
Koldewey, Robert, 222
Kolff, Willem, 291
Kölreuter, J. G., 96
Korh, William, 375
Kossel, Albrecht, 203
Kovalevskaya, Sonya (Sofya) Vasilyevna, 189, 202, 208

INDEX

Linton, Ralph, 292
Liouville, Joseph, 146
Lippershey, Hans, 59–60
Lister, Joseph Jackson, 140
Lister, Joseph, 179
Li Tianyuan, 387
Livingstone, David, 150
Locke, John, 66, 78, 83
Lockyer, Joseph Norman, 183, 206
Lodge, Oliver Joseph, 214
Loeffler, Friedrich, 202, 221
Loening, Grover, 243
Lomonosov, Mikhail V., 90, 96
London, Fritz Wolfgang, 263
London, Heinz, 328
Longitude measurements, 34, 48
Lorentz, Hendrik Antoon, 212, 217
Lorentz-FitzGerald contraction, 217, 224, 231
Lorentz force, 217
Lorenz, Edward N., 326–27
Lorenz, Konrad, 334
Loschmidt, Johann Joseph, 132, 177
Love, Augustus, 176
Lowe, Thaddeus Sobieski Coulincourt, 179
Lowell, Percival, 192, 231
LSD, 289
Lull, Richard Swann, 246
Lumière, Auguste and Louis, 217
Lunar eclipses, 33, 44
Lunar formation, theory of, 194
Luria, Salvador Edward, 288, 292
Lwoff, André-Michael, 333
Lyceum (Athens), 16, 26
Lyell, Charles, 140–41, 144, 154
Lymphocyte adhesion molecules, 356
Lynen, Feodor Felix Konrad, 307
Lyot, Bernard Ferdinand, 267
Lysenko, Trofim, 267
Lysergic acid diethy lamide. See LSD
Lysomes, 314

M

Macadam, 128
MacArthur, R. H., 335
MacCready, Paul, 353
Mach, Ernst, 184, 205, 228
Mach number (PHYS), 205
Mach's principle (PHYS), 184
Macintosh, Charles, 134
Mackenzie, K. R., 285
Maclaurin, Colin, 87, 92
Maffei, Paolo, 343
Magellan, Ferdinand, 47, 145
Magnesium sulfate, 80
Magnetic effect of electric convection, 187
Magnetic storms, 95
Magnetism, 10; tempered steel, 220
Mahler, Ernst, 250
Mail delivery, 66, 86; express delivery service, 154; parcel post service, 198; Pony Express, 174; postage stamps, adhesive, 158
Maiman, Theodore Harold, 325

Maiuri, Amadeo, 239
Makela, Bob, 354
Malinowski, Bronislaw, 248
Mallet, Robert, 160
Malpighi, Marcello, 71, 74–75, 77
Malthus, Thomas Robert, 114
Malus, Étienne-Louis, 123
Manchly, John William, 296
Mandelbrot, Benoit, 350
Manson, Joseph, 385
Mantell, Gideon, 135–36, 145
Mantoux, Charles, 235
Manufacturing: assembly line, 244; jigs, 114
Maps, 3, 7, 11; geologic, 168; Mercator projection, use of, 52; ocean, 374; satellite, 356; weather, 78, 155, 176
Marconi, Guglielmo, 218, 226
Marco Polo, 37
Marcus, P. I., 315
Marggraf, Andreas Sigismund, 95
Marignac, Jean-Charles de, 204, 233
Marinsky, J. A., 297
Mariotte, Edme, 71
Mariotte's law (PHYS), 71
Markov, A. A., 232
Marks, Hertha. See Ayrton, Hertha Marks
Mars, 72, 105–6, 192, 386; distance from earth, 75; space exploration, 330, 343, 346, 350, 371, 384
Marsden, Ernst, 244
Marsh, Othniel Charles, 184, 193, 198, 206, 209
Marshall, Alfred, 210
Martin, Archer, 291
Martin, Arthur J. P., 309
Martin, Pierre Émile, 175
Marx, Karl, 182
Maser, 312, 316
Maskelyne, Nevil, 97
Maslow, Abraham, 227, 328
Mason, John, 170
Mason jar, 170
Maspero, Gaston, 198
Mass action, law of (CHEM), 182
Mass spectrometer, 251
Masters, William Howell, 334
Match: phosphorus, 142; safety, 163
Matlack, Timothy, 108
Matrix mechanics (PHYS), 258
Mattioli, Pietro Andrea, 49–50
Maunder, Edward Walter, 214, 340
Maupertuis, Pierre-Louis de, 90
Maury, Matthew Fontaine, 163, 165
Mauss, Marcel, 260
Maximum ionic density, theory of, 297
Maxwell, James Clerk, 165, 168, 172, 174, 179–80
Maxwell-Boltzmann statistics (PHYS), 174
Maxwell's equations (PHYS), 179, 207
Mayans, 20, 24, 31, 46, 50, 148
Mayer, Julius Robert von, 152, 157
Mayer, Maria Goeppert, 300–301
Mayo, Elton, 266

INDEX

INDEX

INDEX

INDEX

Ricardo, David, 128
Richards, Dickinson Woodruff, 288
Richards, Theodore William, 243
Richardson, Owen Willans, 224
Richer, Jean, 74–75
Richter, Burton, 332, 348
Richter, Charles, 275, 318
Richter, Theodor, 176
Richter scale, 275
Ridley, Henry, 267
Riemann, Georg Friedrich Bernhard, 161, 163
Riemann hypothesis (MATH), 168, 348
Riemann surface, 161
Ritter, Johann Wilhelm, 117, 119
Rivera, Thomas, 260
Rivers, W. H. R., 233, 246
Robbins, Frederick Chapman, 299
Roberts, Ed, 349–50
Robinson, Lockhart, 172
Robot, 324; honeybee, 374
Roche, Edouard-Albert, 159
Roche's limit (ASTRO), 159
Roch-Lecours, A., 362
Rocket propulsion, mathematics of, 251
Rockets, 261, 266, 276, 291, 304
Rock strata classification, 115
Roebling, John Augustus, 155, 201
Roebling, Washington Augustus, 201
Roentgen rays, 219
Rogers, Alan E. E., 349
Rogers, Carl Ranson, 227
Rohwedder, Otto Frederick, 264
Rollerblades, 357
Romagnosi, Gian Domenico, 119
Ronalds, Francis, 133
Röntgen, Wilhelm Conrad, 217, 219
Rorschach, Hermann, 253
Rosch, Eleanor, 359
Rose, William Cumming, 306
Rosenberg, Steven, 373
Rosenbusch, Karl, 187
Rosenfeld, Otto. See Rank, Otto
Rosenman, Ray, 340
Rosetta Stone, 115, 132
Ross, Colin, 372
Roth, Thomas F., 331
Rowland, F. Sherwood, 348
Rowland, Henry Augustus, 187, 199
Rubber, 44, 62, 100; synthetic, 261
Rubbia, Carlo, 362
Ruddman, William F., 374
Rudman, Daniell, 378
Ruhmkorff, Heinrich Daniel, 165
Rulein von Kalbe, Ulrich, 44
Rumely, Robert, 357
Ruska, Ernst August Friedrich, 272
Russell, Bertrand, 227, 238
Russell, Henry Norris, 240, 275
Rust, John, 263
Rust, Mack, 263
Rutan, Dick, 369
Rutherford, Daniel, 94, 99

Rutherford, Ernest, 220, 226, 232, 240, 245, 251
Rutherford, L. M., 172
Ruyson, Fredrick, 72
Ryle, Martin, 314, 316

S

Sabatier, Paul, 220
Sabin, Albert Bruce, 311
Sabine, Wallace Clement Ware, 218
Saccharin, 195, 320
Sack, David, 372
Safety boiler, 182
Safety pin, 159
Sagan, Carl, 361
Sager, Ruth, 329
Sainte-Claire Deville, Henri-Étienne, 166
Sakel, Manfred, 266
Salam, Abdus, 338, 347
Salk, Jonas Edward, 311
Saloman, A., 243
Samuelson, Paul, 302
Sandage, Allen, 324
Sanger, Frederick, 308, 356
Sanger, Margaret, 201, 248, 314
Sapir, Edward, 201
Satellites, artificial, 329, 341, 354, 356, 361;
  commercial communications, 328; Soviet Union,
  317; United States, 319, 321; weather, 324, 334
Saturn, 60, 70, 75–76, 105, 108, 168, 221, 275,
  290, 362, 373; space exploration, 347, 354,
  356, 358
Sauria, Charles, 142
Saussure, Ferdinand de, 249
Saussure, Horace Bénédict de, 97, 103
Saussure, Nicolas-Théodore de, 120
Savery, Thomas, 80, 84
Scale, platform, 141
Scarpa, Antonio, 112, 120
Schachter, Stanley, 307
Schaefer, Vincent, 294
Schank, Roger, 361
Schechtman, D., 364
Scheele, Carl Wilhelm, 99, 101–3, 105–6
Schiaparelli, Giovanni, 192
Schizophrenia, 330, 357; diagnosis, 366, 372;
  therapies, 266, 271, 278
Schleiden, Matthias Jakob, 156
Schleiden-Schwann cell theory, 156
Schliemann, Heinrich, 185, 190, 194, 203
Schmidt, Bernhard V., 267
Schmidt, Maarten, 324, 329
Schönbein, Christian Friedrich, 150, 154
Schrieffer, John N., 318
Schrödinger, Erwin, 261
Schrudde, Josef, 232
Schultze, Max, 174
Schwabe, Heinrich Samuel, 151
Schwann, Theodor, 146, 156
Schwartz, David, 220
Schwarzschild, Karl, 231, 249, 313
Schwarzschild, Martin, 308
Schwarzschild radius (ASTRO), 313

INDEX